BEST NEWSPAPER WRITING 2002

WINNERS: THE AMERICAN SOCIETY OF NEWSPAPER EDITORS COMPETITION

Featuring
Community Service Photojournalism Award
and Companion CD-ROM

EDITED BY KEITH WOODS

The Poynter Institute
and
Bonus Books

06 05 04 03 02   5 4 3 2 1

International Standard Book Number: 1-56625-185-0
International Standard Serial Number: 0195-895X

The Poynter Institute for Media Studies
801 Third Street South
St. Petersburg, Florida 33701

Bonus Books
160 East Illinois Street
Chicago, Illinois 60611

Book design and production by Billie M. Keirstead,
Director of Publications, The Poynter Institute

Cover illustration by Jeff Papa of Phillip Gary Design,
St. Petersburg, Florida.

Photos for the cover illustration were provided by The Associated
Press and are used with permission. Photo credits: AP photographers
Stephen J. Boitano (Pentagon), Suzanne Plunkett (running crowd),
and Gulnara Samoilova (debris-covered people); AP stringers Carmen
Taylor (World Trade Center) and Gary Tramontina (Flight 93).

Photos in the Community Service Photojournalism section were
provided by the photographers. Photos of winners and finalists were
provided by their news organizations.

Printed in the United States of America

For Danny Pearl, reporter, *The Wall Street Journal*; William Biggart, free-lance photojournalist (New York); Azizullah Haidari, photojournalist, Reuters (Afghanistan); Pierre Billaud, reporter, Radio France Internationale; Johanne Sutton, reporter, Radio Television Luxembourg; Ulf Strömberg, photojournalist, TV4 (Sweden); Julio Fuentes, reporter, *El Mundo* (Spain); Volker Handloik, free-lance reporter, *Stern* magazine (Germany); Harry Burton, photojournalist, Reuters TV (Australia); and Maria Grazia Cutuli, reporter, *Corriere della Sera (*Italy). All were killed trying to tell the story of terrorism that began to unfold on the morning of September 11, 2001.

Simplicity and safety nets

MAY 2002

After Jimmy Carter was inaugurated as president in 1977, he directed the Secret Service to stop his bullet-proof limo on Pennsylvania Avenue. He got out and, to applause from the crowd, walked the rest of the way to the White House. My lead in *The New York Times* was four words:

"The President walked home."

Years later, a deliciously good *Philadelphia Inquirer* writer named Jill Gerston astonished me by reciting that lead from memory. Why on earth, I wondered, had she remembered it? Because, she said, she wished she had written it.

Gerston had been assigned to cover the same parade. To convince readers of the importance of the event, she had loaded her lead with elaborate language and dangling clauses. She said she had learned something from reading my lead: The bigger the news, the less it needs the writer to embellish it.

Learning from other writers, even when those writers have no idea they are teaching, is the essence of this series of books called *Best Newspaper Writing*.

And the volume you hold contains far better examples than mine of the power of creative simplicity.

Jim Dwyer's "Objects" were remarkably moving tales of simple items that became important to survivors of the World Trade Center attacks. Three of those stories—centered on a plastic cup, a snapshot, and a squeegee—were cited by the American Society of Newspaper Editors as the most admirable short writing in 2001.

I won't spoil the pleasure you'll have reading Dwyer's work. I will crib from the letter Peter Applebome of *The New York Times* metro desk wrote to nominate Dwyer's stories:

"A few weeks after the attacks, [Dwyer] heard a story. It concerned someone he knew who had worked on the 68th floor of one of the towers. The man had fled the building, taking only a pen from his office. He held up well until a few days later, when he lost the pen and almost instantly became unglued, as if all the tortured emotions surrounding the event had been transplanted into that pen."

Dwyer didn't merely find similar stories. He had the wit to tell them with the power of understatement. The key to the effect of these stories, Applebome's letter suggested, is that Dwyer wrote "with quiet, respectful restraint. You'll find no overwriting here, no grand flourishes, not a syllable that draws attention to the writer instead of the subject. What you may notice, however, is their attention to detail, their surgical precision of language, and their ability to treat profound matters in a wholly unpretentious and accessible way."

Amen.

This is the 24th time Poynter and ASNE have collaborated to honor the *Best Newspaper Writing* and the second time these books have incorporated ASNE's homage to the best photojournalism focused on community.

It is worth pointing out—especially for all the journalists who don't have, or fear they don't have, editors who encourage staffers to take risks—that these winning entries were selected by editors who understand the importance of trusting writers and photographers. The judges, led by N. Don Wycliff of the *Chicago Tribune*, were:

Andrew Alexander, Cox Newspapers, Washington
Gerald M. Boyd, *The New York Times*
Milton Coleman, *The Washington Post*
Gregory Favre, The Poynter Institute
Karla Garrett Harshaw, *Springfield* (Ohio) *News-Sun*
G. Maria Henson, *Austin* (Texas) *American-Statesman*
David A. Laventhol, *Columbia Journalism Review*
Pamela K. Luecke, Washington and Lee University
Walker Lundy, *The Philadelphia Inquirer*
Anthony Marro, *Newsday*, Melville, N.Y.
Tim J. McGuire, *Star Tribune*, Minneapolis
Gregory L. Moore, *The Denver Post*
Richard A. Oppel, *Austin* (Texas) *American-Statesman*
Michael Parks, University of Southern California
Sharon Rosenhause, *Sun-Sentinel*, Fort Lauderdale
Madelyn A. Ross, *Pittsburgh Post-Gazette*
Edward L. Seaton, *The Manhattan* (Kan.) *Mercury*

They were aided in selecting the photojournalism award by Carolyn Lee of *The New York Times* and four experts in photojournalism:

John Beale, *Pittsburgh Post-Gazette*
Susan Gilbert, *The Charlotte* (N.C.) *Observer*
John Glenn, *The Atlanta Journal-Constitution*
Patty Reksten, *The Oregonian*, Portland

* * *

While it surely is true that writers and photographers can benefit from the content of this book, it is even more valuable for editors—especially mid-level editors who might come to work each day afraid to make bold decisions. For years, the most gifted journalists in America have been saying in these *Best Newspaper Writing* books that they would not have been able to do such fine work if they had not been empowered by editors who were willing to abet them when they took risks.

For example, *Best Newspaper Writing 1996* is full of such tributes to editors who lead. Martin Merzer of *The Miami Herald* said his editors "give you the freedom to try something a little different." Ken Fuson of *The Des Moines Register* wrote a story that consisted entirely of a single sentence with 90 words, and credited his editor, Randy Essex, with getting it onto the front page: "He didn't roll his eyes. He read it and liked it. When it was time for the news meeting, he put the entire story on the budget. That's what they call 'closing the sale,' and I appreciated it." Tom Hallman of *The Oregonian* praised his editor, Kay Black, for being "enthusiastic and encouraging, two things writers need when they attempt anything other than a standard news story. Reporters can take risks when they have a safety net."

This is a book not just for the risk-takers but also for those of you who are, or could be, their safety nets. Jill Gerston would approve.

Cheers,
Jim Naughton, President
The Poynter Institute

Acknowledgments

A book that brings together so many people, ideas, and published works—and does it in fewer than four months—requires a tremendous amount of coordination and cooperation from people whose names do not appear on the cover. Most of that cooperation and coordination is orchestrated by publications director Billie Keirstead. Assisted by copy editor Vicki Krueger, Billie oversaw the production of this book from beginning to end.

At the beginning was the American Society of Newspaper Editors contest committee, led by *Chicago Tribune* public editor N. Don Wycliff, whose members chose the winners and finalists appearing in these pages. Thanks also to ASNE executive director Scott Bosley and publications assistant Suzanne Jenkins, who make it easier each year to collect materials and speed up the time it takes for the book to reach the public. The Associated Press again provided the pictures used on the cover.

A great thanks to The Poynter Institute faculty and staff who each year give time and imagination to this project. Faculty colleagues Dr. Roy Peter Clark, Aly Colón, Dr. Karen Dunlap, Kenny Irby, Pam Johnson, and Christopher (Chip) Scanlan each interviewed a winning journalist and wrote the accompanying Writers' Workshop sections. Multimedia editor Larry Larsen produced the CD-ROM. Helping to edit the text were proofreaders Sarah Kennedy, Dan Puckett, and Kathleen Tobin. As always, Poynter's chief librarian David Shedden compiled the bibliography that appears in the back of the book. Poynter president Jim Naughton, program assistant Jeannie Nissenbaum, and design editor Anne Conneen also had important roles in the book's production.

The writers whose work is honored here contributed their thoughts and insights as well. It's that extra slice of wisdom, from interviews with the winners to the "Lessons Learned" written by finalists, that gives the *Best Newspaper Writing* series all the value it has.

Contents

Commentary

Community Service Photojournalism   **383**

The best of writing
in the worst of times

Two hours. Three sites. Four planes. One overwhelming, unimaginable story.

The tragedy of Sept. 11, 2001, dominates this edition of *Best Newspaper Writing* in a way that no story ever has. It was pounded out on deadline, mourned and cursed in columns and editorials, followed up in short stories and long ones.

In that way, the 24th edition of this series holds a unique slice of history between its covers. More than that, though, it holds frozen a stretch of time when writers reached for the noblest potential of their craft. Their work provides proof that journalism can be at its best, even when—especially when?—humankind is at its worst.

The reporters and editors thrust into the middle of the world-shaking events came at them from different places at different times. Together, the stories of winners and finalists alike form a three-dimensional picture of the breaking coverage and its aftermath. Some writers were at Ground Zero. *The Wall Street Journal*'s Jon Hilsenrath saw United Airlines Flight 175 roar over his head and smash into the second World Trade Center tower. N.R. "Sonny" Kleinfield saw the same scene on TV in *The New York Times*'s newsroom, then rushed into the midst of chaos. Bryan Gruley watched from the *Journal*'s Washington, D.C., office and constructed the newspaper's lead story from there.

Others wrote about the aftermath.

Anne Hull of *The Washington Post* touched the story weeks later as she visited Mexican and Middle Eastern immigrants swept up in the percussive aftershocks of terrorism. Columnist Steve Lopez of the *Los Angeles Times* helped readers connect the dots between a life lost in one of the four planes and a quieter, more anonymous death on the other side of the country. Editorial writer John McCormick of the *Chicago Tribune* wrote of war and prayer and their odd coexistence as the U.S. military aimed its wrath and weapons at Afghanistan.

The writing throughout this book is inspirational and

the scope of coverage instructive. Stand too close to the Big Story, stand as close as Jon Hilsenrath stood, and it might be hard to find the "instructive" things. What, after all, guides your pen when buildings fall, and they crush your sense of what is real and what is possible? And to what will these lessons apply if no one can imagine ever again covering a story in which passengers revolt against hijackers and contribute to crashing a commercial airliner, perhaps saving the White House or the U.S. Capitol? How do you learn from what Kleinfield called "something that has no parallel"?

The answers were in the journalism.

■ **Just report.**

When they couldn't get in touch with the office, couldn't reach family, and didn't know what might happen next, reporters and editors said they did what came naturally. They interviewed. Listened. Observed. And wrote it down—on a hotel pad, a business card, whatever they had available.

■ **See the cosmic and the microscopic.**

While Gruley and more than 50 reporters and editors put together the newspaper's lead story, *The Wall Street Journal*'s David S. Cloud and Neil King pushed beyond the moment of the attacks to consider the global implications of terrorism and retaliation. On deadline, the story that emerged proved remarkably prescient.

In the weeks that followed, Jim Dwyer got microscopic. Inspired by the story of a life coming apart when the smallest of things is lost—a pen, a memento from the collapsed trade center—Dwyer took the tiniest of details and turned them into short, profound prose.

■ **At cultural intersections, look in all directions.**

With the country in the grips of a jingoistic, foreigner-unfriendly nationalism, journalists found stories that challenged readers to think hard about the prejudices and stereotypes raised when the buildings fell. Hull and Lopez wove tales about America's outsiders that appeal not to readers' sympathy but to their sense of shared humanity.

There is more to this text than stories related to Sept. 11. In writing about the "lost boys" of Sudan, *The Boston Globe*'s Ellen Barry rendered in words the naiveté, wonderment, and sometimes sad acculturation of teenagers unmoored by war in the Sudan and unnerved by life in the United States.

Photojournalist J. Albert Diaz of *The Miami Herald,* sure that there was an extraordinary story in the profoundly ordinary world of suburban Broward County, told the tale in pictures of maxed-out expansion that threatens to destroy the very paradise suburbanites seek.

Hull's signature entry in Diversity Writing is a masterful narrative in a classic frame: a Washington, D.C., neighborhood in transition finds the well-heeled rubbing elbows with the less fortunate in the unlikely environs of a pricey food store. Unlike many stories in the genre, though, Hull's is full of three-dimensional characters and a truth so complex that it overflows the borders of cookie-cutter story frames.

Here, then, is a celebration of journalism's triumph in a time of terror, another benchmark for those in search of writing excellence. Each sentence is an opportunity for growth, whether it's the story that earned the writer a place in this book or an insight from the journalist about how a detail, a quote, an idea, or a phrase was hatched.

If you ever wondered what makes writing work, read on. The answer is in the journalism.

ABOUT THIS BOOK

Through recorded conversations, follow-up calls, and e-mails, members of the Poynter faculty produced the interviews that follow the stories honored in this book. For the sake of clarity, flow, and brevity, some of the answers have been compressed and reordered and some questions have been edited or added.

Electronic versions of the winners' and finalists' stories were provided to Poynter by ASNE for publication in this book. They may differ slightly from the stories that originally appeared in print.

Best Newspaper Writing editors made minor changes in stories for style and grammar. Where editors found errors of fact, those were corrected after consultation with the writers.

Best Newspaper Writing 2002

N.R. Kleinfield
Deadline News Reporting

N.R. "Sonny" Kleinfield, a senior writer on *The New York Times* metropolitan staff, has made a career out of long-form journalism. During one span he might be writing about a stock club at a city high school, following the teenagers' investment careers for a year before writing about it. Or he might be reporting for nearly a year on the intricacies of race and the hip hop culture. Or he might be following medical school interns through their first year in the program.

Whatever the story, it was sure to take a long time. If he was called on to do a daily, it usually meant covering a plane crash or, as was the case in 1993, a terrorist bombing. If Sonny Kleinfield was writing on deadline, he was writing about disaster. So it was natural that he would be called upon to chronicle the incomprehensible events in New York on Sept. 11, 2001.

Kleinfield has worked for the *Times* since 1977. In that time he has been part of three Pulitzer Prize-winning coverage teams, beginning with the coverage of the terrorist bombing of the World Trade Center. In 2000, he was part of the Pulitzer-winning series on race relations, "How Race is Lived in America." In 2001, he contributed to the work that earned the *Times* a Pulitzer for public service, one of a record seven Pulitzers claimed by the newspaper in 2002.

Kleinfield has shared two Polk Awards and has won the Meyer Berger Award, the Gerald Loeb Award, the Robert F. Kennedy Award, the Deadline Club Award, and the Amos Tuck Award. His story in 1997 about a severely disabled man's drive toward independence was a finalist in the 1998 American Society of Newspaper Editors Distinguished Writing Awards competition.

Kleinfield has written for such national magazines as *The Atlantic Monthly*, *Harper's*, *New Times*, *The New York Times Magazine*, and *Esquire*. He has written seven books, including one about the development of the MRI scanner and another about a race car team's drive to win the Indianapolis 500.

He is a 1972 graduate of New York University and worked for *The Wall Street Journal* for five years before joining the *Times*. He lives in New York with his wife, Susan Saiter, and teenage daughter, Samantha.

His winning stories combine the practiced hand of a journalist who has covered some of New York's biggest stories with the local sensibilities of a writer intimately familiar with the things that make a city home. In these two stories, he succeeds in approximating the voice of the readers, conveying the shock, horror, and mind-blowing confusion that hung over the city long after the smoke cleared.

—Keith Woods

A creeping horror

SEPTEMBER 12, 2001

It kept getting worse.

The horror arrived in episodic bursts of chilling disbelief, signified first by trembling floors, sharp eruptions, cracked windows. There was the actual unfathomable realization of a gaping, flaming hole in first one of the tall towers, and then the same thing all over again in its twin. There was the merciless sight of bodies helplessly tumbling out, some of them in flames.

Finally, the mighty towers themselves were reduced to nothing. Dense plumes of smoke raced through the downtown avenues, coursing between the buildings, shaped like tornadoes on their sides.

Every sound was cause for alarm. A plane appeared overhead. Was another one coming? No, it was a fighter jet. But was it friend or enemy? People scrambled for their lives, but they didn't know where to go. Should they go north, south, east, west? Stay outside, go indoors? People hid beneath cars and each other. Some contemplated jumping into the river.

For those trying to flee the very epicenter of the collapsing World Trade Center towers, the most horrid thought of all finally dawned on them: nowhere was safe.

For several panic-stricken hours yesterday morning, people in Lower Manhattan witnessed the inexpressible, the incomprehensible, the unthinkable. "I don't know what the gates of hell look like, but it's got to be like this," said John Maloney, a security director for an Internet firm in the trade center. "I'm a combat veteran, Vietnam, and I never saw anything like this."

The first warnings were small ones. Blocks away, Jim Farmer, a film composer, was having breakfast at a small restaurant on West Broadway. He heard the sound of a jet. An odd sound—too loud, it seemed, to be normal. Then he noticed: "All the pigeons in the street flew up."

It was the people outside, on the sidewalk, who saw

the beginning. At 8:45, David Blackford was walking toward work in a downtown building. He heard a jet engine and glanced up. "I saw this plane screaming overhead," he said. "I thought it was too low. I thought it wasn't going to clear the tower."

Within moments, his fears were confirmed. The plane slammed into the north face of 1 World Trade Center. As he watched, he said, "You could see the concussion move up the building."

"It was a large plane flying low," said Robert Pachino, another witness. "There was no engine trouble. He didn't try to maneuver. This plane was on a mission."

Dark spots fell from the sides of the buildings, and at first it wasn't clear what they were. Sarah Sampino, who worked across the street, noticed black smoke outside and went to the window. "We saw bodies flying out of the windows," she said. "It was the 85th floor. I used to work on that floor."

James Wang, 21, a photography student snapping pictures of people doing tai chi at a nearby park, looked up and saw people high in the north tower. They seemed like tiny figurines, and he didn't know if they were awaiting rescue or merely looking out. "They were standing up there," he said. "And they jumped. One woman, her dress was billowing out."

Inside the towers, people felt it without knowing what it was. At about 15 minutes to 9, Anne Prosser, 29, rode the elevator to the 90th floor of Tower 1, where her global banking office was. As the doors opened, she heard what seemed like an explosion. She didn't know it, but the first plane had just hit several floors above her.

"I got thrown to the ground before I got to our suite," she said. "I crawled inside. Not everybody was at work." She said she tried to leave but there was so much debris in the air she couldn't breathe. Port Authority rescuers finally steered her to a stairway.

Tim Lingenfelder, 36, an office manager at a small investment banking firm, was sitting before his computer terminal on the 52nd floor of Tower 1. He had just sent an e-mail to his sister in Minnesota. Nothing special—just how was she and what he had had for breakfast.

The windows rattled. He heard a loud noise. The entire building shook. He looked up. Outside the windows, he noticed rubble falling, and he thought, "That can't be from here."

Only two others were at work, a father and son who were both bond traders. They said they had better get out. They hurried to the stairs and, along with flocks of others, began their descent.

"When I got to the 18th floor, my cell phone rang," Mr. Lingenfelder said. "It was my sister. She said a plane had hit and to get out now."

On the 32nd floor, the entourage was stuck for about 20 minutes because of smoke. Everyone ducked into offices on the floor to catch their breath. Mr. Lingenfelder peered out the window and saw a body lying on the roof of the hotel.

They returned to the stairs and made it out onto the plaza. Rubble and debris was all around. On the street there was endless paper and unmatched shoes.

John Cerqueira, 22, and Mike Benfante, 36, were working on the 81st floor of 1 World Trade Center when they felt the collision. "People were freaking out," said Mr. Fanter, a sales manager. "I tried to get them in the center of the office. About 40 people. I led them to the hall down the steps."

He continued: "We stopped on the 68th floor. I could hear people screaming. There was a woman in a wheelchair. John and I carried her down from the 68th floor to the 5th floor, where we got out. We started to see people jumping from the top of the World Trade Center."

Teresa Foxx, 37, works at an investment banking firm a block from the World Trade Center, and she had dropped off her 15-month-old daughter, Trinity, at the Discovery Learning Center on the plaza level of 5 World Trade Center, the building adjacent to the two towers. While she was in her office, Ms. Foxx heard the blast and immediately knew it was a bomb. "Ever since I enrolled her in the World Trade Center, I keep thinking about the bombing that they had there," she said.

She grabbed her purse and went outside and began running toward the daycare center. Other people were speeding toward her, crying and screaming. She was crying herself. She had to get her daughter.

By the time she got to the center, the children had been evacuated several blocks away. She hurried over there and found her daughter. "I just grabbed her and held her," she said. "I was still crying, the other parents were still crying, but we all got our children."

When she got home, Ms. Foxx told her husband, "Now I understand why people run into burning buildings."

Within about 15 minutes of the first crash, the second plane struck the neighboring tower.

People in the street panicked and ran. Some tripped, fell, got knocked down, were pulled up. People lost their keys, their phones, their handbags, their shoes.

Brianne Woods, a student at Pace University, was walking to class, and as she passed a Burger King not a hundred feet from the trade center she heard a blast and felt the ground shake. She ran to a bank, where people were banging on the glass, breaking it, trying to get inside. "I saw a guy bleeding from the head right by the bank," she said. "People were getting stomped on under the crowd. I saw a lady with no shoes; her feet were bleeding. I was probably in there for about 10 minutes, and I was hysterical."

Her brother worked in the World Trade Center and she didn't know if he was in there. She learned later that he had not gone to work.

She happened to have her cat, Oliver, with her, and she began wandering around, clutching her cat carrier, dazed. "I saw two people jump out," she said. "It was horrible. I felt I was in a bad nightmare."

Then a calm set in again. For blocks around, all the way up to 14th Street, the sidewalks were a mass of people, eerily quiet, for the incomprehension had struck them mute. As emergency vehicles, sirens blaring, sped downtown, people stood and gaped at the towers with holes in them. Many people were steadily inching downtown, not imagining anything worse was to come.

Marilyn Mulcahy, 31, had a business appointment at 9 at an office on Broadway a few blocks from the World Trade Center. She got off the subway at Chambers and Church Streets. She saw what she believed were pieces of a plane engine on the sidewalk, police officers running tape around it. She saw the holes in the towers and was dumbstruck.

Reason dictated caution, to get out of the area, but

she was overcome with shock. Almost unknowingly, she walked to the office where her appointment was. Everyone had left. Even so, she took the time to scribble a note that she had been there and would call later.

Back on the street, fear caught up with her. She changed out of her heels into flat shoes she had in her bag and ran uptown.

On the corner of Vesey and Church Streets, across from the Borders Books and Music store in the corner of the trade center, a small-boned woman, her hair caked with blood, was sitting on the curb, shaking uncontrollably. One eye was clouded over. A man in a business suit was lying on a stretcher, being loaded into an ambulance. Emergency workers came to comfort the woman. Five feet away, another rescue worker crouched down next to a heavyset woman who was breathing through an inhaler and hugged her.

Some trade center workers blessed their luck at being late for work. Kathleen Dendy, 50, had gotten her hair cut and so never got to her office at her usual 8:30. She worked on the 99th floor. Rajesh Trivedi, 40, a computer programmer, normally reported at 7, but he had to drop his son off at school and so didn't get in. He worked on the 80th floor.

A plane was heard overhead and people looked up. Another one, they thought. "No, it's a fighter," someone said. "Ours."

"Are you sure?" a woman asked.

Many people were busy on cell phones, trying to reach friends and relatives they knew in the buildings or to alert their own loved ones that they were all right. But the circuits overloaded. Fear mounted.

And then it got even worse.

Police officers warned people in the vicinity to move north, that the buildings could fall, but most people found that unthinkable. They stayed put or gravitated closer.

Abruptly, there was an ear-splitting noise. The south tower shook, seemed to list in one direction and then began to come down, imploding upon itself.

"It looked like a demolition," said Andy Pollock.

"It started exploding," said Ross Milanytch, 57, who works at nearby Chase Manhattan Bank. "It was about the 70th floor. And each second another floor exploded out for about eight floors, before the cloud obscured it all."

Seth Bower was on Broadway when the force of the collapse knocked him over onto other people. Bodies fell on top of him—not all of them, he thought, alive.

A plume of smoke reminiscent of an atomic bomb rose upward and then descended to street level and sped uptown. People began running, chased by the smoke. The air rained white ash and plaster dust, coating people until they looked ghostlike.

Some people were screaming, and many were in shock. "Don't breathe the air," people shouted. "It could be toxic." People held their breath or covered their faces as best they could with cloths or their shirts.

Lisle Taylor, 26, a recruiter with Goldman, Sachs, had just gotten out of a nearby subway stop and saw hundreds of pieces of paper in the air. She thought it was a marketing campaign. Then she looked up and saw the tower collapsing. "A woman grabbed my hand," she said. "She was saying the Lord's Prayer."

For several blocks, everything was black. People found their eyes burned. Many wondered if they were seeing the very face of death.

Michael Clinch, a security officer for an Internet company, left his office soon after the first plane struck and was standing on Broadway talking to a police officer when the first tower fell. He saw a woman running, grabbed her and pulled her under a sport utility vehicle with him. "We got under the truck and waited until it got light again," he said. "There were cars just blowing up. They were trying to get equipment off this emergency truck and get it into a building and all these cars just blew up. One would blow up and set off the next one. It got so bad we just couldn't do anything anymore and we had to get out of there."

Ten or so blocks north of the towers, the smoke had been outrun and it began to dissipate into the air. People stopped, turned and looked downtown. As the air cleared, an unthinkable sight presented itself: empty space where a 110-story tower had been.

People gasped. They trembled. They sobbed.

"It can't be," an elderly woman said. "It just can't be.

Where did it go? Oh, lord, where did it go?"

Many of the onlookers stayed put, frozen in horror. Slowly, the next thought crept into their consciousness: The other tower would come down too.

Several people voiced the thought: "Get out of here, the other tower's going to fall."

People started walking briskly north until the premonition became real—another horrifying eruption, as one floor after another seemed to detonate. Another giant cloud, soot, smoke streaming through the avenues. Again, people ran.

Many of them stopped at Canal Street and watched the smoke dissolve. People cried at what they saw: a crystalline sky with nothing in it.

"Oh my God," Tim Lingenfelder said, "there's nothing there."

That was when he lost it and began to cry.

People stood, numb, transfixed by what had to be a mirage. "All that were left of the buildings that you could see were the steel girders in like a triangular sail shape," said Ross Milanytch. "The dust was about an inch and a half thick on the ground."

Onlookers gathered in clumps and tried to understand. People with cars opened the doors and turned on the radios, and knots of people leaned close to hear what was happening. The news came across of the plane at the Pentagon, the plane in Pittsburgh.

"It's like Pearl Harbor," said a middle-aged man at a small parking lot on Canal Street. "It's Pearl Harbor. It's war."

"It's sickos," someone else said. "Sickos."

"This is America," a man said. "How can it happen in America? How?"

A young man came around imploring people to report to St. Vincent's Manhattan Hospital to donate blood.

Lines five, eight deep developed at pay phones, but many of the phones didn't work. Most of the downtown businesses were closed. People borrowed cell phones, but the heavy phone traffic made communicating hard if not impossible. Countless people spent hours not knowing where a wife, a husband or a child was.

For hours, people lingered, uncertain where to go or

what to do in a no longer plausible world. Some felt compelled to leave Manhattan, taking ferries to New Jersey. A man holding his weeping wife headed toward the Manhattan bridge, telling her, "Let's walk over the bridge to Brooklyn. They can't hurt us in Brooklyn."

Late in the afternoon, hundreds of rescue workers remained outside where the trade towers once loomed, watching the stubs of the buildings continue to burn into infinity. Several stories still stood, but it was hard to judge how many. Above the second story was nothing but an intense orange glow.

"It's eerie," said Monet Harris, 22, a transit worker. "You always look for those two buildings. You always know where you are when you see those two buildings. And now they're gone."

A city awakes, only to reflect on a nightmare

SEPTEMBER 13, 2001

New York woke up to another day yesterday, but it wasn't another day. It couldn't possibly be.

It was a city of less. Less traffic, less noise, fewer people, less activity, less momentum, less certainty, less joy.

The dawn did not erase the preceding day's agony — no dawn could — and so New Yorkers ate their meals, did the dishes and put out the trash, the mundane tasks of life, but nothing felt the same. The city seemed ever so much more fragile and unfamiliar.

On a day when work meant so much less than family and human companionship, when the very constructs of what it meant to live in New York came under question, New Yorkers spent much of their time in somber and heartfelt reflection.

The most glaring difference yesterday, of course, was less skyline. No one could glance downtown without feeling chills from the absence of the trade center towers. But in countless smaller ways, the reassuring signposts of daily life were not there.

It was a city of quiet.

People who lived near the city's busy airports, accustomed to the repetitive ear-splitting roar of jets arriving and departing, awoke to a day of uncomfortable silence. Smaller sounds resounded, for the bigger ones were gone.

Traffic was sparse, and sirens, one of the background noises of city life, seemed so much louder and more ominous than ever before.

It was a city of lonely commutes.

Richard M. Morris's workday always begins when he squeezes onto Metro-North's final rush hour train at Croton-on-Hudson, the last express stop before Manhattan. The train is usually a sardine can by then, people having boarded on the succession of earlier stops. Mr. Morris, a corporate lawyer, barely finds room for his 6-foot-3 frame.

But when he took the train yesterday morning, he had

rows of seats to himself. Even the front car, typically crammed with those eager to conserve a few precious commuting steps, was just about empty.

Mr. Morris continued his routine yesterday out of willpower rather than need. His office was closed. He did not need to come in. "The one thing you know the terrorists want is to disrupt our lives," he said. "I'm not going to give them that. I'm trying to regain some normalcy."

It was a city of eerie contrasts.

On the Upper West Side, there was a powerful but artificial sense of another day. In the morning, a playground in Riverside Park teemed with children playing on swings and in sandboxes in the sparkling sunshine, under the watchful eyes of parents. Along the promenade, people sat reading the papers, biking and skating. But there was an odd hush. Smiles were rare.

By the time one gravitated down to West 55th Street, the complexion changed. Suddenly, there was the evacuated, closely protected aura of a war zone. Police checkpoints and barricades appeared along the bikeway and the West Side Highway, continuing all the way to Lower Manhattan. Traffic vanished. One could travel for blocks and see only a city bus or an occasional taxi.

Lower Manhattan had the feel of an abandoned town. Everything closed. The streets and sidewalks nearly empty.

It was a city of postponements.

It was matinee day on Broadway—shows in the afternoon and evening—but all the theaters were dark. Nothing at the Golden or the Imperial or the Shubert. Nothing at the Lunt-Fontanne or the Palace. Performances canceled "due to circumstances beyond our control."

Two middle-aged women studied the notice on the door of the Lunt-Fontanne, where *Beauty and the Beast* usually plays, and one said, "No, no show today." Her friend said, "I didn't think so. How could there be a show? Who would show up? Who could perform?"

No one journeyed to the observation deck of the Empire State Building to look at the stunning cityscape. The entire building was shut down.

The stock exchange tape on the side of the Morgan

Stanley offices at Broadway and 48th Street reported no stock trades. There were none to report. Instead, there was information on an employee assistance phone line and pleas to give blood.

No parents had to rise early and bundle their children off to school. There was no school. Some classmates arranged their own little gatherings to bond and distract themselves from events beyond their comprehension.

It was not a day for shopping.

So many stores were closed entirely, not sure when they would open. On the doors of the Virgin Megastore in Times Square, a notice said simply, "We are closed until further notice."

Macy's Herald Square, the world's biggest store, was open, but the aisles were thin in the late morning. The Gap across the street was closed. Outside, a half-dozen police officers ate sandwiches and drank from jugs of water propped on a parked car.

Barbers sat idly outside barber shops, talking quietly. It was not a day to get one's hair cut.

Midtown parking lots, usually bursting with cars, sat nearly empty. On 37th Street, between Eighth and Ninth Avenues, was a row of parking lots, promoting their exquisite convenience to Madison Square Garden, Macy's, the fashion district and the convention center. Any weekday found them packed with cars.

In the late morning an attendant at S&R Parking said he had 11 cars, all monthlies. No day parkers had arrived. "Normally, there would be 71 cars," he said.

The next lot down was closed and had no cars in it. The same story at the next one. At Park Right, where $5.92 got you an hour, George Hernandez, the manager, just shook his head. "Five cars," he said. "Just five."

On a normal day, the lot was full by 10 in the morning. "That's a hundred cars," he said. "Today, forget about it. It's bad news."

Mr. Hernandez lived in Queens and always drove to work, but there was limited access, so he took the subway. "Empty," he said. "Plenty of room to stretch out."

It was a city of reflection.

For everyone, the magnitude of what had happened was still being absorbed. People fumbled with what they would or would not do from now on. A man walking down Lexington Avenue in Midtown in the early morning kept saying, "I'll never go downtown again. Worked there 15 years. I'll never go down there again."

Measuring the city's will and its grit is never easy. Throughout its eventful history, periodically marred by tragedy, New Yorkers have always stood up with uncommon resolve and resilience, but this was unlike any other disaster, and many people felt shaken to the core. They found themselves having epiphanies.

Danny Klein, 27, was outside Madison Square Garden, wearing a T-shirt inscribed, "We will rebuild," a sentiment somewhere in the hopes of everyone in the city.

"I wore it because we are going to rebuild," he said. "I wanted to drape my body in the American flag is what I wanted to do."

There were people full of militant feelings, and there were people who expressed restraint.

"I'm a 47-year-old guy who just saw the World Trade Center blow up, and I don't want another innocent 47-year-old Afghani to look off his terrace and see something blow up," said Doc Daugherty, an actor who lives six blocks from the World Trade Center. "You think like you were going to go into a hate mode and instead I'm like more in a peace mode—I mean, can we talk about this?"

Even blocks from the epicenter of the horror, on Reade Street near Hudson, some people who managed to enter the area went on as always. Grace DiTomaso placidly tended the potted geraniums in front of her Italian restaurant, Luca Lounge Cucina. "A little hose and they'll be O.K.," she said as she plucked dead leaves from them. She didn't even look up as emergency vehicles rolled up Hudson.

"Normal routine, don't you need it?" she said. "I think you do."

It was a city of oddities.

At one of the souvenir shops that line Fifth Avenue in the mid-40s, several people were congregated around the racks of postcards, buying cards with the World Trade Center on them.

It was a city of occasional panic.

After a trained dog gave signs of sniffing explosives

on the 44th floor of the Empire State Building late last night, the police evacuated the area. Some jittery New Yorkers ran down Seventh Avenue away from the building. Others stopped on street corners to watch, saying they wanted a last look at the building. But it was all a false alarm.

It was a city of reassurance.

Among all that was different, there were of course the things that were just as they always were. They stood out in stark relief.

Like every other day of familiar and unfamiliar happenings, mail carriers pushed their wheeled carts through the streets, and the sight of them seemed comforting.

One man walked up to a mailman near the large post office building across Eighth Avenue from Madison Square Garden and asked if delivery would be normal today. The mailman didn't miss a step. He said, "Sure. The mail's coming today. The mail comes every day."

And for all the things that there were less of in New York yesterday, there were some important ones that there were more of. There was more grief, of course, but also an omnipresent feeling of compassion, a desire for companionship and a yearning to believe something redemptive could come out of horrific tragedy.

"For the first time in my life, I want a partner just so I don't have to go through this alone," said Jennifer MacLeod, 40, a media consultant.

Rather than stay home the night of the tragedy, she volunteered to work at a friend's understaffed bar, serving drinks, the first time she had waitressed since college. "It was really satisfying to be around other people," she said. "I also oddly felt I was doing a public service."

Most Wednesdays, Felicia Finley, 29, glues on fake eyelashes for her role in *Aida*, the Broadway musical. But yesterday, she felt paralyzed. "I started to get dressed," she said, "then I started watching television and sat back down and started crying."

When the show resumes, she feels she will be renewed. "It's given me a newfound appreciation of what I do for a living," she said. "People need to feel inspiration and hope, and if I can do that, you better be sure that I'll be the first one to do it."

Writers' Workshop

1) For hours after the World Trade Center's twin towers collapsed, Sonny Kleinfield feared that his wife had been killed in the collapse. He also feared for his own safety. Discuss how journalists should handle such personal concerns while trying to do the job they have been assigned.

2) Journalists are often asked to speak to people mourning the loss of loved ones, but rarely is a reporter asked to interview people confronting such a dizzying array of emotions as must have greeted those in New York fleeing the terrorist attacks. What considerations should journalists bring to bear when interviewing people in the wake of disaster?

3) The writer begins nine sentences in his second story, "A City Awakes, Only to Reflect on a Nightmare," with the same phrase, "It was a city of...." What is the effect of this repetition of theme?

4) Consider the tone of Kleinfield's two stories. Both are told in a voice that borders on opinion writing. That tone is set in the leads of both stories. "It kept getting worse," the writer says in the first story. "It couldn't possibly be," he writes in the second. What is the value of such a conversational tone rich in familiarity? Is there a downside to such writing?

Assignment Desk

1) Kleinfield's first story, "A Creeping Horror," moves chronologically through the unfolding event, told partly by the writer, partly by those he quotes. Note the details the reader learns from reading the quotes. Try writing an event story chronologically, using quotes to tell parts of the story.

2) In his second-day story, "A City Awakes," Kleinfield had the challenge of describing what he called "the absence of things." Read the story and identify the ways, directly and indirectly, that Kleinfield describes what isn't there. Write an observation-based story about a part of your town or campus on a day when very little is happening, describing the place by observing "the absence of things."

3) Telling stories so packed with varying emotions makes it all the more difficult to identify the theme that will influence reporting and direct writing. Kleinfield said he found that the overarching emotion of "A Creeping Horror" was disbelief, and that theme is carried out both in the words of the writer and in the quotes from his sources. Before writing your next story, identify one emotion that sets the theme for the story, then find the details and quotes that bring that theme to readers.

4) Read Kleinfield's explanation in the interview for using city landmarks such as Borders Books and Burger King to describe buildings that were part of the World Trade Center complex. Try writing a scene describing a place in two ways: first using the official designations of building names and street names, then using the common references people in that community might use.

A conversation with
N.R. Kleinfield

KEITH WOODS: How did your day begin on Sept. 11?

N.R. KLEINFIELD: Part of my day was dictated by the fact that it was primary day in New York. Normally I don't get involved much in politics or covering elections or anything like that, but it was an unusual primary day for New York because of the recent end of term limits here. Because it was such an unusual race, I got enlisted to do a story about how that mechanism of voting went — whether there were problems with voting machines breaking down and so forth.

I happen to live about four blocks north of the World Trade Center and so, normally, I would have been home when all this happened; but because of the election, I was in the office at 8 a.m. and happened to be looking at wires to see what was going on. On the wires, a plane had apparently collided into the World Trade Center, and I went over to a TV in the office and saw the picture of the smoking tower. Like most people, I assumed it was a small plane that had accidentally hit it. I remembered the famous case of the plane that hit the Empire State Building and thought it was something along those lines.

As I was sitting there watching it with a couple of other people, we saw the second plane go into the second tower, and, of course, like anyone else who saw it at that moment, it was immediately obvious that it was a deliberate terrorist attack. And then the desk here started to mobilize. There weren't very many editors in, and so people who normally would not be doing assigning hurriedly decided to call in people. I was immediately told to forget about the primary and to go down to the trade center and plan on writing a story about the scene from there. I decided I didn't want to take a subway, in case it went down where I didn't want it to go, so I took a cab. I got out of the cab and just started running toward the trade center. I got to just below where I live — about three blocks from the trade center — when the first tower started to come down. I got caught up with all the other people who suddenly turned around and started running in the other direction. Everything became pitch dark, and you had no idea whether it was smoke and dust and pulverized debris that was coming toward you or if the building itself was in the smoke. There wasn't much time to think. The thought was going through my mind whether I was trying to outrun the building, which certainly in retrospect would have been impossible. If the tower had come down sideways and in that direction, it probably would have come down as far as Canal Street.

Which is where you were?

I was well below Canal Street. I was only three blocks away. Everybody just turned around, just stood there and watched as the smoke lifted, and then it was the horrifying and astounding sight of just emptiness in the sky. You saw it lift, and you kept expecting at some point to see part of the building. Maybe the top came off halfway down. There was just nothing there, and people just stood there awestruck, as I guess I was, too.

What were you thinking was happening while all of this was going on—everything from who was behind it to what was going to happen next?

There was very little thinking about what had happened before, what was going to happen next. One of the interesting things was that everyone knew the first tower had come down, and we knew a similar thing had happened to the other tower. It had to be plainly obvious in our minds that, if one tower came down, the other tower was going to come down, too. And yet everybody just stood there. Nobody moved, including me. People were so numbed by it, so in shock by it, that they weren't even thinking, "The other one's going to come down. Let's get further away to safety." We just stood there for the next 45 minutes until the second tower came down; and then everybody, in a similar way, turned around and started moving and watched the same thing happen all over again. It all did happen in distinct stages. There were these lulls between them, short ones at first and then longer ones. During the lulls, I was talking to people and found out where they were and heard their thoughts, but it was almost impossible to try to put it all together in your mind and to make any larger sense of it because it was just too astonishing.

How do you switch from the citizen of New York, who is watching the World Trade Center fall, to the reporter for *The New York Times*, who has to ask people questions while they've got questions of their own?

Well, I guess two forces came into play. Part of it was just instinctual. It was what I was down there for. It was what I do and it just became natural. Maybe it became even more natural in a totally numb state to just start talking to people and looking for people who had come out of the towers and everything. It hadn't even begun to really penetrate my mind about how many people might have still been in there.

I was also thinking about my own personal situation. Before I went down there, I called my wife [Susan Saiter] to see if she had heard about it, and she hadn't been home. Once I was down there, once the towers came down, I was thinking about where she might be. She often jogs in a nearby area. My daughter, Samantha, just started school the day before. She was Uptown, so I knew she was fine. And since we live there, the World Trade Center is basically our shopping mall. And my daughter and Susan had been shopping in the World Trade Center the night before for school clothes. As they often do, they had bought a lot of things and then made choices and things were going to be returned. I remember when I left that morning, there were a bunch of bags next to the door of things that she was going to return to the stores at the World Trade Center that morning, and it was in my mind that she might have been inside the trade center at that time.

I had no cell phone or anything with me. One thing I was trying to do was use phones when I could. I was calling my voice mail at work because I knew that she would call to say she was okay as soon as she was able to. I did that in between talking to people. One thing I didn't know was the amount of communications breakdown. I knew a lot of cell phones weren't working and some pay phones weren't working. But I didn't realize lines had just become over-extended. I only found out much later that the lines at the *Times* became overwhelmed and you couldn't even make calls into them. But, anyhow, I was worried. I knew the best thing to do was to keep busy, and that's why I tried to deflect my concern for my wife by interviewing people.

When did you reach your wife and find out that she was okay?

Much later. I stayed down there for hours talking to people. After a couple of hours had gone by and there was nothing from her, basically my mood shifted. I had no doubt that she might have been there. Then I was sure that she had been there. I mean, there was no rational explanation. I'm a very rational, logical person, and there was no rational explanation for why she wouldn't have called after that amount of time. The only explanation was that she was unable to, and so I became convinced that she had been there and was possibly killed.

The logical question would be how, then, could you go on?

I'd done a lot at this point. For a few hours I could operate on the assumption that there was a difficulty and all, and then it was getting to the point at which I felt I probably should get to the office. My concern had mounted tremendously, and I actually walked back to the office from down there. All during that time there were still no messages, which increasingly convinced me what had been the outcome; and of course, if that had been what had happened, I certainly wouldn't have written a story that day or done anything beyond that. I can't imagine who would. But when I got into the office a little after 1, there was a message from Susan that said she was okay and that she had been out jogging and had been caught in a mob of people who were just shoved uptown and onto ferries. She ended up over in Hoboken, N.J., with no money. She didn't have her phone. Nothing. And she had made some attempt to call and couldn't get anyone on the line and then just never had any chance to.

How do you approach people in the middle of all of this in a way that gets them to turn their attention from either their immediate safety or their deep concern for what's happening to having a conversation with a reporter?

Well, you know, with something of this magnitude, it's almost that people are looking to talk to someone else. I say "this magnitude" as if there were many things to compare it to. But when you have some disaster with a plane crash or earthquake or something like that, I generally find that people are looking to talk to someone else. It doesn't take any effort or any urging or art to get people to talk in that sort of situation. Everybody was grasping for some understanding of what had happened. Everybody needed to know so much more than what they saw.

As we were standing on the streets, there were these fighter jets going overhead, and no one had any idea if they were our fighter jets, if they were Iraqi fighter jets, or what. But everybody assumed they were additional enemy forces. People were listening to radios in cars that were parked on the street and they were hearing the reports of the Pentagon and they heard about the Pennsylvania plane and also the rumors that there were several unaccounted-for airplanes in the air. Nobody knew what was next. They had seen a number of stages of things that got worse and worse and worse, and there was obviously no conviction that that was the end. Nobody knew what direction to go—whether to go inside, to go outside, to go below ground, above ground. Nobody knew what was safe. People were looking for further information. So getting people to talk didn't take anything.

Did you go back toward the trade center after the second tower collapsed?

I stayed in a fairly narrow range of streets. I didn't go down to the site or anything like that, which very quickly became impossible to do. But there were quite a number of people who had been in the towers who'd come down many flights of stairs who were where I was. That was the lowest area where a lot of people had congregated, and so it seemed there was more than enough to do there.

Were you in communication with the editors as you were thinking through the focus of this story?

No. I talked to nobody at the paper until I physically got back to the office.

Did you make attempts to consult with people at the newspaper? And would that be a normal way of operating for you anyway?

You know, in some stories, yes, but not necessarily in something like this. I knew we probably had a tremendous amount of manpower dispatched all over the place. I imagine there probably was tremendous confusion at the office. I didn't feel I needed any guidance down on the street.

As you recount the story to me, I hear the lead of your story develop over and over again; that sentence that says, "It kept getting worse." When did you know that was going to be the lead and the focus of the writing?

I suppose when I came back into the office and I sat down with the metro editor and a couple of other editors. As I started to articulate what I'd seen, it naturally came out that what had happened had happened in these stages; that each stage was worse than the last. So at that point I thought it was clear that that's how I would start the story.

To whom did you speak first among the editors there?

I spoke with the metropolitan editor, Jon Landman.

Was any part of that conversation especially helpful in getting you to the point at which you were ready to write?

I'm not normally a deadline writer, but I've done many of the big disasters that have happened to New York for whatever reason. I've done plane crash scenes and I've done big crime scenes and things like that. I think the editors knew that I knew the general outlines of how to go about doing a story like this. The main focus of consultation with them was to be clear about what the parameters were, or what my story was as opposed to what might be in the slew of additional stories that would be done. It was more clarifying the boundaries of my story than how to write it or how to structure it.

You've talked a lot about your own emotions and the emotions you saw on the street. It seemed that several feelings informed your writing. What were the emotions you tried to capture?

Probably the overarching emotion was disbelief, the horror of it and how unimaginable, how unthinkable it was. I mean, any one aspect of it might have been thinkable. But the combination of the various episodes that came together, one after the other, just put it beyond what was imaginable. Hitting the building with one plane? Maybe you could have come to understand that and think that it was not too far-fetched. Maybe the second plane—that puts it onto another order of magnitude. And one tower coming down. And the second. The death tolls. What everything looked like. There are days when this feels like it happened two years ago, and there are many days when I'm still not sure it happened. It just still remains an unreal event to me in so many ways. And that was such a dominant thing for me, that it was obvious it was a dominant thing for everybody. People went to bed that night, woke up the next day, and said they just still couldn't come to accept that it was at all possible.

You use some fairly powerful, descriptive words that carry a great deal of emotion: "Trembling," "unfathomable," "gaping," "flaming." You convey very strongly in the story the sense of panic, disbelief, uncertainty. I wonder how free you have to be as a writer to put that amount of emotion into a story, since we're generally asked to be more separate from the event than you are in this story.

Right. There are certainly borders we are accustomed to

being within. One doesn't want to overstate something. One doesn't want to, let's say, personalize something. You go out the first time you've been to a plane crash and you see the scene, and I think you have a tendency to overstate it because you've never seen anything like it and you have no context. In so many ways it's going to seem so much more horrible than it was. I mean, you go to your first car accident and somebody died in it, and it can be brought into an emotional event beyond the true context that it should be presented.

The Sept. 11 attack was something where it would be pretty hard to overdo it, and I had had grounding in these other things. I covered other things that were pretty awful and I've seen pretty awful scenes. But people voluntarily jumping out of the building, knowing they would die by jumping out of the building? People making a conscious decision with someone else that they're going to hold hands and they're going to jump together? There's almost no language that could seem too purple or too overwrought in this case, and I think the real challenge was to not *understate* it. If one were going to err in writing about this, it would have been to play down the emotions and to some extent play down the horror and the disbelief of it all. I'm not sure how you could have gone that way.

You use commercial landmarks to help the reader know where you are as you're describing things: Burger King, Borders Books. What role did the landmarks play in the writing of this story?

I think it gave readers grounding. The trade center is obviously a well-known institution throughout the country and the world. Within the city, the actual details of the trade center and what is where are so well known, you don't meet me at Tower 2, it's, "Meet me in front of Borders," "Meet me at Express," "Meet me at Starbucks," and so forth. People are even hard-pressed to know which is the North Tower, which is the South Tower, and you never hear the addresses spoken. One North? People weren't sure what was 7 World Trade Center when that building came down, but they knew it in the way that people know directions in a small town. You know,

"Turn at the windmill" and things like that. People escaped through Borders. They saw that the books were still standing, and they came through that. It allowed people to immediately visualize what had happened where, whereas more generic descriptions wouldn't have done it. Even streets. People don't even know the streets so much. They thought of what places were at these various boundaries. It was logical for me because that's how I thought. As I said, the trade center was my neighborhood, it was my shopping mall. In a way, it was a way of personalizing the building itself.

You build tension and drama with foreshadowing in "A Creeping Horror," even though everyone who's reading it knows what has happened, at least at the most basic level. And you begin that with the lead paragraph and come back to it again later in the story when you say that the calm had set in again. How much of this is intentional and how much of it is just the way the story flowed from your pen?

I suppose some combination of those two things. As I mentioned before, I tend to think in very logical terms, and I tend to organize in my mind, do outlines or things like that, or put down paragraphs and then rearrange them many times. To one extent, I'd seen that this sequence was already organized, but in my mind I had organized how it would unfold. As I went through what information I had, it became pretty straightforward to me — what went where and how it would happen. I suppose it was more natural than it was consciously thought out. But it was probably a little bit of both.

How much did you leave out?

I remember that when I came in, I was thinking, "This is going to be the scene story of all scene stories, so it's going to go very much longer than normal." But I wondered what was enough. I mean, shouldn't it have been 5,000 words? Shouldn't it have been 10,000? I'm not sure I felt that I had left out something that really missed capturing some sense of what happened. There was a very good interview that happened to be with the daughter of [editor] Jon Landman, and she was able to express very vividly, with fascinating detail, the attempt by the teachers to have the students continue to go about their day while they're probably quietly panicking. I never was able to get that in. That's the one thing that still sticks in my mind; that with another 200 words I ought to put that in.

How much time did it take you from the moment you walked in the office until the time you hit the send button for the last time?

Well, the funny thing is we have pretty late deadlines. But because there were all sorts of new production issues with this paper—because there was so much copy and everything else, so much demand on the editing side—the deadlines were actually earlier than normal. So I had to finish this, at least to make the earliest editions, somewhere around 6:30 or 7.

And when did you start writing?

I probably started writing at 3 o'clock and it was done in stages. I wrote part of it; I did more reporting; I looked at other feeds that came in—of which there was an unbelievable quantity. I did very little looking at anything else, like wires. I just never got around to doing that.

You said that you don't do an outline, you kind of put down random paragraphs and then reassemble them. What's your style?

I mostly operate in my head. I don't write down outlines, but I guess I do mental outlines. I almost always write the top of the story at once. If I don't, I know I will struggle for many hours on it. I either know it or I never know it. Once I've written the top of the story, I usually start out writing somewhat from memory, even putting in details and people and quotes. And then I will go through my notes and confirm them. I have a pretty sharp memory on remembering things fairly verbatim. Generally, the first time through I will write the skeleton—everything I can remember and the order I want to put it in, often just marking spaces for things that I don't entirely remember but I know I have something that I want to go there.

How does that process serve you?

It's always been the most efficient way of doing things. I don't really know a lot about the various techniques of how people work because I don't really talk to them much about it. But I know some people go through their notebook and they just write page after page. Whatever they're going to use from their notebook, they start putting it down on paper and then reorganizing and all. I just find it more efficient to start writing from what I remember and then going to my notebook and finding the things that I had put down and want to use. As good as my memory is, I will often find surprises; things that I didn't know I had or didn't think were as good as they seemed to be once I looked at them again, and I'll insert them. But it's always worked. I can write more quickly in this process than any other. I guess early on I had tried other ways of doing things. I'm a very efficiency-minded person and that's proven to be the most efficient for me.

In the second story, "A City Awakes," you again decided a vehicle for telling this story and it's a very clear vehicle. When did that occur to you?

When they asked me to do that story, I left the office and just wandered around aimlessly. As someone who's lived in New York his whole adult life, you're always verging toward superlatives when you're thinking about New York. You're always thinking about how it has more of almost everything than other places. Good and bad. You're always thinking about excesses and mixed dreams and everything. As I wandered around, I noticed what was different. It just seemed that everything I noticed, whether it was big or small, was muted. Everything was on the opposite extreme of what I often thought about. There wasn't too much traffic. There was too little traffic. There weren't too many pedestrians. There were too few pedestrians. There weren't too many crowds to get into the Broadway theaters. There were no shows. There wasn't too much noise. There was too little noise. You never notice the sirens in New York because they're just part of it. They become background noise because they're drowned out in part by everything else. They just stood out in stark relief that day because there wasn't very much traffic. There weren't cars double-parked outside the parking lots. The parking lots were empty. So in every respect this city was less than it normally was, and it just seemed so clear to me that that was the story of the day.

What was the assignment you got from the editors when you left the building?

Well, the assignment was basically to write about the mood of the city, the feel of the city. That was the sum total of it.

The story seemed more heavily weighted toward observation than the first, with a much stronger-than-average editorial voice. How did you come up with that structure?

I don't know that I went through any sort of strong thought process on it. But I guess it's pretty much that it was a similar thing to the first day's story in that there was just no context. There was no comparison for this. It just seemed that to try to convey it took something more, it took something a little different than you might normally do. It's not writing about the day after the Thanksgiving Day parade when a lot of balloons crashed or something. It wasn't enough to just quote a few people who couldn't possibly put into words, a day later, how the city felt or what the city was. It needed to be some of that, but I just felt that it was something that had to be told in a more essay-ish way and a somewhat more "felt" and emotional way. I guess part of it was just an unintended natural reaction. Anybody who was here and anybody who was particularly close to it was just feeling differently than they had ever felt. And your own sensibility about the thing, if you were close to it, was very strong. I couldn't help but have a lot of confidence about my sense of it because I was as close to it, involved in it, and was as much a part of New York as one could be. It would be no better told, and maybe lesser told, by just stringing together a bunch of quotes from people. It was easily captured by just describing scenes, because the scene that I was trying to capture was the absence of things. And since I was writing so much about voids, it was more language than actual details. I was writing about lack of action, lack of activity, and so I just had a sense that it could be captured best by the proper structure and use of words and selection of events, or lack of events.

Well, there were quite a few details, although "details" is an odd word here because they were details about the *absence* of details, in this story. How did you go about collecting them?

Again, it was sort of random. I just went out and wandered around for hours. It's what caught my eye, what made sense as being unusual, and I wanted to very much capture the things that are so familiar and so taken for granted that were different. That was what was on my mind more than anything else.

There's a measure of trust that you had to have in your own instincts here and your own experience that would give you the confidence to write from it. Were you conscious that you had to listen to yourself in this case?

Yes. If you were somebody who was new to New York or somebody who didn't understand the city or the ordinary day-to-day flow of the city or hadn't seen the city in reaction to major events, you would probably have had to fall back on things and people that could give you context. I mean, I've lived in this city for a long time. I'd seen it through so many different things. I couldn't help but think that what struck *me* as odd about this city that day is what *was* odd about the city that day. If you were a tourist, [you] couldn't tell everything that was odd. But it was so striking. The feel of the city was so striking that day, that for someone who's been there for a long time, it was just obvious.

✿USA TODAY

Jack Kelley

Finalist, Deadline Reporting

Jack Kelley has been reporting for *USA TODAY* since the newspaper's first edition. He was hired after graduating in 1982 from the University of Maryland. In the time since, he has reported from 90 countries and interviewed 36 heads of state, including Cuba's Fidel Castro, the Palestine Liberation Organization's Yasser Arafat, Tibet's Dalai Lama, Jordan's King Abdullah, and Pakistan's Pervez Musharraf.

As a foreign correspondent, he has covered many of the most significant conflicts of the last decade. He reported on the Persian Gulf War, the Soviet coup, the Somalia famine, the Arab-Israeli peace accord, the Rwandan massacre, the South African elections, the Haitian invasion, the Russian war in Chechnya, the assassination of Israeli Prime Minister Yitzhak Rabin, the Bosnian war, the Zairean civil war and coup, the Serb massacre of ethnic Albanians in Kosovo, the NATO bombing of Yugoslavia and Kosovo, and the U.S.-led war in Afghanistan.

His writing has earned him a National Headliner Award and the Society of Professional Journalists' Sigma Delta Chi award, both in 2002. He also was a Pulitzer finalist in 2002 for beat reporting. His wife, Jacki, is senior vice president/advertising for *USA TODAY*.

In "Explosion, Then Arms and Legs Rain Down," Kelley writes from the scene of a bloody bombing in Jerusalem, using chilling description and quotes to pull readers into the harrowing, grisly moments before and after a suicidal Palestinian man stepped into a crowded restaurant and detonated a bomb.

Explosion, then arms and legs rain down

AUGUST 10, 2001

JERUSALEM—It was a scene out of a war movie.

The blast was so powerful it blew out the front of the Sbarro pizza restaurant on Jaffa Street. It knocked down people up to 30 yards away and sent flesh onto 2nd-story balconies on the next block.

Traumatized women, some with nails from the bomb embedded in their faces, arms and chests, huddled on the street corner and cried. Men stood motionless in shock. Children, their faces burned, walked around screaming, "Mom, mom, where are you?" Blood splattered the walls and dripped onto sidewalks.

Thursday's suicide bombing, which killed at least 15 people and injured nearly 90, struck downtown Jerusalem at the busiest time of the day—as the lunch hour was ending, at 2 p.m. I happened to be walking near the restaurant when the suicide bomber struck.

It was the deadliest attack in Israel since the suicide bombing of a Tel Aviv disco June 1 that claimed the lives of 21 young Israelis. With so many people critically injured, it threatens to become the most deadly attack since violence erupted here in late September.

Officials warned that the death toll could rise. At least 10 people were in critical condition, including a 4-month-old child.

An entire family—a couple and their three children—were killed, relatives said. The family had lived in a settlement in the West Bank.

Two foreign tourists were among the dead, Israeli public radio reported. The radio identified them as Judith Greenbaum, 31, from New Jersey and Giora Balach, 60, from Brazil.

Hanna Tova Nachemberg, 31, of Riverdale, N.Y., was critically wounded with shrapnel in her chest, according to Rabbi Avi Weiss of the Hebrew Institute of Riverdale.

Three French tourists also were injured.

"The bomber knew what he was doing," Jerusalem

Mayor Ehud Olmert said as he helped teams of Ortho-dox rabbis gather pieces of flesh from the street. Under Jewish law, people's bodies must be placed in their graves whole, or with all parts accounted for.

"This is a massacre," Olmert said.

The militant Muslim group Islamic Jihad, in a telephone interview with *USA TODAY*, claimed respon-sibility for the attack. It identified the suicide bomber as Hussein Omar Abu Naaseh, 23, from the West Bank town of Jenin.

The militant Muslim group Hamas also claimed credit for the bombing.

"We want this successful operation to prove to the terrorist (Israeli Prime Minister Ariel) Sharon that we can, and we will continue to, get him and his fellow pigs and monkeys where it hurts the most," senior Islamic Jihad official Abdallah al-Shami said.

Sharon convened an emergency meeting of his Secu-rity Cabinet immediately after the bombing and vowed to carry out a retaliatory attack against militant Muslim leaders. Israel has been targeting Palestinian extremists and assassinating them. It says they direct the terrorism.

Soon after the bombing, Palestinian Television re-ported Israeli tanks were shelling homes in Gaza.

Later in the day, Israeli soldiers took over a Palestin-ian security building in Abu Dis, which is next to Jerusalem.

The Israeli military sealed the entire West Bank and was moving troops into Jenin, the suicide bomber's hometown.

PALESTINIAN FLAG COMES DOWN

The Israelis also closed nine Palestinian Authority offices in East Jerusalem, including Orient House, the unofficial Palestinian foreign ministry. Seven Palestinian officials were brought out of Orient House early today and taken into custody by the Israeli military. Soldiers took down the Palestinian flag and replaced it with the Israeli flag.

Also, Israeli F-16 warplanes fired missiles at a Pales-tinian police building near Ramallah in the West Bank early today, Palestinians said. There were no casualties, but the building was destroyed. It was the first F-16 attack since May. Until now, Israel had confined its retaliation for Palestinian attacks to tank and helicopter strikes on Palestinian police positions.

"We hold (Palestinian Authority Chairman Yasser) Arafat responsible for this madness," Israeli government spokesman Danny Naveh said. "He has given the green light to Islamic Jihad, Hamas and the other terrorists."

But Palestinian Authority spokesman Yasser Abed Rabbo, who denounced the bombing, blamed Sharon for carrying out "Mafia-style" assassinations of nearly 60 militant Muslim leaders since September. "Sharon has inflamed the Palestinian people with his terrorist, gangland-style assassinations," Rabbo said.

The popular Sbarro restaurant, like other shops and eating places along Jaffa Street, was packed at lunchtime, so I and an Israeli official I was scheduled to interview decided not to eat there.

Several customers, including three mothers and their infants in strollers, stood outside on the sidewalk, eating their pizza and plates of spaghetti. Dozens of pedestrians pushed their way around the women or were forced to walk along the busy street next to the crowded buses.

Among those I could see fighting their way into the restaurant was a young man wearing a white T-shirt and dark sport jacket. A black pouch, similar to a small camera case, was attached to his waist. He appeared to be a Palestinian.

Once inside, he stared at the fluorescent menu board and at the red, green and white tiles, as if to survey his surroundings, one of the restaurant workers said later. He then asked the restaurant clerk how long he would have to wait for a plate of take-out spaghetti. As the clerk answered, witnesses said, the man reached inside his pouch and calmly detonated what turned out to be a bomb.

The explosion was deafening and sent out a burst of heat that could be felt far down the street. It blew out windows and threw tables and chairs into the air. Victims' arms and legs rained down onto the street.

Three men, who had been eating pizza inside, were catapulted out on the chairs they had been sitting on. When they hit the ground, their heads separated from their bodies and rolled down the street. Dozens of men, women and children, their bodies punctured by nails from the bomb, began dropping in pain. One woman had six nails in her neck. Another had a nail in her left eye.

Two men, one with a 6-inch piece of glass in his right temple, the other with glass shards in his calf, fell to the ground bleeding. A passerby tried to comfort them but broke down crying. As he walked away, he tripped on a decapitated body and fell.

Next to them, a man groaned in pain. "Help me, please. I'm dying," he said. His legs had been blown off. Blood poured from where his genitals had been. An Israeli soldier, upon seeing him, gasped "Oh, God," dropped his gun and vomited. The man bled to death less than a minute later.

'THERE COULD BE ANOTHER BOMB!'

Police officers began arriving, yelling into their handheld walkie-talkies and shouting instructions for bystanders to leave. "There could be another bomb! There could be another bomb!" a police officer yelled into a megaphone. He began to cordon off the area.

Few could hear him over the screams of the injured, the sirens of approaching ambulances and the shrill blare of dozens of car alarms set off by the explosion.

Suddenly, a Palestinian man ran up to an injured Israeli as if to help. An Israeli soldier butted the Palestinian in the chest with his rifle, knocking him to the ground.

"I'm a nurse! I'm a nurse," the Palestinian yelled. As he got up, another Israeli soldier threw him against a wall, grabbed him by the neck and placed him under arrest. Two other soldiers hauled him off, hitting him in the head as they walked.

"Terrorist!" a nearby police officer yelled, pointing at the man.

Meanwhile, yards away, a little girl about 3 years old, her face covered with glass, walked among the bodies, calling out her mother's name. Seconds later, she found her. The girl told her mother to get up. But the mother, apparently already dead, didn't respond. The girl, still unaware of what had happened, was led away, in hysterics, by an Israeli policewoman.

Inside the blackened shell of the restaurant, a policeman pointed to what he said was the top of the head of the suicide bomber, which was lying on the floor. The nose and mouth were missing. The teeth appeared to be lying nearby.

"You've killed us all, you bastard," the officer said, pointing to the head.

He then tried to kick the head, but was stopped by another officer. The man spat at the head as he was led away.

Dozens of ambulances arrived over the next 30 minutes to cart off the dead and injured as relatives began arriving. Rabbis, with white gloves, raced around the street picking up pieces of flesh. One rabbi found a small hand splattered against a white Subaru parked outside the restaurant.

"It's of a girl," Rabbi Moshe Aaron said. "She was probably 5 or 6, the same age as my daughter." He gently put it into a bag.

"I wish I could say there won't be anything like this tragedy again," Aaron said. "But it's just a matter of time until another bomber kills more of us. It'll be like this until the end of time."

Lessons Learned

BY JACK KELLEY

I have always thrived on being on the front lines. But this time, I got a little too close.

I had walked into the Sbarro pizzeria in downtown Jerusalem with an Israeli security official who specialized in the growing phenomenon of suicide bombers. He didn't have much time to talk, but agreed to chat over a slice of pizza.

As soon as we entered the restaurant, we knew we had made a bad choice. The line at the counter was so long that it extended out the door. We decided to go elsewhere.

As we walked out, I accidentally bumped into a man wearing a dark sport jacket, white T-shirt, and black pouch strapped around his waist. He appeared to be a Palestinian.

I apologized to the man for my misstep. He nodded as if to acknowledge it. I continued walking down the street. He entered the pizzeria.

The Israeli official and I walked about 30 yards. Suddenly, we heard a deafening explosion. It was so powerful it blew out windows, sent flesh flying up to two blocks away, and knocked us to our knees.

"It's a *shaheed*!" the official said, using the Arabic word for martyr, or in this case, a suicide bomber. "That guy was a *shaheed*!"

I looked back at the pizzeria and saw the bodies of three men, catapulted from the restaurant still in their chairs, hit the ground. Their heads, which separated from their bodies as they hit the street, rolled toward the curb. Then, an arm fell from the sky. A leg landed atop a car.

I looked at my watch to determine the time of the blast (1:58 p.m. local time) and raced back to the pizzeria.

I was standing amid blood, flesh, and glass. There were dozens of injured people around me. All I wanted to do was to put down my notebook and administer first aid.

There was little I could do. Everyone around me was already dead or dying, including the man who looked at me and cried, "Help me, please." He was lying on the street and bleeding where his genitals had been. I felt helpless. Seconds later, he died.

I realized I was the only reporter there. I felt a responsibility to be the eyes and ears of the world and to describe everything I was witnessing. While there had been dozens of suicide bombings in Israel, rarely had a reporter been in the middle of one.

I wrote down in my reporter's notebook everything I saw, heard, and smelled. "Details, details, details," I kept reminding myself. "*Show* the reader what is happening, don't tell. Instead of reporting that the bomb was packed with nails, describe the nails embedded in the eyes of the victims."

I worked quickly. I was running on adrenaline. I knew I had only about five minutes of reporting before the Israeli police would order me out of the area. I focused on three scenes that I hoped would illustrate both the tragedy of the pizzeria and the larger Israeli-Palestinian conflict:

■ The desperate attempt by a Palestinian nurse to help the victims;

■ The burst of anger by an Israeli policeman as he came upon the decapitated head of the suicide bomber;

■ The solemn ritual performed by a rabbi of picking up pieces of flesh left behind.

I raced back to my hotel. I filed news stories for USATODAY.com and *USA TODAY*'s domestic and international editions. (*USA TODAY* publishes a minimum of three domestic and three international editions each day.) I taped audio accounts of the blast for our Internet site and *USA TODAY* Live, a service that provides feeds to Gannett television stations. The demands of meeting these deadlines forced me to remain calm.

Several hours after the blast, I went into shock. I couldn't remember anything about the attack. I had to listen to the audio accounts to jog my memory of what had happened. I was not as tough as I thought.

As I wrote my stories, I kept reminding myself, "Keep it simple, stupid. Use short sentences, action verbs, and direct quotes. Take the reader from the beginning of the bombing to the end. Don't overwrite, overthink, or overdramatize. Just let the story tell itself."

I reported only the facts. In the Middle East, reporters

often are criticized for biases, real or perceived. But it's hard to argue against something you see yourself.

I'm convinced that some stories stay with you forever. This is one of them. For the first two nights after the bombing, I was too scared to sleep. I worried about the nightmares awaiting me and agonized over the pain and suffering of the families of the 15 people killed in the attack and the 130 others injured. I stayed up drinking Diet Coke and coffee.

Still, I wouldn't have traded being on the front lines for anything. As a journalist, that's where I belong.

John Bussey

Finalist, Deadline Reporting

John Bussey has been foreign editor of *The Wall Street Journal* since 1994, responsible for the paper's overseas correspondents and coverage.

A 1979 graduate of Dartmouth College, Bussey joined the *Journal* in 1983 as a reporter in the Chicago bureau and later worked in the paper's Cleveland and Detroit bureaus. In 1988, he became a writer and editor on the front-page staff in New York. He was subsequently chief of the combined *Wall Street Journal* and *Asian Wall Street Journal* Tokyo bureaus, and then economics editor, again based in New York.

Before joining the *Journal*, he was a reporter for the *South China Morning Post* in Hong Kong while on a Henry Luce Foundation fellowship. He also was a reporter for the *Charleston Gazette* in West Virginia and an assistant to the marketing director of *The Washington Star* in Washington, D.C.

His first-person account of the Sept. 11 terrorist attacks in New York mixes high-pressure reporting, a writer's eye and ear for detail, and spare but revealing commentary to reproduce the frightening minutes of death and uncertainty.

One journey through desperation and chaos

SEPTEMBER 12, 2001

NEW YORK—If there's only one sight I'll remember from the destruction of the World Trade Center, it is the flight of desperation—the headlong leap from the topmost floors by those who chose a different death than the choking smoke and flame. Some fell swinging their arms and legs, looking down as the street came up at them. Others fell on their backs, peering upward toward the flames and sky. They dropped like dead weight, several seconds, hopeless and unhelpable.

Always the same end. Some crashed into the plastic awning over the entrance to the north tower. Others hit a retaining wall. Still others landed on lampposts and shrubbery. After the 80-floor drop, the impact left small puffs of pink and red drifting at ground level. Firefighters arriving on the scene ran for cover.

In the movie *Armageddon*, the asteroid pierced New York buildings sending shrapnel out the other side. That, remarkably, is exactly what it looked like from the street, when the first plane hit the north tower of the World Trade Center.

The first warning was the sound of jet engines, flying low over the island of Manhattan. A second or two later, what seemed like a sonic boom.

From the sidewalk, behind the building that houses *The Wall Street Journal*'s offices just across the street from the World Trade towers, I didn't see the first plane dive into its target. But I saw the result: an arc of debris, brilliant orange and aflame, coughed from the building southward, landing blocks away.

By the time I'd gotten to the ninth floor of the *Journal*'s building and taken a position at a window in the northeast corner, diagonally across an intersection from the World Trade Center, the conflagration was well under way. Great clouds of smoke pushed skyward. Intense flames were consuming higher floors above the crash site. Debris was falling onto the streets—huge chunks of metal clanged as they hit the earth. Office papers littered the ground. Cars in a nearby parking lot—a full two city blocks from the explosion—were aflame.

I called our partner, CNBC, the business news television service, and began reporting the scene from inside our offices, beneath the burning structure. Then suddenly—as suddenly as the first explosion—I saw the second tower erupt in flame, sending more flame and debris crashing southward. This time, the television cameras, located in midtown Manhattan and pointed south, caught the image of a commercial jet veering into the second tower.

Evacuations were emptying buildings on both sides of the street, and fire trucks, Emergency Medical Services vehicles and police cars were crowding the area in front of the World Trade Center. Traffic was halted many blocks north and south.

Then, as the fires worsened, and the smoke got blacker and thicker, the first of the office workers began to jump. One at a time, a few seconds apart.

Unknown to the dozens of firefighters on the street, and those of us still in offices in the neighborhood, the South Tower was weakening structurally. Off the phone, and collecting my thoughts for the next report, I heard metallic crashes and looked up out of the office window to see what seemed like perfectly synchronized explosions coming from each floor, spewing glass and metal outward. One after the other, from top to bottom, with a fraction of a second between, the floors blew to pieces. It was the building apparently collapsing in on itself, pancaking to the earth.

This was too close. Uncertain whether the building would now fall on ours, I dove under a desk. The windows were pelted by debris, apparently breaking—I'd never know for sure. The room filled with ash, concrete dust, smoke, the detritus of South Tower. It was choking, and as more debris rained down onto and into the building, the light of the day disappeared. I crawled on the floor and braced myself under a desk deeper in the office. But the air was as bad.

With my shirt now over my mouth in the blackout of the smoke, unable to do more than squint because of the stinging ash, and thinking that this is what it must be like on the upper floors of the towers, I realized I had to move. I stood up from under the desk and began feeling the wall and desks, trying to orient myself in the now pitch-black cubicled world of our modern office. Disoriented, I twice passed by the entryway to this particular corner of the ninth floor. And then I was through, by accident, into a larger space, with more air.

The smoke had spread over the entire floor, which had been evacuated minutes before. In the emergency stairwell, still thinking that it was a matter of time before our building was crushed, I breathed in my first clear air. At ground level, though, it was a different story.

Outside on the sidewalk, the scene looked like Pompeii after the eruption of Mount Vesuvius. Inches of ash on the ground. Smoke and dust clouding the air. My throat stung as I worked my way past ambulances and EMS workers who had been caught outside when the tower collapsed. The emergency workers were trying to find colleagues. In the silence, as the ash fell like snow, radios crackled: "Steve, Steve, where are you?"

One fireman bashed through a door of a diner, and a handful of us took refuge from the outside air. We opened the restaurant's cooler, distributed water bottles, and took some outside to give to the ambulances. I asked what had happened to the people evacuated from the *Journal*'s building, my colleagues. Did they get away? No one knew.

I stepped into one ambulance with water and asked for a surgical face mask. I was handed several, and later passed them to coughing, spitting emergency workers in the street. The mask would be my life saver.

Because as I walked down the street, getting my bearings, and moving closer to Liberty Street, which opened out onto the trade center compound, the second tower was weakening. I heard a pressing metallic roar, like the Chicago El rumbling overhead. And then the fireman next to me shouted: "It's coming down! Run!"

Run where? I had no idea, so I did the best thing at the moment: I ran after the fireman.

Four of his colleagues joined us, plus another civilian or two on the street. We sprinted behind the wall of a nearby apartment building as the North Tower collapsed two blocks away. "Stay away from glass windows," he shouted as we ran, but what he said next was drowned out by the roar passing right through us. We flattened ourselves against a metal doorway, this small group, trying to be one with the building, as chunks of concrete and metal fell from the sky behind us and roared up the street and into the building's courtyard all around us. Debris fell against the shirt on my left shoulder—I couldn't push it any harder against the building.

After two minutes, we all went down, in a collective crouch, and tried to breathe. The building had stopped falling. The roar had subsided. But the smoke and ash seemed as dense as tar, far worse than in the building when the first tower fell. We all were wearing the tight-fitting surgical masks which, with shirts pulled up over our faces, made the difference.

Hyperventilating from the sprint and the fear, the group concentrated on not panicking. Our leader, the fireman who warned of the glass, yelled out in the dark: "Is anybody hurt? Try to breathe through your nose!"

In the blackness, he tried his radio: "Mike! Mike! Where are you?" No answer. Again, and no answer. My hand was on his trembling back, the better to brace myself, and I thought about asking him how long these blackouts and ash clouds could last. Then I realized the full ridiculousness of the question. How would he know? How often does a 110-story building collapse to the ground? I honestly wondered whether I'd survive long enough for the air to clear.

Mike finally answered the radio and was wearing a respirator. He also had a flashlight. And so eventually he found us. Blinded by the ash in our eyes, we stood up as a line, each put a hand on the shoulder of the guy in front, and let Mike lead us out of the darkness into the lobby of a building 20 steps away.

We poured water into our eyes, and shook ash from our clothing and hair. I looked for Mike to thank him, but he had already left to help an injured EMS worker on the street.

A young man in the lobby, apparently missed in the evacuation, held his daughter, a little blond-haired girl perhaps two years old. She was crying.

An older man who had also sought shelter was raving uncontrollably nearby. We calmed the older man, and the girl stopped crying.

The Wall Street Journal
Team Deadline News Reporting

It took a moment for Bryan Gruley to recognize what was happening. A commercial jetliner had crashed into one of the World Trade Center towers and the mammoth building was ablaze. Now another plane was on the television screen and a fireball was exploding out of the second of the twin towers. Then the telephone was ringing, and a *Wall Street Journal* reporter was letting everybody know that the Pentagon had been hit.

Gruley, like the rest of his colleagues at the *Journal*, went from horrifying realization to hard work. His job on another day was to help *Journal* writers get their stories in shape for the front page. Now he had to get there himself—with the country's biggest story in decades—and he didn't have a lot of time to do it.

Gruley is a senior editor in the newspaper's Washington bureau. He joined the *Journal* as a reporter in

1995 after working for 11 years at *The Detroit News*, where he covered business, including the auto industry and the Detroit newspapers' efforts to get a joint operating agreement.

On Sept. 11, Gruley, a 1979 graduate of Notre Dame University, was called upon to capture the devastation of terrorist attacks in New York, Washington, D.C., and rural Pennsylvania. His story, based on the reporting of more than 50 *Journal* reporters and editors, moves readers through the unfolding tragedy, which is brought to life by gripping anecdotes and riveting quotes.

The *Journal* staff, with its New York offices abandoned and left badly damaged and inaccessible by the collapsed World Trade Center buildings, also summed up the national response to the attacks in one story and in another provided insightful, dead-on analysis of the national security and military challenges ahead. That comprehensive coverage, under the most adverse of circumstances, also earned the *Journal* a Pulitzer Prize.

Among those contributing to stories written by Gruley, June Kronholz, Christina Binkley, Clare Ansberry, Neil King, and David S. Cloud were:

Ann Davis, Jon Hilsenrath, Mark Schoofs, Emily Nelson, Phil Kuntz, Gary Fields, David Rogers, Tom Hamburger, Rachel Zimmerman, Bruce Orwall, David Wessel, Kevin Delaney, Joanne Lublin, Gordon Fairclough, Lynn Lunsford, Paul Barrett, Dan Golden, John Wilke, Jackie Calmes, Laura Johannes, Stefan Fatsis, Matthew Rose, Jed Sandberg, Carla Robbins, Raju Narisetti, John McKinnon, Greg Zuckerman, Georgette Jasen, Ted Bridis, Michael Orey, Scot Paltrow, Helene Cooper, Jonathan Friedland, Andrew Caffrey, John Hechinger, Steve Power, Kate Kelly, Jathon Sapsford, David Bank, Rachel Silverman, Jeff Trachtenberg, Greg Hitt, Kortney Stringer, Russell Gold, Alexei Barrionuevo, Wendy Bounds, Kathryn Kranhold, David Armstrong, Jerry Guidera, Tim Aeppel, Patricia Davis, Robert Guy Matthews, Aaron Lucchetti, Shawn Young, Tom Lauricella, Jim Vandehei, Robin Sidel, Ianthe Dugan, Jim Browning, Antonio Regalado, Charles Gasparino, Peter McKay, and Lisa Vickery.

—Keith Woods

Nation stands in disbelief and horror

SEPTEMBER 12, 2001

They were like scenes from a catastrophe movie. Or a Tom Clancy novel. Or a CNN broadcast from a distant foreign nation.

But they were real yesterday. And they were very much in the U.S.

James Cutler, a 31-year-old insurance broker, was in the Akbar restaurant on the ground floor of the World Trade Center when he heard "boom, boom, boom," he recalls. In seconds, the kitchen doors blew open, smoke and ash poured into the restaurant and the ceiling collapsed. Mr. Cutler didn't know what had happened yet, but he found himself standing among bodies strewn across the floor. "It was mayhem," he says.

Around the same time, Nestor Zwyhun, the 38-year-old chief technology officer of Tradecard, an international trading firm, had just stepped off the New Jersey commuter ferry and was walking toward the World Trade Center when he heard a sound "like a jet engine at full throttle," he says, then a huge explosion. Smoke billowed in the sky and sheets of glass were falling everywhere. "I stood there for two seconds, then ran," Mr. Zwyhun said.

More than 100 floors above him at the trade center offices of Cantor Fitzgerald, someone put a call from the company's Los Angeles office on the speaker phone. What was happening there? The Los Angeles people heard someone say, "I think a plane just hit us." For more than five minutes, the Los Angeles people listened in horror as the sounds of chaos came through the speaker phone, people screaming, "Somebody's got to help us....We can't get out....The place is filling with smoke." Then the phone went dead.

Three hundred miles to the south, in Washington, D.C., a jet swooped in from the west and burrowed into the side of the Pentagon building, exploding in a tower of flame and smoke. Mark Thaggard, an office manager in the building, was there when the plane hit. People started running this way and that, trying to get out. "It was chaotic," Mr. Thaggard says. "It was unbelievable. We could not believe this was happening."

The nation stood in shock and horror yesterday after three apparently hijacked jetliners, in less than an hour's time, made kamikaze-like crashes into both towers of the World Trade Center and the Pentagon, killing hundreds, maybe thousands, of people and leaving countless others maimed and burned.

The streets of downtown Manhattan were strewn with body parts, clothing, shoes and mangled flesh, including a severed head with long, dark hair and a severed arm resting along a highway about 300 yards from the crash site. People fleeing the attacks stampeded through downtown and streamed across the Brooklyn Bridge while looking over their shoulders at the astonishing sight of the World Trade Center collapsing in a pile of smoke and ash.

Andrew Lenney, 37 years old, a financial analyst for the New York City Council, was walking to work a few blocks from the trade center when, he said, "I saw the plane out of the corner of my eye. You're accustomed to a plane taking up a certain amount of space in the sky. This plane was huge. I just froze and watched the plane.

"It was coming down the Hudson. It was banking toward me. I saw the tops of both wings," he said. "It was turning to make sure it hit the intended target. It plowed in about 20 stories down dead center into the north face of the building. I thought it was a movie," Mr. Lenney said. "I couldn't believe it. It was such a perfect pyrotechnic display. It was symmetrical."

Outside the Pentagon, hundreds of workers who felt the building shake on impact poured outside amid spewing smoke. Inside, lights had switched off and alarms were blaring. "We heard a loud blast, and I felt a gust of wind," said a civilian Pentagon worker who asked not to be identified. "I heard a loud explosion, and somebody said, 'Run, let's get out of here.' And I ran."

The president learned of the initial plane crash in New York before joining a class of schoolchildren in Sarasota, Fla. At 9:04 a.m., Chief of Staff Andrew Card whispered word of the second attack into his ear as Mr. Bush was reading to the children. About a half hour later, he appeared on television to inform the nation that terrorists were behind the tragedy. He said he had ordered a full-scale investigation to "hunt down and to find those folks who committed this act."

Shortly before 9 a.m., American Airlines Flight 11 from Boston, hijacked by suspects with knives, slammed into one trade center tower. Eighteen minutes later—as millions watched the first tower burn on live national television—a second hijacked jet crashed into the other tower. By midmorning, the south tower had exploded and collapsed, raining debris and sending choking dust and smoke across lower Manhattan. Within half an hour, the second tower caved in.

As that scene unfolded, a third hijacked jet crashed into the Pentagon. The side of the building caved in, with secondary explosions bursting in the aftermath and huge billows of smoke rising over the Potomac River, where they could be seen all the way to the White House.

A fourth plane, also hijacked, crashed about 80 miles south of Pittsburgh. United Airlines said it was a Boeing 757 en route from Newark, N.J., to San Francisco. It crashed in a remote field, killing all 45 on board. Virginia Rep. James Moran, a Democrat, told reporters after a military briefing yesterday that the rogue plane could have been headed to the Camp David presidential retreat in the mountains of Maryland.

The FBI, with 20 agents at the site, said that it was treating the crash as a crime scene. Early reports indicate that there were no ground fatalities.

In Pennsylvania, Daniel Stevens, spokesman for the Westmoreland County public-safety department, confirmed that its 911-call center received a call from a man aboard United Flight 93 over Pittsburgh at 9:58 a.m. The caller, claiming he was locked in a bathroom, said "the plane is being hijacked," and repeatedly stressed that his call was "not a hoax." Mr. Stevens said he thinks the call was bona fide. On the same flight, a flight attendant from Fort Myers, Fla., called her husband on a cellphone shortly before the plane crashed.

A federal official said a crew member on one of the American flights called the company's operations center and reported that several crew members had been stabbed and relayed the seat number of one of the attackers.

The crashes shattered a placid, clear morning in New York and Washington. By early afternoon, fighter jets were patrolling Manhattan, and downtown New York hospitals were turning away people offering to give blood because of long lines. With cellphones not working, people swarmed pay phones and huddled around radios. And the trade center towers had disappeared from the skyline.

Vincent Fiori was on the 71st floor of the first tower that was hit. "I'm sitting at my computer and I heard a rumble and my chair spun around," he said. Most people weren't sure what had happened. On the street, people gazed up at the gaping, smoking hole in the building, some holding handkerchiefs over their mouths, more curious than frightened.

The mood changed quickly when the second plane hovered into view and swerved into the other tower. Mr. Zwyhun, the Tradecard executive, was on the upper deck of a ferry, returning to New Jersey, when he saw the second crash and realized "this wasn't an accident."

Panic ensued, as stock traders, secretaries, construction workers and store clerks ran for cover. But there was bizarre calm, too, as some businesspeople rescheduled meetings on cellphones. Police showed up in numbers, ordering everyone to move uptown as fast as possible.

The top floors of the buildings were engulfed in smoke, and people began leaping from windows, one at a time, hitting the ground, shrubbery, and awnings. On the Brooklyn Bridge, dust-covered New Yorkers trooping homeward jammed the pedestrian walkway. A man in shorts and a T-shirt, running toward Manhattan with a radio to his ear, shouted "The Pentagon is burning, the Pentagon is burning!" and a young woman talking on her cellphone shouted, "My mother works there. I don't know where she is. What is happening? What is happening?"

Pedestrians streaming off the Williamsburg Bridge were met by local workers who had dismantled office water coolers, stacked mountains of plastic cups and hauled cases of water to the foot of the bridge. Tom Ryan, a burly ironworker who was handing out cups of water, said, "Our lives are never going to be the same. Now we're going to go through the same things as other countries."

Ferries, police boats and pleasure craft cruised up to the side of the promenade near the towers to whisk people away—children and the injured first.

Paul and Lee Manton, who moved to New York only a month ago from Australia, were holding their two children, ages 3 and 5, and frantically trying to find out where to go. The family lives near the towers, and after the planes hit, Mr. Manton stared out his window at the flaming buildings. "I said, 'These are going to go down,' and just as I said it the building started falling." Fifteen minutes later, he and his wife rushed their children outside in search of escape.

For more than 45 minutes after the second plane smashed into the second World Trade Center tower, the skyscrapers still stood—burning but apparently solid. Workers in the nearby buildings flooded out, and the promenade along the Hudson River was where many of them went. When the tower started to cave, it began with a low rumble. Slowly, amid a dark cloud of smoke, the debris rained down. "My God, it's falling," someone shouted. Mesmerized, no one moved.

A firefighters union official said he feared an estimated 200 firefighters had died in rescue efforts at the trade center—where 50,000 people worked—and dozens of police officers were believed missing.

Father John Doherty, a Roman Catholic priest, was on the street not far from the Marriott Hotel adjacent to the World Trade Center. "I was buried and dug my way out," he said, speaking on a stretcher in Battery Park City a few blocks south of the ruins. He paused to spit, and out came a wet, gray wad of ash. In the pitch dark of the smoke, he said, he made it to safety only by following a guard rail that runs along the riverside. "It's only the finger of God that saved me," he said.

Timothy Snyder and two other employees of Thermo Electron were in their 85th floor office in the North Tower of the World Trade Center when the plane hit three floors above them. They didn't know it was a plane; Mr. Snyder believed it was a bomb.

"We were just working," he says. "All of a sudden,

we heard this slamming sound that was so loud. The debris started falling outside the windows, and the door to the office blew open. The building started swaying, and it was hard to say if the building would remain standing. I was in my chair, and I just grabbed onto my desk.

"After five or 10 seconds, the building stopped moving, and we knew we had to leave. We all grabbed our bags and headed out." They walked down to the 78th floor where they were guided to another stairwell, crossing a lobby with a bank of elevators. The marble walls of the lobby were buckled.

As they walked down, the stairwells were crowded but calm. "There was air you could breathe," he says. "We didn't feel we were being suffocated." They were guided through the mall under the World Trade Center. Just as they came out, World Trade Center Two collapsed. "Being in the cloud of smoke was like being in this very dense, unbreathable air that was so black no sun was getting through." He ran for safety and made it.

"We feel, since the plane hit only three floors above us, amazingly thankful we're all alive. But there were emergency workers going up those steps while we were going down. They were trying to save others and they didn't make it."

In New York, officials set up a triage center in Jersey City, N.J., in front of the Datek Online Holdings building on the Hudson River. At Chelsea Piers, a recreational complex along the Hudson River, emergency officials set up a makeshift trauma center in a cavernous room that appears to be used as a set for TV shows and films. "Trauma" was spray-painted in orange letters over one entryway, and inside there were more than 50 beds — many converted from fold-out tables and lit with the aid of television studio lights. Some 150 surgeons, in town for a medical conference, reported to the trauma center and were prepared to take patients. Emergency workers prepared several dozen volunteers who were to be assigned one-on-one to accompany patients as they came in for treatment.

But as of 4:30 p.m., more than seven hours after the first plane struck one of the World Trade Center towers, there weren't many patients — only a handful of emergency personnel had come in for treatment of minor injuries. One emergency official, communicating through a bullhorn, told the waiting doctors, nurses and emergency medical technicians that the New York Fire Department at the scene wasn't permitting rescue workers to head into the rubble. "It's still too hot," the official said. And the city's hospitals still had vacant beds.

Mike Athemas, a 46-year-old volunteer fireman, headed downtown [after the attacks] and didn't leave until midafternoon. "Everywhere you turned, there was someone taking bodies out of the rubble," he said. Making matters worse, documents that had been blown from the building were catching fire and igniting vehicles outside the World Trade Center. "There were 20 cars and trucks—police cars and emergency vehicles—on fire," said Mr. Athemas. One New York city firefighter sobbed aloud, "My company is dead. They're all dead."

After the first plane hit the World Trade Center, New York City firefighter Craig Gutkes was part of a ladder company in Brooklyn that was called in to Manhattan. When he was still on the Brooklyn side, his company saw the second plane roar over their heads, "It sounded like a freight train," he said. They watched that plane plow into Tower No. 2. When he arrived on Liberty Street, "It was like a war zone when we got there. There were body parts all over the street."

In midtown, in front of St. Bartholomew's Church, an Episcopal church, assistant rector Andrea Maier stood in the street in white vestments, handing out a specially printed prayer for peace to the dazed throngs walking uptown. Dozens of people prayed inside the church. Special services for peace were being held every hour to accommodate people walking in off the street to pray. "We'll just do this all night if we have to," said the church rector, the Rev. William Tully.

Amir Chaudhary, a 24-year old taxi driver, watched the second tower collapse from across the Hudson River in Jersey City. "In a blink of my eye the twin towers were gone. There was no boom even. Didn't hear anything. Guys were on their knees crying, begging me to give them a ride away. I feel like maybe it's a bad dream: If I wake up, I could get the twin towers back."

Although the White House was not damaged, its people were not untouched by the tragedy. Barbara Olson, wife of

U.S. Solicitor General Theodore Olson, was on board the Los Angeles-bound airplane that took off from Dulles Airport and crashed into the Pentagon. Ms. Olson, a frequent political commentator, used a cellphone to call her husband just moments before she died. Late in the day, President Bush took time from his security briefing to call Mr. Olson and offer his condolences.

Before sending his aides home, Sen. John Warner of Virginia recalled to them, "I was in Washington when I heard about the Japanese attack on Pearl Harbor. This is another Pearl Harbor, and now your generation will have to meet the challenge."

By yesterday evening, military vehicles were patrolling the city, and police had cordoned off a three-square-block area near the White House.

In Arlington, Va., abutting Washington, fishermen plunking for catfish at a marina near the Pentagon said they could feel the heat from the explosion. The White House, the Capitol, and the Treasury and State departments were evacuated shortly after the crash at the Pentagon. "Get out! Get out!" police yelled as they swept through federal buildings. As legislators streamed out of the Capitol, the memorial chimes across the street played "God Bless America."

Hour of horror forever alters American lives

SEPTEMBER 12, 2001

By June Kronholz in Washington, Christina Binkley in Los Angeles, and Clare Ansberry in Pittsburgh

An hour of terror changed everything.

Far from the World Trade Center or the Pentagon, Florida shut down its state universities yesterday. San Francisco closed its schools, as well as the TransAmerica building and pedestrian access to the Golden Gate Bridge. Major League Baseball games were canceled.

The popular, needlelike Stratosphere tower on the north end of the Las Vegas strip was closed; so was the Paris casino's mock Eiffel Tower. University of Virginia psychologist Dewey Cornell canceled his lecture on student threats and violence inside the schools—so his audience of principals could go back to their schools to deal with the violence outside.

"You just thought America was the safest country," said Jesse Strauss, a 13-year-old eighth-grader at Pelham Middle School in a Manhattan suburb. His mother added, "Our world as we know it isn't going to return to normal for a long time."

Yesterday's terrorism darkened, marked and forever altered the way Americans live their lives.

"We are going to have to learn what a lot of other countries have gone through: to manage fear at a cultural and national level," said Charles Figley, a professor of trauma psychology at Florida State University. "We're getting a lesson in the way fear works."

In a country long proud and even boastful of its openness—a country where an ordinary citizen can stroll through the U.S. Capitol unescorted—the terrorist attacks are likely to force Americans to watch their steps and look over their shoulders. We already do a lot of that. Metal detectors now mark the front door of many government buildings, and security guards are a fixture in the lobby of most large office buildings.

'IT'S A TEST OF US'

But tightening still further carries its own danger of allowing terrorists to change a fundamental of American life. "It's a test of us," said Fred Dutton, a former aide to John and Robert Kennedy who now represents the government of Saudi Arabia in Washington. "Are we going to become insecure, and feel the need to have a less open, government-controlled society?"

"The worst thing we could do is say, 'This is the way things are going to be from now on,'" said Robert Butterworth, a Los Angeles psychologist who heads a disaster response network. Avoiding crowds, popular events and high profile venues like Disneyland or Sea World—which also closed yesterday—is a logical response, but we also "have to figure out constructive things to do," he insists.

Retaliation is another logical response. Indeed, President Bush promised as much. In an example of the country's mood, a scrawled sign outside a blood bank in New York ordered, "Mr. Bush, Bomb the bastards now."

But retaliation carries the risk of setting off a tightening spiral of violence and counterviolence not unlike the Middle East or Northern Ireland. Unlike countries that have had to learn to live with violence, "We are new at this," said Florida's Dr. Figley, who heads a project that has trained trauma teams in Yugoslavia. "My fear is we will overreach and make things worse rather than better by retribution, revenge, racism and marginalizing ethnic groups."

DOUBLE SECURITY AT SERVICES

That fear is especially true for Jews and Arabs. In Brookline, Mass., Congregation Kehillath Israel, like many other Jewish congregations, plans to double the security detail at next week's services for Rosh Hashanah, the Jewish New Year, and the Yom Kippur holy day 10 days later. Police cars will be stationed outside, and uniformed and plainclothes police inside.

"I think I now understand what it is like to live in Jerusalem," said the congregation's rabbi, William Hamilton.

Meanwhile, the city of Dearborn, Mich., moved to ensure there isn't a backlash against the city's large

Arab-American population by setting up an emergency operations center and putting 22 extra police officers on patrol.

Fear of terrorism is likely to lead Americans to tolerate more government surveillance—such as overhead video cameras at sporting events—than they have to date. "It's very likely in the wake of today's events that we're going to see a greater acceptance on the public's part—and on the court's part—to approve certain kinds of police tactics," said William Stuntz, a Harvard Law School professor.

"Today represents a real change in the world," he added. "It's not possible ever to think of these issues the same way."

In Redding, Calif., the chief of police, Robert P. Blankenship, agreed. "We're not going to be as comfortable and as secure as we once were. Looking at the TV, it's obvious now that we're vulnerable," he said.

Stepping up security isn't always possible, though. Fairfax, Va., already posts police officers in its secondary schools; unarmed security officers patrol the district; school doors are locked, teachers and staff wear identity badges. The effectiveness of metal detectors and surveillance cameras isn't proved, and anyway, they "create in kids the sense of a jail," said Daniel Domenech, the superintendent.

VIOLENCE FROM THE OUTSIDE

Inner-city schools have spent heavily on security technology in the past decade; the Houston school district even has its own SWAT squad. School security has long looked inward for a threat—to students carrying weapons or picking fights. But rising violence from the outside—from disgruntled parents or former employees—is drawing increased attention.

In the wake of the events yesterday, much of the U.S. was closed down—the federal government, schools, airports, the Hoover Dam near Las Vegas and the 47-story Bank of America building in downtown Miami. Also shuttered were the International Monetary Fund and the World Bank; their fall meetings, scheduled for later this month and a planned target of antiglobalization protests, may be canceled, a bank official said. Other institutions and facilities also will reopen amid greater security, re-sulting in increased frustration and delays.

How to explain the day's inexplicable events to their children will be a huge dilemma for parents. "You're not going to be able to keep this one under wraps," said Dr. Butterworth, the trauma psychologist. But he warned against using the tragedy as a teachable moment—a common response in the schools to huge national devel-opments—and overwhelming children.

A further fear is the possibility of copycat incidents that often follow acts of highly publicized violence. Some people "deal with their fears by making other people afraid," said University of Virginia's Dr. Cornell. Indeed, a New York school was evacuated shortly after the planes hit the World Trade Center tower because of a bomb threat. And in Las Vegas, 30,000 people at the In-ternational Banking Expo were turned away from the city's convention center after a bomb threat was called in from a pay phone on the center's premises.

Maxine Boarts, 71, a real-estate agent from Pitts-burgh on a weeklong vacation in Las Vegas, wasn't planning to leave until Friday, but is worried about get-ting a flight home—"if we're not afraid to" get on a plane then. Watching TV from a bar on Bally's casino floor, she said she and five companions considered rent-ing a car to drive home should they need to, but couldn't find a car to rent. It would be a multiday car trip, "but we'd be alive when we get there."

Ms. Boarts wondered if the events will disrupt her grandson's wedding plans next June, but is more con-cerned about the effect this will have on the nation's psychology. "We'll look at people so differently now," she said. "We're an open people. We're the kind that would talk to anyone. Now, it'll take a second thought."

A few things didn't change yesterday. Gambling at nearly all Las Vegas casinos continued at near normal volumes, although many gamblers watched CNN as closely as their cards. Merrill Lynch & Co. pressed ahead with a media and entertainment conference for about 500 investors at the Ritz-Carlton Hotel in Pasadena, Calif., after heated argument in the lobby between those Merrill officials who wanted to cancel it and Jessica Reif Cohen, a Merrill first vice president, who didn't.

And Americans, as they have in past moments of shared national tragedy, rolled up their collective sleeves. So many volunteers showed up at a Rockville Centre, N.Y., blood bank that overwhelmed staffers began handing out numbers, then turning away donors with anything but O-negative blood, which is accepted by any recipient. Nonetheless, dozens of would-be donors sat in a line of folding chairs that snaked around the building, waiting their turn.

Death toll, source of devastating attacks remain unclear

SEPTEMBER 12, 2001

By David S. Cloud and Neil King

By successfully attacking the most prominent symbols of American power—Wall Street and the Pentagon—terrorists have wiped out any remaining illusions that America is safe from mass organized violence.

That realization alone will alter the way the U.S. approaches its role in the world, as well as the way Americans travel and do business at home and abroad.

The death toll from the hijacked jets' attacks that destroyed the World Trade Center in lower Manhattan and damaged the Pentagon was impossible to gauge immediately. But it could eclipse the loss of life the country suffered in the Japanese attack on Pearl Harbor, when more than 2,300 perished.

It wasn't immediately clear who was responsible for the attack, though official attention focused on Middle East terrorist Osama bin Laden and his organization. One U.S. official said intelligence agencies already had gathered "strong information" linking Mr. bin Laden to the attacks. If the bin Laden organization isn't directly responsible, U.S. officials suspect, it could have sprung from a network of Islamic terror groups he supports and finances.

The gravity of the challenge to the country was summarized by Sen. John McCain, a Vietnam War veteran, who said: "These were not just crimes against the United States, they are acts of war."

Yet a war against terrorism is unlike a conventional war, and in some ways is far scarier. As a traumatized nation saw in gruesome detail on its television sets, terrorists attack civilians, not soldiers. And while the wars of the past century involved nation-states that could ultimately be defeated, a war against terrorism involves a less distinct enemy, whose defeat will be hard to ensure.

President Bush nearly promised armed response in his response to the tragedy. "America has stood down enemies before, and we will do so this time," he said in nationally televised address from the Oval Office. In a pointed warning to terrorists as well as to nations such as Afghanistan, which hosts Mr. bin Laden, the president declared: "We will make no distinction between the terrorists who committed these acts and those who harbored them."

Leaders of the House of Representatives and the Senate—shuttered yesterday amid the threat—plan to reconvene today in a special session to consider a bipartisan resolution condemning the terrorist attacks.

The sheer sophistication of the terrorists was remarkable. The FBI is operating on the assumption that there were multiple hijackers on each of the flights that struck New York and Washington. They apparently were armed with knives, and investigators believe that in at least two of the planes they "corralled and put in the back" the regular pilots, leading to the assumption they were experienced in handling jets. The FBI has been poring over airport security videos and flight manifests, and officials said they are finding strong leads to the identities of the hijackers from the names found there.

Last night, a law enforcement official said the FBI was seeking warrants to search a former residence of one of the hijackers in Daytona Beach, Fla. The official added that airport video surveillance, as well as names on the manifests, suggested that the hijackers were of Arab nationality. In some cases they were armed with box cutters in addition to knives. One passenger, Barbara Olson, the wife of Solicitor General Theodore Olson, telephoned the Justice Department in an attempt to reach her husband during one of the harrowing flights and said passengers were being held in the back of her plane before it smashed into the Pentagon.

In a clear sign of the operation's professional nature, a government official said the hijackers knew how to shut off the planes' transponders, which transmit airline flight number, speed and altitude. The official said it wasn't clear when the transponder in American Airlines Flight 11 from Boston, the first plane to strike the World Trade Center, was turned off, but it happened before it hit its target.

Meanwhile, average Americans far from the attack

sites already are feeling the aftershocks. Many suddenly are worrying about a matter that had never previously occurred to them: the safety of their cities from coordinated attack. Shortly after the World Trade Center attack, Peggy Smith, an office administrator with the law firm of Conley Rose & Tayon, left her downtown Houston office clutching computer-tapes and copies of account data for safe-keeping. "This is the end of the world as we know it," she said. "The United States will never be the same."

Underscoring that sentiment, American F-16 fighter jets were scrambled and two aircraft carriers were dispatched, not to some distant foreign destination, but to protect the skies and seas around Washington and New York. For the first time ever, all airline flights were grounded across the country. Financial markets were closed.

The events occurred without any apparent warning, prompting immediate questions in Washington and elsewhere about a failure of U.S. intelligence. How did such a broad and coordinated attack on multiple sites occur without U.S. intelligence officials getting wind of it? How were so many commercial airplanes hijacked and diverted hundreds of miles out of their flight paths toward the nation's largest population centers? "Today our government failed the American people," said Rep. Curt Weldon, a Pennsylvania Republican.

Yet there were some hints of trouble that were, in retrospect, under-appreciated. A senior U.S. intelligence official who left the government earlier this year said that the joint FBI-CIA counter-terrorism center had been receiving what it considered solid intelligence during the past two months pointing to possible imminent attacks by Islamic extremists. The intelligence consisted of a noticeable uptick in communications activity among Islamic extremist groups.

Some officials believed, though, that the attacks were likely to occur overseas, as did recent attacks against American embassies in Africa and against the USS *Cole* in Yemen. "We've known for the last two months that something was planned; just nobody knew where," the former senior official said.

At the same time, there had been heightened concern

for several weeks about a possible attack on a military target in the Washington area, said a current U.S. official. For that reason, checkpoints at Fort Myer and Fort Belvoir, both in the Washington area, have been more strict. At the White House, even the cars of members of Congress have been checked for explosives, and there was a partial evacuation several weeks ago when a car suspected of carrying a bomb was spotted outside the executive mansion. "Who the hell would think they would fly airplanes?" one official asked.

There are multiple reasons to suspect Islamic extremists, which explains the immediate focus on Mr. bin Laden or liked-minded compatriots. Earlier this year, in a Manhattan courtroom only a short walk away from the World Trade Center, four of his followers were convicted on all charges in the 1998 bombings of two U.S. embassies in Africa. At one point, sentencing had been set for today, though that had been postponed.

At the same time, Sheik Omar Abdul Rahman, the spiritual leader of Al-Gama'a al-Islamiyya, Egypt's largest militant group, sits in a U.S. prison in Minnesota for his role in planning an earlier but failed attempt at terrorism in New York. His followers have been seething ever since he was convicted in 1995 for his role in a plot to stage a series of terrorist attacks in New York, and officials say he may have helped inspire a bombing in a parking garage of the same World Trade Center destroyed. "I've never forgotten about that blind sheik and what a symbol he was to radical Islamists," said Robert Blitzer, the FBI's former domestic terrorism chief. "This could be revenge."

Ties between Sheik Abdul Rahman's followers and the bin Laden world appear to have tightened. Just last month, the foreign minister of the Taliban, the Islamic organization that effectively runs Afghanistan and harbors Mr. bin Laden, suggested the U.S. could trade Sheik Abdul Rahman for several Western aid workers under arrest in Kabul.

The violence raging between Israel and Palestinians has given Islamic extremists more reason to be agitated at the U.S. Such anti-American entities as Iraq and the Hamas and Hezbollah extremist organizations have rallied to the side of the Palestinians, railing against both

Israel and its American ally.

In any event, the attacks themselves were so intricately planned and so vast in scope that they transcend any past terrorist action. Some experts speculated that the enormity of the plot could even point to the involvement of a hostile government, such as Iraq or Iran.

Many experts, though, agreed the simultaneous nature of the attacks and other trademarks pointed to the larger terror network run or somehow inspired by Mr. bin Laden.

The list of non-state actors even remotely capable of pulling off such an attack is quite small. The only group generally known for staging simultaneous, complex terrorist attacks is Al Qaeda, the loose organization led by Mr. bin Laden. The U.S. has indicted him for the two 1998 embassy bombings in East Africa, and U.S. officials say that evidence points convincingly to his involvement in the bombing last year of the USS *Cole* in the Yemeni port of Aden.

Other groups such as Hamas on the West Bank, or Hezbollah, in Lebanon, have staged truck bombings and suicide attacks in Israel and elsewhere across the region. But no one has ever pulled off a series of attacks of this magnitude. Nor, experts say, are either of those groups prone to targeting Americans, despite the fact that anger is now high toward the U.S. across the Arab world.

James Steinberg, former deputy national security adviser under President Clinton, said he believed that an attack of this size was likely the work of several groups within Mr. bin Laden's greater orbit. Of those, he listed the Algerian-based Armed Islamic Jihad and the Al-Gama'a al-Islamiyya, Egypt's largest militant group. Mr. bin Laden's Al Qaeda has been known for several years to be in close contact with operatives from a wide range of militant groups across North Africa and the Middle East.

Other terrorism experts said the attacks, in their sheer audacity, bore many trademarks of the bin Laden strategy. The African embassy bombings, one in Tanzania and the other in Kenya, occurred less than 10 minutes apart, while the attacks on the two World Trade Center towers happened within 18 minutes. The fact that the World Trade Center was at the center of the plot also points to the actors behind the 1993 trade center bombing, many of whom were later found to have had close ties to the bin Laden network, according to U.S. officials involved in the investigation.

Yet some experts also said the complexity of the operation made it unlikely that Al Qaeda could have pulled it off without help from other terrorist organizations more experienced at hijackings and the technical problems of overcoming airport security. Al Qaeda has been building ties with groups like Islamic Jihad, the Iranian-backed Palestinian terrorist group, which has threatened attacks against U.S. interests recently in response to Israeli use of U.S.-supplied fighters and helicopters on the West Bank.

One official noted that several of the crashed jets were laden with fuel, which would make it more difficult for hijackers who took control of the jets to maneuver them unless they were experienced or had some training at controlling large airliners.

"If it turns out that bin Laden claims responsibility for these attacks, he couldn't have done it without help from professionals, like Islamic Jihad," said Robert Baer, a former CIA officer and Middle East specialist.

Certainly the attack would signal a frightening increase in Al Qaeda's deadly skills. Its previous attacks have used truck bombs and other crude devices. Other attacks linked to the group have been plagued by problems. More than a year before the bombing of the *Cole*, another attempt to bomb a U.S. warship failed when a boat carrying explosives sank. A Los Angeles airport bombing was thwarted altogether.

On a more ominous note, some former terrorism officials also speculated that the attacks may reveal that Mr. bin Laden now has a large and sophisticated domestic terror network operating within the U.S.

"It is not to be ruled out that there are tacticians, bomb-makers and plotters now fully active in the U.S., many of whom have been here for years," said Daniel Benjamin, a former counterterrorism official in the Clinton White House.

The diffuse and overlapping organization of today's terror groups became particularly clear after the aborted millennium plot in December 1999, when U.S. border agents arrested an Algerian crossing into Washington state with a trunk-load of explosives. Tentacles of that plot, which targeted the Los Angeles airport and other sites, extended from Canada and cities across the U.S. to actors in Algeria, Sudan, Egypt and Afghanistan.

In a bizarre twist, some experts suspect that the bin Laden organization may also have had a hand in a suicide bomb attack against Ahmed Shah Massoud on Sunday in northern Afghanistan. Mr. Massoud leads the opposition force fighting Afghanistan's Taliban leaders, who control about 90 percent of the country. The Taliban have given refuge to Mr. bin Laden since the mid-1990s. There are conflicting reports as to whether Mr. Massoud survived the blast.

For many Americans, a more tangible and bitter image of anti-American sentiment abroad will be the scenes of some abroad celebrating the terrorist attacks on Americans. In the West Bank, thousands of Palestinians took to the streets to herald the attacks and express their happiness. And in Sierra Leone, Pakistani members of a United Nations peacekeeping force were laughing, smiling and slapping hands at the mission headquarters in Freetown.

If the attack was launched by a non-state entity, choosing when and where to retaliate may not be easy.

After the bombing of two U.S. embassies in East Africa in 1998, President Clinton ordered cruise-missile strikes on a site where Mr. bin Laden and his top lieutenants were supposed to be meeting. As it turned out, the meeting had ended and the strikes came too late.

"The big question for everyone now is how much intelligence do we have? Do we have the kind of intelligence that we need?" said retired Gen. Dennis Reimer, former Army chief of staff and now head of the Oklahoma National Memorial Institute for the Prevention of Terrorism.

The U.S. could move more easily to punish any state that abetted Mr. bin Laden, especially Afghanistan, which has refused repeated demands to turn him over. A devastating military strike on the Taliban's headquarters could be one course.

Afghanistan's Taliban leaders were clearly very nervous about that possibility, denying Mr. bin Laden's involvement and calling for American "courts" to seek justice. A series of explosions last night in Kabul, the Afghan capital, apparently were part of internal fighting between the Taliban and its internal foes, and not part of any U.S. response to the terrorist attacks.

Writers' Workshop

Talking Points

1) Reporters must often decide whether to include gruesome facts in stories about such tragedies as murders and automobile accidents. Bryan Gruley, like others writing about the Sept. 11 attacks, faced such a decision. He chose to use some of the details, including "a severed head with long, dark hair." What should guide a journalist's decision about when and how to use such information?

2) Gruley had to rely almost exclusively on information that *Wall Street Journal* reporters filed from the field. He could not talk to them and could not afford the time necessary to communicate with them by e-mail. What challenges do you think are created by that kind of reporting? What might a journalist do to ensure accuracy under such circumstances?

3) Read David S. Cloud and Neil King's story about the fallout from the attacks. Discuss how they handled the speculation—far from confirmed on that day—about Osama bin Laden and his Al Qaeda network. How successfully, under deadline, did the writers handle the balance between helping readers understand *why* while not extending beyond what they knew?

4) Gruley tells the story of the New York attacks with two narrative vehicles: He uses anecdotes to re-create the moment when the planes hit the buildings, each time adding new insights through quotes. He also moves the story geographically from the site of the attacks to the edges of Manhattan and beyond, tracking the movement of fleeing people. What effect do those writing vehicles have on the tone of the story?

Assignment Desk

1) Deadline stories always present journalists with the significant challenge of getting to official sources and nailing down facts that are complete and verifiable. Imagine that a plane were to crash into a landmark building in your town. List the official sources, by name and contact number, whom you'd need to reach.

2) Quotes, Gruley said, are just facts. In his story, he uses quotes collected by *Journal* reporters to add details not otherwise found in the story. Look through a collection of your most recent stories. How many quotes would fit Gruley's definition? How many are just filler?

3) The ending of Gruley's story was changed during editing. Its original ending quoted a young Arab taxi driver, Amir Chaudhary, saying he wished it was all a bad dream from which he'd soon awaken. The edited version ends with the phrase "God Bless America." Read Gruley's thoughts on the ending in the interview, then rewrite the ending, including the final quote but finishing with Chaudhary. Compare the two. Which works better and why?

A conversation with
Bryan Gruley

KEITH WOODS: Sept. 11 will be one of those dates on which everyone remembers where they were when they heard about the attacks. Where were you?

BRYAN GRULEY: I was in early. I was sitting at this desk, and from where I'm sitting I can see a television about 50 feet away. I saw a bunch of people gathered around it, so I walked over there. I remember I was standing next to Bob Greenberger, one of my colleagues, and we were watching the first tower burn; and, of course, we both thought it was just something innocuous, some commuter plane or some goofball in a Cessna flew into it.

And then we saw the other plane, and I remember I didn't get it at first. I thought it was some sort of reconnaissance plane sent up by the cops. I saw it. It circled and then it disappeared and the building exploded. I couldn't really tell how big it was. I didn't realize it was a 747.

When the building exploded, I thought it was just some sort of secondary explosion from the original crash. But Greenberger, who has done stories on terrorism and such, immediately got it, and he said that it was a terrorist attack, and then it dawned on me that that was a second plane.

We were having this staff thing—we call it the wire breakfast—to plan the Column Five feature that runs on Fridays. As it happens, our guest that day was a guy from the Clinton administration who had worked on terrorism. We didn't have our meeting. We all filed into [Washington bureau chief] Alan Murray's corner office and started talking about what we were going to do. This was obviously a terrorist attack; and, as we were sitting there, somebody's cell phone rang. It was Ted Bridis, who was then one of our reporters—he has gone back to the AP since then. He was driving in from Virginia and saw the third plane hit the Pentagon. That's how we heard about it. Which is really scary. In retrospect, you say it was all over then, but we had no idea that it was all over.

At this point in New York, the senior leadership of
***The Wall Street Journal* is scrambling, trying to figure**
out where to go to even set up to talk about stories.
You didn't have the same kind of chaotic situation in
D.C., did you?

No, because everything's working here. I remember we
met and our conclusion that morning was that we would
do a story, a "leder." We didn't know that there would be
banner headlines and stuff. We were operating under
our normal expectation that there would be two leders
and one of them would be a leder on how this changes
the world.

Define a "leder" for me.

The leders are the Column One and Column Six stories.
We were figuring that Jerry Seib, who has a lot of exper-
tise in terrorism and military and that kind of stuff, would
pull together a leder on what this means going forward,
how this changes things for the United States. And Alan
assumed that New York would put together a leder on
what happened up there, and we would file some stuff to
them about what happened at the Pentagon. It seemed, at
that point, the main thing was up in New York. So there
were various assignments given to various people around
the bureau. Some people were sent out as close as they
could get to the Pentagon site, and other reporters were
told to start making calls—particularly to the military, but
also to the intelligence agencies, the FBI, and others—to
figure out what was going on.

I imagine that there had to be some dueling loyalties
here. I'm wondering how you manage when the
journalist wants the story, but the citizen has to be
concerned about personal safety and family.

Let me give you a personal anecdote. My daughter,
Kaitlin, called me. She's a freshman at Elon University
in North Carolina. She called me from school, crying
and telling me to get out of the district. I told her not to
worry, I'm probably in the safest place in the world now,
because I assumed that the military had buttoned down

this city as tight as possible. And by then the planes were all out of the air. One of the first things I did after all this happened was call my wife and say I'm okay and we're going to put out the paper. I mean we knew we had to put out the paper and we *wanted* to put out the paper. What we didn't know that early in the day was that it was going to be a little harder than normal. It was just a really heavy day. For everybody.

What were some of the critical decisions that helped the staff to respond, both to the reporting and the writing challenges that you faced?

Well, from my ivory tower perspective in Washington, I think the most important decisions were made by the reporters in New York City and here, particularly those in New York, who immediately set to work reporting. Some of these people were getting off the ferry or getting out of cabs, some of them were actually in our building up there. Without any instructions from their bosses or anybody else, they just started working. They got out their notebooks, started interviewing people, and gathering the information that made that story. To me, that's the most important decision that was made that day, and it wasn't a top-down decision because it couldn't be. That is the best evidence of Paul Steiger's leadership of the paper, that, when the bosses were essentially out of the loop, the players got on the field and played.

And when did you get your charge as the person who would do the rewrite?

Alan said we needed to put together a leder for the Europe edition, and we needed it done by 2 o'clock. Normally it's 3. So I did it. I used memos from Neil King and David Cloud. I was finishing up the European leder when Alan stopped by my desk and said, "New York is not going to be able to do a leder. We're just not in touch. You're going to have to pull that together." I just said okay, because by then there were reporters who were showing up on e-mail.

From New York?

Primarily from New York. I remember my e-mails just clicking down. They were sending e-mails to all staff. It clogged up the e-mail for a while because all these e-mails were going to everybody on the staff, hundreds of people. But they were doing it because they didn't know who they might hit and who they might not hit, so they wanted to make sure somebody heard. It would say this is so-and-so, I'm okay, here's where I am, and here's what I have so far, and I'll file you some more. So I had a bunch of those. Soon as I finished with the Europe leder, I started converting the story, but mostly I just started fresh.

Was this one-way communication—them sending information and you using it?

For the most part, mainly because I didn't have time to communicate with them. I mean, e-mails were coming in just one after another, literally, and you had to separate out the ones that were just saying, "Here's so-and-so and I'm okay." I'd look at those and move on and get the ones that sent a memo of real reporting. And I just started plucking those out and building this enormous Word file that ended up being 600-plus inches long.

With so much information coming in at once, what tools did you use to manage all of this?

Well, physically what I was doing was taking stuff out of these e-mails and throwing it into a Word document I called "Terror." At some point, I printed it out and I threw it here on my desk, and I just started looking through it and circling things I absolutely wanted to use, the things that were just terrific little tales. And, unfortunately, that got cumbersome. I didn't have the time because more e-mails were coming in as I was doing that, and I didn't want to miss a really good one. At one point, I had to say, "All right, I'm not looking at any more stuff. I just can't. I'll look at those later for a later edition. I have enough great stuff to move on."

You're circling things, you're deciding what will go in, what will not go in, on the fly. Even then you've still got to take a 29,000-word document and make it

4,000. What was the rest of that process?

Well, I just started writing. Sometimes that's just the best thing to do. I started with over 29,000 words. I had over 300 inches of notes—that would be 12,000 to 15,000 words—when I wrote the first version, and then more was coming in. But at some point I just stopped looking at it all, so probably the last 10,000 words came in and I didn't even look at them.

There were a couple of things that Alan wanted me to do. He wanted me to make sure that I had a little bit of interplay between New York and Washington high in the story. He didn't want it to be all New York. It was really just a matter of falling back on what always works, particularly when you have a story that unfolds in chronological order, as this did. Just fall back on the chronology. Move from the attacks in New York City and up through Manhattan, and that's sort of how the story moves: from the center of the attacks northward, with some exceptions.

How much time did you get for this assignment?

I remember I didn't start this story until 4 o'clock. I had the lead and Alan looked at that and he said, "Great, go for it." I asked how much time I had. He said, "You have to have it in by 5." I work on a lot of projects now, and Murray was giving me hell: "You don't have two weeks to write this." Murray likes to yank my chain.

Two hours would have been nice.

Well, as it turned out the whole story didn't get up there until a little before 7. And I was filing it in short bursts.

Was it a single write-through then? I mean, no chance for rewrite, no chance for revision?

No. I had very little time. I mean, Alan was gently prodding me, and sometimes not so gently. So I would send him little chunks, six or seven paragraphs at a time, and he'd keep pushing me for more. And that's pretty much how I proceeded.

Did you have any chance at all to do reporting in the middle of all of this?

No. If I had questions that could be answered by somebody here, I'd just yell out. For example, I had some question about how many companies and people worked in the World Trade Center, and I just asked John Wilke, who sits next to me, if he could do this for me, and in 15 minutes he had it done. That was the extent of my reporting. I just had to write. The final story was 52 inches—3,000 words—so about one-tenth of what we started with.

That's a significant editing down.

Hey, when you're using an ax, it's easy. It wasn't like I had 30,000 words and I had edited it down, which would have been harder. It was coming in and I was building: Here's a great anecdote. Here's a great anecdote. Here's a great anecdote. My plan was, write a terrific lead, then give them bang, bang, bang, three—I'm Catholic, I always think in threes—three kick-ass anecdotes. I had three, and it was nice that they all came at the moment of conception, so to speak, when the planes hit, because that was the greatest moment of shock for everybody. Then I would back off and tell a little bit about Washington and then back off and tell the news and then just go tell the story. And then it was just a matter of pulling things out and putting them in order. I remember flipping paragraphs up and down and trying to put them in some sort of order and transition so they would make sense.

How quickly did that plan come into focus for you?

I don't know if it really came into focus. I just sort of did it. It was in my head, but you write a lot of these and edit a lot of these narratives. It's just easy—if you have the stuff, I mean. I had unbelievable stuff to choose from.

How difficult was it to decide what level of detail to use when you're writing about such things as a severed head and other body parts?

Well, at the *Journal* we usually go for understatement. But I thought if somebody wants to take these details out, I'll let somebody else do it. I think they should be in there because this is what this is about, and this is how horrible this was, and it was such an unfamiliar sight to Americans. These are the kinds of things we see on the evening news and we click the channel and go over to Letterman or whatever, and now it was real, it was in our streets, and we had to confront it. Nobody ever asked me about it. There was no hesitation as far as I know. I wrote it and it went in as I wrote it, as it was reported. The heads and bodies, the severed arm were reported by Jon Hilsenrath, who must have been right there.

Why is it that the fourth airplane isn't mentioned until the 15th paragraph?

Why is it? I don't know. That's the short answer. Even though it took place in a span of two or three hours, it felt like a span of a few seconds, but I know I didn't think I had to write news, like "This happened, that happened." I did want to get the fourth plane in before the jump. I did not. But it wasn't a conscious decision, and no editor asked me about it. I think we thought it would be dealt with. The David Cloud and Neil King story was going to be more newsy, and there would be five or six stories on the front page. My charge was simply to take our readers there and tell them, show them what had happened. So in retrospect, might I move that one-sentence reference up? Yeah, I might. I might. I'd have to think about it first. Because when you move the sentence up, then you want to deal with all the to-and-fro over the calls to the planes, which are very dramatic and which we got very late, everybody got very late.

Some of that, I'm assuming, was the nature of doing the story from top to bottom in pieces the way you were doing it.

Yeah. And when you're doing it in pieces like that, you're less cognizant of where things are in relation to the jump. I do these seminars around the empire about how to write leders, and I tell people over and over again, "If you're writing a narrative, get back to the narrative before the jump, the jump, the jump." It's crucial, because that's a trap door for readers. If you start a story with the idea that you're taking your readers inside someplace that they've never been—a day-trading room or a war zone or something—and then you pull away from the scene, you can get bogged down in explaining the significance, and quoting this source and that analyst. The reader gets to the jump and he's like, "Well, I thought this was going to be a narrative." Now he's in some explication. He's bored, so he doesn't go back. You gotta get back. I always tell them get back, get back, get back. Maybe in retrospect I would want to put that plane in before the jump, but I prefer to get back to the narrative, which I did succeed in doing before the jump.

You mentioned earlier that you were trying to take people to that point of awareness, then move forward. It seems throughout the story that each time we visit a new person, we go back to a couple of minutes before the attack and then take them through it again, except this time it's a different story.

What was so fascinating and horrifying about this day was the juxtaposition of normalcy with chaos. So it was important to show, for example, Paul and Lee Manton, who had just moved to New York. They're holding their two kids, and so now you have a picture of them in their house or their apartment or whatever it was—that normalcy—and suddenly they're frantically trying to find out where to go. I would think this is an example of one of those circle-backs. You have a character. You try to say here's who they were, here's who they are now. Because they've changed. I mean they didn't change in nature, but their lives changed in an instant. I can't say I had a conscious thought about that. It just sort of came naturally.

What were some of the most interesting things you left out of the story? There must have been some things that you just said, gee, if I had another 10 inches, I'd really like to get this in.

There were some things on the margins that would have

been nice to have in, but I think I got the best representative scenes. There were other good things from people, but they were similar to stuff that was already in: a simple detail like the water at the end of the Brooklyn Bridge, which I love. The cups, the people helping one another. Then, as it happens, this ironworker's there and gives this summing statement that America's never going to be the same again. I'm sure I had other Brooklyn Bridge stuff, but it just seemed like that did it, that accomplished what we were trying to do.

Were you thinking geographically that way?

Yeah, I can say that I was. This image of people streaming out of New York City reminded me of the many images we've seen of refugees from Somalia, Bosnia, Kosovo, name it. In fact, one of my friends, Mark Fritz, wrote a terrific book about this, and he embedded these images in my mind of refugees, and that's what I thought of. And I thought that's such an alien image to America: people bolting their homes, some of them their businesses, and streaming across this great Brooklyn Bridge, looking over their shoulders, and seeing this while they're fleeing from their own city and seeing their towers being destroyed.

Tell me how you landed on the ending.

The original ending was the cab driver. I just loved his plaintive quote: "I feel like maybe it's a bad dream: If I wake up, I could get the twin towers back." That's originally how I ended it. Now, I'm not a big fan of endings in quotes. If you look in today's papers, 99 percent of the features will end with some quote that says, "And that's how my story was today."

Is that why you don't like them?

Yeah, I think they're overused and they're cliché and most of the time they tell me nothing new. I want to learn something new. I love stories that end with action. But that said, I just thought his quote drew the image very well of the twin towers being gone. I did not notice, but

Marcus Brauchli, our national news editor, sent me an e-mail saying, "How interesting that you ended with an Arab." I hadn't noticed that. It wasn't intentional at all. That said, Larry Rout, who edited the story in New Jersey, took it and flipped it around and ended it with "God bless America," which is just fine. It ends with action, which I liked. And it has the other virtue that we didn't have to go from New York to Washington to New York again. The New York section ends with Mr. Chaudhary, and then we go to Washington and we're gone, we're out of the story.

There is even some irony in the fact that it went from ending with an Arab to ending with something as American as "God bless America."

Sure, sure. Larry did it, and that's cool. You know, this was not a night for fighting.

In retrospect, can you imagine any training or preparation that would have made it easier to do your job?

How do you train somebody to do this? It'd take years, I think, or at least you'd have to have experienced a bunch of these stories. I haven't been in this particular kind of story, but I've been in my share of stories that had to be written in a matter of minutes, let alone a matter of hours. I couldn't have done this when I was 25 or 30 years old. It certainly wouldn't have been easy for me. I'm not saying it was easy, but I never really panicked or anything. It was just a matter of putting it in order. As always, writing is almost 90 percent reporting. It's all getting the stuff. If you have the stuff, it's a lot easier to write than if you don't. And I certainly had it.

What did you learn from this story that would be important to students?

You know, one thing I noticed in reading it over this morning was—and this is a great credit to the reporters here—we let several of these people just talk because they were so good at doing it. Sometimes quotes don't work as well as a writer's own description and observation. But sometimes they really work well. I think in this story they worked well. Andrew Lenney's long description: "It was coming down the Hudson. It was banking toward me. I saw the tops of both wings." You know, the reader saw this and didn't see it. So they lock in with him where he was. But then he starts to tell them things they didn't see and then there are people in the Pentagon and there was the priest. I think in this story those things worked. It was almost like TV. You can see those things and feel them. That was helpful and, again, that's just great reporting. That's not writing per se. The choice to put the quote there is writing, but mainly these are just facts. Quotes are really just facts.

How did you acknowledge the reporters who helped in the story?

You know, I thanked some in e-mails when I could. When we won the award two weeks ago, we ran a short story. I sent a note to Tim Lemmer, who helps run our web page, Dowjones.net, where I knew we'd have our own announcement, and I sent him the names of all the people who contributed, especially the ones in New York. They're my heroes because a lot of them risked their lives. Without them we don't have a story.

There's no byline that could accommodate that, that's for sure.

No, and we did the right thing not having a byline on that story. There was some talk late in the evening about what we should do. I said there's so much good work here that I don't think we should single out anybody.

Recalling deadline with
The Wall Street Journal

Jon Hilsenrath, economics reporter

I went into the office early on Sept. 11, planning to get some work done before heading over to the Marriott Hotel in the World Trade Center complex for an economics conference. I was at my desk when the first tower went up in flames just before 9 a.m. I have trouble hearing, so I didn't hear the first crash. But I heard a colleague screaming in the library, and I ran over and saw the tower in flames.

I ran down to our ninth floor to try to find an editor who might be getting going on our coverage. I found Paul Steiger, our managing editor, and John Bussey, our foreign editor, just starting to get mobilized. I told Paul I was ready to contribute, and will always appreciate the priority of his instructions: First, he said, I should not put my life in jeopardy. Second, he said, I should grab a notebook, get outside, and try to figure out what was going on. I didn't have a sense of the magnitude of what was unfolding, but the fact that the first thing he said was, "Don't get yourself killed," suggests in retrospect that he did.

I hurried to get outside and made my way to a pedestrian bridge that led over the West Side Highway to the foot of the World Trade Center complex. As I went outside, I called my wife, Cristina, to tell her that there was a fire at the World Trade Center, but that I was all right and she shouldn't worry.

At that point, I didn't know what had caused the fire, but I suspected it might be a plane. Sure enough, as I crossed over the highway on the pedestrian overpass, I saw what looked like aircraft wreckage lying on the street, just south of the towers. I went to check it out and saw much more: chunks of flesh all over the road; an arm severed at the elbow, the index finger outstretched as if pointing. Near it was a decapitated head with long, dark hair covered in what looked like a bandana.

I'm no war correspondent, so covering a scene like

this didn't come naturally. My first instinct was to search for small details. Small facts are much more powerful than fancy prose. As I scribbled in my notebook, a police officer came up and told me to clear away; debris was falling from the building and I could get hit. Normally I would try to find a way to get around him, but this situation was so grave, something told me that I should listen to him.

Just then I heard a loud, ominous rumbling in the sky. I turned and saw a giant commercial jet banking low. It flew right over my head, roaring full throttle toward the towers. I was 200 to 300 yards away and knew immediately that the city was under attack. As the second tower burst with a fiery explosion, I was running south to get out of the way of falling debris.

I called Cristina again, assuming she had just watched this on television, knowing I was right there. She asked me to get out of there, smartly reasoning that the buildings could fall. But I tried to assure her that I was safe and insisted I had a job to do. For the next 30 to 45 minutes, as I tried to interview eyewitnesses and people fleeing the building, a crowd formed and we watched as both towers burned, spewing black smoke, and people jumped from the upper floors to their deaths. At first, I had a hard time distinguishing between debris and falling bodies, but I soon came to the grim realization that the debris had a way of fluttering to the ground, while the bodies accelerated as they fell.

It was hard to stay focused. I set my mind to interviewing people who were inside the buildings. They experienced things that eyewitnesses like myself hadn't. The street just south of the tower was literally covered in shoes left by people running away.

After a few interviews, I made my way back toward our office, reasoning that we might be organizing our reporting efforts there. I was about a block away in Battery Park City when another terrible rumbling sound came. Everybody started running in my direction. Until this point, I was shocked but not scared. But now things got truly frightening because all I saw was running and all I heard was rumbling. I didn't see the building collapsing because our office building obscured the view. I thought another plane was coming at the area, but I didn't know where it was coming from or where it was going. So I ran, like everybody else, south and toward the water.

Then I saw a giant cloud of dust engulfing the southern tip of Manhattan. There was no avoiding it. I realized the WTC had collapsed, and having just watched dozens of people falling from the towers, many of them presumably jumping as they choked on black smoke, this also was a very scary moment.

The sun disappeared, and it was like a surreal snowstorm in there. Suddenly quiet, you could only see a few feet in front of you. A steady flow of tiny white debris rained down. But you could breathe if you covered your mouth with your shirt. I slowly made my way south, and then around the southern tip of Manhattan toward the South Street Seaport, with so many others, orderly, and refugee-like.

In the midst of all of this, I was working my mobile phone madly, trying to get back in touch with Cristina to tell her I was okay, and then to editors to try to call in a report from the scene. But as I joined this march away from Ground Zero, I became very conflicted about what I should be doing. As a husband and father of two beautiful kids, my instinct now was to get out of there. At the same time, I realized that I was walking away from a scene where thousands of people would be dying. How could I leave? What about my responsibilities as a journalist?

Then the second tower came down, and my brother got through to me on my phone and said the Pentagon had been hit, and that rumors were everywhere that several other planes had been hijacked. I found a man nearby, covered from head to toe in soot, standing near the South Street Seaport. He had been in one of the towers and escaped. But his son was a policeman. This man thought his son would be down there. He wanted to go back. I interviewed him. And then I left the scene.

Deadline Tip:

I'm still not sure what journalistic lessons to take out of that day. It was so extraordinary. On a very basic level, it reinforced a lesson you learn in your first reporting job. People and small details illuminate stories, and so they are the essence of good reporting.

Phil Kuntz, assistant Washington bureau chief

I was in New York for meetings, staying at the World Financial Center Marriott about two blocks away from the trade center. My meetings were later in the morning, so I was sleeping in. I was on the 27th floor.

The first explosion woke me up, and I started watching the fire. I didn't know at the time that it was a plane. I called up my bureau chief in D.C., Alan Murray, and he told me to try to do a phone interview with CNBC. I got them on the phone and we were getting set up, but somehow our wires got crossed and I lost them. While I was watching the fire, I saw the second explosion. That's when I realized it was a terrorist attack. For the next five hours, I had no way of reaching anyone in Washington, so my colleagues there had no idea what had happened to me.

We got evacuated from the hotel. I started interviewing people in the lobby and later on the street as we headed south away from the towers. I was taking notes on scraps of paper—the hotel note pads from my room—talking to as many people as I could. I was feeling rather helpless, trying to pay attention to my own safety while also trying to talk to people.

While interviewing a guy about six blocks south of the trade center, I decided to move about a half-block west because I wanted to see the damage to the second building—the one I saw get hit. Just as I did so, the building fell. I was soon engulfed in a cloud of smoke and ash.

We all headed south to Battery Park, and we came to a restaurant—a glass-encased restaurant in the park. The people inside were panicked themselves, and they didn't want to let anyone in. Eventually somebody emerged from the crowd with a hammer and he broke the window and I helped kick in the glass. At that point, the manager opened the door and people barreled into the restaurant. Once we were inside, the restaurant workers were great, passing out water and drinks. The manager later apologized, saying he was unsure what to do and wanted to prepare the restaurant for the huge crowd, which included numerous school children, toddlers, and several dogs. Most people, including me, were covered with ash. I interviewed more people at the restaurant.

They started bringing ferries to wherever they could pull up and escorting people onto the boats to take us to Jersey City. It was like a refugee scene there, with people wandering around, covered in ash, asking where they could get a hotel or a car. The hotels were filled and the rental cars were all sold out. I wandered around until I found a school about a half-mile inland. I walked up to an adult, who happened to be the principal, and I said "I'm a journalist and I need a phone and e-mail." She said, "My office is yours for the rest of the day." I typed up my notes, and by shortly after 2 o'clock, I sent in a memo that recounted my day and the accounts of witnesses I had interviewed. It turns out that Bryan [Gruley] used the anecdote about the guy I was interviewing right before the building fell. It ended up being the story's lead anecdote.

Deadline Tip:

In a situation like this—and who knows if there ever will come another situation like this—e-mail is a better way of communicating. I wasted a lot of time trying to reach people by phone when I should have been looking for a computer hooked to the Internet.

Ann Davis, reporter

I heard about the attacks while listening to National Public Radio at home in my apartment on the Upper West Side. The phone worked only sporadically, but whenever I got a dial tone, I called as many friends and colleagues as possible. It was easier to get a connection to a number outside New York, and I called one of my best friends in Los Angeles to tell her I was safe.

At that point, no other media outlet, as far as I am aware, had reported on what happened in the final minutes before 658 people perished at Cantor Fitzgerald, the giant bond brokerage house on the top floors of Tower One. I knew my friend's father used to run one of Cantor's offices, and her brothers had worked at Cantor in New York, so my main concern was making sure everyone was okay.

Her family was fine, but they had just heard about the deaths of hundreds of friends from grief-stricken brokers at Cantor in Los Angeles. At the time the first plane hit, Cantor offices in Dallas, Los Angeles, Darien, Conn., and elsewhere had been on conference calls with several Cantor trading desks in New York. The Los Angeles office heard someone say, "I think a plane just hit us." For more than five minutes, outside offices heard people yelling that they couldn't breathe, and literally dying, before the phone cut off.

This was a deeply personal tragedy for my friend and not the kind of situation in which I could press for great detail. At the same time, it was an experience shared by hundreds of people at Cantor offices worldwide, and one of the most poignant stories about the victims to emerge. So I described what happened in e-mails to *Journal* colleagues. It was one of the lead anecdotes for the next day's paper and gave other colleagues a jumping-off point to report further on the event. It also led to my collaboration with others on a much longer front-page story about Cantor in October.

Wall Street bond firms weren't my beat. I just happened to tap into this part of the Sept. 11 story. The sounds of chaos from Cantor trading desks was one of the saddest things I heard that day, and I was reminded that I should listen to anyone and everyone who had information about what had happened.

From there, my reporting was almost all on the Internet. I passed on tidbits as I learned them. It was the only efficient way for me to make a difference. We were participants. Anything that happened to anyone we knew was part of the story. Our sources were friends, doormen, shopkeepers—not the people we usually turned to. It totally changes the way you think about doing your job.

Deadline Tip:

The lesson for me was to remember that everyone in your life can be a source of information. The difference with friends is that you have to realize what is personal to them and what they are comfortable sharing. You have to be careful not to exploit those relationships. I never quote friends in my stories, but I do sometimes use them as a barometer, for perspective. My friend, her father, and brother had hundreds of friends killed that day. It was amazing to me that they had to go through that. At the same time, they appreciated the fact that the media were grieving with them.

Mark Schoofs, foreign correspondent

My role that day was small, just one of hundreds who tried to do our jobs. I was exhausted. I had been up at 2 a.m. trying to call Tanzania, then I'd gotten up again to try to catch people at the end of the business day in Tanzania. At just about 8:45, I got out of my apartment, bleary-eyed, and looked up and saw this gigantic hole in the World Trade Center. It was immediately electrifying, like shock had run through my body. I thought, "Oh, my God, I need to do something." I ran back into my apartment and called family members and told them I was fine, not to worry.

I got on my bike and headed downtown. It was remarkable how the events of the day didn't seem to sink in. Here I was, driving my bike into this absolutely silent exodus of thousands and thousands of people walking uptown, quietly. It was something biblical, like something out of a movie.

I was sure this was a terrorist attack from the time I saw the first tower. It was a perfect day, and planes don't run into skyscrapers on days like this. The second plane was only confirmation. I remember being very happy that the towers hadn't fallen. The terrorists hadn't totally won.

When I got downtown near the World Trade Center along the Hudson River, I got off my bike and started interviewing people. I was really lucky that I didn't get down there so fast that I was in danger when the buildings fell. But at that moment, when the buildings started to fall, nobody said anything. Everybody knew what was happening, but they were silent for a second. People only started to scream a couple of moments after, and then even more when that cloud started coming toward us.

The only thing I could think of at that instant was not that I would get killed, not that the building would fall on top of me, but, "Oh, my God, this is going to be so unpleasant." I still had the bike in one hand. A nanny was nearby with a baby, and the nanny was completely panicked, screaming, and crying. So I took the baby. Then a man came behind us, saw that my hands were full, and he took the baby and we all moved away. In that exchange, I lost my notebook. For the rest of the day, I took notes on business cards and numbered them so I'd know what order the notes were going in. Everything in the story that was mine came from those business cards. Thank God, I had a lot of them in my backpack. The impact of it all still hadn't hit me. It had this feeling of being incredibly surreal.

Then I was interviewing a priest who had been injured and was lying on a stretcher. All of a sudden he turns his head and spits up this big wad of ash—it looked like a lump of wet cement—and at that moment it really hit home that many, many people were dead or dying.

There's no way to assimilate a 110-story building collapsing. But when I was talking to this priest, and he suddenly did this very physical, grotesque act—spitting out a lump of pulverized skyscraper—that act somehow made the whole event real. Human beings, hundreds or thousands of them, were buried in the rubble, suffocating on that dust, or already crushed into dust themselves. This was about life and death, and I needed to focus very clearly to bring that home. This was obviously going to be the greatest human tragedy that New York had ever endured.

I think the challenge for me was not fear, probably because I didn't witness the intense carnage that my colleagues did. For me, the challenge was confusion—not being able to take in what had happened. When I first got down there, I had a person telling me that they saw people jumping out of the building to their deaths. I wasn't sure whether to believe that. I needed to verify it.

After both towers had fallen, I headed back toward Ground Zero. It was like the surface of the moon. Dust covered everything, and it really did look like another planet. It was quiet. It was just quiet. There was nobody crying for help.

I figured we'd put out a story, so I had to file. I didn't

know where to file. I managed to get a call through to my father, and I asked him to call around to our bureaus around the country and find out where I needed to file. I told him to have them contact me at my Yahoo e-mail address, since I didn't think the *Journal*'s e-mail would work. I went back to my apartment and filed. Then I went back out.

I went to hospitals and medical stations, but there were no patients. There were dozens of ambulances and scores of gurneys, but no patients. It began to dawn on me that this was one of those events in which you either lived or died, with very few people in between.

All you can do in that kind of circumstance is write what you see and try to make the best understanding you can, knowing you would have to wait for the Big Understanding.

Deadline Tip:

What I learned is that you can always improvise. There is always a way to get the job done. [Assistant managing editor] Jim Pensiero went out and set up an entire computerized newsroom in less than a day. [Foreign editor] John Bussey stayed at the window, recording what he saw, until the tower collapsed and he had to dive under his desk to avoid the storm of flying debris crashing through the windows. There's always a way of getting the job done. You just have to be willing to improvise a bit.

St. Petersburg Times

Kathryn Wexler   Amy Herdy

St. Petersburg Times

Finalist, Team Deadline News Reporting

Lois Marrero was a hard-driving Tampa police officer who did not suffer fools well and battled the department brass with the same verve that she brought to the city's streets. When she died on a muggy July morning, ambushed on a robbery investigation before she could draw her gun, she became the department's first female officer killed in the line of duty. The *St. Petersburg Times* sent a team of reporters to cover the breaking story and recount the life of a 40-year-old cop with an equal number of admirers and detractors. Tampa reporters Kathryn Wexler and Amy Herdy produced a profile of the courage and brashness that propelled Marrero toward her death in an apartment complex parking lot. The story also let readers see the controversial side of an officer—once stripped of her rank and fired—who'd successfully sued the department to win her job back. Working deftly around the edges of the tragedy, the reporters were able to tell readers a little about Marrero's life as a lesbian, a difficult societal issue in the best of times, but one that would take on increasing relevance in the weeks to come as the department wrestled with questions of family death benefits. The story is sensitive without being sentimental, straightforward without trampling unnecessarily on the badge or the woman who wore it so boldly.

Officer's small size hid feisty spirit

JULY 7, 2001

By Kathryn Wexler and Amy Herdy

TAMPA—Lois Marrero was never one to duck a fight. It made her life difficult at times. It also made her a cop with the right stuff, colleagues said.

Marrero was fired in 1997. Police brass determined she had lied about attending a law enforcement seminar when she was really on vacation.

The spirited, petite Latina refused to go quietly.

She sued the Tampa Police Department, claiming the real reason they yanked her badge was that she had fired off a six-page letter of grievances—to the chief of police, no less.

As a whistleblower, Marrero didn't want just money. She wanted her job back.

She got it. The department reinstated her, but stripped her of her rank as sergeant.

In the quasi-military culture of police work, bucking the system is left to the hardy few. Marrero was one of the fighters—both inside the department and out. She hated injustice on the streets. And she didn't tolerate it within her organization either, officers said.

"She was a battler," said police spokesman Joe Durkin. "She had get-up-and-go."

In her private life, she was nurturing and devoted. Tampa Officer Mickie Mashburn was Marrero's companion the past 10 years. They were on the phone Friday morning, reveling in their plans to see a WNBA basketball game in Orlando later that night. Marrero had to hang up abruptly.

"I've got a (radio) call and I've got to get out there quick," Marrero said. It would be the last call Marrero would respond to. She ended the conversation the way she always did.

"She told me she loved me," said Mashburn, 48. "It has me in peace that way."

Marrero, 40, had 15 months left before retirement.

She was training for another marathon. And though she was nearing the end of a rocky and often unhappy career, Mashburn said, she was as driven as ever.

Just two days ago, Marrero was investigating a report of a suspicious auto repossesser a block from where she would be shot, when she saw one dog attack another. She darted over.

"Get the dog collar or I'm going to handle the dog myself," she warned the owner, said Karen Breit, the person who had called about the repo man.

"She was very outgoing and bubbly. But you could tell she didn't take any c___ from anybody," Breit recalled. "She had no fear."

With 19 years on the police force, she had a firm handshake and a sharp mind. "Very good personality," Capt. Jane Castor said.

Marrero cultivated her tough, street-wise reputation. Her diminutive size—she was 5-foot-1—never held her back. In fact, it was something she traded on.

"She would tell us stories about her stature and some of the drunks she had to deal with," said Scott Paine, a former City Council member. "They'd look down at her and snicker and say things like, 'You going to make me, lady?' And then she would."

Said Officer Craig Harridge, "I don't think that Lois would back away from anything. She had a heart that was twice as big as her physical size."

In her early years, Marrero was a rising star. Supervisors wrote in evaluations in the 1980s that she was a "model officer."

She and another officer were recognized publicly in 1988 for doing what would prove to be the future of police work, community-oriented policing. Assigned to Ybor City, at the time a crime-ridden district, Marrero and her partner, Dana Singer, got the electric company to fix street lighting. They went after the city to condemn dilapidated buildings. Police officials praised them for making Ybor City safer.

"When she did her shift, the people of Tampa always got their money's worth," said Officer Josh Pinney, who worked with Marrero about five years ago in community affairs.

By the mid 1990s, she was head of the unit that

fought gang activity.

But she was soon making waves of a different kind. The letter she sent to the chief, dated June 25, 1997, was remarkably fiery for an underling.

Among a litany of complaints, Marrero was angry Holder didn't order a formal investigation of an officer for allegations of stealing uniforms from the department.

"Sir, once again there is No consistency here," Marrero wrote.

When she was fired three months later, police officials criticized her for conducting her own investigation of the Police Athletic League, an officer-staffed outreach program, instead of going through other channels.

Though reinstated, Marrero felt she had been wronged, not vindicated, Mashburn said.

Tampa Mayor Dick Greco showed up Friday at the hospital where Mashburn and family members were mourning. Mashburn told him he wasn't welcome. The mayor hadn't shown any support for Marrero during her travails, she said.

"She loved her job so much and it tainted it for her," Mashburn said.

Maj. Scott Cunningham said Friday that residents had been calling all day to say Marrero stopped frequently to talk. "One citizen called and said, 'Lois was with me just yesterday.'"

The size of her commitment will be long remembered, he said. "Her memory will be a lot bigger than her stature."

Times staff writers Christopher Goffard, Graham Brink, Angela Moore, Babita Persaud, and David Karp and researcher John Martin contributed to this report.

Lessons Learned

BY KATHRYN WEXLER

I met Lois Marrero several years ago, when she was a feisty little cop with a big chip on her shoulder. She was as controversial in death as in life; whatever opinions co-workers had of her, they were strong.

The force of her personality made her a potentially colorful profile. I tried to capture her spirit and her flaws.

Some thoughts on writing a piece like this:

■ **Nix the hero cliché.** An easy crutch when covering the violent death of a police officer, or anyone in uniform, is to write a profile of The Hero. It's trite. It's usually also a lie. Officer Marrero was brave, but she was bitter, too. Delicately revealing her frailties may have made her less sympathetic. Ultimately, though, I think it reinforced her humanity.

■ **Talk, talk, talk, even off the record** (and even if your newspaper, like mine, doesn't allow the use of anonymous sources in published stories). Plenty of officers didn't like Officer Marrero. And they certainly didn't want to be quoted as saying something negative about a cop just killed in the line of duty. But talking to them on background gave me a better sense of her personality and the trials she faced.

■ **Get to the mother lode source.** Crime reporter Amy Herdy begged maybe a dozen officers she knew to page Officer Marrero's grieving domestic partner (and fellow police officer) for her. Finally, the partner, Mickie Mashburn, called back. Mashburn relayed details of their life: how they had planned to see a basketball game that night, how Marrero was training for a marathon, how they ended their last conversation lovingly. Mashburn also told how she had rebuffed Tampa Mayor Dick Greco, who she felt hadn't stood by Officer Marrero in life. Amy fed the scene at the hospital to me by phone, and it nicely rounded out the profile.

■ **Zero in on any primary relationships.** Officer Marrero was gay, a fact she hid from no one. High up in the story, I described her as "nurturing and devoted" to

Mashburn. Since it was important to her, it deserved a prominent spot in her obituary. Mashburn, Officer Marrero's domestic partner, later told us Amy Herdy was the first reporter to address her as a grieving partner.

■ **Think theme**. Hopefully, a reader will come away from the profile thinking one central thing about Marrero: that she was a fighter. Writing the profile with that in mind made the story more cohesive. And, in fact, it's clear that that trait determined much of how she lived.

Los Angeles Times

Geraldine Baum   Maggie Farley   Matea Gold

Los Angeles Times

Finalist, Team Deadline News Reporting

From their offices on the Pacific coast, editors at the *Los Angeles Times* geared up on the morning of Sept. 11, 2001, to cover a story on the other side of the country, a story without precedent or peer. Reporters were dispatched, assigned, and reassigned as the terrorist attacks moved from New York to Washington to the outskirts of Pittsburgh. Editors carved out working space and divided the labor to handle the crush of information that would come rushing in as the day unfolded. There were decisions to be made: Who would handle rewrite? What stories needed to be done? Who would check for redundancy as each deadline approached? On the ground in Washington, reporter Matea Gold, reeling from the realization that terrorists had just hit the Pentagon, plowed forward with reporting on the panic and uncertainty in the nation's capital. In New York, reporters Geraldine Baum and Maggie Farley moved against the human tide to get to the center of a story that seemed to worsen with each passing minute. Together with more than three dozen *Los Angeles Times* staffers, they wrote history on deadline.

Terrorists attack
New York, Pentagon

SEPTEMBER 12, 2001

NEW YORK—In the worst terrorist attack ever against the United States, hijackers struck at the preeminent symbols of the nation's wealth and might Tuesday, flying airliners into the World Trade Center and the Pentagon and killing or injuring thousands of people.

As a horrified nation watched on television, the twin towers of the World Trade Center in lower Manhattan collapsed into flaming rubble after two Boeing 767s rammed their upper stories. A third airliner, a Boeing 757, flattened one of the Pentagon's five sides.

A fourth jetliner crashed in western Pennsylvania. Authorities said the hijackers might have been trying to aim the plane at the presidential retreat at Camp David, Md., the Capitol or other targets in Washington.

The assaults, which stirred fear and anxiety across the country and evoked comparisons to Pearl Harbor, were carefully planned and coordinated, occurring within 50 minutes. No one claimed responsibility, but official suspicion quickly fell on Saudi fugitive Osama bin Laden. Unexplained was how the terrorists boarded the jets and overpowered the crews.

Federal law enforcement sources said the FBI conducted searches and served subpoenas, some in south Florida. One official said agents were investigating the possibility that some of the terrorists were pilots who had been trained "for this kind of action."

The FBI was sifting through hundreds of tips pouring into a toll-free hotline and a Web site and pursuing dozens of leads.

Addressing the nation Tuesday night, President Bush vowed to "find those responsible and bring them to justice." This country, he said, would retaliate against "those behind these evil acts" and any country that harbors them.

Altogether, the four downed planes carried 266 people. All were killed. Scores of people jumped to their deaths or died in fires and the collapsing superstructure at the trade center. New York Mayor Rudolph W. Giuliani said earliest reports counted 2,100 people injured, about 150 of them in critical condition.

Estimates of the death toll at the Pentagon ranged from 100 to 800.

At nightfall, more than nine hours after the attack, a 47-story annex to the 110-floor twin towers at the trade center collapsed as well. It too had caught fire, but by the time it fell, all of its occupants had been evacuated.

At a late-night news conference, New York authorities said more than 300 firefighters and three dozen police officers were missing. Many had rushed into the towers after the airliners hit, only to be trapped when the buildings collapsed.

Among the dead were the New York fire chief, his chief of special operations and a first deputy commissioner.

Some of those still in the rubble reportedly called officials or family members on their cell phones, and some trapped police officers made radio contact with headquarters. But because of fires and unstable debris, rescue attempts were halted after dark.

Bush placed U.S. forces around the world on highest alert and flew from a visit in Florida to secure military bases in Louisiana and Nebraska before returning to Washington to address the nation. Vice President Dick Cheney, Cabinet members, congressional leaders, and the president's family also were taken to secure locations.

It was the worst siege of terrorism waged against the United States in its history. It shut down the federal government in Washington and the financial markets in New York. It closed all airports across the nation for the first time, as well as some Amtrak rail lines in the Northeast. It put off the primary election in New York and closed Disneyland. It halted Major League Baseball for a day, as only World War I and D-day have done before.

America tightened security at its borders and at embassies and military sites around the world. The National Guard patrolled Washington and New York. Bridges and tunnels into Manhattan were closed. Authorities evacuated the Capitol Building, the State Department, the CIA building, the United Nations and the Sears Tower in Chicago. Hoover Dam was closed to visitors. Patrols increased along the trans-Alaska oil pipeline.

Even in Europe, authorities evacuated high-rise buildings as a precaution.

Members of Congress, after being briefed by FBI and intelligence officials, said bin Laden was the suspected mastermind. "They've come to the conclusion," said Sen. Orrin G. Hatch (R-Utah), "that this has the signature of Osama bin Laden." He is the fugitive Saudi terrorist under indictment here for the bombing of American embassies in Kenya and Tanzania. Bin Laden has been granted asylum by Afghanistan.

That nation's hard-line Islamic Taliban rulers condemned the attacks in New York and Washington and rejected suggestions that bin Laden was behind them. In London, editor Abdel-Bari Atwan of the *Al-Quds al-Arabi* newspaper said he had heard that Islamic fundamentalists close to bin Laden were planning a major operation but that he did not take the threat seriously.

"They said it would be a huge and unprecedented attack," Atwan told Associated Press, "but they did not specify."

Anger across the United States brought talk of retaliation. "These attacks clearly constitute an act of war," said Sen. John McCain (R-Ariz.).

He was echoed by Adm. Robert J. Natter, commander of the U.S. Atlantic Fleet. "We've been attacked like we haven't [been] since Pearl Harbor."

"This is the second Pearl Harbor," said Sen. Charles Hagel (R-Neb.). "I don't think I overstate it." Nearly 2,400 people died when the Japanese attacked Pearl Harbor on Dec. 7, 1941. It drew the United States into World War II.

Governments around the world offered condolences and pledged solidarity in the fight against terrorism. Palestinian leader Yasser Arafat said he was horrified by the attacks. But in the West Bank town of Nablus, about 3,000 people took to the streets, chanted "God is great" and handed out candy in a gesture of celebration.

Russian President Vladimir V. Putin called the attacks "terrible tragedies." China said it was "horrified." Pope John Paul II condemned the "unspeakable horror" and prayed for the victims and their families.

The sequence of events that stunned New York into grief-stricken agony began at 7:59 a.m. EDT, when

American Airlines Flight 11 took off from Boston's Logan International Airport. The flight carried 81 passengers and a crew of 11 westward toward Los Angeles International Airport. Fifteen minutes later, United Airlines Flight 175 left Logan, also bound for Los Angeles. It carried 56 passengers and a crew of nine.

What transpired inside both aircraft in the minutes that followed remains unclear; it never may be known. Later in the day, however, federal authorities would speculate that the planes were chosen by their hijackers because their transcontinental loads of jet fuel effectively made them flying bombs.

Atty. Gen. John Ashcroft said the hijackers of Flight 11 were armed with knives. Other reports indicated some flight attendants on Flight 175 were stabbed.

A ROUTINE START TO DAY AND THEN CHAOS

What is known for certain is that Flight 11—the first aircraft to strike the World Trade Center—was hijacked somewhere over upstate New York, made a hard left turn and flew for approximately 14 minutes until it struck the Manhattan landmark.

Flight Explorer, a Virginia-based company that sells Federal Aviation Administration radar data to airlines, was tracking the flight. According to Walter Kross, one of the company's technical specialists, the 767 was flying at 29,000 feet near Albany, N.Y., when it veered to the southeast.

The plane's speed dropped from about 450 knots to 340 knots. The Boeing 767 flew faster as it headed for the New York area, reaching a speed of 500 knots. It then slowed to about 300 knots as it approached the World Trade Center.

About 8:30 a.m., it slammed into the building.

"It had to have been hand-flown," Kross said, suggesting that at least one of the hijackers was skilled enough to pilot the aircraft with precision.

A thunderstorm Monday night had cleared the air over Manhattan and the sunlight of a warm September morning was glinting off the Hudson River as the business day began in the city's highest buildings.

Clyde Ebanks, vice president of an insurance company, was at a meeting on the 103rd floor of the World

Trade Center's south tower when his boss said, "Look at that!"

He turned and saw a plane go past and hit the north tower.

Carnage and chaos ensued.

Peter Dicerbo led his 44 colleagues from the First Union National Bank down 47 flights of stairs. He staggered away from the building, his clothes torn; the workers were stunned, dazed and coughing.

Less than 20 minutes later, the United Airlines jet struck the other World Trade Center tower.

"The minute I got out of the building, the second building blew up," said Jennifer Brickhouse, 34, from Union, N.J., who was riding an escalator into the trade center when she "heard this big boom."

"All this stuff started falling," she said, "and all this smoke was coming through. People were screaming, falling and jumping out of the windows."

At least one couple were seen leaping hand-in-hand from the tower's upper stories.

Three miles away, across the East River in Brooklyn, sheets of office paper fluttered out of the sky.

At 9:50 a.m., an hour after the first crash, the first World Trade Center tower collapsed in smoke and rubble.

There were reports of an explosion right before the tower fell, then a strange sucking sound, and finally the sound of floors collapsing. Then came a huge surge of air, followed by a vast cloud of dirt, smoke, dust, paper and debris. Windows shattered. People screamed and dived for cover.

"I heard the largest, loudest collective scream I've ever heard," said Melissa Easton, who was watching from the roof of her Chinatown apartment building about 20 blocks away.

Not long afterward, at 10:30 a.m., the second tower of the World Trade Center collapsed.

The top of the building exploded with smoke and dust. There were no flames, just an explosion of debris, and then more vast clouds swept down to the streets. People were knocked to the ground on their faces as they ran from the building.

Hyman Brown, a University of Colorado civil engineering professor and the construction manager for the

World Trade Center, said that flames fueled by thousands of gallons of aviation fuel melted the towers' steel supports.

"This building would have stood had a plane or a force caused by a plane smashed into it," he said. "But steel melts, and 24,000 gallons of aviation fluid melted the steel. Nothing is designed or will be designed to withstand that fire."

In addition to the more than 200 missing firefighters, police officials said nearly 100 of their officers were similarly unaccounted for. Brian Stark, a former Navy paramedic who assisted rescuers, said paramedics had been told that hundreds of police officers and firefighters were missing from the ranks of those sent in to respond to the first crash.

Giuliani said the 2,100 injured included 1,500 "walking wounded" who were taken by boat to New Jersey, and 600 others who were taken to New York hospitals. It could take weeks to dig through the rubble for victims. "I have a sense it's a horrendous number of lives lost," Giuliani said. "Right now we have to focus on saving as many lives as possible."

Hundreds of volunteers and medical workers converged on triage centers, offering help and blood. So many people lined up to donate blood that many were turned away.

The city took on the eerie hush of a metropolis under siege. With public transportation shut down and major bridges and tunnels closed to traffic, walking became the only way to get anywhere. Thousands clogged Manhattan bridges, leaving the city on foot. Throughout the metropolitan area, people stunned by the day's events strolled about as if in a daze.

More than nine hours after the attack, an annex in the complex—7 World Trade Center—continued to burn. At 5:20 p.m., that building collapsed. Blocks away, crowds roared with astonishment.

"People stared open-mouthed and were in shock," said bystander Russ Baker.

Jesus Soriano Jr., 34, of Brooklyn, said he was there when the twin towers fell.

"I felt the first building collapse. I saw the second tower collapse," Soriano said. "It collapsed from the outside in."

"Those terrorists are real cowards," he said.

Tyler Catalana, 23, a resident of Mill Valley, Calif., who is studying architecture in New York, said he saw the north tower collapse into itself.

"It looked like a nuclear war," he said.

Catalana said that when the dust began to settle, "it looked like the surface of the moon."

Much of lower Manhattan was evacuated as officials feared potential gas leaks and falling debris could cause further casualties.

Like refugees fleeing a war-torn nation, tens of thousands walked across the Brooklyn Bridge and along a nearby highway as they sought safety.

Some people wore paper masks to block out the dust. People gathered around cars listening to news over their radios. Others washed off the dust with the water from open fire hydrants.

Giuliani said the New York Stock Exchange was intact, but he doubted it would reopen today, because it was necessary to keep lower Manhattan clear for emergency vehicles. Public and parochial schools in the city were scheduled to be closed.

"New York is still here. The World Financial Center is still here," the mayor said. "We have undergone tremendous losses and we will grieve for them horribly. We are going to prevail."

Three large trucks arrived at the city morgue in the afternoon with extra supplies. A spokesman said that bodies were expected later.

Families searching for missing relatives were directed to an office where city employees took information. Extra medical examiners were summoned to the morgue.

The most severely burned were taken to a center at New York Presbyterian Hospital on Manhattan's upper East Side. Elective surgery at the hospital was canceled. Patients in the emergency room watched the disaster on television.

Tiffany Keeling, 32, of New Mexico was treated at Bellevue Hospital for smoke inhalation and head injuries. She said she was attending a training seminar for financial consultants on the 61st floor of the south tower of the trade center.

"We were looking out the window and the entire sky was filled with paper," she said. "We thought it was a ticker tape parade."

Then, Keeling said, she noticed a huge cloud of smoke billowing from the north tower. "Fireballs were falling to the ground, which I now know were people."

Keeling and the other trainees headed for the stairs. When they were between the 59th and 58th floors, a voice on the building's public address system said the north tower was the only structure in danger and that everyone could return upstairs. Half of her group went back up. She and others continued to the street.

"People were coming down from the top floors in every condition you could imagine," Keeling said, through tears.

"I heard a woosh like air getting sucked in a vacuum. I grabbed my jacket and got as close to a planter as possible and started feeling little things on my back like hail, and they got bigger and bigger until the air was solid debris."

Keeling said she turned to a man who walked down the stairs with her and asked: "Are we dead?"

She said only 75 of the people who attended her training group were accounted for.

Denny Levy, 36, a videographer, witnessed the impact from the ground.

"I saw this plane flying low over the buildings down the center of Manhattan," said Levy, who was uninjured. "It went toward the World Trade Center. It sounded like its engine was broken. Your brain tricks you. I thought it went past the building, and then it went a little to the left and took a plunge at the building.

"Then there was this burst of stuff coming out of the building. There was no fire and no explosion. I wondered why the plane was making so much noise and was so low.

"You could tell it was a passenger plane, that it was in trouble or trying to get close for a view. You'd never think a plane would go dead center into a building. It was like a missile.

"I thought it was an accident, except he took a sudden left. He went right for it. It was so creepy. I thought,

'Oh, my God, I just saw 300 people die.'"

John Kelly, 38, a furniture designer, said he looked out a window of his apartment after hearing the first explosion.

"My wife says, 'Oh, my God, they hit the second building.' I looked. The plane went through the building, and there was a blast out two sides. It was like exit wounds in all directions.

"I saw people jumping, bodies flying through the air. I saw people waving white flags. It was horrible.

"Police and ambulances were everywhere, and within seconds there was no one. You saw everyone running, running, running. You saw shoes, sunglasses on the street. People dropped their stuff and ran.

"It was like a nuclear explosion."

A CRUSHING BLOW TO SYMBOL OF STRENGTH

As a stunned nation attempted to grasp the horror of television images from New York, a third hijacked airliner crashed into the Pentagon, bursting into flames and delivering an incendiary blow to the symbol of America's military might.

American Airlines Flight 77, a Boeing 757 with 58 passengers and a crew of six aboard, hit the west side of the building at 9:41 a.m. EDT, half an hour after it left Dulles International Airport en route to Los Angeles.

"I glanced up just at the point where the plane was going into the building," said Carla Thompson, who works in an Arlington, Va., office building about 1,000 yards from the crash.

"I saw an indentation in the building and then it was just blown-up up—red, everything red," she said. "Everybody was just starting to go crazy. I was petrified."

Within 20 minutes of the crash, the White House, the Pentagon—the world's largest office building—and the U.S. Capitol were evacuated.

What began as an orderly exodus from the nation's defense headquarters turned to panic as evacuees made their way to parking lots.

"People were just milling around in a daze," said Ginger Groeber, a civilian Defense Department official who had been in the Pentagon watching television reports of the attacks in New York when the building was hit.

"These people were panicking out there," she said. "People were looking for their staffs. Nobody's cell phones were working."

The District of Columbia government shut down. Many private firms also closed and sent employees streaming home, causing traffic nightmares.

As parking garages closed and cars poured out, one woman grabbed the door of a lone car going in.

"Don't park," she yelled, her face twisted in fear. "They're hitting the Pentagon! They're hitting the Pentagon!"

Naval officer Clyde Ragland, who works near the Pentagon, was stuck in his office because the streets outside were clogged with traffic.

He and his co-workers were watching television reports of the disaster in New York when "we gazed out our own windows and, to our horror and disbelief, saw huge billows of black smoke rising from the northeast, in the direction of D.C. and the river…and the Pentagon."

Ragland described billowing black smoke and "what looked like white confetti raining down everywhere." He said it soon became apparent "that the 'confetti' was little bits of airplane, falling down after being flung high into the bright, blue sky."

"Everything is confusion right now, but there was no panic. Just stunned disbelief," Ragland said.

Streets surrounding the Capitol Mall were paralyzed as people tried to get away from the federal buildings, worried that they would be targeted next.

Federal workers raced down the steps into the subway, only to be greeted by a sign flashing: "Security alert! The Metro is closed until further notice. Please try to call a relative or a taxi if you need a ride." The subway reopened by midday.

But with phone lines jammed and no taxis to be found, many people tried to hurry away on foot, exchanging rumors about the attacks.

"We never thought this could happen," said Mary Shea, 58, an FAA program analyst, as she stood outside the L'Enfant Plaza subway stop. "What a shock, what a shock."

Long lines formed around pay phones.

"My mom works at the Pentagon, my mom works at

the Pentagon," one man repeated over and over again, rocking back and forth, urging the line to speed up.

Abigail Harrington, an employee at the District of Columbia Department of Health, stood with a large group of people on 7th Street, peering down the road for a bus she hoped to catch to pick up her daughter from school.

"I feel horrible," said Harrington, clutching her hands together. "I can't reach my husband on his cell phone. I don't know what's going on. You never think that something like this can affect the world's biggest superpower. It's really, really scary. It really is."

Secretary of Defense Donald H. Rumsfeld was in a wing of the Pentagon opposite the point of impact. He told reporters that he felt the shock and went outside where volunteers were helping to carry away the injured.

Rumsfeld refused to estimate the casualty toll at the military's nerve center. The plane crashed into a newly renovated portion of the building that had not been fully reoccupied.

Authorities estimate that 23,000 people work in the Pentagon, and Rumsfeld vowed that the building would reopen for business today.

Barbara Olson, the wife of U.S. Solicitor General Theodore B. Olson, spoke to her husband twice by cell phone from the hijacked airliner before it crashed.

She told him that all the passengers and crew, including the pilot, were forced to the back of the plane. The only weapons she mentioned were knives and cardboard cutters.

Olson said his wife made no reference to the nationality or motive of the hijackers.

Barbara Olson had originally planned to take a Monday flight to Los Angeles but changed her plans to have breakfast with her husband Tuesday, his birthday.

The plane that crashed in Pennsylvania, United Airlines Flight 93, took off at 8:01 a.m. EDT from New Jersey's Newark International Airport, bound for San Francisco. On board the Boeing 757 were 38 passengers, two pilots and five flight attendants. The early stages of the flight seemed normal, with the plane charting a westerly course that brought it to northern Ohio.

But as the jet was flying due west just below Cleveland, it made a sharp U-turn. Radar tracked it passing just south of Pittsburgh.

At 9:58 a.m., a 911 operator in Pennsylvania's Westmoreland County received a call from a man who said he had locked himself in a bathroom on a hijacked airliner. "We are being hijacked, we are being hijacked," the man said over his cell phone.

At the same time, flight attendant CeeCee Lyles, a mother of four, dialed her cell phone and told her husband, a Fort Myers, Fla., policeman, that her flight was being taken over by hijackers.

The Westmoreland County dispatcher, Edward Milliron, said his office was taking information from the passenger in the bathroom when the line went dead.

"We lost them," he said. "Two or three minutes later, we lost them."

Milliron said area residents began calling to report that a passenger jet was flying low over their homes. The plane crashed at 10:06 a.m. in a rural area near Indian Lake, about 80 miles southeast of Pittsburgh.

"I felt it. My house was shaken by it. I thought a truck hit my house," said Rev. Sylvia Baker, who lives about two miles from the crash site. "When I saw it wasn't my house, I was sure it had to be my neighbor's house."

The plane went down in an open field near a coal strip mine outside Shanksville, a hamlet of 235 people nestled in the wooded hills of western Pennsylvania. Mark Stahl of nearby Somerset said it carved a large black hole in the field and that smoke and flames billowed out.

"I didn't know what to think. It was shocking," Stahl said.

Reporters said the crater was about 40 feet wide and more than 8 feet deep. The largest debris from the plane was no bigger than a phone book. The crater was cordoned off, and officials said the task of removing bodies and the debris would not begin until this afternoon.

After a briefing by the Marine Corps, Rep. James P. Moran (D-Va.) said the plane may have been turning toward Camp David or Washington targets in its flight path when it went down. The crash site was 85 miles northwest of Camp David in the mountains of Maryland.

Response to the tragedies came from a number of

quarters, some calling for swift retaliation while others urged moving ahead cautiously.

Former Secretary of State James A. Baker III said the United States should strengthen its intelligence capabilities.

"In effect, we unilaterally disarmed our intelligence capabilities," Baker said. "We need human intelligence to penetrate these groups."

Richard Holbrooke, former U.S. ambassador to the United Nations, said it would take the cooperation of numerous countries, including Russia and states in the Middle East, to bring those responsible to justice.

"Any nation seen to harbor or aid and abet these people must be treated as co-equally responsible," he said.

Larry Johnson, a former State Department counterterrorism official, said the United States must wage war against those who launched the attacks.

"This is a declaration of war," Johnson said. "You don't go in for a tie here. If these guys want to cross the line this way, so be it. But so will we. We can't go back now. If we don't act, the U.S. will be seen as unable to fight."

But John L. Martin, the former chief of the internal security section at the Department of Justice, urged restraint.

"Any kind of retaliation must be very restrained, and methodical, deliberate and accurate," Martin said. "Or else it's going to worsen the situation."

Rep. Dana Rohrabacher (R-Huntington Beach) called the attacks a "day of infamy" for the nation's intelligence community.

"For the national security apparatus to have missed this is the biggest intelligence blunder in our lifetime," Rohrabacher said. "The people we pay billions of dollars to have left us at the mercy of international terrorists."

Brian Jenkins, a Rand Corp. expert on terrorism and international crime, said in Santa Monica: "We've seen elements of this event before. Thirty years ago, almost to the day, Sept. 6, 1970, four hijackings, one of which failed, involved the Popular Front for the Liberation of Palestine, who held hostages in the desert outside Jordan. It was a multiple coordinated hijacking.

"And we've had concerns that hijackers might crash into a major city. Algerian extremists in Marseilles [in]

1994 wanted refueling. French Intelligence, listening, feared they would take off and crash into Paris.

"Today, versus 30 years ago, the acts are large scale and often indiscriminate. The World Trade Center event today combines the two."

At UCLA, David Rapoport, editor of *Terrorism and Political Violence*, an academic journal, said there has been nothing like today's attack "in the history of terrorism."

Rapoport said the attack required "extensive planning by numerous individuals."

"The organization capable of this act has managed to elude our intelligence. We were not looking at the right organizations. And if we were, our failure is even greater."

Contributing to this report were Times staff writers Ricardo Alonso-Zaldivar, Geraldine Baum, Stephen Braun, Richard T. Cooper, Megan Garvey, Judy Pasternak, David G. Savage, Esther Schrader, David Willman, Robin Wright, and Aaron Zitner in Washington; John J. Goldman and Thomas S. Mulligan in New York; Eric Slater in Chicago; and Edward J. Boyer, Richard Lee Colvin, Thomas Curwen, Abigail Goldman, Ardith Hilliard, J. Michael Kennedy, Jeff Leeds, Hilary E. MacGregor, Eric Malnic, Richard E. Meyer, Diane Pucin, Mary Rourke, Tim Rutten, Henry Weinstein, and Nona Yates in Los Angeles.

Rick Meyer   Scott Kraft

Lessons Learned

Recalling deadline with Rick Meyer, rewrite

Most of us were out the door and headed for the newspaper before the second plane hit. By 7 a.m., we'd gathered at the national desk.

Reporters were already scrambling in New York, Washington, and Pennsylvania. We needed a rewrite team in L.A. That meant Tim Rutten, Ed Boyer, J. Michael Kennedy, and me — all of us veterans of assorted wars, hurricanes, floods, bombings, and plane crashes.

Deadline Tips:

■ Organize the body of the story ahead of time. One of us would write the New York section, another would write the Washington section, another the Pennsylvania section, and another the intro. This meant files from our New York reporters would go to the New York writer and so on. The intro writer would get a look at all the incoming files and cherry-pick what he needed for the top and for the setup of what was coming below.

■ Rewriters need to work within earshot of one another. So we ran three editors out of an office large enough to accommodate the four of us. Files began arriving. Good stuff. This is when rewrite people realize, every time, that whatever they turn out is only as good as the reporting they get. This time it was beyond good. Geraldine Baum, Maggie Farley, and Matea Gold outdid themselves. Reporters ought to get the bylines. They are the ones who are out there being rained on, lied to, and sometimes shot at.

■ While you're on the phone with the reporters, checking the facts, resolving the inconsistencies, and asking for more about this or that, someone else needs to coordinate your story with other stories. In this case, it was Marc Duvoisin, an assistant managing editor, who kept us from colliding with sidebars being written in our New York bureau, our Washington bureau, and here in Los Angeles.

We did the story four times. We wrote it for the Extra. We rewrote it for the national edition. We rewrote it for our home edition. Then we updated it for our 11 p.m. replate. Each time, the intro writer combed down through it to give it a single voice.

Recalling deadline with Scott Kraft, national editor

It was a few minutes after 6 a.m. in Los Angeles (9 a.m. Eastern time) when editors on the national desk, on the phone from their homes, began talking about deploying reporters. We knew we needed to move quickly.

First, we took inventory. We have eight reporters based in New York, and, lucky for us, seven of them were in town (though only four were in Manhattan, a fact that would become important when that borough was sealed off). Geraldine Baum had alerted us that she was bound for the World Trade Center from uptown; Maggie Farley was headed to the scene from her home in Brooklyn; and bureau chief Josh Getlin was bound for the office in midtown to anchor the New York coverage.

The story seemed, at that early juncture, to be confined to New York. So Tom McCarthy, the deputy bureau chief in Washington, dispatched several reporters from Washington to New York by car as reinforcements. We would recall most of them to Washington an hour later when the Pentagon was struck, and redirect two to western Pennsylvania when a plane crashed there.

By 7 a.m., reporters and editors from many departments had gathered around the national desk in Los Angeles. Stories were being suggested and assignments made. But the first order of business for us was to choose a writer for the main story. That was an easy call—Rick Meyer. Rick is a longtime Los Angeles-based national correspondent known for his considerable talents as a narrative writer. He's fast, of course. But he's also a clear, concise, and lyrical writer. Rick sat down at a computer terminal with one assignment: weave the work of dozens of reporters from as many locations into a powerful main story.

Deadline Tips:

■ Identify your best rewrite people and use them often. We've found that the conditions in which a rewrite person is invaluable are: 1) when the story breaks late and the reporter won't have time to both report and write the story; 2) when two or more reporters are headed for two or more locations; or 3) when the story, though breaking early in the day, is moving so quickly that it will require reporting at the scene through deadline.

■ Assign people to watch TV and take notes. On a big, breaking national story, TV stations (especially local ones at the scene of the news) frequently get access to officials, victims, and witnesses. Assign several folks to monitor different channels. We use reporters if they are available. If not, a library researcher, an office assistant, or a copy clerk can be pressed into service. They should all send their memos to the rewrite person.

■ Ask two experienced editors who are not involved in the coverage to back-read all of the day's stories. They will catch inconsistencies as well as duplication.

■ Editors should try to be wary of the one-reporter-one-story trap. You'll want to assign dozens of stories in a major breaking news event. But you won't necessarily want to run them all separately. Some won't pan out, and others will inevitably overlap. Look closely at them as deadline approaches. Running separate stories on overlapping themes will confuse readers. So try to take the duplicative stories and ask one of the authors to merge them.

On the scene in Manhattan with Geraldine Baum

I had just dropped my children at school 100 blocks north of the World Trade Center when I heard that the first plane had struck. I immediately left a message for the New York bureau chief that I was heading down there.

By subway, commandeered car, and taxi I made it to Lower Manhattan by 9:30 a.m., and began walking down Church Street toward the towers. I could see them smoking and flaming like two Roman candles ahead of me, but what I saw up close was incomprehensible.

As I made my way south, I saw scores of stunned witnesses and survivors walking north covered in gray ash. Some of the escapees were in clothes half falling off; others were missing a shoe. I kept stopping them for their stories. There was Walter, the insurance agent who had walked down 86 flights of Tower One. Almost in a trance, another man was striding briskly in the middle of the street carrying his briefcase. His Oxford shirt was filthy and unbuttoned. I tried to get his story—he'd walked down 70 flights—but in a very businesslike tone he said he was in too much of a hurry.

Then I heard the first tower drop.

A loud rush of air and an explosion made me jump. I looked up from my notebook and there it was, tipping east and then down. I froze, and then saw a black and gray billow of smoke rushing toward me. It didn't register what was happening until I saw dozens of police cars backing up at high speed on Church Street. I ran away, too. I stayed close to the buildings because I was afraid I'd be stampeded. I tried to get into a deli, banging on the glass door. But the men inside wouldn't open up, probably afraid they'd be swamped by smoke. Finally I made it into a building lobby.

When the dust settled outside, I found my way back to Church Street, where I immediately checked for the second tower. It was still standing. But people were tumbling out. I made slashes in my notebook every time a body dropped. One, two, three were down. Then two people seemed to fall together. Seven, eight, nine...12.

A little while later, a cop stopped me to ask if I had heard that the Pentagon had been hit and other planes were heading to cities all over America. No, I hadn't, and

I wasn't ready to believe him. The Pentagon? I decided to just keep reporting, do my job, take notes, take in as much as I could.

Every hour or so over the next 12 hours, I found a phone and called in notes. My cell wasn't working, but I begged to use others' and found pay phones. "The basics, Geraldine," I kept telling myself. "Do the basics." I gave quotes, descriptions, survivors' names, phone numbers, and details from eyewitnesses' accounts.

My instinct as a reporter was to try to understand what was happening around me. But really, for one of the first times in my career, I just couldn't. I couldn't absorb it all, so I took on what is the primary function of a reporter anyway: to witness and describe.

On the scene in Brooklyn Heights with Maggie Farley

We could feel the air shake in our Brooklyn Heights apartment just across the water from Lower Manhattan when the second plane hit the World Trade Center, and we knew then it was terrorism. From our brownstone's roof, a neighbor videotaped the second plane exploding into the building, and his pictures were spectacular in their clarity and horror. I called the *Times*, and two frames from that video—the plane approaching the tower, then entering it in a fireball—ran on the front of our midday Extra. CNN quintupled the *Times*'s bid for the video footage, and the scene became one of the defining images of the attack.

That was the last easy phone call. Almost immediately, the lines overloaded, but I managed to log on to the Internet and I kept the line open all day. I filed every few hours by e-mail, dictation, or Net2phone. Some reports made it through; others didn't.

I tried to walk over the Brooklyn Bridge toward the smoking site, but the bridge was thronged with thousands of ash-covered people surging the other way. A policeman looked at the police pass resting on my eight-months pregnant belly and said, "Are you crazy? Oh, you're a reporter. Same thing."

So I interviewed people as they streamed off the bridge. Some, in shock or in tears, couldn't talk. Others couldn't stop.

One man in the ghostly procession, blanketed in ash to his wingtips, escaped as the building fell. He was a Muslim, and he was angry because blame was already beginning to settle on Osama bin Laden. At a mosque nearby, he performed his ablutions before the noon prayer, but this time the ritual cleansing had an extra dimension as he scrubbed the ash from his face.

On the scene in Washington, D.C., with Matea Gold

I was in a Washington hotel room the morning of Sept. 11, preparing to cover the Los Angeles mayor's first lobbying trip there. I was about to head out the door when, on the TV, I heard one of the morning news anchors gasp. I turned to see an image of one of the World Trade Center towers smoking. As I watched, a plane flew into the second tower.

I stared, stunned. The mayor was in a meeting at the White House. I was supposed to meet him at the Department of Transportation in a half hour. I rushed out and jumped in a cab.

The streets around the National Mall were eerily empty. A man selling T-shirts on the sidewalk had his ear pressed to a portable radio. "They just hit the Pentagon," he said as I approached, his face twisting. "What the hell is happening?"

Suddenly, federal workers came pouring out of nearby buildings. Everyone had been told to evacuate.

For the next several hours, I did the only thing I could: report. I found a group of shell-shocked Federal Aviation Administration analysts staring at the sky, looking for more planes. "This is Armageddon," said one.

After walking through the chaotic streets for hours, I made my way to the hotel where the mayor was staying and found one of his aides in his room, frantically packing. The mayor had been hustled out of the White House and taken to a bunker with other officials. I called the desk in Los Angeles and fed what I had seen.

"Did you hear?" the aide told me as I hung up. "The towers collapsed." I could see the Pentagon burning. I headed back out.

Jim Dwyer
Short Writing

Jim Dwyer is a native New Yorker who writes about New York for *The New York Times*. His career, values, and style are so grounded in the city that he has earned those three references to New York in that first sentence. For Dwyer, the standard dyad, "New York, New York," seems one short of the mark.

Who else but Dwyer, in the face of New York City's greatest catastrophe, would focus his writing on the small, everyday objects that have stories hiding inside them: a window washer's squeegee, a photograph recovered from the rubble, a plastic cup for water. After the events of Sept. 11, 2001, Dwyer's work captured the attention of the nation, and earned him his second ASNE Distinguished Writing Award.

Dwyer won his first in 1991 for his *Newsday* columns. Having crafted hundreds of columns over the last two decades, Dwyer has perfected the art of the short newspaper story, the category for which he has earned this year's prize.

Dwyer was born in Manhattan, grew up in a working-class environment, and attended the city's parochial schools. He decided to major in science at Fordham University with hopes of becoming a doctor, but came under the influence of a Jesuit priest and writer, Ray Schroth. At Columbia Graduate School of Journalism, Dwyer studied under Donald H. Johnston and Melvin Mencher, who, like Schroth, mentored Dwyer in both the craft and moral dimensions of journalism.

Dwyer honed his reporting skills at *The Hudson Dispatch* in Union, N.J., *The Daily Journal* in Elizabeth, N.J., *The Record* of Hackensack, N.J., *New York Newsday*, the New York *Daily News*, and finally, *The New York Times*. In addition to his ASNE awards, he has won a Pulitzer Prize and a Meyer Berger award. He also shared in *The New York Times*'s 2002 Pulitzer Prize for public service. He is the author of a book on the New York subways and co-author of books on the first World Trade Center bombing and on the causes of wrongful convictions within the criminal justice system.

—Roy Peter Clark

A soothing cup of water, a vessel of plain kindness

NOVEMBER 22, 2001

Before strangers decided to bring cups of water to other strangers, the very air had become an accomplice to the hijackers. "It was like ground-up glass going down your throat as you were trying to catch your breath," Norma Hessic said.

"Like burning embers from a fireplace, it was big chunks," John Cerqueira said. "I couldn't even close my mouth. It was literally stuffed in every orifice. In your ears, your eye sockets."

"You couldn't see in front of you," Jeff Meisel said.

"It was black," Dee Howard said. "All I could do was pray and run."

For one infernal moment that morning, only the cold laws of physics ruled. The trade center towers, traveling at 50 miles per hour in powder form, chased thousands of people through the streets of Lower Manhattan, whipping into the soft tissues of their throats, trying to crush them from the inside out.

In the next instant, men and women emerged from shops and doorways, with cups of water, gauze, flashlights. Life was shoving back, seeking its own equilibrium.

Ms. Howard stood on the corner of Chambers and Centre Streets, a few blocks from the trade center, clutching Imez Graham, a friend from work. They had lost their building. They had lost their way home. They had lost their shoes.

Linda Mauro, leaving work at the Municipal Building, saw the two women powdered in white from their heads to their bare feet. She found some water and made them drink. They would not go into any building, so she walked with them, buying two pairs of slippers in Chinatown.

The Chinese shopkeepers opened spigots in their sinks, found some cups and passed drinks to Ms. Howard, Ms. Graham and thousands of others streaming past.

Norma Hessic stood on Church Street, near the Millennium Hotel, screaming in the darkness. "Someone stuck his hand out at me. He said, 'Take my hand and don't let go,'" she remembered. "He took me three or four blocks, to an abandoned food cart; there was water and juice there. My throat was burning up."

Jeff Meisel fled along Broadway to Nassau Street, where Chino Chaudhary, the owner of an Indian restaurant called Diwan-E-Khaas, was pulling down his rolling gates. Mr. Chaudhary stopped and grabbed people stumbling past. "He dragged us into the store," Mr. Meisel said. "Made everyone go downstairs, to big slop sinks, to wash off. He gave you bottles of water. He wouldn't let you leave until it had cleared outside. He wouldn't hear about money. I never was in there before."

As John Cerqueira and a friend, Mike Benfante, descended from the 81st floor of the north tower, they saw Tina Hansen in a wheelchair, behind a glass door on 68. Mr. Cerqueira, 22, and Mr. Benfante, 36, carried her down 68 floors, out to an ambulance. No more than five minutes later, the building collapsed, all but suffocating them.

They staggered onto West Street, where someone handed them water. "I think it was the Jewish ambulance guys," Mr. Cerqueira said. "They gave me oxygen. We were sharing it."

The refugees streamed north. Aniko and John Delaney collected their daughter, Sophie, 2, at the Trinity Church day care center, two blocks from the trade center. Covered with soot, the family rolled Sophie up Sixth Avenue, then spotted an outdoor food station, staffed by people from Da Silvano restaurant at Houston Street. As fast as the workers could make sandwiches, they were handing them away. The owner, Silvano Marchetto, brought his cordless phones outside so the escapees could call home.

"We were parched," Mrs. Delaney said. "Water was the No. 1 thing we were looking for. He had it all out on the tables outside. Right on the path of all the people heading north."

With little Sophie fretting and crying, Mr. Marchetto sent the Delaneys from his restaurant to his apartment so they could wash up and Sophie could take a nap.

All this, and much more like it, happened anonymously in the minutes and hours right after the attack, without a word of instruction or a second of preparation.

None of those who helped felt they were special. "Just a tiny microcosm of what was going on," said Linda Mauro, who found water and slippers in Chinatown for Dee Howard and Imez Graham. "They wanted to hug me, then stopped because of the ashes. I said, 'Don't even worry about it.' We hugged."

"Not just us was helping," said Chino Chaudhary, who dragged Jeff Meisel and others into his Indian restaurant on Nassau Street. "Everybody was. From the Duane Reade, anyone with a shop."

"Nobody complained about nothing," said Silvano Marchetto, the Florentine with the restaurant in Greenwich Village, who fed perhaps a thousand people that day.

The moment a war begins is chiseled into history. Acts of grace linger only in the memory of small things.

After Theresa Leone escaped from the north tower, she made her way home to Morris Park in the Bronx.

That night, in her bag, she found a plastic cup that had been full of water when someone—a stranger, she doesn't know who—handed it to her as she passed the restaurant supply district along the Bowery.

"I'm going to hold onto it," Mrs. Leone said. "I don't know why. The whole thing means so much. I was privileged."

From the rubble,
a picture and a friendship

OCTOBER 23, 2001

Tim Sherman spotted the photograph near the end of his first day of digging, on the Friday after that Tuesday. The time of day, he recalls, was "after dark." He had been on the move since dawn. A gang from his job at the Middlesex Water Company had come to New York to help, with strong backs and water main know-how and willing spirits. In a way, there was nothing to do.

Around them, smoke heaved from shapes no human hand could form. However many tons of stuff were on the ground, the landscape fell heavier and longer on the eye. "There is no God," he remembers thinking.

The Middlesex crew grabbed hand tools and faced the wreckage at Liberty Plaza. "Digging. Bucketing. Whatever needed to be done," Mr. Sherman said.

Late that day, he raked a pile of ash, then saw the picture. Frozen in time and in 8 by 10 inches of vibrant colors, three cute kids stared at him from the ground: one boy just old enough for braces, another boy a few years younger, and a toddler sister.

The picture was sopping. He stuck it on a wall to dry, but it slid off. "If you put it back up there, it'll just fall again and get lost," a co-worker told Mr. Sherman, so he stashed it away. "This could be the last thing a mother or father saw before they died," Mr. Sherman would say.

Over the next two weeks or so, the fraternity of hard work, warm meals and caring people changed Mr. Sherman's opinion about God. Back in New Jersey, his hometown paper, the *Home News Tribune*, ran an article about the water company crews helping out. The paper also published the picture Tim Sherman had saved.

* * *

All day after Brian Conroy saw the salvaged picture in the newspaper, he had a hard time concentrating on his job, managing a sales territory for Arnold Bread and Thomas' English Muffins. He knew those faces—knew the kids. Those were George Tabeek's children, and George worked at the trade center for the Port Authority.

Years ago, a decade or more, Mr. Tabeek owned a piece of a restaurant in Edison. Mr. Conroy tended bar there once a week. The Tabeek boys would visit their dad while he was watching the register. At closing time, the two men would share a pizza and news about his children. They were good friends, but work friends, so when the restaurant closed, they went about their lives.

Mr. Conroy recalled that the Tabeeks lived in Brooklyn, and he found two listings for them. On one call, an answering machine picked up. Mr. Conroy put the phone down. At the second number, a woman said hello.

Yes, this was the Tabeek household.

Mr. Conroy explained who he was, but fumbled trying to state his business. He cannot say if his heart was pounding or had simply stopped.

The woman finally figured out whom Mr. Conroy was talking about.

"Oh," she said. "Oh. George. He's right here. Do you want to speak to him?"

Mr. Conroy fell silent. The little hairs rose along his arms.

* * *

About 10 years ago, George Tabeek took his children to the Sears where his sister worked in the photography department and had the children sit for a portrait. Dana would have been about 3; Steven, 11; and young Georgie, 14.

The picture of the children followed him as he moved through jobs at the Port Authority, as Georgie became a New York City police officer, as Steven went to Saint John's University, and as Dana started high school at Bishop Kearney.

Mounted in a gold frame, the portrait sat on the edge of his credenza, in his office on the 35th floor of 2 World Trade Center. Mr. Tabeek, an engineer, was one of the people with the keys to everything. When he looked out the window across the plaza to the great spread of New York, in the corner of his view was an 8-by-10 picture of his children.

That awful morning, he had the good luck to be stopping for a doughnut in the plaza when the first plane hit. He then tested that fortune, running up 22 floors with firefighters to rescue people. He was inches from a fireman, Lt. Andrew Desperito, when the second building fell and took Lieutenant Desperito.

He told all this to Brian Conroy, the old friend he had shared pizza with in the life before. Mr. Conroy then told him about Tim Sherman the water worker, and the wet picture he had found buried in the ash.

For the first time in weeks, Mr. Tabeek said yesterday, he thought about the picture that sat in the corner of his window view, the small piece of his remembered sky.

He wanted it.

"I'll get it," Mr. Conroy said, and he did.

X-ray reading

BY ROY PETER CLARK

One way to learn from the stories in this book is to use your X-ray vision. After all, Superman was also a newspaper reporter.

X-ray reading allows you to see through the text of the story. Beneath the surface grinds the invisible machinery of grammar, language, syntax, and rhetoric, the tricks of the trade, the tools of making meaning.

While good writers do not always intend the effects they create, it helps the reader to assume that they do. For example, put on your X-ray glasses and read my first sentence above. You'll see that the most interesting words ("X-ray vision") in the sentence come at the end. That's a trick I learned from reading books on writing, but also from reading good writers.

To encourage the development of your X-ray reading skills, I have marked up a story by Jim Dwyer. The words I've written in the margins represent what I see below the surface of the story.

It may be interesting for you to compare and contrast my notations against Dwyer's reflections upon his own work. If X-ray reading appeals to you, use it to analyze the two other Dwyer stories, and then the other works in this collection.

Fighting for life 50 floors up, with one tool and ingenuity

OCTOBER 9, 2001

Now memories orbit around small things. None of the other window washers liked his old green bucket, but Jan Demczur, who worked inside 1 World Trade Center, found its rectangular mouth perfect for dipping and wetting his squeegee in one motion. So on the morning of the 11th, as he waited at the 44th-floor Sky Lobby to connect with elevators for higher floors, bucket and squeegee dangled from the end of his arm.

The time was 8:47 a.m. With five other men—Shivam Iyer, John Paczkowski, George Phoenix, Colin Richardson and another man whose identity could not be learned—Mr. Demczur (pronounced DEM-sir) boarded Car 69-A, an express elevator that stopped on floors 67 through 74.

The car rose, but before it reached its first landing, "We felt a muted thud," Mr. Iyer said. "The building shook. The elevator swung from side to side, like a pendulum."

Then it plunged. In the car, someone punched an emergency stop button. At that moment—8:48 a.m.—1 World Trade Center had entered the final 100 minutes of its existence. No one knew the clock was running, least of all the men trapped inside Car 69-A; they were as cut off 500 feet in the sky as if they had been trapped 500 feet underwater.

They did not know their lives would depend on a simple tool.

After 10 minutes, a live voice delivered a blunt message over the intercom. There had been an explosion. Then the intercom went silent. Smoke seeped into the elevator cabin. One man cursed skyscrapers. Mr. Phoenix, the tallest, a

---

Margin annotations:

a thematic lead for story and series

great, funny word in a serious story

beginning of "tick-tock," dramatic passage of time

detail lends authenticity

first of several dramatic short sentences

reminder of original theme

series of short sentences builds suspense

detail with color so readers can see

an extension of his body

quote that also advances the action

now passage of time has life-or-death meaning; reminds me of adventure movies

a wonderful, significant name

Port Authority engineer, poked for a ceiling hatch. Others pried apart the car doors, propping them open with the long wooden handle of Mr. Demczur's squeegee.

There was no exit.

They faced a wall, stenciled with the number "50." That particular elevator bank did not serve the 50th floor, so there was no need for an opening. To escape, they would have to make one themselves.

Mr. Demczur felt the wall. Sheetrock. Having worked in construction in his early days as a Polish immigrant, he knew that it could be cut with a sharp knife.

No one had a knife.

From his bucket, Mr. Demczur drew his squeegee. He slid its metal edge against the wall, back and forth, over and over. He was spelled by the other men. Against the smoke, they breathed through handkerchiefs dampened in a container of milk Mr. Phoenix had just bought.

Sheetrock comes in panels about one inch thick, Mr. Demczur recalled. They cut an inch, then two inches. Mr. Demczur's hand ached. As he carved into the third panel, his hand shook, he fumbled the squeegee and it dropped down the shaft.

He had one tool left: a short metal squeegee handle. They carried on, with fists, feet and handle, cutting an irregular rectangle about 12 by 18 inches. Finally, they hit a layer of white tiles. A bathroom. They broke the tiles.

One by one, the men squirmed through the opening, headfirst, sideways, popping onto the floor near a sink. Mr. Demczur turned back. "I said, 'Pass my bucket out,'" he recalled.

By then, about 9:30, the 50th floor was already deserted, except for firefighters, astonished to see the six men emerge. "I think it was Engine Company 5," Mr. Iyer said. "They hustled us to the staircase."

On the excruciating single-file descent through the smoke, someone teased Mr. Demczur about bringing his bucket. "The company might not order me another one," he replied. At the 15th floor, Mr. Iyer said: "We heard a thunderous, metallic roar. I thought our lives had surely ended then." The south tower was collapsing. It was 9:59. Mr. Demczur dropped his bucket. The firefighters shouted to hurry.

At 23 minutes past 10, they burst onto the street, ran for phones, sipped oxygen and, five minutes later, fled as the north tower collapsed. Their escape had taken 95 of the 100 minutes. "It took up to one and a half minutes to clear each floor, longer at the lower levels," said Mr. Iyer, an engineer with the Port Authority. "If the elevator had stopped at the 60th floor, instead of the 50th, we would have been five minutes too late.

"And that man with the squeegee. He was like our guardian angel."

Since that day, Mr. Demczur has stayed home with his wife and children. He has pieced together the faces of the missing with the men and women he knew in the stations of his old life: the security guard at the Japanese bank on the 93rd floor, who used to let him in at 6:30; the people at Carr Futures on 92; the head of the Port Authority. Their faces keep him awake at night, he says.

His hands, the one that held the squeegee and the other that carried the bucket, shake with absence.

another quote that advances the action

the atom bomb stops ticking at ".007"

Three examples encompass all the lost

now things are really serious — he dropped his damn bucket!

powerful word at the end; the "absence" is not just in his hands, but stands for the absence of the dead and missing

Writers' Workshop

Talking Points

1) Jim Dwyer won his award for writing stories about everyday objects that have stories inside them. Discuss this as a strategy for covering big stories. Think of stories you have covered in which you could have focused on small objects to represent larger themes and events.

2) Discuss Dwyer's ethical notion that stories must present evidence to create a pathway to "reproducible results." In other words, Dwyer names sources and attributes information so that you could check him out if you wanted. Study the attribution in these stories and see how it compares and contrasts with other writers in this collection.

3) Dwyer says that in order to write these stories tightly, he must focus on the action and minimize character development. That said, discuss the characters who populate these stories. What little things have you learned about them? How does Dwyer shine a light on their values and personalities?

4) In order to save space and move the stories along, Dwyer prefers quotations that also convey action. Read these pieces and discuss how this strategy of quoting affects the reader. What value is gained by having a character describe parts of the action?

Assignment Desk

1) After reading these stories as models, find an object that has a meaningful story hiding inside it. Write that story for your publication.

2) Make copies of Dwyer's work to create a file of excellent short newspaper stories. Whenever you see a jewel of a story in a newspaper or magazine, clip it out and add it to your file. Let your colleagues contribute to your collection. Read these any time you feel that your writing is getting flabby.

3) Read over some of the shortest stories you have written. Revise them with the purpose of making them tighter and more focused.

A conversation with
Jim Dwyer

ROY PETER CLARK: Are you still writing "object" stories from Sept. 11?

JIM DWYER: I am. I think I've done about eight or nine, and I kind of do them sporadically.

Can you do a quick inventory of the objects you've done?

Besides the squeegee, the paper cup, and the photograph, there's a pair of handcuffs [that were used to dig out of the rubble], a hanging IV line, a torn paramedic sweatshirt, a bag of daffodil bulbs, a blind man's cane.

I have more that I'm thinking about but haven't done: an answering machine, the voice of the dead person on it and having to change that. But I don't quite feel prepared to invade that particular space just yet, and I may not. Ever. We'll see. And I will only invade it if invited.

I read that you got the idea for these stories from a man who lost his pen. What was that about?

I wrote a book about the first World Trade Center bombing and made a number of acquaintances and friends during that work. One guy who got out of the building on Sept. 11, I had interviewed that week and did a piece about him. He was composed—stunned like all of us—but very together. A week or two later I heard from a mutual friend that this man, Chuck, had fallen apart, and I asked what had happened. And he said he lost his pen. I said, "What do you mean he lost his pen?" He went in his pocket and couldn't find the only thing he had taken out of the trade center where he had worked for 25 or 30 years. And Chuck fell apart when he couldn't find his pen.

Then another friend pointed out to me how on the backs of all the fire trucks there were new coils of hose because so much hose was lost and torn at the trade center that day so that all the trucks had this new stuff on the back of them.

Then there was some discussion about this guy, Larry Silverstein, who had gotten the lease on the entire trade center just a short period of time before the attacks, and he had paid three billion dollars for this, and I thought what about that three billion, did he write a check for three billion dollars? What's that like? So I thought these three things would all make interesting stories because they were about something besides the nominal topic. But I didn't write any of them. I proposed it as a series of pieces to an editor here and he bit, and then I made a higher rule, which was that things not only had to be evocative, but they had to have had some actual role in the narrative that was being told.

So they could not be, for instance, like the steel crossbeams that some saw as religious, or they could not be flags or other purely symbolic totems. They had to be functioning things that were part of people's life-scape or memory in a very real, significant way. That was my own unenunciated but practiced rule.

And the first one was?

The squeegee.

The squeegee. Wow. You hit the big time. Let me ask you about short writing. Do you have some tips or some secrets for how to keep things short? Does it come from the original conception of the story? Do you write long and then cut it back? Tell me a little bit about how that works for you.

I think if you cut it back, you're almost always better off than thinking short to begin with. If you think short, you may lose good material. You'll get the best stuff if you write a little bit longer or think a little bit longer, and then bring it back.

What writing shorter forces you to do is to think about the essence and core of the story, the marrow of the story. People told me very interesting stuff. For instance, all these guys who escaped from the elevator with the squeegee, they all told me fantastic things about getting home that day and meeting their wives and the joy of being alive and embracing what they thought was lost, and it was great stuff, but that's another story.

Trying to keep it to one story at a time is a very rigorous and rewarding discipline. By writing short you're telling that story and that story only. Now, what does it do for you with character? In these cases, most of these things are about plots, stories, narratives. We have a rule here at the *Times*: We never refer to things in print as newspaper "stories." That's a style rule, which cracks me up, but I guess it's part of the discipline of the thinking here, which is that we refer to them as "articles" and "news reports." But of course, everybody calls them stories.

Stories are stories. All of these things have events and actions that are driving them, so there's not a lot of character development in them. Just not a lot of space for it. And that's one of the prices you pay, that you don't have a rich sense of who these folks are. You get little tiny strokes about them, at the most.

Do you have more tips or secrets for writing short?

I used to carry around a list of rules that I made up after my first year of writing columns and, unfortunately, it was in my wallet that was pickpocketed about four years ago.

I see an "object" story coming on.

Yeah, if I ever got my wallet back. I'd love to have those rules back, too. But what happened was I read my first year's worth of columns and got fed up with them all, and made a list of instructions for myself that included 1) save something good for the end, 2) never put numbers in the lead, and 3) always cut a hundred words.

That would keep your stories shorter for sure.

Yes, and it keeps you out of tangents, keeps you out of the distractions.

I want to ask you a question about the hugeness of

the events and the smallness of the things you were writing about. Were you going against the grain consciously, or was it the only way to get at this monstrous event?

I found it the only way in. I went down there very early after the towers collapsed and found myself bewildered because there was no ordinary geometry around. That lack of normal shape, I guess, set my brain thinking about finding the recognizable.

I knew a lot of people who were lost that day, both the people who worked in the towers and people who were responding as rescuers, guys I went to high school with. And I have a daughter who goes to school down the block. And it was a big deal, you know. It was a huge deal. I also spent about an hour that morning on the phone with a guy who was trapped on the 86th floor, couldn't get out. Over the course of an hour, we talked several times trying to get people to him, and I was explaining to him, having spoken to the engineer who designed the buildings, that a plane would not take down this building. And, you know, those were all things that happened in real time and, unfortunately, that guy didn't get out. Nor did a woman who was working in the office with him. So there was a lot of stuff for all of us to process.

I don't know how to even phrase this question...but do you think the absence of a more conventional detachment altered the way you wrote these pieces, or were you able to re-establish some kind of strategic distance?

I felt that there was plenty of opportunity to step back and craft these things carefully. I didn't feel like there was any kind of emotional splurge in them.

Were you emotional when you were writing them or reporting them?

Well, when I was reporting them, yeah. But mostly I was just trying to craft the stories. It's very hard to do that.

Let's talk about the crafting for a minute. I found the language to be really interesting. It's mostly understated focusing on the things that happened. But there's some movement in these stories. You move up the ladder on occasion. The stories gain a little "altitude." You're almost a little philosophical at moments. Is that fair to say?

Certainly. In that one about the water cup, I thought that was almost homilistic, to tell you the truth. I feel a little bit awkward about that. But with the others, I was very conscious about trying to dehumidify them and keep the sentimentality or even emotion out of them. But there are moments near the end of both the photograph story and the squeegee story that I was writing toward.

In other words, you knew ahead of time where you wanted the story to end up?

Right. I try to connect the dots, to get to some place that's outlined ahead of time in my head. In the squeegee story, it was the guy's hands shaking; in the photograph story, it's about his remembered sky. Why was this photograph important to me and to him? How does it qualify as an object that's important? It's because it had this function for him, that it was stuck in the corner of his window, and when he looked out the window, it was in the sky for him. So that was what I was trying to build toward in that one. And in the other one, I was trying to get to this interesting woman from the Bronx [Theresa Leone] who spoke about holding onto her cup.

How early in the process might you gain a sense of what your ending is going to be?

Well, I usually stick it up as the lead and say, "Well, maybe I'll save that for the ending."

Is it ever during reporting?

Yeah, probably in the photograph story. I was thinking about the ending when I was speaking to the guy who lost the picture. Where was the picture? He said it was always at this certain spot, and I knew that that was going to be the goal line.

Now that leads me to a couple of questions about reporting. Basically you're writing about events that you didn't witness—and about places that no longer exist.
So what kind of reporting does that require? What kind of questions does it require to evoke the kind of detail and perspective that you manage to get into these stories?

In the case of the elevator, I talked to those guys for hours and had the interesting experience of seeing them interviewed on the *Today* show a couple of days after my piece ran, and not being able to follow what they were saying, and being very heartened by the idea that there's something left for the people in the *Jurassic Park* of print to do, you know, which is to carefully piece together narratives.

When you talked to Mr. Demczur, for example, can you give me an example of the kind of question, the kind of back and forth that went on just trying to figure out what's up with this bucket and this guy? Did you have to really milk him to get details?

Well, first we talked about the incident in general, and then we went over it in excruciating detail, and then we talked about tools. And I had an idea in mind that perhaps he had stashed it in the sky lobby—that's the 44th floor where he picked up the elevator that morning. But I think he told me he didn't. I think he told me he took it with him into the cafeteria.

Then we started talking about the bucket and how long he'd had it. He was kind of amused by my questions about it. What the hell difference does a bucket make? Well, it makes a little difference. And actually there's a great footnote to that story, which was that a couple of days afterward I got contacted by the company that supplied the squeegee to the company that Mr. Demczur squeegeed for, and they are—you'll be happy to know—the company that invented the squeegee. In

1936, an Italian immigrant named Ettore invented the first and what it claims is still the best squeegee, and the biggest selling squeegee, in the world, and they wanted to get in touch with him because, for people who have long and diligent service to the Ettore Company, they give a special prize of a gold lapel squeegee pin. So not only did they come to me, but they flew to New York and they gave all these guys gold lapel squeegee pins with diamonds and rubies in them. But they also gave ten grand to one of the relief funds and they had a dinner for them, just very nice. I think his uniform is now in the Smithsonian.

So I am very pleased by that story. And I, myself, got an incredible facsimile of the squeegee pin without the jewels in it. I got the three-dollar version. So I took that as my gelt.

That's great.

So anyway, to return from the tangent from Mars, the reporting in all of these cases was to make sure the thing happened the way it did. In this case, everything people told me more or less checked out with one another. There were some minor discrepancies on certain points, but, for the most part, everybody told the same story and, without a question, the squeegee was a key part of the escape, and without question, he brought his bucket down several flights of stairs with him, and they just got out. Some will say it was two or three minutes; some would say it was 10 minutes. But they all got separated in the staircase. So there were multiple tellings of the story in more or less similar ways by people who had not had a chance to get together and cook up a story. And the same happened for the other guy, for the picture.

I have the three stories in front of me and I've got them marked up a little bit. I've done a little "X-ray reading," which is my way of saying that I'm trying to read the text to look underneath and see the machinery working. I want you to either support or disabuse me of some notions about what you were trying to do technically in the story.

Now on one of the stories, you begin with the ac-

tion. **You begin with Tim Sherman spotting the photograph. So it begins right in the middle of things. Why not begin the squeegee story: "None of the other window washers like his old green bucket"?**

Instead you begin with the very evocative, "Now memories orbit around small things."

I didn't have that lead originally. I put it in there because my editor, Jon Landman, read the piece without that in it and said, "You know this is just another escape story. Why are we doing this? You're not explaining that this is a series of stories about objects, and you've got to explain that." All that kind of critique. So I said, "Okay. Pipe down, here you go." I don't know. It was a good criticism and a fair criticism.

And it works, I think.

You really make time work for you in the story. I've heard someone recently call this device a "tick-tock." You give the time: "…8:48 a.m.…no one knew the clock was running." You refer to the final 100 minutes and then at the end, "Their escape had taken 95 of the 100 minutes." I don't want to overstate it, but there's a cinematic quality to that in which an adventure is heading toward some sort of dramatic climax. It's *High Noon*, right?

Oh, yeah, for sure. I think it's a tried-and-true technique, and so I have a decent respect for hackneyed techniques, and so…

You mean "classic" techniques.

Yeah. So, yeah, that was exactly why. If you stick a clock into almost any story, it moves it along.

I notice that there are moments, especially dramatic moments, when your sentences get shorter and shorter, and in some cases, the sentences are so short that they become short paragraphs. They're one-sentence paragraphs.

"There had been an explosion. Then the intercom went silent. Smoke seeped into the elevator cabin.

One man cursed skyscrapers....
   "There was no exit....
   "No one had a knife."
   All those periods slow things down in a way that builds the suspense. Were you intending that effect?

No, not particularly. I just wanted people to have a very clear sense of each action. It may be to slow it down in the sense that if you make it a longer sentence or more lyrical, you will delay people's sense of the moment that you're describing. To be as abrupt and plain as you can be, I think it chisels it right into people's consciousness.

There was no exit. They're stuck, they got the door open, but then there's a blank wall. It's like you're upping the ante. Or the facts are upping the ante.

Yes. And the reason that one is its own paragraph was to set up the object three paragraphs below it. It was a way of setting the paragraph about the squeegee in higher relief and to do that, I felt I had to emphasize that there was no other tool available.

No one had a knife.

No one had a knife. So I wanted to have that be its own paragraph, but I didn't feel right for some reason having that be its own paragraph unless there was already some rhythm of one-sentence paragraphs in place, so there being no exit is a pretty dramatic moment.

I figured you ripped off Sartre.

No. I wish I were that well read. I'm not. I also have a pretty strict rule for myself, which is never to start a sentence with "there was" or "there were." And yet somehow I decided that if I obeyed that rule I wouldn't have a short, punchy sentence there, so I permitted myself to break the rule.

I thought you also did something really interesting toward the end of the piece when Mr. Demczur finally drops his damn bucket. That worked so well just

because it was like it's attached to his arm, right? And, finally, things got urgent enough that he was willing to leave it behind. So I thought that all of the references you made to his attachment pay off in this moment of desperate urgency.

Yeah, well, that's the game. It's to paint the ball in the brightest colors possible so you can follow it all the way through.

Nice description. Tell me about your idea that journalism is the business of providing "reproducible results."

Yes, I'm in favor of that.

You once said that you've "become more and more persuaded that you have to have a fingerprint for the story that people can check."

Yeah, especially in these kinds of dramatic human-interest stories that are so extreme. You have to have DNA, you have to have fingerprints. You have to have evidence that any reporter or any citizen can go back and look at and say, "Yep, that's what happened."

It's not enough for you to be able to produce that kind of evidence for your editor?

I'm happier as a reader having it in the stories. I may be an overly skeptical person, but I remember when I was a kid in college reading Lillian Hellman's *Pentimento* and saying, "This thing's a phony." Every possible point of proof is covered up. You know, that was the book that became the movie *Julia*, and it turned out to be a total fake. If you can blend the attribution as gracefully as possible into the text, then why not?

Let me give you an example and see how you react to it. You watched the documentary *9/11* on CBS last night [Sunday, March 10]?

Yep.

My wife and I were watching it, and I kept saying to her, "Oh, shit, that young guy is going to wind up dead," and she said, "Oh, you don't think so, do you, because they're talking to him now?" And I said, "Yeah, but they're talking to him before Sept. 11." You remember how they kept bringing back characters to speak so that you knew that they were alive?

Yep.

But they delayed until a dramatic high point the fact that the young firefighter was the last one back, the last to walk back to the station.
    You do that very well in the story about the photograph.

Yeah, and I didn't even think about it, to tell you the truth. I was just trying to let the story unfold as it did first for Tim Sherman and then Brian Conroy. That's just how it happened.

But you had the choice…

…of blowing it out earlier.

Yeah, you had the choice of introducing George Tabeek earlier than you did, right? As a living, breathing person.

In the story there are two typographical breaks.

Three dots, yeah. Why did you use those?

That was my choice because this event took place in three parts. The saga happens…

It's a three-act play.

It was a three-act play, and that is a nonverbal way of signaling we have a new scene.

Well, I just want to reinforce that it worked for me as a reader because the little hairs rose on the back of my neck when it turned out that this guy was...

Was alive.

...was alive. And you created the stimulus for my worry, my care, and the delay. It's dramatic for the reader, but of course it was also dramatic for Tim Sherman when he had to make the call.

Yeah, those were his exact words about the hairs standing up on his hand.

So, in that case, you took part of a quote and turned it into a piece of action.

Right.

We all know where it came from so that you have produced the evidence in a way that you're really comfortable with.

Yeah, I'm pretty comfortable with it. And I was a little bit concerned about not manipulating readers.

Jim, did you go to Catholic school? Catholic high school?

Yes. I went to Loyola on 83rd Street in Manhattan. I grew up in Manhattan.

So let's talk about your parable of the photo. I thought it was really, really interesting as I was reading: "However many tons of stuff were on the ground, the landscape fell heavier and longer on the eye. 'There is no God,' he remembers thinking."

Right, right.

And I said to myself, "Is a good Catholic boy gonna let that stand?" And then, "...the fraternity of hard work, warm meals and caring people changed Mr. Sherman's opinion about God."

Yes, God makes a comeback.

But here we're talking about events that are so unspeakable, the kind of things—like the Holocaust—that make people ask the big, meaning-of-life questions. You were conscious of that when you were writing this, it seems.

Oh, yeah, for sure. There's an awful lot happening for these guys. Between the existence of God and the loss of friends and memories of time gone by and all this.

I want to turn for a minute to the piece about the cup of water. I want to talk about the overall structure of the piece. You clearly think of structure. You mentioned the last piece had three parts. Here you begin this piece with a series of quotes from four or five different characters, and you pick up most of them, if not all of them, lower in the story.
      I said to myself, "I wouldn't introduce the piece with so many characters," and then it occurred to me, "unless I was writing about an event that is so chaotic that people are just moving in all different kinds of directions." So it seemed as if you were trying to create a sense of the confusion and frenzy that was clearly so much a part of these people's experience.

Yeah, that was the idea that people from all different—I mean it's not made explicit here, but people who were geographically splayed were having these similar observations about their senses being assaulted and the difficulty of escape.

The characters are a microcosm of some of the diversity of the city in terms of the names of people and the language they use and those kinds of things.

Right, right, and that's just how it was. I mean it wasn't meant to be uplifting in any particular "rainbow coalition" type way; but that was how it turned out, that was who was there, that's who works down there.

The quotes are very distinctive. I think some writers

might have been tempted to clean them up. One quote says, "Not just us was helping."

And then Silvano Marchetto says, "Nobody complained about nothing." So one of the things you're trying to do with those quotes is to reflect character and ethnicity and...

And what they had to say. You know, it's just what they said. It wasn't a lot of normalizing, I guess. You can't sandpaper it down, people's voices.

Some reporters do though, right? Don't you read stories in which everybody sounds the same?

Yeah, of course. It's why papers die, because they become this endless dial tone of monotonous voices saying monotonous, regular things.

The other thing that you let your quotes do is advance the action. "He took me three or four blocks, to an abandoned food cart; there was water and juice there. My throat was burning up." You mentioned that as sort of a strategic element in your selection of quotations.

Correct. To make sure that you have the advantage of attribution being coupled to the narrative.

I notice in several sentences that you list things in groups of three: "In the next instant, men and women emerged from shops and doorways, with cups of water, gauze, flashlights." And just down below that, "They had lost their building. They had lost their way home. They had lost their shoes."

The rhythm of three, it has a sort of encompassing effect.

Yep. It works somehow in these pieces. It works anywhere, I think, in writing. It's the natural pealing of the brain, I think.

Tell me about Theresa Leone. Was she surprised when you called? Was everybody surprised when

you called them?

Some were. Everybody wants to talk about this, or did at that point. And I think they were surprised I had found them.

Theresa may not realize that she has the honor of being your "kicker."

She's a kicker, yeah. When my 15-year-old daughter was coming home after they evacuated her school, she was given water by people on the way home and she had a long walk. She had walked miles and miles. But that was a consistent theme with people. Every one of them, virtually every one of them spoke about how instantly good people were, and they were producing this water. And that's something, you know, I'm grateful that my daughter had something to drink when I couldn't get to her, and I'm glad I was born and reared on this little island. I'm glad this is how we behave when we're put to it.

[Editor's note: Theresa Leone is Roy Peter Clark's cousin. Dwyer learned of Leone's story while being interviewed by Clark for a fall 2001 story on Poynter Online.]

Michael Phillips

Finalist, Short Writing

Michael Phillips covers international economics, development, and AIDS for *The Wall Street Journal*, working since 1996 out of the newspaper's Washington, D.C., bureau. He covered U.S. military operations in Afghanistan in 2001.

Phillips joined Dow Jones in January 1995 as a reporter for the Dow Jones Emerging Markets Report newswire, based in Washington.

He began his journalism career in the fall of 1986 as a free-lance reporter for *The New York Times*'s Sunday New Jersey section. For several months in late 1987, he was a reporter for United Press International in Boston before becoming a free-lance reporter in Dakar, Senegal, in 1988. He joined States News Service during the fall of 1988 as a reporter, and, from Washington, covered regional news first for New Jersey and later for Minnesota and Florida. In 1991 he became a foreign correspondent for the Associated Press in Madrid, and was dispatched to cover conflicts in Somalia and Angola.

Born in Minneapolis, Phillips received a bachelor's degree from Harvard College and a master's degree from the Woodrow Wilson School of Public and International Affairs at Princeton University. While at Princeton, he was a reporting intern for UPI in Nairobi, Kenya.

Writing one of his short dispatches from southern Afghanistan, Phillips takes a moment of boredom and silliness to underscore the tension that grows when young soldiers are stationed in the desert to protect an air base seized in the war.

Over the hump: Tense, bored Marines watch camels

DECEMBER 6, 2001

CHARLIE COMPANY'S PERIMETER, Southern Afghanistan—The Marines first spot the intruder through the lime-green glow of night-vision scopes.

It ambles across the sand, circles a foxhole and disappears back into the desert. The lieutenant alerts the sergeant, the sergeant alerts the corporals, and soon the entire Third Platoon is scanning the horizon for a suspect camel.

"It's the Taliban cavalry-suicide camel," says Lance Cpl. Chris Tone, 21 years old, from Anaheim, Calif.

Specialized Marine hunter-killer units this week started cutting off possible Taliban escape routes out of their stronghold in Kandahar. But the young grunts of Charlie Company, Battalion Landing Team 1/1, 15th Marine Expeditionary Unit face night after night of cold, boredom and frustration, defending the perimeter of the desert air base they helped seize last week.

The four Marines of Second Team, First Squad, Third Platoon hold a segment of the line facing Kandahar, but haven't seen an Afghan. So far, the occasional incursion by a stray camel has been the only action. The team is wary, nevertheless, in case the creature could be rigged with explosives. It also poses a threat to helicopters and cargo planes if it ambles onto the heavily used airstrip.

Second Team spends day and night in a 6-foot by 10-foot foxhole. When their sergeant orders them to "stand to," they place their weapons atop some sandbags and peer out into the desert. The Marines will stand-to until headquarters declares the area secure enough that two of the men can sleep while the other two keep watch.

It's 7:45 p.m. when Lt. Victor Lomuscio, 25, of New York's Long Island, puts the platoon on camel watch. The platoon sergeant radios his other fighting positions, but the suspect has slipped away.

"If he's out there, [it] isn't moving," says Cpl. Alex Velazquez, 22, of Washington, D.C. The moon isn't up yet, and the night-vision scopes, which turn midnight into noon when there is a bright moon, are less effective searching for a stationary target in low-light conditions.

After the camel scare, the Marines grow quiet. They still aren't permitted to stand down, since Marine sniper patrols are out in the desert and must pass through friendly lines, something that can only be done with everyone up and watching.

The stillness is soon broken by gunshots from Bravo Company's lines to the right. First a few rifle shots, then a burst from a machine-gun. A medic runs up with a message from the platoon commander that the platoon is still on full alert. The sergeant heads to the command post for more information and returns with word of another camel assault. Bravo Company fired to scare at least one camel away from the runway, while a C-130 Hercules circled overhead waiting for space to land.

A stand-down is ordered, but the camel watch continues through the night. When the morning sun starts to heat the desert landscape, the off-duty Marines emerge from their sleeping bags. "Unidentified vehicle approaching from south to north," the lieutenant announces, relaying a radio message from the command post. The mortar teams quickly reset their weapons to hit targets beyond the Bravo positions and the troops don their Kevlar helmets and flak vests.

In the distance, five Humvees and a pair of fast-attack vehicles streak into the desert. They break into groups, then come together in a line, leaving puffy trails of dust. In Charlie Company's command post, the lieutenant relays their report: "It's the damn camel."

Lessons Learned

BY MICHAEL PHILLIPS

■ **Watch people do their jobs.** People like to talk about what they do and how they do it. What makes them proud of their work? What do they hate about it? What are the tricks that get them through their shift? The Marines brew foxhole Frappuccino out of powdered cocoa, coffee, and non-dairy creamer. They make postcards out of their Meals, Ready-to-Eat cartons. They fantasize about girls and beer, topics of endless interest to young men far from home. To be frank, they are waiting to see if they have what it takes to face combat and kill someone. Failing that, they might like to take a shot at a camel. Granted, Marines on the front lines in the Afghan desert have more innate news value than many things closer to home. But the same approach works elsewhere. I seem to remember a great story years ago about the guy whose job with the county was to scrape up roadkills. How do parking-meter monitors deal with being hated? What do airport firefighters do while waiting for a disaster they may never see? You may not want their jobs, but it can be interesting to spend a day or two watching them cope.

■ **Don't go to bed.** Night stories have an air of mystery for the diurnal among us. They also create a natural narrative structure because you can follow your subject's activities from dusk to dawn. In this case, several reporters embedded with the 15th Marine Expeditionary Unit spent the night on the Camp Rhino perimeter, a defensive line about a kilometer outside the compound and dirt airstrip the Marines had seized a week earlier. With the encouragement of the Marine public affairs officers, most spent a couple of hours in a foxhole, then called it a night. I was inclined to do the same, but by the time I got to the journalists' tent, there was no room left. I couldn't get into my sleeping bag or straighten out my legs. Freezing and sleepless, I stumbled over a colleague and went to spend the rest of the night shooting the breeze in the Charlie Company command post. That bit of serendipity and insomnia helped complete the narrative.

■ **Spend time with your sources before they commit news.** Every reporter knows the importance of building relationships with sources. That's especially true when dealing with sources such as the military, who have a deep suspicion of the press. One excellent way to overcome, or at least minimize, that reticence is by visiting when you don't want anything from them. Marines, for instance, spend lots of time training before they ship out. That rarely makes a good news story, but the Marines appreciate it if you show up and watch them conduct exercises. The approach might work with firefighters or Coast Guard patrols or police riot squads. You'll learn their language, their concerns, and all about their capabilities. And they'll be more likely to keep you in mind when it comes time to decide which reporters to take on real missions.

■ **No news is (sometimes) news.** At the time the camel story was written, reporters at Camp Rhino were irked that the Marines' sometimes-ludicrous ground rules kept us from writing the hottest news stories. The military, for example, sometimes barred us for "security reasons" from reporting on events we had witnessed, then announced those same events at Pentagon news conferences. Ours were valid complaints, but on occasion the lack of news itself can be newsworthy. The Marines were the largest U.S. ground force in Afghanistan then. Trained to storm beaches, they were deep in a country with no coastline or even much water. Yet while special-operations troops were battling Al Qaeda and Taliban fighters, the Marines were, for the most part, guarding an isolated airfield used as a base by the commandos. The Marines were frustrated by being so close and yet so far from the action, and Charlie Company's boring nights illustrated their quandary. But let's face it, the story wouldn't have been very entertaining were it not for the camels, and their arrival was just dumb luck.

Being a reporter is more fun than almost anything else you can do for a living. Who else (besides Marines) gets paid to spend nights in a foxhole in the Afghan desert, chatting with Marines, peering through night-vision goggles, and searching for camels? We get to see a little bit of so many things in life.

The Charlotte Observer

Peter St. Onge

Finalist, Short Writing

Peter St. Onge has been a general as-signment reporter for *The Charlotte Observer* since 1999. He came to the *Observer* from *The Huntsville* (Ala.) *Times*, where he was an ASNE finalist in 1999 in the Deadline News Re-porting category for his coverage of a Jonesboro, Ark., school shooting hearing.

A 1991 graduate of the University of Missouri, he is a two-time Livingston Award finalist and multiple award winner in the Associated Press Sports Editors competition, including first place this year in Enterprise Reporting.

His short features in the *Observer* are mined from traditional sources, from overheard conversations, from neighbors and strangers. In his writing, he employs all the tools of the longer narrative, each story set apart with a twist and an original turn of phrase.

As in other stories he has written, there's a surprise waiting for the reader in "A Teacher, a Student, a Lesson About Life," set up as much by St. Onge's understand-ing of what his readers are thinking as by the clever way the story unfolds.

A teacher, a student, a lesson about life

MAY 20, 2001

The dance teacher wasn't a teacher that night. He was just Sam, a 29-year-old at a south Charlotte club looking for some turns on the floor.

The student wasn't a student yet. Meredith was a regular at the club, and on that Saturday night she noticed that Sam was one of the best dancers out there. Sam had spotted Meredith, too, but when he approached her table later in the evening, he asked another woman to dance. She declined, and he turned to Meredith.

"Are you asking because you feel sorry for me?" Meredith said, on the way out to the dance floor.

"I'm asking because your friend said 'no,'" Sam replied.

They danced, one couple in one club on one Saturday night in Charlotte. Meredith liked how Sam moved so gracefully to the music. She also liked how Sam told her she was "awesome" on the floor. When the second song was over, they found seats off to the side, and they talked for a long while.

Sam told Meredith he was from Indiana and that he had moved to Charlotte 10 years ago to live with his father. Meredith told Sam she had spent all her 31 years in Concord. They talked about traffic and dance clubs and, of course, music. They laughed when each revealed a secret love for Elvis Presley.

Sam also told Meredith he was a dance teacher at a Fred Astaire studio in Pineville and that she should come by for a couple of introductory sessions. Meredith was apprehensive; she had always loved to dance, but lessons? She thought she might feel foolish. She worried others would stare at her out there on the floor.

She decided she'd worried long enough about stares.

Now, on a cool Wednesday evening, Meredith Stallings pulls her van into the studio parking lot for her third session. Sam Hall waits for her at the door. "We both agreed at first that this would be kind of weird," Meredith says, rolling her wheelchair toward the building.

Meredith is paralyzed from the waist down with spina bifida, a disease that inhibits the development of vertebrae. In the past, she says, people smiled when they watched her dance, but those smiles seemed always on the edge of pity. Sam smiles at her differently.

"There's a whole lot of stuff I didn't think I could do," she says. "It's years of being told you can't do things, or years of thinking you're not supposed to. Now I know you just need to say I can do it."

She hopes Sam knows what he's taught her in the past few weeks. She hopes her new friend knows what so many of us never do: That a small brush of kindness can color so much of someone's life.

Sam wants Meredith to understand something, too. At the studio, he teaches mostly elementary dance steps, moves he mastered long ago. Now he adapts the moves to Meredith's wheels, and he finds himself researching dance, looking at music a different way. "I think we're teaching each other," he says.

And so they move to the middle of the hardwood floor, and the teacher reaches for the student's right hand with his left. The studio's speakers offer the shoop-shoop of Jackie Wilson's "Lonely Teardrops." The teacher begins a shag step. "How about this?" he says.

He pushes toward the student, and she swings to her right. He pulls on her hand, and she turns to her left.

"You got it," Sam says.

"OK," Meredith says.

"Just say you will," the song says, and right then it seems that simple.

Lessons Learned

BY PETER ST. ONGE

Two short lessons from a short story:

■ **Lesson No. 1: Look for the narrative**—even in the 500-word range. When I first heard about Meredith Stallings, I was reluctant. Certainly, hers was a nice story: a woman in a wheelchair stretching her boundaries. But such a feature also seemed on the brink of patronizing. After all, why shouldn't she learn to dance?

When we met, Meredith told me the story behind her developing friendship with Sam, the dance instructor. Later, Sam also talked about the night they met—and how he, too, had benefited from this dance partnership. A narrative revealed itself: This was a story of a friendship beginning with a risk on a dance floor, then flourishing with a different risk on another dance floor.

It also was a good reminder that our nut graphs often have moments leading up to them—and moments that follow. Pursue them.

■ **Lesson No. 2: Don't be afraid to surprise.** Readers didn't learn about Meredith's wheelchair until the seventh inch of a 12-inch story. That's a significant tease —in this case one that included an intentionally vague headline and unrevealing art.

The trail of crumbs begins in the lead, where I introduce a "teacher" and "student." In the third paragraph, Meredith worries about Sam feeling sorry for her. Why? You have to read on to find out.

A warning: The payoff should be worth the mystery.

Another warning: Be choosy about when you tease readers. Don't, however, be stingy with surprises. I'm graced with an editor who believes readers like to get gifts throughout stories. Sometimes they are revelations, big or small. Sometimes they are mysteries answered. Look for those opportunities. Be a giver.

Anne Hull
Diversity Writing

Anne Hull considers it a privilege to watch people's lives unfold. She thrives on field work. It excites her to capture the raw, uncut experiences of people she writes about.

"When you're in the field, you're living someone else's life and seeing it through their experiences. I take that as a gift," said Hull, a national reporter for *The Washington Post*.

It is a gift of immersion she relishes. She never tires of it, even when it leads her to offbeat places and in strange directions. When she was a national correspondent for the *St. Petersburg Times*, she stayed in a trailer without plumbing in a Kentucky "holler." For another assignment, she rode buses for five days without getting off. Any discomfort faded with the thrill of being there.

Her interest in such stories was nurtured when, as a

high school senior, she went to work at the *St. Petersburg Times* as a "copy kid" and met narrative journalists David Finkel (now with *The Washington Post*) and Tom French. They encouraged her to read the "new journalism" writing of such authors as Tom Wolfe and Gay Talese. Those journalists, she said, told intimate stories in unconventional ways, conveying the truth of people's lives more completely than conventional, "what happened" news.

"It spoke to truth that was larger than a single event. It wove in people, context, histories, sociologies, and the fullness of life," said Hull, who spent 17 years at the *St. Petersburg Times* before joining *The Washington Post* two years ago. "It seemed to get to the bottom of people and their motivations...a kind of fullness of truth."

In the following stories, Hull finds a fuller truth about Muslims and other immigrant groups affected by the terrorism of Sept. 11, 2001. She also captures people in the crosscurrents of a city in transition when a high-end food store enters a low-end neighborhood.

She is there. And because of that, so, too, are her readers.

— Aly Colón

[Editor's Note: This is the first year Diversity Writing has been recognized as a permanent category in the ASNE competition. The Freedom Forum, which has partnered with ASNE on many diversity efforts, funds this award.]

Divided feast

APRIL 1, 2001

Cecilia Crawford had never heard of the luxurious organic grocer Fresh Fields until one came to her neighborhood. Unemployed and 28, she was like most of the others who filled out job applications. They were Giant people, or Shoppers Food Warehouse people, or corner market people.

The new Fresh Fields near Logan Circle was spectacular: a 61,000-square-foot cathedral that cast its auric glow over P Street NW.

But in this neighborhood? This neighborhood was more Popeyes and bulletproof windows, arroz con leche and $3.29 fried whiting in greasy carry-out joints that played "Bad Bad Leroy Brown" on scratchy AM radio.

All Cecilia knew was that she could earn $7 an hour at a job that didn't require a bus ride. She tied on her new Fresh Fields smock and her knockoff lunar Nikes, and took her place at the end of a cash register bagging groceries. Doe-eyed and maple-skinned, smiling that beguiling smile, even though most of the items moving toward her on the conveyor belt were mysteries.

A jar of green paste with a turtle on the lid for $4.99. A ball of white something floating in milky liquid for $10.62.

Occasionally, one of the cashiers would turn to a customer, holding up a bunch of leafy greens. "What's this?"

"Just plain kale."

After a while, Cecilia stopped looking at the register to see how much things cost, and she stuck to sacking. The five-pound bag of Pleasant Morning Buzz coffee beans went next to the Pilsner Urquell on the bottom, then the octopus salad, the fresh mozzarella, then two avocados, then fresh basil, and a Burt's Beeswax lip balm last.

The crowds surged. They came for staples and they came for curatives. A man stood morosely in the specialty food department one afternoon, his basket containing

$150 French champagne, a brick of Belgian chocolate and several artisan cheeses. He was to sign his divorce papers in two hours.

With the cars double-parked outside, it became apparent there was a new drug on P Street. It was called food.

* * *

On a brilliant Sunday a month after the grand opening, the P Street Fresh Fields is a scrum of consumerism: The cash registers are doing 20,000 transactions a week.

At the cheese counter, a husband stares at the pecorino foglie di noci, aged in walnut leaves in ventilated caves. "I can't find good old standard Swiss cheese," he tells his wife.

"Well," she explains, "I don't want good old standard Swiss cheese."

On this Sunday morning, they want tulips and rotisserie chicken and warm baguettes. Butcher paper is wrapped with square corners around heavy steaks. Even the delicate things are more beautifully frail on Sunday, like the Malpeque oysters glistening on ice. A feeling floats down the aisles that good things will come of all this.

The plaintive hope is best spoken by a tall blonde standing at the bakery counter. She's holding up a pre-boxed cherry pie and asking, "How do I make it so it's all crunchy and golden and warm?"

Fresh Fields understands the dream, but usually in places like Bethesda and Georgetown. Not on P Street, home of Best-In Liquors and its large sign warning, "DO NOT URINATE HERE, VIOLATORS WILL BE ARRESTED."

The arrival of Fresh Fields is part of the larger story of a rebounding city, particularly in areas such as Logan Circle on the edge of the Shaw district, once scarred by rioting after Martin Luther King's assassination and unable to recover until the rejuvenating river of pinot noir began to flow.

By the early 1990s, a ripping economy was pushing the affluence of Dupont Circle eastward. Construction of a new downtown convention center started to push revitalization from the other direction. Sandwiched in between was a residential real estate market gone atomic. A former methadone clinic at 14th and Q streets NW was turned into $300,000 luxury condo units that sold out in four hours.

The area still had its share of soup kitchens, homeless shelters and armed robberies. But in 1997, an unlikely retailer began scouting the area for property.

Whole Foods Market Inc., which had bought Fresh Fields in 1996, was expanding nationally. Whole Foods had helped catapult the health food store from dusty grain bins to gleaming meccas offering organic, natural and gourmet foods, all swaddled in Earth Day politics. ("Ultimately, each of us creates our own reality," the employee handbook explains.) Ferociously anti-union and publicly traded, Whole Foods pulled in $1.6 billion in sales in fiscal 2000; its 2.875 percent profit margin is double the grocery industry average.

The company began eyeing a site on the corner of V and 13th streets NW. But when a group of Logan Circle citizens—white Victorian home rehabbers—learned of Fresh Fields' interest, they launched a campaign to persuade the company to consider P Street instead. The group produced a 52-page demographic study that showed the 1997 market price of a home within half a mile of the P Street site was $342,000. It flooded Whole Foods' headquarters in Austin, Texas, with more than 3,000 written pleas.

Fresh Fields' own "psychographic" figures revealed that dining and entertaining were core values in the gentrifying P Street radius, which was increasingly white, gay and affluent.

In 1999, Fresh Fields broke ground on a rat-infested lot at 1440 P St. It would be one of the largest stores in the company, with 37,000 square feet of shopping area and a parking garage for 151 cars. Hoping for a visual echo, the architect studied the abandoned auto showrooms that lined 14th Street in the 1940s. A glass facade would throw light everywhere, creating a colossal blast of radiance on P Street. Galvanized steel beams were left exposed in the ceiling. The aisles would be roomy and wide, mocking the Lilliputian lanes of cramped city markets. Special bulbs were used to create a natural warmth, not the cold blue of other grocery stores.

Groupies monitored the construction site as if it were a sacred dig. When the glass front went in, they pressed their noses to it and tried to guess how much longer.

"It was kind of like the early reports of the Spanish and Portuguese telling us of another land," says Dave Cercone, a historian who lives a block away. "It was like a burning tower for all of civilization."

And then it opened last December. A man newly sprung from a five-year federal prison stint returned to his old neighborhood and stood agape when he saw the buttery basilica on P Street, later remarking that he felt like he'd been away for 20 to 30 years.

On this Sunday morning, the store is something to see: brunch hunters in leather jackets, scruffy pagans, matching male couples and worshipers from the nearby AME Zion, cooling their gospel throats with power smoothies in the juice bar.

And yet there's the sense that all parties are grappling with one another's folkways. Those most mystified are the employees. While nine department managers and other experienced hands have come to the P Street store from other Fresh Fields locations, the majority of the 300 hires are from the neighborhood. They live in the shrinking inventory of affordable housing, Section 8 apartments and much-prized rent-controlled units. For them, grocery shopping means 69-cent chicken thighs on sale and Donald Duck orange juice and bread that's either white or wheat. This is a whole new galaxy.

* * *

"Do you have Luna Bars?" a customer asks.

"What are Luna Bars?" the employee asks back.

"You know, sort of like Clif Bars."

Or: "Do you have low-fat brie?"

In these early days, the hunters always seem to know more than the employees. A slender woman with silver jewelry approaches the bakery counter. Her tone is determined. "The Fresh Fields honey buns are usually this high," she says, holding her fingers four inches apart. "These are down to here."

The baker explains, "It's the way they been poofin' lately."

"The way they've been what?"

"Poofin'."

"Define poofing," the woman says. "That's obviously your term."

Cecilia Crawford stands at Register 5, bagging groceries and taking it all in. She can't remember what they buy or how much they spend. But she wonders where they go from here. "A big house with a great living room set," she says, imagining. "Totally nice."

Like the city itself, she's rallying, trying to forget her old fast-food apron and welfare. She's arriving early and doing extra. "Paper or plastic?" she asks, a hundred times a shift. Some people bring their own cloth bags and she fills those. Some have Italian baby strollers with special wire racks and she fills those.

"Paper or plastic?"

She bags organic baby bella mushrooms, yellow pear cherry tomatoes, watercress and sirloin for a total of $64.75. She bends over to say hello to a baby in a velvet hat.

"He's gorgeous," Cecilia tells the mom.

"Oh, thank you," beams the mother.

The next customer says to his shopping partner, "I feel like I'm in Communist Russia when I'm in that Safeway. There's nothing in the store." Cecilia bags his fingerling potatoes, eggplant, smoked salmon and pasta.

When her shift ends, she punches out and unties her smock in the break room. She exits the candescence and begins her walk home in the dark. Three blocks later, she comes to her building and presses the buzzer.

Upstairs, a few women in bathrobes are watching TV, tossing out answers at *Who Wants to Be a Millionaire*, which strikes Cecilia as funny, "seeing as how we're here." Here is N Street Village, a homeless shelter and residence for women. Three times a week, Fresh Fields donates soon-to-be-expired groceries to feed the residents, one of whom is Cecilia Crawford.

* * *

More than 2,300 people applied for the 300 jobs at the P Street store. In produce alone, 600 were screened for 21 positions. A knowledge of risotto and orzo was not a prerequisite, nor was grocery experience. One person had cleaned bathrooms at the National Zoo. Another worked at Linens 'n Things.

"I'd much rather have someone happy and smiling over someone with a long face and 10 years in the grocery business," says store manager David Schwartz. "I can train you to cut meat. I can't train you to enjoy life."

In the nonauthoritarian culture of Fresh Fields, the bluejeans-wearing store manager's name tag simply says: David. Wiry and spring-loaded, after seven years with Fresh Fields David believes intimidation squelches employee creativity. He acknowledges those who come from a "culture" of standing at a cash register and pushing pictures of combo meals may struggle with the self-empowerment atmosphere of Fresh Fields. And, he readily admits, "you are not gonna get everyone to have the love."

He's right. Not all employees catch the fever. "Everybody wants to raise their children healthy, but we can't afford it," says one bakery worker, who will later quit. "Five dollars for milk 'cause it's in a glass jar?"

After several weeks of operation, some 30 original employees are gone, for a variety of reasons. What's left are the best, David says. "Look around the store and what you'll see are shiny happy people."

Food has a joyous narrative at Fresh Fields. Little signs explain the journey of a piece of cheese or the bio of an organic orange. But the most remarkable stories belong to the employees.

For Cecilia Crawford, Fresh Fields is her comeback after a long drop. She quit Bowie High School in ninth grade, unable to read even a few words. She signed up for welfare at 18 with her first child. By the fall of 1999, she was 27 with four kids and an impending eviction notice.

"I went to Child Protective Services," she says. "I did what I had to do."

Her children were placed in foster care in Prince George's County. Without them, she wandered into the District, where an aunt lived, but instead found herself at a notorious cluster of tin-can trailers where drugs were sold and dewy condoms hung in the morning weeds. A door was open and she went to it. The trailers became her blurry encampment. To get away, she walked around the Washington Monument or caught warm buses to nowhere.

Women who stayed around the trailers often walked to N Street Village for medicine or food. Cecilia would follow them but never go inside. One day she did. She was given a bed.

"I don't think I talked to anyone for a month," she says.

That was a year ago. She still lives at the shelter. Twice a week she takes the bus to reading class, having learned long ago to use landmarks, not letters, to navigate by. She sees her kids once every four weeks. She cashes her Fresh Fields paychecks at the liquor store and banks most of it through her caseworker at N Street Village.

To get her kids back, she needs a place to live. There are 13,000 people ahead of her on the District's Section 8 waiting list. Like everyone else, she tries her luck in Maryland.

One Saturday Cecilia has off, she leaves N Street Village with the classified ads neatly folded in her purse. She wears a Winnie the Pooh fleece pullover, something she pulled from the pile at N Street Village. She is accompanied by a dignified older woman, another N Street Village resident whose matching shoes and hat belie her homeless status.

Together, they conquer a Metro ride, a bus ride and a quarter-mile walk, which brings them out to Landover Hills. When Cecilia reaches the rental property the landlord announces she's nearly the 20th person to come through in the last hour, probably because his ad said, "Sec. 8 OK." Walking back to the bus stop, a dog snapping through a chain-link fence, the two women are quiet.

"Sure is far away," the older woman finally says.

Cecilia tries to figure the commute time to Fresh Fields. Ninety minutes.

"No way," she says. Not in defiance, but in defeat.

When she returns to N Street Village, she goes to bed and sleeps into Saturday night. Above her is a gold framed photo of her kids. Among her personal trinkets is her unread Fresh Fields employee handbook, which explains its philosophy on wages this way:

"Drawing a paycheck is nice, but it's not the whole meaning of life. We believe we offer each of our Team Members an opportunity to fulfill a higher purpose: helping to make the world a better place."

* * *

On P Street, the world is becoming a better place. Developers with scrolled blueprints pace off the sidewalks, taking in the retail glory of Fresh Fields. Next door at Best-In Liquors, owner Amare Lucas is trying to capture some of the spillover.

"Look," he exclaims, proudly waving toward his new inventory of premium vodkas, "Ketel One!"

Inside Fresh Fields, customers are eagerly posting their comments on the community bulletin board.

"A beacon in the night!"

"So very happy to have another high quality store in the DC. Thank you from Columbia Hts. resident and customer."

"In town to protest from Brooklyn. I protest that my hood doesn't have such a store!"

"Great store. Please add a white wine chiller like the one at your Georgetown store."

"What's the deal with the olive rolls. Lackluster. Try olive roll samples from your Wisconsin Ave. and Arlington store."

"Please have a bigger diversity of goat or sheep's milk cheeses at a price of less than $10."

"Would like you to explore different coffee creams, like Irish cream, French vanilla, etc."

"Need more French bread. (baguettes). You always seem to be out. This is a 'basic.' Thanks."

"Incorporate solar panels on your roof top. Love, the green people."

"I really like this store...but I prefer the bulk bin presentation at the Georgetown store."

"The trash cans in the 'dining areas' are not big enough (the holes through which we insert our trash) to accommodate a plate from your hot bar. This means I have to fold the plate, thereby getting oil all over my hands."

"Great store. Very impressive. But outside a lot of light shines up. Looking for aliens? I'd rather see stars."

"Why no thyme?"

* * *

Sales numbers are posted daily in the back. P Street is doing nearly half a million in sales a week. Of the 28 stores in the mid-Atlantic region, the P Street store has blazed to the front of the pack in wine, cheese and flower sales. At the same time, the store is trying to combat its upscale reputation in the neighborhood by offering a wider selection of its value-oriented private label "365" line, from colas to sandwich cream cookies to macaroni.

"We're becoming everyone's grocery store," says assistant store leader Andy Smock. "We didn't want to become classist."

But resisting the pinwheels of stuffed salmon laid out on marble in prepared foods is proving too much for some. Shoppers at all income levels are cutting deals with themselves to rationalize. "If you go to the Palm or Smith & Wollensky, you're gonna pay $35 for one steak," says one customer.

An organic Haas avocado at Fresh Fields sells for $1.99; across the street at the small market an avocado costs 99 cents. Organic certification isn't the only price booster, according to store management. Customers expect better-tasting and better-looking food at Fresh Fields, which carries a higher waste percentage than traditional grocers because it culls out aesthetic duds.

For the uninitiated, the prices at Fresh Fields are eye-opening.

"This is for the rich and famous," says June Augustin, a Trinidadian local who wanders in to check out all the excitement. "Like, this okra is $6.99 a pound. You get it for $2.99 a pound at Giant. Look at the tuna! $17.99 a pound! I'll go to the wharf."

Even some of the most devoted customers express concern over Fresh Fields being plunked down in this neighborhood. And yet here they are, shopping basket in hand.

"All my friends have been debating this place," says Lida Husik, an artist who is white. "It makes me nervous to see this gentrification. At the same time, this is the best black bean vegan soup I've had in a long time."

"I have mixed emotions about this place," says Lori Harris, a legal secretary and African American who works downtown and stops at Fresh Fields on the way home to Hyattsville. "Yes, it's nice to have Fresh Fields here. But the flavor of the neighborhood starts to change. It's admirable, it's cool that they hired local workers, but when the workers can't afford to shop here, what does that say?"

In her own basket, there rest lobster Newburg in

phyllo and Yukon Gold potato chips.

"It's that pull," Harris admits.

Other shoppers dismiss the hand-wringing. "There were porn shops and hookers here 10 years ago," says Kevin Callwood, an international business consultant who is African American. "That's the kind of heart of the neighborhood they want? This store represents that era is over."

Not totally over. Duron Paints across the street is still used as a labor pickup point, and when work doesn't come the men sometimes drink beer in the bushes, which often devolves into shouting matches at 11 in the morning. The others sun themselves against the brick wall of Metro Supermarket, the small grocer across the street from Fresh Fields that sells frozen ham hocks and tortilla husks. In the shadow of Fresh Fields, the Metro market is a grimy orphan, but it has been the neighborhood grocer for years.

One cold morning, an intoxicated man curls up in the men's room at Fresh Fields. When he awakens he begins pestering customers in the Jamba Juice bar. He's asked to leave, and then proceeds to pass out in the entrance, as a groomed standard poodle looks on. Shoppers step around him. D.C. police are called.

"Oh, this one again," sighs the cop. "And he's heavy. You always drunk, baby."

Before the P Street store opened, management wondered about the Fresh Fields custom of offering free samples. Would the homeless nosh their way through the chocolate babka? As it turns out, the most aggressive samplers appear to have homes.

There is the woman in a boucle coat who reaches for a toothpick and begins spearing cubes of Madrigal Baby Swiss. Stab, stab, stab, stab, stab, until she has a decent kebab. Standing at the platter, she goes through three toothpicks.

There is the man who stands over at the hot bar and repeatedly dips his spoon into the communal serving pan of lamb stew. The entire pan is tossed as soon as he walks away.

"You'd think they'd be discreet, but they just get to eatin' like they at home," says Ron Wilson, in prepared foods.

There is the regular P Street grazer, a distinguished 60-ish man with silver hair, who one night begins his circuit in produce, tossing a fistful of complimentary cherry tomatoes into his mouth. Walking with hands behind his back, regally strolling, he approaches the bing cherries, which are not complimentary but sell for $4.99 a pound. He enjoys several. Then he serpentines back to the hot bar for minestrone soup. In cheese, a few cubes of Gouda. And then a piece of hearty prairie bread. Next stop: butter pound cake.

The employees aren't supposed to scold. Occasionally, another customer will do it for them. A woman in the bakery once pointed at an abuser and shouted, "HE'S TOUCHING THEM WITH HIS HANDS!"

As time passes, the employees are less afraid to draw the line. One day, a woman comes to the prepared-foods counter with her own bowls from home. Dubious of recycling, she insists her own containers are the solution.

"Ma'am," says employee Linda Holmes, citing sanitation rules, "we are not going to lose our jobs to save the earth."

* * *

The culture of Fresh Fields—the hippie vibe, the organic emphasis, the peer review that substitutes for bureaucracy—is often lost on the immigrant strivers. They walk by the in-store yoga video, impervious to the yoga master's calming instructions. *Breathe. Open your chest*. Many hold two jobs, and Fresh Fields is just Act II in a very long day. Those speaking the least English start in the kitchen. New tasks are pantomimed rather than explained. One Eritrean woman escaped from her burning village. Another fled to a Sudanese refugee camp. Now both assemble turkey-and-muenster wraps at Fresh Fields for $8 an hour.

Martha Claros had never heard of Fresh Fields when she saw the ad for the new store on P Street. She lived nearby in a highrise called King Towers, where the dim hallways are filled with the sounds of Spanish cartoons and forks scraping against plates. Languid Africans in sandals share elevators with Salvadoran girls carrying Britney Spears book bags.

For the last 13 years, Martha Claros had worked as a housekeeper, most recently at McLean Gardens, where she and her team cleaned 27 condos a day for $6.25 an hour. A job in the Fresh Fields bakery for $8 an hour with medical benefits was beyond her dreams. And no more catching the bus to work. King Towers is five blocks from Fresh Fields.

Martha, from Bolivia, had nearly perfected her English but had no real knowledge of bakery work. She knew biscotti softened when dunked in hot liquid, or so a doctor whose house she cleaned had told her.

Her face is coppery with two dark eyes. She wears the sort of spongy-soled navy shoes worn by a 47-year-old who has lived on her feet. They are her splurge: Easy Spirits. She has a 7-year-old son named Javier. After she puts him to bed at night, she reads up on prairie bread, muesli, pane paisano, pecan raisin, oatmeal rustic, rosemary sourdough, spelt, dairy-free vegan muffins; the list is endless.

"I want to show them all my appreciation," she says, explaining her diligence. "This is the first time in 13 years that I will have something. I already started saving for Javier's college. I think age 7 years is a good time to start. Fifty dollars a month."

At the bakery counter, Martha works with five African-American women, a woman from Senegal and a white guy from Annapolis. The bakery is often under siege. It's wedged between the juice bar and the sushi area and sometimes the very calm Salvadoran sushi chef just smiles as he shapes his rice balls, watching the customers bunch up in impatient hordes for warm baguettes.

Martha's brow is damp with perspiration as she hustles around taking peanut bars from a large pan and placing the singles in plastic containers. As she cuts pumpkin bread for samples, a woman in a leather jacket approaches. "Hi, can you make a recommendation? I'm having a dinner that will be largely a Thai Asian dinner. Would a sesame semolina be your best recommendation?"

Martha scrambles to remember her bread book. "You know," she says, with slight nervousness, "French baguettes go with everything."

Another customer wants to know the difference between sourdough and rosemary bread. "Well," Martha ventures, "the sourdough is plain and the rosemary has rosemaries in it."

A woman in a hurry cuts in front of the waiting bakery customers. "Excuse me," she calls out to Martha. When the other customers turn in disbelief, the woman flashes a winning smile and apologizes. "I'm *very* focused on a chocolate torte," she explains.

When Fresh Fields first opened, the women in the bakery were astounded by the money being spent. But by month three, they are dulling to the pageant. "They may not eat the $20 cheese every day," Martha points out, in defense of expensive cheese. "Maybe a slice every other day."

Senegalese-born bakery employee Fatou Dieng regales her co-workers with tales from her days at Dean & De Luca, the gourmet market in Georgetown. Fresh Fields is nothing, she tells her rapt crowd.

"The raisin pecan bread is $9," Fatou says, in her lilting French accent. "Go there and say, 'Hello, I'm looking for raisin pecan bread, how much is it?' They will tell you. The jalapeno cheddar corn? Eight dollars. And the brioche loaf is $9. You say $9 and they don't even listen to you. The money is there. Strawberry shortcake? $38. They don't care, $38, $58, they don't care."

Martha's eyes widen. "Do they pay in cash?"

Fatou folds her arms over her white bakery smock. "Sometimes the customers come in with their housekeepers and just throw it in the cart!"

The women shake their heads. Fatou goes on. "Before I came to America, what I was seeing on TV was the best place in the word," she says. "The big houses, the malls. You didn't know, except the dream they show you on TV."

Martha offers the immigrant creed. "Fatou, you work hard, your dreams come true!"

But Fatou isn't buying it. "It's like, 'You come and jump in the money. The money is waiting for you.'" Then she is quiet.

Martha punches off at 8. "*Hasta la vista*, ladies," she tells her bakery colleagues.

"Same to ya, sweetheart," a co-worker waves.

On her walk home, Martha passes Logan Circle. It is practically bucolic under the moonlight. Five years ago,

Martha wouldn't have walked this strip alone at night. "Now," she says, "thanks God, all those things are in the past."

She hasn't noticed that the refurbished crack houses with crown molding around Logan Circle are going for $499,000. Nor does she realize that real estate agents are using Fresh Fields as a selling point. But lately she sees the newly painted walls in her own apartment building, and a spruced-up lobby. Twice in the last year her rent has increased; now it's up to $460 a month. To stay ahead of the curve, she cleans houses on her days off.

When she tries to remember her last real day off, she pauses, counts in Spanish, and then announces a date four months earlier.

* * *

"If you're a guy, what do you want, a steak with a bone or without?" asks the sleek blonde with the Kate Spade purse.

His red apron strings tied around his waist, Sean Lucas leans over the silver counter. "Get a thick one with a bone in it."

The two rib-eyes go into a basket next to the asparagus. The wine is waiting at home. It's Tuesday night.

The concept of "celebrating life" is something else again at Fresh Fields. Every night is a celebration, as Sean is learning. Behind the meat counter, he thumbs through *Saveur* magazine for recipe tips so he can bond with the customers.

When he works mornings, he stumbles onto his porch at 3:30 a.m. and buckles his belt in the cold. The birds are still hiding in the branches. He lives off Benning Road, east of the Anacostia, and he hoofs eight blocks to the bus stop for the 4:18. His main hope is to not get robbed on the way. When a car with a fender-rattling bass beat goes by, he lifts a wary head. "I haven't heard too much about robberies lately," he says. "The main thing is shootings."

At 25, Sean knows how to glide anywhere. He used to be a concierge for K Street lawyers, shagging their dry cleaning and flowers. Before that, he graduated from the Duke Ellington School for the Arts and did a year at the Corcoran art school until he couldn't afford it anymore. Not much about his new job at Fresh Fields makes him think about his favorite painter, John Singer Sargent, but he sees pride in his work. "Like in the movies, like *Rocky*, you know the scene where the man moves to the city and he's struggling? He got a job cutting meat."

Behind the meat counter, Sean is helping another new guy get the hang of the good life.

"See, Donis here, he's got good intentions but he's not in the routine of thinking and doing," Sean explains one Friday night.

Donis Arias came in off the streets to work at Fresh Fields. He did a brief stint as an anti-gang counselor, but mostly the corner was his thing. He is short and husky, with a tufty goatee. He wears a delicate ring a girl gave him on Valentine's Day, and a bracelet that says "EL SALVADOR."

Donis didn't have money for dinner three months ago; now he lords over tens of thousands of dollars of Coleman beef. Cattle fed the best grains. No hormones. No antibiotics. Yet none of it appeals to Donis. "To me, I can't eat this kind of food," he says. "My mom got me used to Giant."

Sean shakes his head in disappointment, and says of Donis, "All of us are limited as far as what we can expound on."

But it's Friday night, and the carnivores are knocking, so Sean and Donis try to serve. Donis weighs out a pound of chicken maple breakfast sausage. Sean wraps four lamb chops in butcher paper and then a porterhouse. "Y'all gonna eat good tonight," he tells his customer.

"It's not all for tonight," the customer says, a tad defensive.

Donis is bent over some chicken when he suddenly straightens. Thumping over the storewide sound system is a song by the teen rapper Lil Bow Wow. This may be urban P Street, but Lil Bow Wow? Donis wigs out. "Listen to that, man, it's ghetto music in a Fresh Fields!"

A co-worker dismisses the notion. "That's not ghetto music."

Donis gestures toward the aisles. "That's the way *they* see it."

A slender man breathlessly appears at the counter.

"I'm looking for a meat hammer," he says. "I'm making veal scaloppine and it needs to be thin."

Donis tells the customer they don't sell hammers. The customer gets a sad face. Donis just looks at him. The customer wonders if someone could thin out the veal. Donis goes in the back and starts pounding. When he returns, he hands over the package. "Here you go," he says. "Nice and beat up."

Sean rides Donis, trying to make Donis have better customer contact. He gets after him to pronounce his consonants. "Don't forget, Donis," Sean says, holding up a rib-eye. "Tell 'em to rub some oil on it and season it well."

Donis grins mischievously. "Tell 'em to put some barbecue sauce on it."

Sean has flecks of meat on the sleeves of his white smock. He doesn't keep his sleeves rolled up old-school style with rubber bands like his boss. But he wants to learn all he can. He makes $8 an hour and hopes to move up in the company. One day he'd like to be on the other side of the counter.

"I wish I had the money for that kind of steak." he says. "I wish I could make that amount of money to entertain guests."

He's working solo one evening when a man and a woman shopping for a dinner party try to decide. This time, it's Wednesday night. "How are the boneless sirloins?" the woman asks.

Sean holds up three monster steaks. The woman appraises them. "I'm feeding seven people," she says. "Better do four."

"Nothing wrong with that," Sean says, ringing up the meat: $68.68. To go with the steaks, there will be mushroom cream sauce, potatoes, endive salad and red wine. Sean surrenders the package. The woman needs both hands. "It's like I'm taking home a mini-calf," she says, smiling.

"Yeah, a calf, huh?" Sean says. The couple walk away.

Sean leans over the meat counter. "Hey," he calls, "tell me how it turns out."

* * *

Each Fresh Fields customizes itself to fit what it calls

the "palate of different markets." By the third month of operation, the P Street store is selling high-end produce that no other store could (black trumpet mushrooms for $29.99 a pound), but at the same time it's ringing up astronomical numbers of chicken wings on the hot bar.

The customers? Impossible to categorize. LeDroit Park mavens stand in line next to retired radicals living in group houses in Mount Pleasant. There are Logan Circle loft-dwellers buying beer like Tetley's English Ale ("this can contains a floating widget") standing beside Rasta vegans buying rice milk and red bananas.

But the store goes far beyond food. Gay men claim it's the best new scene in town. Others say it can be the saddest place in the world when shopping for just one.

Some customers feel themselves inexplicably pulled toward the building. "I'm out and about, doing my thing, yada, yada, yada, and for one reason or another, I find myself here," says John Grimberg, a political consultant who lives two blocks away.

The P Street store has become the utopia that management had been aiming for. The only requirement is money. Which is the one factor that cleaves the utopia, as far as the employees are concerned.

"What in the world are they doing with all that food?" asks bakery clerk Evelyn Lyles. "Are they buying for themselves or a houseful? Most of 'em I picture being bachelorettes and bachelors, livin' alone and eatin' good. Kinda lonesome, though."

In the bakery, Martha Claros now knows ciabatta from pane paisano. When a 35-ish man appears at the counter one evening holding a recipe, Martha is eager to suggest a bread. Her colleague, Gloria Pullen, who wears her bakery cap side-cocked, tries to get a peek at the recipe. Shrimp and fennel.

"Mmm, hmm," Gloria says, though she has no idea what fennel is. "That should be good. You got to run that off for me."

"Uh, yeah," says the customer. "Can I have a loaf of the kalamata olive?"

"Okay, baby."

Bread in basket, the man walks away, and Gloria is still trying. "You got your chardonnay?"

What do the women talk about during a down moment

in the bakery, when the demand for bread and tarts momentarily subsides? Kids and money. All are renters and all have the anxious feeling lately the city is changing in ways that imperil their modest lives.

"Me and my girlfriend have been real good about trying to stay on top of things," says baker Tracie Brashears. "We just conversate about it late at night when the kids are in bed. Some people leaving D.C. are going to Clinton, Maryland; Fort Washington, Maryland; Upper Marlboro. They have so many incentives to move you. I love my city. You are not going to run me out."

On a busy afternoon, Martha Claros has gotten permission to use her 30-minute break to attend a parent-teacher conference at Javier's elementary school, which is six blocks from Fresh Fields. But the bakery is getting slammed and the hours tick by.

"Do you have ciabatta?" a customer asks.

"Ciabatta? Yes, ma'am," Martha says.

"Do you have ciabatta rolls?"

"No, ma'am."

Javier's teacher will only be at school until 7 that night. At 6:30, Martha tries to make a break for it when a regular customer appears at the counter wanting half of a tiramisu cake. "It was an expensive cake and I didn't want to lose the customer," she would later say. The whole time she's walking to the freezer and then letting the cake thaw slightly before halving it she's thinking, I'm dying to know how Javier is doing at school.

She hands over the tiramisu. The clock in the bakery says she has 23 minutes before her parent-teacher conference window closes. Martha hurries through the crowded store to reach the time clock, passing Sean Lucas at the meat counter, who is forcing some pearl of wisdom on Donis.

Outside, it's misting. Martha has 15 minutes and five blocks to go. She does something she never does. She hails a cab, paying $5 to reach Javier's school. The light is still on in the classroom.

Javier is doing well, the teacher says, but he talks too much.

As Martha walks home to King Towers that night through the puddles, the luminosity of Fresh Fields is a far-off candle.

* * *

With silver hair and a leather bomber jacket, Wayne Dickson proudly strolls past Fresh Fields. In 1986, Dickson and his wife moved into a four-story Victorian house two blocks away, and for the next decade they toughed out the bleak years of stepping over syringes on their curb. It was Dickson who helped power the campaign to bring Fresh Fields to P Street. Now he finds himself there every day.

"Men love it," says Dickson, president of the Logan Circle Community Association. "It's got a lot of big stuff. Hunks of bread, big steaks, great big wide aisles."

His wife likes it, too. "You can go and get a baguette and ride home with it in your bicycle basket," says Carol Felix-Dickson.

Fresh Fields is great, but it's just a start, Dickson says. He envisions a "Main Street USA" in these blocks and along 14th Street. A hardware store, a garden store, an upscale bicycle shop, a bakery.

The arrival of Fresh Fields has created a noble moment in the regentrification story. Carl's Barber Shop three doors down has picked up new business, including first-time white customers.

And yet the moment can't last. When Dickson stands in front of Carl's Barber Shop, he spreads his arms joyfully.

"You can just imagine what this could become," he says, surveying the drab storefront. "First-floor retail, living space above."

Through the front window, owner Carl Lewis can be seen clipping hair and telling stories.

Dickson values diversity. But he is realistic. "It's an economic fact that when there is gentrification that some people get squeezed out," he says.

A week later, a large banner goes up across from Fresh Fields. Hung on the vacated Columbia Lighthouse for the Blind building, the banner is a 30-foot-high photograph of a luxurious loft with blond wood floors and contemporary furniture. Underneath the image are the words "FINE URBAN LIVING" and the name of a development company.

* * *

The same afternoon the banner goes up, Cecilia

Crawford leaves N Street Village for her 3-10 shift at Fresh Fields. In the coming weeks, there will be unexplained absences. Like many of the new hires, she will struggle with the structure and demands of a job. But today she's right on time. She knows most of the regulars along 14th Street. She often smuggles soaps and shampoos from N Street Village, doling them out to the neediest cases. A few nights earlier, she was walking by the 7-Eleven when a man stepped out of the shadows. Cecilia knew him as the Duckman. She had promised to buy him gloves when she got paid. "Bring those gloves by soon," the Duckman told her. "I got to sleep outside tonight. They're full-up down the street."

On this sunny afternoon, the Duckman is nowhere to be found. Not in front of the 7-Eleven, which will soon become a Caribou Coffee. But Cecilia spots another regular. Rather, he spots her. Standing in the middle of the sidewalk, he strikes a balladeer's pose and begins to sing.

"Cecilia, you're breaking my heart, breaking my confidence, baby."

"Oh, quit that," she says, allowing his fatherly embrace.

On 14th Street, she walks past Any Kind Checks Cashed and the novelty store that sells dusty teddy bears and Kangol caps. At Mid City Fish Market ("Fish morning special. 3 pc whiting 2.99 with 2 eggs and grits") she turns the corner for P Street.

As she makes the final stretch to Fresh Fields, the enormous banner catches her eye. The glossed wood floors. The sun pouring in. The luxurious couch.

"What is *that*?" she says, her face tilted up.

"I want my apartment to be so gorgeous," she says.

Inside Fresh Fields, she takes her station at the end of the cash register. The items start coming down the belt.

"Paper or plastic?"

In N.C., anxiety and animosity put an edge on an old dream

NOVEMBER 25, 2001

GREENSBORO, N.C.—Every flag, every "God Bless America" sign flashing at every barbecue joint reminds Alma Chavez that she is suddenly on the outside. Again.

"Something weird is going on," she says, gunning her Chevy Silverado to work one November morning.

Chavez recently started a $9-an-hour job as a receptionist at a storefront law office in an industrial section of Greensboro. The lawyer wanted to tap into Guilford County's exploding Hispanic population, so he hired Chavez, and one of her first duties was to make a sign for the window: "HABLAMOS ESPANOL."

Now the Spanish-speaking men in cowboy boots and feed caps stack up in the lobby, pouring out their woes to the lipsticked 23-year-old behind the counter.

"Mr. Spaulding," Chavez says, calling for her boss, "we got a client with a situation."

No more factory work. Her English is as perfect as her blizzard-white Payless sneakers under the desk.

But her immigrant dreams lost their altitude when foreign terrorists struck America. After a decade of historic immigration, the United States slammed the gates on outsiders and began to reconsider those within its borders. No one knows how long these anxieties will last, nor the restrictions that have followed, but Chavez can feel the new chill in the air.

So she's lying low, going straight home from work to eat eggs and tortillas with her family. They don't venture out after dark, afraid that someone will mistake them for Arabs. Chavez is a legal resident, but her fiance is undocumented and, to make matters worse, out of work. Jobs were getting scarce before Sept. 11, and now the bosses want workers with papers. At 21, strong and ready to sweat, he stays home with the baby, his silent cell phone hooked to his baggy khakis. They've canceled a Christmas trip home to Mexico; he would almost certainly get caught trying to sneak back across the newly tightened U.S. border.

"I didn't know who or what the World Trade Center was," Chavez says. "Now I know."

She knows, too, who was responsible. And when she sees Middle Eastern immigrants around Greensboro, her resentment rises.

"They messed it up for us," Chavez says.

'AM I WELCOME HERE?'

When Yasir Hassan arrived last summer to attend the University of North Carolina at Greensboro, his mother and sister accompanied him from Pakistan, filling his cupboard with spices from home, labeled in Urdu in their delicate script. Greensboro was a strange land indeed. He noticed the wooden signs nailed to the hickories and oaks and wondered, "Why are all the trees named Jesus?"

Within a month, though, Hassan was living on Cocoa Puffs and watching Montel Williams before classes. On Fridays, he and his Pakistani roommate would cruise the strip between Wal-Mart and RaceTrac, "hollering at girls, just freaking out; it's very luminous at night."

But like Chavez, Hassan felt his place in America change after Sept. 11. He was no longer an international student in a FUBU sweat shirt who contemplated the benefits of titanium wire over gold in computers; he was dark and Muslim and studying in the United States on a visitor's visa—and in possession of a Pakistani passport that spelled his name Yasir, Yasser and Yassir.

"You cannot imagine the trouble this has caused," he says.

Because one of the terrorist hijackers had entered the United States on a student visa, Hassan suspected that his file would be reviewed by school officials, and he was right. Of the 13,000 students on campus, 500 were foreign, with 24 from so-called terrorist-sponsoring countries. An FBI agent called to check in with the international student program director.

"Am I welcome here?" Hassan asked his student adviser. The answer was yes, of course. Campus leaders beefed up security and held forums on Islam, co-sponsored by the 20-member Muslim Student Association. Hassan didn't belong to the group but took comfort in its presence. The campus became his haven.

Beyond the university gates is where his real troubles started.

Late one Friday night, Hassan and his roommate, Kashif Khan, were visiting with two American women in the front yard of their house. Two trucks and two cars pulled up and several men unloaded. They asked where one of their friends was. He has already left, Hassan answered. The next thing he knew, he was surrounded and heard the words, "You dirty Pakistani bastards." He looked over and saw Khan on the hood of a car, being beaten. Hassan was on the ground when a beer bottle crashed into the side of his skull.

Khan was still coughing blood the next day when a friend urged them to report the incident to the police.

"I covered my head and several guys kept beating for 2 minutes until the dad of my friend came out when they ran," Hassan wrote in a criminal complaint Oct. 6. The two women identified one of the attackers; a magistrate executed an arrest warrant for him. A police officer advised Hassan to buy a cell phone for security.

A month later, Hassan still has the faintest mark on the right side of his forehead from the beer bottle. He is sitting in the scrappy apartment he shares with Khan, with computer parts stacked along a wall. One of the things he loved about Greensboro when he first arrived was the way strangers greeted him for no apparent reason.

"Now the only people who speak to us think we are Mexican," he says.

'I DON'T LIKE IT'

Greensboro, population 224,000, is in the central piedmont of North Carolina, where candidates for office hold "pig pickin's" and screen doors slam in the waning days of fall. The Shriners recently decided not to wear their turbans and blousy pants at the upcoming Jaycees Holiday Parade out of respect for the victims of Sept. 11.

But beneath the Andy Griffith Americana is a mini-Ellis Island with more than 120 nations and 75 languages represented in the Guilford County schools.

If any place was vulnerable to the aftershocks of September's terrorism, this was it. Porous borders, student visas and refugee resettlement programs had brought the whole world here.

Of Guilford County's 420,000 residents, between 30,000 and 40,000 are first-generation immigrants or their children, according to the UNCG Center for New North Carolinians. A flourishing economy and Greensboro's progressive streak—with five colleges in the area and a Quaker mayor—helped light a fire under the melting pot.

And then Sept. 11 happened, creating an instant forum for anti-immigrant voices.

Outside the library on the UNCG campus, a Lebanese business major was assaulted by two white men shouting, "Go home, terrorist!" He withdrew from school and returned to the Middle East.

If Hassan's only security was in being mistaken for Mexican, at least he had plenty of cover, thanks to the wave of immigration Chavez belonged to. No state in the country has gone through a faster Hispanic immersion than North Carolina, with a 655 percent increase in the past decade. Half of the state's quarter-million Hispanics are undocumented, a distinction that mattered little in the low-wage, labor-guzzling economy of the 1990s.

But after Sept. 11, a résumé built on sweat was no longer good enough.

"There's a broad public consensus that immigration is about more than plucking chickens and picking melons," says Dan Stein, executive director of the Federation for American Immigration Reform, a Washington-based anti-immigration group. "It's about protecting communities...knowing who's who in America."

After Sept. 11, President Bush stopped talking about granting amnesty to 3 million Mexicans living illegally in the United States. Because of the weakening economy, U.S. employers lost interest in expanding the foreign guest worker program. In South Carolina, the state attorney general was suggesting that the Immigration and Naturalization Service should deputize local law enforcement to round up the undocumented.

"No one wanted to listen to Pat Buchanan in 1996 when he called for a moratorium on immigration," says Charles Davenport Jr., an op-ed columnist for the Greensboro *News & Record*. "Now, people are willing to think about it."

Davenport says he had watched his town transform

overnight with immigrants, many of whom refused to assimilate. He wants Marines stationed every 20 feet along the U.S. borders.

"If you walk into Food Lion at 8 at night, you may well be the only English speaker in the whole place," Davenport says. "I don't like it. I feel like I'm in another nation. It's not hostility; it's a sorrow for the culture that I know."

BAD TIMING

That Food Lion is where Chavez often shops. On a Sunday morning in November, Chavez and her family are gathered around the kitchen table, eating bowls of *menudo* and folding together tacos and washing it all down with Cokes. Half the house is hung over from late-shift factory work. Chavez's sister fills comforters with stuffing at an assembly plant; her mother wraps holiday gift sets at another. The family has come a long way since crossing into the United States at an unguarded border checkpoint in 1991, heads ducked low and bodies scrunched on the van floorboards.

In 2000, after years in Chicago and getting their legal resident cards, they moved to Greensboro, where they bought a $57,000 house in a racially mixed neighborhood. Now they're practically home-grown, right down to the pacing Rottweiler.

But Chavez's boyfriend, who asked not to be named, had the bad timing to arrive in the United States 18 months ago, paying a "coyote" $1,600 to guide him across the desert. In Greensboro, he got a $600-a-week construction job and met Chavez. She liked the spray of freckles across his nose and his hair, black as motor oil, which she cut in the bathroom with a towel over his strong shoulders. They exchanged rings and had a baby this year, cramming into a front bedroom in the Chavez house, where they live now, their door still taped with the pink ribbon that announces, "It's a Girl."

And yet there is the feeling that a moment has ended.

Until Sept. 11, the state Department of Motor Vehicles had one of the most lax residency requirements in the country. Illegal immigrants from around the Southeast would drive to North Carolina to get their prized piece of documentation. With a driver's license, they

could cash a check or open a charge account. It legit-
imized them beyond their under-the-table wages.

But with the discovery that at least seven of the terrorist hijackers had obtained identification cards through
the Virginia DMV, North Carolina quickly passed a law
requiring proof of residence, effective Nov. 1.

Unfortunately, Chavez's boyfriend has neither a tax-
payer ID number nor a Social Security card.

"He never got it; now he can't," says Chavez, frustrated by his procrastination.

But unemployment is his bigger concern. When
Chavez meets a woman whose husband works construction, she asks about a job for her boyfriend. Is he legal?
the woman asks.

When the Sunday dishes are cleared away, Chavez
and her boyfriend go out for baby formula. They drive to
the newly developed part of Greensboro, a concrete
hatchery of Petsmart and Super K and Service Merchan-
dise. "You can tell which stores have the best prices,"
Chavez says, looking out the window. "The empty parking lots mean prices are too high."

In Kmart, they pick up a flier, studying a 40-piece
dinnerware set in Summer Harvest for $19.99. "We love
coming over here and checking things out for our new
home," Chavez says. But who are they kidding? On the
drive home, they pass the China King buffet, where they
used to go on Sundays when her boyfriend had a job.
The parking lot is packed.

'THIS IS THEIR LIFE SAVINGS'

Hassan has still not told his family in Pakistan about
the beating. Attending university in America is his father's dream. A middle-class Pakistani annual income is
the equivalent of $10,000. The University of North Car-
olina charges international students $5,500 a semester,
more than three times the in-state tuition of $1,700. Last
year, foreign students accounted for 3.4 percent of total
enrollment in U.S. colleges and universities, but they
paid nearly 8 percent of tuition and fees, according to
the National Association of Independent Colleges and
Universities.

"This is their life savings we blow away in two semes-
ters," Hassan says one November morning. He had

stayed up very late with his roommate the night before, drinking black tea and eating boiled eggs, scheming how to get rich enough someday to repay their fathers.

But the mood is subdued. After the assault, Khan has asked his adviser if he could take a semester off, but the adviser warned that his student visa might not be renewed in this unpredictable climate.

With lawmakers talking about a moratorium on student visas, Hassan and Khan, like Chavez and her boyfriend, have scratched their plans to go home for Christmas. What if the United States won't let them back in?

They are fighting homesickness and an end-of-semester shortage of funds. Their cable service has been stopped for nonpayment. "This is the darkness before dawn," Hassan says.

The cell phone they bought after the assault makes them feel safe. One school night, they leave campus and drive to the Four Seasons Towne Center mall with another student of Pakistani descent. It's wonderful being out, away from the library. They wander through Abercrombie & Fitch, beneath the posters of shirtless blond heroes in football pads. At American Eagle Outfitters, one of them holds up a T-shirt with the word SOBER. "You should get this," Khan teases Hassan, one alcohol-abstaining Muslim to another. At Dillard's, they study a 10-inch Calphalon omelet pan. Eggs are all they know how to cook.

The next morning, on the way to campus, they pass the High Point Dinner Bell and its "God Bless America" sign and the Country Bar-B-Q with its "America Home of the Free and the Brave" sign. Flags were everywhere, red, white and blue against the Carolina fall.

"It induces the patriotic adrenaline; that's great, every nation should come together like this," Hassan says philosophically, taking in the landscape. "What I fear is they are all going to get together and beat us again. The worst part is they would be singing 'The Star-Spangled Banner' while they are beating us."

'JUST A FIGHT BETWEEN BOYS'

It was all a miscommunication, says the 18-year-old man whose name appears on the criminal complaint signed by Hassan and Khan.

Curtis Bridgman is sitting on his parents' porch one sunny afternoon, holding a guitar in his lap. He wears a sleeveless T-shirt, a joker tattooed onto his right biceps and a silver ring in his eyebrow.

"This was just a fight between boys," Bridgman says. "It wasn't no hate crime."

Furthermore, he says, "it wasn't no seven, eight or nine people. Only four of us." He says no one used a beer bottle as a weapon, and no one used a racial epithet.

His mother comes out on the porch. "We come from a multicultural family," she says, citing a black and Hispanic who've married into their family. "So how could we be racialist?"

Then his father steps outside. "What'd you do, call someone a [racial epithet]?"

"No," Bridgman says. "It's about some Pakistans."

"Some Hispanics?" his father asks.

"No, some Afghans," Bridgman says.

Two High Point Police Department officers finally serve the arrest warrant on Bridgman, charging him with assault with a deadly weapon. He's scheduled for a January court hearing.

'WILL THEY KNOW?'

If some members of Congress have their way, Hassan may soon be carrying a card that includes his fingerprints, retinal scan or facial biometrics. The INS will start more closely tracking all of the country's 550,000 foreign students.

"Will they know when I am at the Krispy Kreme?" Hassan asks.

On the same evening Bridgman is arrested, Hassan is leaning against the fountain on campus. The night is gentle. He has studied and e-mailed half of Pakistan from the computer lab. Still no word on whether he will be issued the student visa he applied for in September. He's sure the school will come through, but less sure about the U.S. Embassy in Pakistan.

Even with the restrictions, and all that has happened to him, Hassan still wants to study here. "An American education is highly respected in Pakistan," he says. He would go back home and work in technology.

But America itself, that's a different dilemma. When

Hassan was a boy in Pakistan, he read Archie comics and imagined America as a magical place. "Later on is when the reality dawns on you," he says. "The chances of meeting Betty Cooper are very remote."

He pauses. "Sometimes life is so bad here that you only wish for an egomaniacal, cheating, low person like Veronica Lodge."

'ALL BECAUSE OF THEM'

"Good morning. Attorney Spaulding's office," says Chavez, deftly juggling the phones in the law office the next morning. She punches another line. "Anthony, thank you for holding."

A potential client hovers at the counter, filling out a narrative of his legal troubles. "How do you spell 're-voked'?" he asks.

Chavez leans forward. "R-E-V-O-K-E-D."

In a week, her mother will be laid off from her $9-an-hour third-shift factory job, making Chavez the biggest breadwinner in the house. Her boyfriend is still out of work. With winter coming, construction is slowing. Some of their friends have pulled up stakes and returned to Mexico.

Her brother was detained and searched at the airport recently. "All because of them," he came home muttering.

The dream doesn't feel so fresh anymore. Chavez leafs through a Harry and David gourmet Christmas catalogue that arrived in the office mail. She eyes the boxes of Royal Riviera pears. "You come over thinking you will just stay a while," she says. "You get caught up in the American dream, which is expensive, and now all messed up."

An American dream, slightly apart

OCTOBER 27, 2001

PATERSON, N.J.—Mohammad Al-Qudah fires up his Weber grill and throws on a few lamb steaks. It's a glorious October evening. He has prayed three times already and will pray twice more before he goes to sleep.

His wife, Nadia Kahf, third-year law student and mother of two, mixes hummus in the blender. She's not wearing the *hijab* she usually wears in public.

They recently left an apartment for this sprawling split-level in the suburbs, proof that Al-Qudah has come a long way since arriving from Jordan in 1989 and cramming into a Paterson boarding house with several other Middle Eastern immigrants.

Yet, on the big-screen TV in the den, he and his wife toggle between CNN and al-Jazeera, wary of the American news filter.

"It's news when one Jewish person dies," Kahf says. "When they massacre 24 Palestinians, nothing. What really bothers me is when they bring on Islamic experts who are not Muslim."

Since the Sept. 11 terrorist attacks, and with the United States dropping bombs on a Muslim country, Kahf and Al-Qudah wrestle with their place in their adopted nation, a land suddenly rippling with American flags and a taste for revenge. The crosscurrents are especially strong in this part of New Jersey, where the FBI believes six hijacking suspects flowed through this year while plotting their suicide missions.

"Terrible, criminal," says Kahf of the murder of more than 5,000 people.

Yet the seeds of the hijackers' motivations are not mysterious to her.

"People in a lot of places hate America," she says. "It's not hard to understand that."

Born in Syria, Kahf arrived here 17 years ago, when she was 12. America seems to have been good to her. But her embrace is tentative. In a study this year titled "The Mosque in America: A National Portrait," 82 percent of American Muslims strongly agreed that high-tech America offered opportunity; 28 percent said the nation was immoral and corrupt.

For Kahf and her husband—taxpayers, registered voters, law-abiding citizens—assimilation is not a goal. After she graduates from Seton Hall University law school, she hopes to specialize in defending Muslims in civil liberties cases. "There are so few Muslim lawyers, even fewer female Muslim lawyers, and even fewer female lawyers who cover," she says, referring to the *hijab*.

"Throughout history," she says, Muslims "will always be separate."

But after Sept. 11, separateness became a liability.

"Do you know who your neighbors are?" a local news segment asked ominously after the Paterson terrorist cell was discovered.

Al-Qudah quickly attached an American flag to his wife's car.

A MINI-RAMALLAH

When Rep. William J. Pascrell Jr. (D-N.J.) met Yasser Arafat in 1998 in Ramallah, the Palestinian leader asked, "How are my people in Paterson?" The city has one of the largest concentrations of Arab Americans in the country; 20,000 of its 160,000 residents are Muslim. Paterson prints its recycling rules in English, Spanish and Arabic.

The heart of the Arab-American community is along Main Avenue in South Paterson, a mini-Ramallah, with *halal* butchers and men drinking tea and scarved women surveying bins of olives. Turkish techno music pumps from the hot-waxed cars of the Jordanian boys smoking Marlboro Reds.

This is where Mohammad Al-Qudah came when he arrived from Jordan. There was the food he knew, and the language he knew and the faith he knew.

Main Avenue is also where Hani Hanjour came looking for an apartment in February, choosing a $650-a-month one-bedroom unit over a mini-mart. It's where alleged ringleader Mohamed Atta visited a travel office in July and bought a one-way ticket to Madrid.

When Kahf learned that a hijacked plane had crashed into the World Trade Center, 20 miles to the east, her first reaction was horror, followed by something equally desperate:

"Please don't let it be a Muslim."

The collateral damage from the attacks takes shape in a third-floor apartment over Main Avenue, where a woman named Ruby Santos pulls back her lace curtains and watches the sky for low-flying airplanes.

"I have nothing against Arabics," says Santos, a Puerto Rican mother of three who grew up happily in the melting pot of Passaic County. "But I don't trust them after what happened."

When a bearded Middle Eastern man wearing an Army jacket boarded her bus, "all the way to Passaic I had a stomachache," she says.

Her 13-year-old daughter, Melissa, rolls her eyes.

Santos folds her arms. "Melissa, you don't get scared when you see an Arabic with a little scarf?"

"Ma, I see them every day, the lunch ladies in the cafeteria."

Santos's younger daughter, Deidre, pipes in. "Mommy, I thought some Arabics were nice."

"Not all of them are bad, baby." Her eyes go back to the window, the darkness beyond it, the place where she used to feel so comfortable. "Those hijackers, they just messed up everything."

'I FEEL GUILTY'

With a day off from law school, Kahf joins a group of Muslim "sisters" to visit a friend with a new baby. All are covered from head to toe in *hijab* and *jilbab*, the smock worn for modesty. One woman pulls up in a black Lexus SUV, her hand wrapped in a bandage.

"How did you burn your hand?" someone asks.

"Not cooking," says Dalia Fahmy, who is finishing her master's in politics at New York University.

"Her stove is so clean, and she's been married two years!" her sister, Dena, chimes in.

They settle around a table spread with baklava, tea, cashews and dried fruit. Talk inevitably turns to the tenor of life as a Muslim after Sept. 11. Immediately afterward, the imam at their mosque suggested that women stay inside, particularly if they wore *hijab*. Fahmy lasted two days in seclusion and then went to Gymboree. "I'm in line and I feel like everyone is feeling weird for me," she says. "At the same time, I feel guilty for the situation."

Sally Amer also stayed home. "Okay, I'll let you lock me down for one day," the pharmacist and mother of two told her husband. On the third day, she went to the mall. A Muslim friend of hers was not so lucky; someone shot an arrow through her child's bedroom window.

Kahf couldn't miss law classes. So her husband taped the flag to her car antenna, and off she drove into the anxieties beyond her driveway.

Not wearing their *hijab* would have made life easier.

"Would Oprah take off her skin color growing up in the '50s or '60s?" Fahmy asks.

The women oppose Afghanistan's Taliban regime, but they are frustrated, too, by stereotypes of Islam. "Americans confuse culture and religion," Kahf says. "With the Taliban, women are not being educated. That's political, not religious, and it's wrong."

Yet Kahf objects to what she sees as American feminist arrogance toward the practice of covering, even among the Afghan women forced to wear *burqas* by the Taliban.

"*Oh, they must be so hot in those tents*," Kahf says, mockingly. "Maybe they *want* to cover."

Several years ago, Kahf applied for a teaching position in the history department at a community college. With a bachelor's degree in political science and a master's in Middle Eastern studies, she thought she had the job. "The director was very happy until he met me and saw my cover," Kahf says. She was rerouted to the ESOL (English Speakers of Other Languages) department.

From the baby shower, the women disperse into the afternoon to put children down for naps, to pick up children from school. Wearing their *hijab*, they move like silken ghosts down the sidewalk. The flag on Kahf's Jeep whips in the autumn breeze.

A few days earlier, her son asked her why so many people were flying flags.

"Because everyone is happy to be in America," she told him.

But not necessarily happy with the country's policies. Kahf opposes the war efforts in Afghanistan. "America really does decide whose life is more important," she says. "Think of it from the point of view of an Iraqi child, or a Palestinian child."

NEIGHBOR AVOIDS NEIGHBOR

Not far from the heart of Paterson's Middle Eastern community, there is a house where retribution is more easily understood. A sign on the front door reads: "Thanks to you for your concerns and prayers. Kenny still missing. I will be waiting for my son now and forever."

Paterson lost one resident in the World Trade Center attack. Kenny Lira was a 28-year-old computer technician who worked on the 110th floor of the North Tower. A Peruvian American, he grew up easily among the Latinos and Arabic kids in this neighborhood.

Now his mother, Marina Lira, sleeps on the couch at night to be near the TV, as if it will deliver the antidote she needs. On CNN, the FBI announces its 22 Most Wanted Terrorists list. The colorful graphic "America Strikes Back" is stripped beneath the 22 photos of dark faces.

"I know that the Muslim religion is not what these people are practicing," Lira says.

Yet she no longer walks to Main Avenue to buy dried cherries and pita bread. "I don't even drive that way," she says. "We drive the other way. A friend said to me, 'I saw them and my anger grew inside.'"

While Lira was in Manhattan putting up fliers for her missing son, a stranger came to her house and spoke with a relative. I'm Muslim, the woman said. My family is Muslim. We apologize for what happened.

"My niece told me this happened, but I did not see it," Lira says. She looks out the front window. The neighbors who used to walk by covered in *hijab* and *burqa* no longer pass her house.

"Why?" she asks. "Why?"

'THIS MAKES ME FEEL GOOD'

The next night, while Lira holds a candlelight service at her house in honor of her son, Kahf is starting dinner.

"Finish your math," she tells her daughter.

"Oh, Mom, I hate math," says Mariam, 9, slumping over her backpack on the kitchen counter. "Fifth-grade math is a killer. Can I just get a zero?"

Kahf calls into the living room to her 5-year-old son. "Abdallah, you said you were just going to play one game of Nintendo."

She hears the garage door open. "Daddy's home."

Mohammad Al-Qudah embraces his children. His wife takes the spinach pastries from the oven and kisses him. "How was your day?" she asks. His gas station business is down 15 percent since Sept. 11.

After dinner, a friend calls. President Bush is on TV. Al-Qudah grabs the remote. Bush is saying that Muslim women who cover their heads should not have to be afraid. Al-Qudah leans forward on the couch and points to the president. "This is very important," he says. "You know, he's been very good on this."

More than his wife, he looks for the positive. He keeps several voice-mail messages he received in the days after the hijackings.

Hey, Mo, this is Jimmy. Want to make sure everything is okay. We're thinking about you.

I know that with what happened, certain Americans will look on Muslim groups unfavorably. We're thinking of you. Thanks, Mo.

"This makes me feel good," he says.

They are part of America, but apart. Kahf does not see this as a contradiction. "This is part of living in a democracy," she says. "This saying, 'America, love it or leave it.' I don't buy it. True democracy is being able to question things, even to criticize things, but always wanting to make the situation better."

The next day, Kahf irons her *hijab* and grabs her keys. A decade ago, local Muslims prayed in a rented room above a restaurant near Main Avenue. Now, the Islamic Center of Passaic County, a former synagogue, welcomes 800 Muslims on Fridays for 1 o'clock prayer. Kahf settles in the back of the mosque with the other women. Kneeling, facing toward Mecca, she bows, her forehead to the carpet.

The imam, Mohammad Qatanani, repeats that Muslims are against terrorists, against what happened at the World Trade Center, but also against "crimes committed against innocent lives in Afghanistan."

From the mosque, Kahf picks up her daughter at the

Islamic school. Mariam is standing on the blacktop with three of her friends, all of whom wear *hijab*. "She looks so grown up in it," Kahf says, beaming.

At home, Mariam goes outside to ride her Razor scooter with a neighbor boy, who by now understands when Mariam is called inside for prayer time. "Come back in five minutes," she will say.

Her father's car pulls into the garage. In a few hours, he will go to the mosque for prayer. He has a business trip to Las Vegas coming up. An airline passenger named Mohammad Al-Qudah! A friend joked that he should show up at airport security wearing a bikini and handcuffs.

"I can't believe you are going," his wife says.

He smiles. "I'm going to do what the president says. I am going to live my life."

Diamonds sparkle in his wife's ears. His son prays beside him on the rug and goes to sleep in zebra pajamas. His daughter began wearing *hijab* to school this year. His business is expanding.

"I was born in Jordan," Al-Qudah says. "But America makes me feel alive."

Writers' Workshop

Talking Points

1) Anne Hull says that in her article "Divided Feast" she wanted to capture the crosscurrents in the Washington, D.C., neighborhood in which the new Fresh Fields store was locating. How does she do that in her story?

2) Subjects bring something to the telling of a story. How does Hull select her subjects in the three stories published in this book? What do they bring to the story?

3) Sometimes Hull identifies her subjects by race or ethnicity. Sometimes she doesn't. What effect does it have on the story?

4) What precautions does Hull take in identifying Alma Chavez's boyfriend in "Anxiety and Animosity"? What ethical issues do you see in identifying him?

Assignment Desk

1) Hull says she likes to read, and reread, certain writers she admires in an effort to learn new writing techniques. Read some writers you admire and identify what techniques they use. Try to apply them in your next story.

2) In "Divided Feast," Hull spends time observing and writing down what happens during a typical day at the Fresh Fields store. Find a store or other gathering place where different segments of the community intersect. Spend time there. Try to capture the "crosscurrents" you observe.

3) Hull tries to build in time to be able to adjust to her subjects' schedules. Pick a subject you'd like to write about. Spend time following the subject's agenda instead of your own.

4) Some subjects may face consequences if you identify them fully. Think of some people whose identity you may have to protect. Draw up a list of questions you could ask yourself to determine if this subject might need protection. What consequences might this person face if your description

made it clear who he or she was?

5) After the events of Sept. 11, one of journalism's natural inclinations was to cover members of the Muslim community to find out what was happening to them. Hull also decided to learn what impact Sept. 11 might have had on other immigrant groups. Can you think of other groups that might have been affected by Sept. 11, or some other major event, than the ones that first come to mind? Make a list of them. How would they be affected and why?

A conversation with
Anne Hull

ALY COLÓN: I wanted to ask what prompted you to write the stories that won the ASNE Diversity Award.

ANNE HULL: The stories from Greensboro and Paterson were not assigned. But in the days and weeks after Sept. 11, the whole country was trying to figure out the effects of what had happened on immigrants. Paterson was the location of one of the so-called terrorist cells. It's the second-largest Arab-American community in the country. It's an obvious choice to write about. What does it feel like to be a Muslim in this community…a suspicious character in this moment in our country's psyche? So I went to Paterson and found a family to write about. What are the small moments of their Muslim lives with the huge backdrop and paranoia of Sept. 11?

For the Greensboro story, we wanted to find a Latino family. North Carolina is one of the fastest-growing Latino states in the country. I picked Greensboro because it's fairly progressive, has a lot of refugee resettlement agencies, and it's a place that has dealt with immigration and done a good job of it.

So the idea was to find a sort of mini-nirvana, see how Sept. 11 is splintering this sanctuary. We found a Mexican family and how they were dealing with the new suspicions. While they weren't Middle Eastern, they were outsiders. We wanted to write about what their lives were like in the days after Sept. 11—everything from being looked at differently in a grocery store to being stopped by police. That sort of thing.

And "Divided Feast"?

I happened to be new to Washington at the time that Fresh Fields was being built three blocks from my house. I watched it with curiosity as the opening date got closer and closer. This is a quickly gentrifying area, and I am one of the white gentrifiers and kind of wrestling with my own feelings in that equation. Also, I was very delighted that this fantastic grocery store would be three blocks away. I wanted to write about the dynamic of change, and that was really a metaphor for the whole city of Washington. It's the poor being pushed out because of housing costs. Washington, according to the census, is getting whiter. It was just the perfect story to do in the perfect moment in Washington's history.

How did this prick your journalistic instinct as you were watching this? What was the catalyst for you?

On one level it's just very obvious. You see this beautiful, shiny palace going up in a blighted neighborhood, and the contrast is startling. As a journalist, you want to find out more about this. It's like seeing a zebra on the White House lawn. It's such a contrast you want to know more about it. So I called the corporate headquarters and asked if I could stay in their store and write about the store's opening. They were kind of wary because they were very sensitive to their role as the dreaded, uppity, gentrifier in a former African-American neighborhood. But I basically laid out why I wanted to write about it and why it was important for the moment. It's an important chapter in the history of the city. There's a real excitement generated around this grocery store. But there's also some apprehension. Let me come and live in your store for two weeks, night and day, and write about the currents drifting, swirling about this grocery store.

How did you persuade them to let you do that?

I explained it would probably be written about anyway. It had been written about in the past in sort of a snarky way. But that was not my intention. It was to write about both the customers and the people who work in the store. Fresh Fields had made a big deal about hiring locals. That was kind of an "in." I wanted to write about the people who worked in the store. I'm not sure they expected the exact outcome of the story. But they're very savvy. They knew the risks they were taking when they let me into their store.

Day after day and night after night, I was there. I began to feel like I was clocking in at Fresh Fields, too. I saw my job as trapping all these crosscurrents. I've never reported a story in which I filled so many notebooks in so short a time. People just wanted to talk about this store and its place in the city at that time.

What were some of the specific things that helped convince them?

Well, one thing I did was show them clips of other stories I'd done that had some complicating racial or class questions. I offered to provide references. They knew it would likely be on the cover of *The Washington Post Magazine,* which I think was working in their favor. I think I told them that I was truly excited about the store coming to the neighborhood, that I lived a few blocks away. I was also very curious to see—there was no question if the store would be a success financially—but it would be great to watch it grow from its birth to the rollicking talk of the town that it would become in a few months. I think they grew comfortable with the idea.

How long were you there?

I probably spent 16 days reporting straight. And then came back and wrote it in probably three and a half weeks. I was there the second week it opened. I read as much as I could on Fresh Fields's philosophy and corporate strategies and did all my research. I hunkered down and just lived there. I couldn't write all the observations fast enough.

So the first couple of days I just hung out in the aisles all day. Then I knew I wanted to identify two or three characters who would each bring something to the telling. One, obviously, was an immigrant.

There are more Salvadorans in Washington. They are the predominant, low-wage workers, having replaced a thinning black working class. I knew I wanted to find a Latino who lived in the neighborhood and had gotten a job at Fresh Fields. I found that character in the woman named Martha, who worked in the bakery.

I knew I wanted to find an African American, and found that by picking Sean in the meat department. The other character was a woman, also an African American, who sort of personified the 1980s of D.C. in that the schools had failed her. She was a welfare mom, got into drug problems, and eventually had to put her kids in foster care. Now, like the city, she was trying to revive. This was her first job in a very long time. So she was hanging her hopes on Fresh Fields, just as customers, in another way, were hanging their hopes on Fresh Fields.

So it was important to find three good characters out of those 300 employees who could each bring something distinct to the telling, and also didn't mind me hanging around them and going to their houses after work.

How did you pick them? Did you just observe them and then go talk to them about that? Or did you have a list of employees?

Number one, they were willing. Number two, they met the criteria that I just explained, that each one would bring something to the table. Fresh Fields would have preferred that I profiled an ex-stock broker who decided to go work at Fresh Fields. But that's not typical.

In Cecilia's case, the grocery bagger, she lived at a homeless shelter. And to have someone living in a homeless shelter and working at Fresh Fields, when Fresh Fields donates its excess food to that very homeless shelter, it's just too rich. You have to have this person in it. And she was articulate and insightful and she was full of hope. I mean, her life was on the ascent and, again, so was the city's. I wanted those two stories to intermingle.

The other characters were both good as well. I said, "I'm going to be hanging around you if that's okay, and I would even like to go home with you, walk home with you from work or take the bus home. I'd like to meet at your house at 3 in the morning, Sean, when you come in to open the butcher case. It's going to seem really weird, but could I do it?" They were all open to it.

After a couple of days of observation, I noticed the way they interacted with customers. By day three or four I was pretty sure I knew whom I was going to follow. I think I had two characters nailed down by the first week and a third character came the second week. But it's crucial to get the right navigators, and a good editor knows that it takes time to find the right person who's going to tell the story.

Did you have a plan or did you develop a plan as you saw things develop?

A lot of reporters have more of a plan than I do. I'm sort of accidental in much of what I attempt, and there are a lot of bad sides to that strategy. But in this instance, it worked because the material was so rich. You had this constant bumping up of white against black, Latino against black, rich against poor, homeless against mansion owner. It was just all this commingling that you couldn't write down fast enough, but you have to have. You have to be aware every single moment. So this was a largely observed story. You just had to be on high alert all the time, looking at everything. If life got slow at the bakery, then you go to the butcher department and see what's hopping there. You just always wanted to be in a high-intensity area of the store.

But I wouldn't capture dialogue and attach a name to it unless they knew I was a *Washington Post* reporter. I introduced myself to everybody instead of just voyeuristically eavesdropping. I just didn't think that was fair, and when I did voyeuristically eavesdrop and used that exact dialogue, I did not put in the person's name.

If you deconstructed the architecture of this story, what were the threads you wanted to make sure became evident to the reader?

Number one is to remind people who can afford to shop at Fresh Fields in this peak economic boom that there's a cost. A lot of people can't shop at Fresh Fields. They don't even know what Fresh Fields is. And they're getting squeezed out of their homes because of Fresh Fields. It was always this sort of pulsing drive to remind people that there are less fortunate. That sounds like the biggest Hallmark greeting cliché, but that is the underlying engine to that story. It's just to remind people of those who have no way of touching the American Dream.

Did you see the story on multiple levels because

you're looking at class, economics, ethnicity, and race—all of those playing through that?

And also there's one extra—sexual orientation. This is an increasingly gay, affluent neighborhood without children and that causes all sorts of conundrums.

How did you decide when to use a racial or ethnic or some orientation identification?

I think it's very important to identify someone by race when you're writing a story like the Fresh Fields story. It means everything. We are not all one homogenous batch. We are distinct. We bring our own histories to who we are, if we've experienced prejudice or not. I think it's really important to identify someone, and I tried to do it in every case that I mentioned a name in the Fresh Fields piece. I didn't catch any resistance from editors for that. So where it mattered, I put it. Where it didn't, I didn't.

I quoted two or three very upwardly mobile African Americans in there who said, "Who wants the old way? This is great. Ten years ago we had prostitutes and crackheads here. Bring it on." Bring on this upward mobility, which implies that they're not really thinking of the older generation of African Americans who are getting squeezed out. I think the story is about class more than anything else, with race as a secondary backdrop.

I was wondering how you picked that particular Muslim family in the "American Dream" story.

I spent five days in Paterson reporting that story. Usually you start on the outside and work your way in. You start with the official world. My first interview was with a congressman from Paterson. I talked to the mayor, just starting on the official edges. But then you start to work your way in. You go to the mosque, which I did, and I met some of the board members of the mosque. I met one in particular who knew what I wanted to write about after we talked for a while. He put me in touch with three families. In the period of a couple of days, I very quickly met all three of those families for a couple of hours each and then settled on the family that I eventually chose to write about. So it's a real time-consuming process and compressed in a very short time.

Did this family meet what you were looking for?

Yes. All sorts of stereotypes were going on about Muslim women being subservient and the kind of gender roles they play within marriages. Nadia [the Muslim woman and wife] was extremely independent. There was an excellent, equal relationship between Mom and Dad. The relationship with the kids was just great. Their faith was extremely important, but their place in America was also important. Nadia's in law school. She hopes to practice law wearing her head cover. They wanted to be American but be themselves within America. Again, it gets to that we are not all sort of one homogenous batch of people. We are distinct and here's why it's important to hold onto those distinctions. They also made the great point that this country is founded on questioning things and why can't you live here and also question it. Because at the time there was an absolute moratorium on anything that wasn't patriotic.

How do you go about representing them as they are, as opposed to how we see them from our own biases or stereotypes?

I think it's something as simple as spending time with people and not always directing the conversation. Letting them shape the conversation. I went to a baby shower. I went to a prayer service. I did little errands around the neighborhood. We went to the bakery. It's letting them set the agenda. They were perfectly ready for me to ask about women wearing *burqas* and head coverings, and she said something really interesting: that it is arrogant of Americans to say that *burqas* are oppressive to women. I just thought she said it beautifully. So it's trying to remain open-minded. It's spending time with them on their terms, on their turf, and not being afraid to be corrected; to have a real conversation as opposed to just a very formal Q&A.

Was that a challenge to do in a short time period and

stay true to the people you're covering?

Well, I should say I went with four pages of questions. I always map out questions and keep them with me and slip them in when I can. Questions are a way to organize your thoughts. One question generates 10 more. You always need to write out questions so you're prepared. But you need to build in time to hang out with whoever you're writing about. If you have two days to report it, it's just going to be two very long days. Unfortunately, it just doesn't work to do it 9-to-5. You have to adhere to their schedule. If they're up at 6 and taking their daughter to Islamic school at 6:30, you need to be at their house and accompany them. Watch the little girl put on her head cover when she gets to the campus. Watch Mom kiss her goodbye. Just be there for everything. You can't get it when you're in your hotel room.

In your story about "Anxiety and Animosity" in North Carolina, you used a narrative that alternated between the Mexican immigrant, Alma Chavez, and the Pakistani student, Yasir Hassan. Why did you decide to do that?

It could be argued that it did not work. I'm not sure I would have done it in hindsight. It's possible I diluted the power of either side by including two. I'm not sure. But everybody at that time was writing about the persecution of Muslims and Arab Americans and Middle Easterners. We wanted to write about the real immigrant face in this country and that was Latinos. Around Sept. 11, we kind of forgot about Latinos, but they are the greatest story numerically. So I went to North Carolina with the intent to write about this Mexican family. I ended up finding Yasir, who had gone through a bad experience. I decided to include that there were a couple of different immigrant groups who were really feeling the heat as a result of Sept. 11, though obviously they had nothing to do with it. Here's what the fallout feels like in a place a thousand miles from the World Trade Center. Yasir and Alma would never meet each other. Yasir drives by Alma's street, but he doesn't know her. Yet they both share the same tension because they're both outsiders.

I was curious about the considerations that went into not naming Alma Chavez's boyfriend, who is undocumented and might be subject to deportation.

It's very touchy. We didn't name him because, you know, I would say there's very little chance the INS would ever come arrest her boyfriend and take him away. The energies and resources are not there to do that, especially after Sept. 11. I don't think they're there to do that, but you cannot assure anyone of that. So while Alma might say it's okay to use his last name, we took the precaution and did not use his last name.

Did you wonder about naming Alma and the fact that they were living together? Would it be easy for the INS to look for Alma and then find him? Did that pose any concern or did they raise that at all?

Not at all. When you're dealing with the undocumented, they often don't understand what could happen, and you need to map out for them what could happen. So when they say go ahead, it's no problem, you need to say, "Well, this is going to appear in the newspaper with this many readers and what if the INS sees it? There's a chance you could get deported." I mean, you need to walk them through the worst-case scenario and you need to do that early and you need to do that often.

And then I always bounce this off an editor. I mean, I've had many sleepless nights worrying about certain people being taken away.

How did you decide to use specific descriptions— Alma puts the towel over her boyfriend's strong shoulders—and how were they relevant?

Description comes from two things: observation and the discipline to write it down. When you observe something, you write it down. You have to be on high alert to smell, to sniff, to hear, you just have to be open to every sensation and you also have to remember to write it down. The hard part is picking the right details because you have so many, and I think that comes from experience. But what I do is read those who do it so well and see which details they pick. There's a reason they pick particular details. If you have a beautiful sentence loaded with three images, it's going to drag down the whole sentence. You just need one. Pick one. That takes discipline.

But the towel over his shoulders implies a couple of things. It implies class, because he's not at the barbershop. It implies tenderness, because she's cutting his hair. And it's a physical description because he has strong shoulders and that comes from having worked.

You describe Curtis Bridgman in your other story in Greensboro as wearing a "sleeveless T-shirt, a joker tattooed onto his right biceps, and a silver ring in his eyebrow." Now those would be the obvious things. But I also would think that there was a reason why you picked those obvious things to include in his description.

It speaks to class. It speaks to rebellion. It is a little bit contrary to the Southern stereotype you might expect.

So when you pick a description, you see it as being integral to the story itself and the advancement of the reader's understanding of that story.

Absolutely. You know, blue sky. What does a blue sky matter unless it's a blue sky at a funeral? I mean, the details have to be like facts.

Are there particular techniques, tools, or approaches you use to make sure you get the most out of observing people?

I think two things, behind-the-scenes-type things, are important: research and reading. I constantly go back and reread William Finnegan. He has a book called *Cold New World: Growing Up in Harder Country*. It's a compilation of stuff he did for *The New Yorker* on the different kinds of underclasses in America.

What struck you as different about these stories?

The thing about the Fresh Fields story, which would be good to incorporate into more of our daily journalism, is the wonder of dialogue and how much it can communicate without the journalist having to paraphrase. I mean, the way people speak is revealing. And when you write about class and race, it's very revealing. I sometimes think we, as journalists in newsrooms, try to think for someone else, and that's not fair and it's not right.

The Sacramento Bee

Stephen Magagnini
Finalist, Diversity Writing

Stephen Magagnini, a reporter for *The Sacramento Bee*, writes about culture, race relations, and the ways those two issues intersect, merge, and collide in northern California and beyond. He spent the last year as a Knight Foundation Fellow at Stanford University, one of two fellowships he has been awarded in recent years.

Magagnini has worked on his current assignment since 1994, joining the *Bee* 18 years ago after a shorter stint with the *San Francisco Chronicle*. He has been telling stories that might fall under the rubric of "diversity" all of his career, beginning when he joined the *Sacramento Union* in 1978, after graduating from Hampshire College, and teamed up with his mentor, journalist K.W. Lee.

He has since written columns and magazine stories, and has served as a projects reporter, writing about crime, corruption, politics, and just about every ethnic group in northern California. He won the ASNE Award for Distinguished Writing on Diversity in 2001 for a series of stories about recent Hmong immigrants.

In this excerpt from the first installment of "Roots of Pain," he steps into the maelstrom of reparations by following a black family's journey back to their ancestry, a trip that takes them headlong into American slavery and its centuries-old consequences. The journey leads through a history of enslavement, emancipation, lynchings, and economic freedom, and culminates with a family reunion where, under a pine tree, a seldom-heard version of the reparations debate unfolds.

Roots of pain: Descendants seek solace for slavery

OCTOBER 7, 2001

Sam Starks is maybe 40 minutes outside Crockett County, Tenn., when the skies turn black and a wall of summer rain crashes into the windshield of the rented Jeep Laredo.

Thunderclaps shiver down his wife's spine. Charlane begs him to pull over—if not for her, then for their baby daughter, Mariah, her brown eyes wide at the tempest.

But Starks has come too far to stop now. His little family has flown 1,500 miles from Sacramento and driven through five states to resurrect the dead, to restore names and identities stolen from their ancestors the moment they were born into slavery.

"These souls cannot rest until they are re-humanized," says Starks.

In Washington, D.C., an all-star team of African-American lawyers and scholars is gathering evidence for a lawsuit seeking reparations for 246 years of slavery and its aftermath.

There is some precedent. Japanese Americans who were interned during World War II have received cash reparations; so have some Jewish survivors of the Holocaust. A few American Indian nations have gotten back some of their ancestral lands.

But the pursuit of slavery reparations—perhaps the last stand for African Americans in the post-affirmative action era—is a long shot, as many Americans question whether money can right wrongs that took place more than 100 years ago.

Sam, a community activist and outreach coordinator for SMUD, and his wife, Charlane, a sixth-grade teacher in Elk Grove, seek something less tangible. They seek reparations of the heart.

IN PURSUIT OF THE PAST

The storm breaks, and an hour later, Sam Starks is standing in a cotton field in the June twilight—perhaps the very plantation where his ancestors made their white masters rich.

Among the knee-high cotton plants, Starks kneels down and feels the freshly soaked earth. Maybe it was churned by his great-grandpa Charlie Jackson, the offspring of a 14- or 15-year-old plantation owner's son and a 15-year-old mulatto slave girl, bought off the docks in Richmond, Va.

Starks wonders how much he would have been worth in 1851. $700? $900? He is a powerfully built man, 5-foot-10 with blacksmith's forearms, engaging, capable and quick. Perhaps too quick to make a reliable slave.

Sam and Charlane's desire to prove their connection to America's slave past puts them in the company of thousands of other African Americans who long to know themselves through ancestors who survived through centuries of being treated first like animals, then like lesser human beings. Ancestors who, through their sacrifices, have given children like 8-month-old Mariah the chance to grow up in an English-style brick house with a big yard in a good neighborhood.

In recent years, increasing numbers of African Americans have embarked on similar quests, says Reginald Washington, the African-American specialist at the National Archives. The Web site AfriGeneas.com, one of several African-American Internet sites Sam has searched, reports that its hits jumped from less than 500,000 a year in 1995 to more than 1.5 million this year.

These roots hunters surf budding genealogy sites on the Internet, scroll through miles of microfilm, scrape weeds off old gravestones, rub their palms on the smooth pews of musty clapboard churches and chase the ghosts of the past.

In homes of aging relatives, they sip iced tea and hear firsthand tales of Jim Crow and hand-me-down stories of slavery. By reconnecting with roots smothered or severed by slavery, they are repairing a part of their souls.

RACE ALWAYS LURKING

Charlane, who has skin the color of latte and hazel-green eyes, grew up in Detroit, where some schoolmates called her "redbone" or "high yellow," taunting her for not being black enough.

Sam's skin is coffee with a few drops of cream. His

father, a veteran of the Korean and Vietnam wars, bought a house in Colonial Heights, an increasingly mixed neighborhood in east Sacramento.

Sam was elected president of his ninth-grade class, graduated with degrees in English and sociology from California State University, Sacramento, and hosts occasional community forums on topics such as "What If Dr. King Were Alive Today?" and "Blacks in the Criminal Justice System." In 40 years, he can't point to a single episode where he was blocked by the color of his skin.

But race always lurks in the background. His best friend in Colonial Heights was a white kid whose parents, Starks later found out, killed a neighborhood petition to keep the Starks family from moving in.

To this day, Starks feels his skin is a force field that must be penetrated before people decide, *Sam's all right.*

"You have to get past this built-in animus or discomfort," he says. "It's in the first handshake, it's the first look in the eye...African Americans are in a constant state of proving—to yourself or others—that you are as good or better than other people."

He and other African Americans call it "the dance." It hearkens back to slavery, when slave traders forced their slaves to sing and dance and look happy to appear less threatening—and thus command a higher price on the auction block.

Starks and his wife are following intently the national reparations movement—a movement gaining steam thanks to Harvard professors Cornel West from Sacramento and Charles Ogletree from Merced; and Randall Robinson, who led the successful U.S. boycott of apartheid in South Africa. Their legal team includes Johnnie Cochran and Alexander Pires, who won $1 billion in 1999 for black farmers shortchanged by the government.

Polls show that the majority of Americans oppose reparations for descendants of slaves who died long ago, especially since they don't feel personally responsible for slavery. Others feel that affirmative action programs and civil rights amendments are a form of reparations.

But Robinson argues in his book *The Debt: What America Owes to Blacks* that those solutions have done little for millions of African Americans "who inherit grinding poverty, poor nutrition, bad schools, unsafe neighborhoods, low expectation" because of slavery "and the vicious climate that followed it. Affirmative action...will never come anywhere near to balancing the books."

Some reparations advocates have calculated America's debt to African Americans at $97 trillion. For Sam and Charlane, reparations are more about recognition of the wounds of the past. "Money can't fix what happened," Charlane says. "You can't put a price on taking away someone's spirit, someone's identity."

"Who was Jesse Stark, who fought for his freedom in the Union's 115th colored infantry?" Sam asks. "Or the Gilberts, who ran so often they were listed as flight risks on the Tennessee slave schedules? Why shouldn't history remember them? Why should they be on the rolls of property, and not in the census of humans? What we're really talking about is an acknowledgment of their Americanness, their contributions to the American dream."

And, Sam adds, "We're somewhat offended that people might think that time would quell the need for justice, the need for resolution."

[The full text of this story can be read on the CD-ROM included with this edition of Best Newspaper Writing.]

Lessons Learned

BY STEPHEN MAGAGNINI

As the reparations debate heats up across America, there have been many fine "talking heads" stories outlining arguments for and against, identifying possible culprits, calculating potential damages.

But there's no easy way to own up to the wrongs of history. No cosmetic surgery, no matter how expensive, can mask scars of the heart.

And that's the story I wanted to tell. Like most Americans, I was taught about slavery in a disembodied way. Yes, the Founding Fathers had slaves, and yes, it was wrong, but those were different times, slaves were an economic necessity, America's great free-market democracy was built on the backs of slaves.

But we barely got a glimpse of what it was like to be enslaved, or the totality of the horror, or its enduring legacy. We didn't feel it. And as a nation, we've never really acknowledged it, except intellectually.

I wanted to get under our collective skin. I sensed that reparations, for many African Americans, was about finding their roots—despite the efforts of slave owners to destroy them—and having those roots honored.

I called Sam Starks, whom I'd known for seven years, and asked him if he knew any African Americans who were going roots-hunting. "Hell, yes," he said. "My wife and I are. Come along."

There's no obvious connection between reparations and roots-quests, but Amy Pyle, my editor, shared my gut feeling that there was a deep connection. It was there when Sam's wife, Charlane, scrolled through the 1880 census and saw her great-great-great-grandfather had been born in Africa. It was there when Sam knelt in a rain-drenched field in Tennessee where his slave ancestors picked cotton. It was there in rural South Carolina, where Charlane's Aunt Laura laid bare generations of whippings, lynchings, and indentured servitude, then predicted, without malice, that "someday, it's all gonna be reversed."

It all came together at a family cemetery in Kentucky, where some 40 members of the annual Starks Family Reunion ruminated on old gravestones and, with the suddenness of a summer thundershower, launched into a lively and spontaneous debate on reparations. I didn't need to say a word. All I had to do was be there. I'd been traveling with Sam, Charlane, and their baby daughter, Mariah, for a week, and by then the Starks clan was calling me "Stephen Magagnini-Starks." In their eyes, I was honoring their history just by being there.

What I learned is that there's no single cure, because people respond to pain differently. Some wanted 40 acres and a mule, or the monetary equivalent. Others wanted jobs and educations that their forebears were denied. But the family griot said no, to give us handouts dilutes our victories over adversity.

By journey's end, I was emotionally invested in the Starkses. I cried over the treatment of their ancestors — many reduced to nameless chattel on slave manifests — and the stain of slavery that may never be erased.

And I wept with pride over their resilience. They are survivors in the best American tradition.

The New York Times

Amy Waldman

Finalist, Diversity Writing

Amy Waldman is co-bureau chief of *The New York Times*'s New Delhi bureau, covering South Asia. She has been at the *Times* since 1997, writing about Harlem and the Bronx until Sept. 11, 2001. For months after terrorists struck the World Trade Center and the Pentagon, she joined many *Times* staffers in reporting on the impact of the attacks. That assignment took her to Russia, Iran, Afghanistan, and England.

Before going to work in New York, Waldman was a free-lance journalist in South Africa, stringing for newspapers and magazines in that region while contributing articles to such U.S. papers as the *Houston Chronicle*, *The Christian Science Monitor*, and *L.A. Weekly*. In South Africa, she reported on the tumultuous, dynamic days leading up to the 1994 democratic elections, covering the events as a stringer for *The New York Times*.

Waldman, a native of Los Angeles and a 1991 magna cum laude graduate of Yale University, has shared an Associated Press writing award, the Newswoman's Club of New York Front Page Award, and the New York Newspaper Publishers Association Distinguished Feature Writer Award.

She won the latter prize for "An American Block," the series that earned her a finalist spot in the 2002 ASNE contest. In the scene-setting opener to the series, "In Harlem's Ravaged Heart, Revival," excerpted here, she gives readers an unvarnished, nuanced look at the remarkable rebirth of a city block once beset with crack, violence, and hopelessness.

In Harlem's ravaged heart, revival

FEBRUARY 18, 2001

Burgers grilling, fruit punch staining baby faces, summer scenting the air. In a courtyard on 129th Street, the tenants are having a barbecue.

The architecture is Mediterranean in feel, a plaza flanked by two buildings freshly painted peach and yellow. To the front, a gate to protect the pristine setting. To the rear, a Technicolor splash of green: a garden with gazebo.

Urania Muniz, a film editor, teaches her 4-year-old to say "Excuse me" before interrupting. Tuesday Brooks, a young woman starting a cable television talk show, sits near Terrence Booth, 25, a retail pricing analyst.

A blues trio rocks, and Janice Anderson, a religious retiree opposed to such entertainment, rolls her eyes. The president of the tenants' association reprimands a child roller-skating in the courtyard. The rules forbid it.

The details of the scene are ordinary, the change they signal extraordinary. Not long ago, there were no rules on this block, West 129th Street between Fifth and Lenox Avenues in Harlem. The courtyard was a vacant lot where drug dealers ran from the police. The adjacent buildings had long been empty, their only fresh paint new graffiti. Ms. Anderson and some of the older folks at the barbecue lived on the block. The rest—black, white and Hispanic young professionals secure in the information economy—wouldn't have dreamed of it.

In 1994, *The New York Times* described 129th Street as "another America," such was its isolation and deprivation. The block, then almost uniformly black, had been bent by poverty, welfare and unemployment, by alienation between men and women, by drug dealing, addiction and violence.

The block's reputation was so fearsome that police dispatchers issued warnings before sending officers. Cabs collected residents only off the block. The walls of tenements blotted out the sky, and the future. Empty lots became the defining image of childhood for a rap producer raised here, who named his record label Vacant Lot.

Change, it seemed, would never come.

But it did. More than six years later, 129th Street is, increasingly, just an American block. It has moved, in Ms. Anderson's turn on a biblical phrase, "from the darkness and into the marvelous light."

The years have brought unprecedented economic growth; a startling decrease in crime; the ebb of crack; the remaking of welfare; an influx of immigrants; a city drive to redevelop the housing stock under its control; and the rise of neighborhood organizations focused on restoration.

Months on 129th Street, from that summer barbecue to the first day of school to a Christmas celebration, showed the dimension of its changes.. Visits at dawn and midnight, conversations in homes and on corners, illuminated their texture and their limitations. Even from July to January, the evolution on 129th Street was remarkable: buildings renovated or sold, jobs lost and found, lives undone or refashioned. It seemed a constantly molting place, reflecting both the churning that is always a staple of poverty, and the ever faster rate of change here.

Change, too, has rippled across Harlem, once the nation's black cultural capital, but more recently a landscape of despair. From 1970 to 1990, central Harlem's population dropped by more than a third. In 1990, its median income was $19,169, compared with $41,415 citywide. Harlem had been severed, in essence, from the island of Manhattan. Now, slowly, it is rejoining it.

The changes have played out differently on different blocks. On some, revitalization has been slowed because a federal program to underwrite home loans fell prey to unscrupulous profiteers. On others, the city has yet to restore derelict housing. And 129th Street itself is a work in progress, with much unchanged for its roughly 1,400 residents.

But the block, which once embodied everything wrong with America's inner cities, today reflects much that can go right. So far, 17 of the block's 35 buildings, from town houses to tenements, have been rehabilitated. The block now has an art gallery, a Mormon church, a racially mixed preschool. A community development office matches residents with jobs. A lush little garden, tended by residents, thrives.

Deliverymen actually deliver food, and cabs deliver passengers. Trees—notable for their long absence—are growing. This fall, the street was repaved, smooth as ice, for the first time in years. Housing was even built on one of the last vacant lots, which had been used for the rap company's poster.

The reduction in crime has erased old fears and thus old borders. New life suffuses the block. Artists, actors and taxi drivers. A mortgage consultant and import-export entrepreneurs. Young black professionals looking for cheap rent. Middle-class, middle-aged black home-owners. Police officers. Africans in glorious robes. Hispanics. Whites.

Many of those profiled in the *Times*'s 1994 series have since experienced transformations large and small. A teenage mother now works for a city official. A young man paralyzed in a drive-by shooting in 1993 left the block in search of better housing while his brother became a rap artist. A studious young man finished college and is in the Navy. His sister, now off the block, and his mother, still on it, found their lives altered, like many here, by the imperatives of new welfare laws. Those laws, which require work in exchange for benefits before they are cut off entirely, pushed many residents into the work force. Their landing has been cushioned by an economy as supportive as a trampoline.

That is not to say that the poor have bounced into the middle class. In 1999, the median household income in Central Harlem was $20,625, barely up from 1990. But the routines of work, combined with better housing and lower crime, have made the block feel more like a middle-class place.

If 129th Street is—in its architecture, geography and population—idiosyncratic, it is also emblematic. Its re-birth has been duplicated in urban neighborhoods from Brooklyn to Houston to Oakland. It has all taken place during the longest and deepest economic expansion in American history. But since previous booms left no impression on this block or others like it, the story of 129th Street's, and Harlem's, transformation is clearly more complex, and often politically contradictory.

Conservatives can point to tough-minded welfare poli-cies and aggressive police work. Liberals can point to the lowering of immigration bars, which brought an influx of strivers, and to the $300 million the city has invested in housing in Harlem since 1994. Government policies like the Community Reinvestment Act pushed banks back into inner cities. A federal empowerment zone helped lure some new businesses, but more came because they needed new retail markets. And then there are powerful, unpredictable human factors, like a younger generation turning against crack, or exhibiting, perhaps, a greater tolerance for integration.

Consider the mix of factors that brought new, better-off residents to 129th Street. As the boom fueled the real estate market, and the city failed to build much new af-fordable housing, prices in better neighborhoods zoomed out of reach. At the same time, housing offi-cials, community leaders and landlords, determined to break Harlem's resolute concentration of poverty, to transform a ghetto into a neighborhood, were recruiting a new type of resident.

The fruits of that effort are perfectly displayed at the block's prize building, 38-44, with its courtyard. Its up-wardly mobile tenants have been picked as carefully as actors for a film. And in a place where doors are left open and stoops are extensions of living rooms, their complex is separated from the street by filigreed iron bars. It is a gated community.

An oasis in the ghetto, one resident says, for much of the ghetto remains intact. Amid the transformed build-ings and transplanted residents, the way up, or out, for many of the block's residents still seems poorly mapped. Limestone facades can be scrubbed. Limited education, racism, defeatist thinking, addiction and a shifting econ-omy are harder to overcome.

Poverty has shadowed residents from welfare to work, while other people's prosperity may price them out of Harlem. And for some, a rising tide has revealed only how low they are marooned.

The drug economy still thrives here, as does the war on it. At twilight, Harlem's fabled street life bursts forth. A gun skirmish over the summer between two Bloods was a reminder of how easily violence can reignite. As the block hovers between ghetto and neighborhood, cultural, racial and class tensions eddy quietly. And some worry that on a block where vast extended families created a village, the gain in normalcy may mean a loss of community.

The block is on the cusp, as is Harlem. A recession or a spike in crime could reverse its progress. And moving forward, for some, has its perils, too. Decades of decline could not erase Harlem's historic black identity. Success may be more powerful.

[The full text of this story can be read on the CD-ROM included with this edition of Best Newspaper Writing.]

Lessons Learned

BY AMY WALDMAN

It is probably rare, and perhaps stupid, to start a series that you are asking readers to spend a lot of time on with a deliberately boring scene. But in a sense, that's what I did.

The writing followed the reporting. I was following up a 1994 series about the same block, so after reading the series, I went up to 129th Street. I walked up and down the block and kept checking the street signs because I was sure I was in the wrong place—it looked so utterly normal. That normalcy—and how shocking it was to find it here—was what I wanted to convey. If on Manhattan's Upper West Side a shootout would be dramatic, here, after what the block had been through, a placid back yard barbecue was equally so.

In a three-part series, totaling nearly 18,000 words, this first section was by far the hardest to write. It had so much work to do. In one section I wanted to show how things were and how they had been before. Since a main goal of the series was to show how policy changes and social trends affected peoples' lives, I needed to give a sense of what those changes were. Because it was based on an earlier series that had focused on a group of characters, I had to briefly indicate what had happened to those people, since I wasn't going to build this series around them.

Most difficult of all was laying out early on the absolute contradictions this block contained, so readers wouldn't feel deceived later. Yes, many things were dramatically better, but many things weren't. Simple narratives are always preferable, but rarely true. The challenge was to explain how both could be true in the same place, and let readers know what they were in for.

I wanted people reading this to experience the mood swings, the exhilaration, and the despair that I had reporting the series—how one day it would seem as if everything was going right on 129th Street, and the next as if the worst problems were the most entrenched.

It might have been easier to write, and easier for a reader to follow, if I had picked a character to start with, or built the series around a few characters. But I decided against that. A central point of the series was how diverse the street had become, how many worlds it now contained. And if life had changed since the first series was written in 1994, I felt the telling of that life had to change, as well.

I had spent months with the residents of 129th Street, and they had opened themselves to me in every possible way. I wasn't going to sugarcoat life there, but I wanted to be fair. I didn't think it was fair to the array of people now living there to have the few stand for the many. So I sacrificed some narrative simplicity for what I hoped would be a more accurate, if messier, portrayal of what life on a block is like.

Ellen Barry
Non-Deadline Writing

Ellen Barry is a staff writer for *The Boston Globe*. After graduating from Yale University in 1993 with a degree in English, she moved to Russia and began her career as a copy editor and feature writer for the *Moscow Times*. She also has been a staff writer for the *Boston Phoenix* and a contributing writer for *Metropolis* magazine. At the *Globe*, her assignments have ranged from roving New England to covering the war in Afghanistan. She now covers mental health issues. In 1998, she received the Association of Aesthetic Plastic Surgeons' Journalism Award.

Every writer has a territory, a unique landscape in which milestones are marked by the writer's curiosity and passionate interest. For Barry, the daughter of a diplomat, that territory is the frontier, whether it's a place, such as the upper, largely "unpeopled" reaches of northern New England, or a state of mind, such as the culture shock that the "lost boys" of Sudan faced when they arrived in Massachusetts in 2001. A gifted absorber of telling detail and relevant action, Barry evokes the dizzying experiences of the newly arrived immigrant. In the words of *Globe* editor Martin Baron, "She made the strange familiar, the familiar strange."

"The Lost Boys of Sudan" is also a triumph of collaboration, an example of what mutual respect for other journalistic disciplines can produce. Barry and photographer Bill Greene immersed themselves in the lives of a remarkable group of tall, slender strangers trying to make sense of a very strange land. Told in their own near-biblical speech and Barry's graceful prose, "The Lost Boys of Sudan" is quintessentially American—a tale of immigrants that, through indefatigable reporting and nuanced writing, documents a haunting reminder of America's promise and its perils.

—Christopher Scanlan

[Bill Greene's photographs that accompanied this story can be seen on the CD-ROM included with this edition of Best Newspaper Writing.]

Strangers in a strange land

JANUARY 7, 2001

*On Dec. 17, a dozen teenage boys left mud huts in the
Kenyan plain for a new life they could only vaguely
imagine. As they prepared to board their first motorized
vehicle for their first airplane flight and their first
glimpse of the West, someone taught them a new word:
Massachusetts.*

KAKUMA REFUGEE CAMP, Kenya—Here, amid the
cracked earth and grizzled acacias of northwestern
Kenya, rumors were running rampant about North
Dakota.

Dozens of boys crowded around the U.N. compound
where someone, somewhere, held a list of the U.S. cities
where they might be offered homes. An older boy asserted that North Dakota is colder than Nairobi, but this
was impossible to confirm. Another was enraptured with
the idea of Albany, and dreamily repeated the phrase
"Albany, New York. Albany, New York," a spot whose
distance he estimated at a million, or possibly 2 million,
kilometers.

And a 17-year-old, John Deng, had his heart set on
Chicago, having learned that it is home to an abundance
of bulls. To the son and grandson and great-grandson of
cattle herders from the Dinka tribe—men who still sing
adoring songs about the horns of their favorite oxen—
Chicago has enormous appeal.

"I see that on some shirts, like Chicago Bulls. We believe that in Chicago we will have a lot of bulls," said
Deng, a young man with a gap-toothed smile who speaks
a formal English akin to that of a BBC announcer.

Within hours, however, Deng would be told the name
of a place that suggests a landscape without cattle:
Arlington, Mass. It would mean nothing to him.

The flights to America are leaving every day now,
screaming out of the bush in a huge cloud of orange
dust, as the great migration of the group known as the
Lost Boys of Sudan gets under way. Heads down, bare-

foot except for shower thongs, the departing boys file into the aircraft as grave as spacemen, sometimes without even looking back at the friends standing five deep against the barbed wire.

As far as their tribes are concerned, they may as well be spacemen. Most had never ridden in a motorized vehicle before leaving for America; their grandparents, some said later, were not necessarily aware that other countries existed.

"They were afraid," said Peter Lagad, a 27-year-old who watched the first groups of boys climb aboard in November. "It was as if they are doing a test on you. It was like getting shot to the moon."

The decision by the U.S. State Department to resettle 3,800 Sudanese boys across America—in places like Arlington and Fargo and Phoenix and Grand Rapids—seems extraordinary on two levels.

It is a testament, first of all, to the power of the story they have to tell: Forced from their homes by civil war, 33,000 boys from the Dinka and Nuer tribes have lived for 13 years as a virtual city of children wandering across Africa. They protected one another, raised one another, and, in the months spent fending off wild animals and enemy soldiers, buried one another.

The story was retold many times, percolating through the international community, and by the end of last year the U.S. government had decided that finding homes for this group of long-limbed 16- and 17-year-olds was a national priority.

The second extraordinary thing will take place over the next year, in the United States, as these teenagers plunge into the Western world of cellphones, traffic lights, and public high schools.

In the days before they started their journey to Logan Airport, the boys received classes in "cultural orientation" from two African women who said they felt a stab of pity at the naiveté of the boys' questions. Would there be a toilet on the airplane? How will I know when it is safe to cross the street? If a girl asks a boy on a date in America, can the boy refuse? How many cows are required to buy a wife in America? Is it possible to get a government grant to pay a dowry?

For some, the trip felt like a leap into pure oxygen. As

the final flights of 2000 were filling up, one young man
of 17 tried again and again, but found he could not bring
himself to leave Africa. His third attempt to board an
airplane to the West collapsed under rainy skies in
Nairobi. Limp, with his eyes shut, the young man folded
his 6-foot-plus frame like a broken umbrella over the
shoulders of an American aid worker.

His friend Bol Thiik explained that his problem was
not physical. Rather, he was convinced that his father, a
well-known magician in his home village, would curse
him rather than allow him to go to America.

"There are many Sudanese who believe that if your
child goes to America or Europe he will not come
back," said Thiik, who shivered through the embroidered robe he had bought for the journey. "It is as if your
child died."

Leaving Africa, the departing boys would shake off
the rhythms of a thousand years. Thirteen years after
they were removed from Dinka cattle camps, eight
years after they settled into refugee life in Kakuma, the
lost boys still structure their lives around invisible herds
of cattle: They gather weekly to sing the praises of their
cattle, and they measure a woman's beauty in terms of a
bride's price; a particularly tall and curvaceous daughter
would thus cost 100 cows.

Asked what the Dinka do for fun, Deng explained
that it is possible, using a hot poker, to mold the horns of
one's favorite bull into extraordinary and hilarious
shapes.

"Then," he said, grinning, "there is a lot of happiness."

CROSSING TO SAFETY

The cattle vanished from their lives long ago. Beginning in 1983, when a tenuous peace in southern Sudan
reignited into civil war, the predominantly Muslim government in the north renewed its campaign against
black Christian separatists in the south.

Male children were drained from the landscape,
snatched up as recruits for the rebel Sudanese People's
Liberation Army, targeted by northern militias, or
forced to flee. Those old enough to remember recalled
joining a moving column of people headed across the

226

PHOTO BY BILL GREENE, *THE BOSTON GLOBE*

border to Ethiopia, passing through strange towns that they still imagine with the eyes of 4-year-olds.

It would be a long time before they could stop walking. Joseph Kuir Maker, a former member of Parliament from Sudan's Christian south, recalled having been sent to organize the boys in Ethiopian camps in the late 1980s. They stumbled in, he said, in groups of 10 and 100, naked and exhausted, and simply lay down on the ground.

Some seemed close to losing their minds, Maker said. He mentioned one child who had stuck in his memory, who would force the other children to sing, and who would beat them if they stopped.

"When children are alone, they can get wild and lose their culture," he said. "You could just see they were dying people. Some of them were skeletons."

Maker and the other adult caretakers, about 300 to look after 33,000 boys, helped to organize the boys into family-like units, but did not quite succeed in protecting them. In 1991, Ethiopia was engulfed in its own civil war, and the boys were driven back to Sudan. This time, they would walk some 300 miles before crossing south into Kenya and eventually arriving at Kakuma; Maker estimates that a quarter of them died.

On the way, on a day they can't unstick from their memory, the whole column of boys crossed the Gilo River with Ethiopian soldiers at their backs and crocodiles under the surface. Many of the children drowned that day. Simon Galuk, a 20-year-old with jutting cheekbones, spent years dreaming about a boy who grabbed onto his foot until he jerked it away. His colleague, as he put it, drowned. At the time, Galuk was 10.

"We crossed the Sahara Desert. That was bad. But not like the tragedy of Gilo River," he said, with an enormous, high-pitched sigh. "The issue of Gilo River was very unique."

Now, the roughly 5,000 boys who survived and stayed together have grown to adulthood at Kakuma, in the 14-day stretches between distributions of U.N. wheat flour. Then, last year, when the rumored resettlement began to seem real, the boys gathered for another great transit. America, Deng was told, "is not a country where someone can just come and kill you. There is a law." He wrote it — AMERICA — in chalk on the wall of his 3-by-4-meter mud hut.

Last month, the adults who had been watching over the young men for 13 years, gathered to send them off to an unimaginable American future. The old men, their eyes misted by cataracts, sat in shady seats of honor and drank glasses of water poured for them from a gasoline can. The elders spoke words of advice into a Sanyo boom box so the young men could carry cassettes of recorded wisdom with them to America.

"Don't go and be attracted by the high life," one bearded and bony man admonished. "Beer is a new thing to you. Don't just go and get involved in that. There are many Negroes in America. Don't think you know them just because of their hair."

Another, a headmaster at the camp's primary school, warned: "I advise you to be very careful with the ladies."

In the afternoons, when the planes departed, Maker and his deputy came out to bid the boys farewell. Maker looked around at these sons of rural cattle-herders — whose T-shirts read "2Pac" and "Harley-Davidson" and "Alabama Conference on Autism" — and saw the raw material of an elite. By the end of the day, they would have seen more of the world than any of their forebears; by next year, they will be some of the best-educated people from their country.

In the Sudanese capital, Khartoum, the justice minis-ter had denounced the resettlement, telling a news service that it "creates a nucleus for a new rebellion," but Maker insisted that these boys are too important to put in danger.

Among them, he is certain, is the future president of southern Sudan.

"They will be in America," said Maker. "They will be a few boys inside of thousands and thousands of white mens and ladies. They are going to see a very big, tall building." He was not worried about them, he said, as they disappeared from view. "They are the people who are going to the safe place."

'OUR SKIN IS SHRINKING'

The week they flew into Logan Airport, a wall of cold air moved into New England, glazing tree branches with ice and freezing the water inside hydrants. The 12 boys who arrived on USAir Flight 6806 were so cold that their teeth pained them. Alith Ayuen, a 17-year-old whose name refers to the gray-brown color of a favorite cow, began to feel that the cold had passed into his bones, and offered a long hand that was cool as marble.

Met at the airport by Lutheran resettlement agents with bags full of clothing, they tucked themselves into ski parkas and knit caps and gloves that they wouldn't take off for days—in an effort, Ayuen said, to prevent their hearts from freezing.

The air was somehow different in America. Some felt so odd that they wondered if they had contracted malaria. John Bul looked down at his own arm, which was chalky from the strange dryness of indoor heating. He announced, in a whisper, what worried him: "Our skin is shrinking."

And so the lost boys found themselves in a fresh wilderness. Placed in local homes by Lutheran Social Services, 12 bone-thin youths began to eat in earnest: whole loaves of bread and peanut butter; six trips to the buffet table in a Worcester Chinese restaurant; glasses and glasses and glasses of milk. Some said they began to feel an unfamiliar buzz of energy in their muscles. In a suburb west of Boston—the Lutheran group requested that the locations of foster homes not be identified and full names of the boys not be used—four Dinka boys sit down at Pastor Ross Goodman's dinner table under an embroidered sampler that reads: "Be not forgetful to entertain strangers, for thereby some have entertained angels unaware."

Bol Thiik opened the small backpack he had brought with him from Africa and took out a bundle of the sticks that they used at Kakuma to brush their teeth. The day after he arrived, 13-year-old Mou Deng walked around clutching a pocket calculator by one corner. There was too much to take in.

"I meet many things of which I cannot explain," said John Deng. "There are a lot of lights. There are a lot of cars. They are like cattle moving. We see a lot of white mens and we are being few. They look the same, I cannot differentiate them. What make me nervous is I see so many white mens and they are not saying hello to me."

"As for the position of the sun," he added, "I give up."

The strangeness was everywhere. The sun appeared to shine without creating warmth. Houses were as hot as Kenya while the air outside was freezing. Four boys staying with Ray Maesto in a yellow ranch home near Worcester went off into gales of laughter at the turns he was constantly making in his car; on the plains of Africa, a trip from one point to another might have taken hours, but it had always been a straight line. They were engines of questions. Why don't black people live outside the city? Why don't American trees have any leaves? Why aren't there any young people in church? Why don't Americans eat dinner at home?

And there was a moment, in Maesto's house, when something happened to Ayuen that he knew would happen: The telephone rang, and for the first time in his life, he picked up the receiver and spoke to the voice inside it. The people who raised him used smoke signals for long-distance communication, or they blew through the hollowed-out horns of bulls, he said.

Ayuen can talk about life with the cattle endlessly, still, but a week after he arrived he had realized he would never return to it.

"When I was there, according to me, it was a good life," he said. "The way I compare the life now, it is very different. I have seen so much more of the world. I would not be happy. That life is bad actually. It is very far from the modern life."

For the moment, the modern life is sweet. But this month is the refugees' honeymoon, says Julianne Duncan, a child welfare worker who spent a year working with the group in Kakuma. Next week, three of the boys will show up for their first day in public high school, a place where men and women talk and touch with a familiarity that unsettles the Dinka. Six months will bring the disenchantment and depression that so often sets in among new immigrants, Duncan said. In a year, they will be able to apply for permanent residency in the United States. But first there is the strange business of building an American life.

On the day after he finally reached America, Bol Thiik, who had watched over his brothers with a statesmanlike gravity through the transit, found himself undone when he walked out of the public library with a book he intended to read.

"The gate started crying," Thiik said, in a tone of wonder.

Gently, his foster mother led him back inside the library, where they scanned a bar code and demagnetized the sticker that had triggered the alarm.

Dinka values, teenage rites

MARCH 18, 2001

OXFORD—In Mrs. Racicot's second-period geometry class, beside a smart-mouthed basketball player and a bubbly, pregnant senior, one of the Lost Boys of Sudan folded his long legs into an empty seat.

In Africa, Philip Jok had been known for springing up from the ground like a grasshopper during tribal dances, so that on a good day, his bony feet flew up to his friends' heads. He was famous for writing long, extemporaneous songs about cattle.

But at Oxford High School on Jan. 18, all that receded into the past as he was issued a paperback copy of George Orwell's *1984*, a three-ring binder, and a combination lock. During the course of that day, he would stare blankly through a class discussion on the last days of the czarist regime in Russia. He had not been informed of Communism's rise, or its fall, until that morning.

And later, in the gymnasium, he would sit on the bleachers as primly as a missionary, collar buttoned, while eighth- and ninth-graders raucously shot baskets in front of him. He had "never seen such a kind of place," he said, or "put that ball in that pocket."

But that didn't matter, either, when he got up and loped across the squeaking floor to the basket. The freshmen, cheeks burning, watched mutely.

"He skies," said Bobby Martin.

Philip Jok has a jump shot.

In moments like this, in classrooms across eastern Massachusetts, Jok and 50 other Sudanese teenagers who arrived three months ago are crossing a divide from a desperate childhood to the protected zone of American adolescence.

When the young men known as the Lost Boys of Sudan came to the attention of aid workers in the early 1990s, they presented a terrible image: a river of thousands of male children removed from their homes in the chaos of Sudan's civil war, rail-thin and often naked, who had walked hundreds of miles in scorching heat.

They grew to the brink of adulthood in African camps, and remained so cut off from the outside world that their journey to America, where the State Department is resettling 3,800 of them, seems a trip not just across continents but through time. When they left their mud huts for the last time three months ago, many had never heard of the moon landing or the atomic bomb, or, according to a spokeswoman for the Lutheran Social Services resettlement program, "what stairs were for."

Throughout the process of resettlement, they have repeated their shared goal so many times that it has begun to sound like a prayer: to learn enough to return to southern Sudan and lift their people out of their premodern state. Eighteen-year-old Bol Thiik strode into Winchester High School with a fully formed idea of what he needed. He sat down with the principal, Susan Morse, and requested instruction in "religion and agriculture."

Months later, the closest he has come is *Catcher in the Rye*, the classic text on the American teenager's search for meaning. For that, as for social studies, tank tops, and the overhead projector, the boys from the Dinka tribe were totally unprepared.

It is a gap that can't be crossed gradually, said Ambrose Beny, 63, a Sudanese-born professor of English literature who, like the boys, grew up in the world of savannah cattle-herders, and then moved to a small town in New Jersey through an exchange program.

"The thing I like about America is that it does not leave you alone," said Beny, who first came to America in the 1960s. "You cannot be neutral about it. How you adjust and adapt to it, that's the real question. Some, of course, will get lost, because they won't make the transition."

How these boys will be changed by living here is anyone's guess, he says, but one thing is certain: They will be changed.

"Give them six months," he said. "Let America do its work."

LIVIN' LA VIDA LOCA

In the Ethiopian camp where Bol Thiik learned to read, there was no paper, so the boys sat in long rows scratching letters in the dirt with sticks. The children were caned if they moved, so they learned to sit for hours on their knees in the sun, naked or nearly naked. Dust was a problem, said Thiik; if it was thick enough that drivers had to turn on their car headlights, school was canceled. In long rows, the little boys learned to repeat and memorize lists of facts.

The schools in America were indoors. There were many classrooms stacked on top of each other. The boys realized, after a few days, no one was being caned.

And suddenly, for the first time in their education, part of the subject matter was themselves.

"Commit to working on two or three of your favorite character traits over the summer," advised one guide for new students at Oxford High School, and Winchester's contained the following advice: "Q: Some people say your friends will change in high school. Is this true? A: From our experience, you tend to grow apart from some of your middle school and elementary school friends, but it is totally natural."

The boys' concerns were more basic. Trained to address their teachers as "master" and "madam," they were astonished and dismayed by American students' casual insolence toward adults. And they were unnerved to see boys and girls kissing in the hallways. Romantic yearning is not a central value among the Dinka, who buy their wives for cattle and sometimes marry four of them. Speaking to a girl in school, or on the roadside, is grounds for punishment, and a young man wishing to talk at any length with a girl is required to arrange it through her parents, Thiik explained.

Those Dinka values met their biggest challenge to date at the Oxford High School Valentine's Dance. Jam'n 94.5 emceed, which meant "Livin' la Vida Loca" and the Bloodhound Gang singing "You and me baby ain't nothing but mammals/Let's do it like they do on the Discovery Channel." The four Sudanese boys had been wondering for weeks just how the Americans dance, and they stepped into a cafeteria strangely swimming with spotlights.

What they saw was astonishing. They paused, trying to figure it out.

"We were just waiting for the organization of the par-

ty," said Alith Ayuen, an 18-year-old with ghostly tribal marks on his forehead. "I saw people dancing and I thought, how are they going to organize that? They told me it is already started. Then we went to the field and danced."

Weeks earlier, the first Dinka venture into the bass-pounding crucible of the high school dance had ended badly. Among the hundreds of teenage boys who were brought into the country before Christmas was a much smaller group of teenage girls, including Aduei, a tall 17-year-old who stands perfectly straight. At her first dance, a classmate drew her so close to him that she tore away in the middle of the dance floor.

"I thought I would lose my culture and I became frightened and I ran away," she said.

At their own dance, a similar moment arrived for William Wol, Samuel Leek, Philip Jok, and Alith Moses. The music slowed, and girls stepped out of the crowd to pull them close.

"The girl who was dancing with me, she came and hooked me like that," said Ayuen. "I think about whether I can just push her back or I can continue. And one of these people were just glancing, watching us."

After the dance was over, they shook their heads disapprovingly over the girls' scanty clothing, which seemed far more provocative than the occasional nakedness of their home villages. Said 16-year-old Samuel Leek, thinking back on his schoolmates at the dance, "They pretend that there are clothes, but there are no clothes."

The boys went into gales of laughter recalling it; it would be wrong to call them traumatized by the event. In fact, by the time the strobe lights went off at 11 p.m. and the cafeteria returned to its former life as a cafeteria, Moses had won a box of chocolates in the dance contest.

They came home dazzled by the crazy freedom of American teenagers, restless, excited, with a hundred things to think about — as Leek put it, "somehow happy but not happy."

'THEY DON'T KNOW THE EARTH GOES AROUND THE SUN'

Three months ago, when the boys climbed off a plane into a world glazed in ice, they could hardly think beyond the pure physical shock. Their skin seemed to be shrinking; they felt that their hearts were unprotected from the cold. On his way to the bus stop on the blue, crescent-mooned morning when he was to start school, Philip Jok still marveled: "I feel my hand not to be my hand."

But when school began, the stress shot off in a different direction. Carlos Akot complained to his teacher that his brain had begun to hurt.

Jolanta Conway, the dimpled, Polish-born ESL teacher at Winchester High School, was watching 18-year-old Akot as he struggled through a standard high-school English text: Ray Bradbury's chilling, futuristic story "There Will Come Soft Rains," which describes a day in the life of a house whose occupants have been burned away by an atomic blast.

Conway knew by the dismay on Akot's face that something was terribly wrong.

She rushed to assure him that none of it was real.

"I tried to explain, 'When you were children, you were imagining things. It wasn't real. This is the same way,'" Conway said. "They asked, 'Why do people do this? Why do people write something that is not true?' Then they were reading science fiction, and I thought, 'Oh, my God.'...I told my husband, 'My brain is hurting, too,' because I had never analyzed a short story like that."

How do you teach a 17-year-old the concept of fiction? Their needs, teachers found, were not quite the same as English-as-a-Second-Language students; most speak stilted, archaic English passed on from missionaries. Nor were they "special needs" students, exactly; many are not only smart but desperately motivated.

They were something else entirely—unaware of basic facts about the modern world, like "someone who has lived out in the woods for 50 years, and then come back," said Kathy Threadgould, who teaches computer science and math at Oxford High School. Early on, one of her Sudanese students asked her why words didn't come out of the mouths of people in photographs.

For months, teachers kept discovering new gaps. At Winchester, two of Conway's Sudanese students finally confessed the heart-racing terror they experienced every time their foster parents drove over elevated highways, which they feared would collapse and kill them.

In Oxford, a tutor organized a trip to a costume shop, to prove to her incredulous students that Barney was not a real talking animal.

"I saw there on TV a cow can speak English, and a dog can also speak English," said Jok, with an amazed laugh. At the costume shop, "all those things, we saw them there. They can just have leather, and they can wear that leather, and you will be seen like an animal. If you are seen in our country, they can say, 'Oh, that is a god.'"

"Me myself I believed them," he said, "but nowadays I never believe them."

To some who worked with the students, those early days were spellbinding. In math, for instance, where they were initially assessed at an eighth-grade or lower level, the students were picking up new concepts incredibly fast, "doing something symbolically that I wouldn't have thought possible," said math teacher Richard Thorne.

"It's interesting to watch how a mind absorbs something," he said. "It's like a tabula rasa."

But at other times, they just seemed painfully dislocated. Four of the Sudanese began classes at Boston English High School, which has so many African immigrants that it offers a bilingual track in Somali. Shortly after they arrived, one teen went to a tutor, Paul Siemering, seized with anxiety over his lost lunch card. Siemering carefully explained that it was nothing serious. Then he took him back to the cafeteria, where a worker explained that she could make him a new card. But the next period, Siemering walked into the library and found the young man with his head down on a desk, sobbing.

"These boys are more culturally and socially deprived than anyone who's ever come in here," said Siemering, who has been tutoring African students at English for 10 years.

"It's almost impossible for regular teachers to grasp their level of innocence," Siemering said. "They don't know the Earth goes around the sun. They don't know who Elvis Presley is. They don't know who Hitler is, they don't know World War II. You might as well be talking Sanskrit. It's hard to go far enough back to start."

Three months into their journey, though, something has started to happen.

David Lual had announced his intention to return to his home village, marry five wives, and herd 500 cattle. Then suddenly he mentioned that he would also like to visit Venice. In the Arlington group home set up by St. Paul Lutheran Church, William Wol, a nearly wordless 18-year-old who lovingly drew cattle in his school notebooks, began dinging on piano keys with a tentative finger.

And Alith Moses—whose home village is still so cattle-centered that paper currency is worthless—started to like the poetry of Edgar Allen Poe. He even said he would consider marrying an American girl if "the kind of relationships that is happening between me and her is very strong, that is like what is happening in that poem 'Annabel Lee.'"

'I CAN'T COME HOME ANYMORE'

Whether or not the boys know it now, there are certain kinds of information that change you permanently, said Ambrose Beny, the professor who was among the first Dinka to receive an education in the West.

"I can't come home anymore," said Beny. "In some ways it would probably be too limiting for me. There are not too many [Dinka]—I mean, there are none of them—who have read Shakespeare or William Faulkner. And I would want to talk about those writers, so in a way, I would be lost."

In the high schools where the Sudanese boys spend their days, other shifts have taken place without anybody's notice. At Oxford High School's sophomore semiformal, to the accompaniment of Sir Mix-a-Lot's "Baby Got Back," 16-year-old Cassandra Rose flushed with pleasure recalling the letter she had received, through an intermediary, from one of the young Sudanese men.

Eyes ringed with the palest blue glitter, Rose wore a pink feather bracelet and decals on her fingernails. She had instantly related to the displacement of the Sudanese students, she said, having transferred to Oxford from Worcester herself.

The note melted her heart with its courtly language, although she had to look up some words, like "consort," and she wondered why he kept referring to her as "obedient girl."

Still, in a high school where male gallantry runs along the lines of "I-think-you're-cute-do-you-like-me," she said, there was something strange and wonderful about the words he used.

"Do not worry about me a lot," the note said, "but I will always be the first one to worry about you."

Illusions fade in reality
of city life

JULY 8, 2001

LYNN—When he was a small boy scampering after calves in the village of Mading, Jok Mading was told that there were people in the world whose skin was white, but he was a clever child and did not believe it.

Sometimes, when an airplane flew overhead, the children would stare up at the line of vapor hanging behind it and say: America. But there were older people—maybe two generations older than Mading—who could live and die in the belief that their people, the Dinka, were the principal residents of the earth.

So it was odd, days after Mading had left Africa at age 19 and been resettled in a rented apartment in Lynn, to find himself addressed—by children, no less—as a "monkey without a tail."

He and 10 other young Sudanese men sat in their cramped apartment in Lynn, conferring about the meaning of this term. Like "nigger"—another word they had heard people yell at them—"monkeys without tails" sounded like a "word of abuse," as Mading put it, and the young men were frozen and alert in the face of it. When he finally was told the definition of these words, Mading sat back slowly.

"I now know the meaning of that word," said Mading, who was wearing a donated Lynn Rotary Club T-shirt. "Now, what can one do? If someone call me nigger, what can I do to it?"

Six months have passed since the first of the refugee group known as the Lost Boys of Sudan were whisked off to new homes in America. In 1987, the boys of Bor and Bahr el Ghazal provinces were driven out of their war-torn villages on a trek that would bring them nearly 1,000 miles across Africa. Since then their lives have been so bound together that they shared a single, government-issued birthday.

But here in Massachusetts, where dozens of Lost Boys have landed, the young men have embarked on different paths. The 40 who came in under the age of 18 joined foster families, often in the suburbs, and are enrolled in high school, with tuition waived at Massachusetts state universities if they are admitted.

Meanwhile, their older comrades—about 90 Sudanese in their late teens and early 20s—are living in groups in apartments around the region and have entered into urban life. The shocks came immediately.

For the first time, the color of their skin was charged with tense meaning. More difficult, though, have been the day-to-day frustrations of looking for low-wage jobs while trying to grasp the most basic facts about American culture, which some pursued by watching television game shows.

There was no way to warn them about America's more complicated truths, said Julianne Duncan, a child welfare worker who, at Kakuma Refugee Camp in Kenya, was the first American most of them knew well.

"It's kind of like trying to explain cold to people who have never experienced cold," she said. "They were really, really focused on what it was going to be like to get on an airplane. The part about after six months, you're going to be depressed...they could absorb certain amounts of it, but not all. People can only learn so much at any one time."

For some, the difference between expectations and reality has felt like a betrayal. A few weeks after he arrived, John Garang, a mordant, clever 22-year-old who has become the informal leader of the group living in the Lynn apartment, sat down to write to Timnit Embaye, the cultural trainer at Kakuma Camp whose job it had been to prepare the Sudanese for life in America.

"I curse the day I joined the process to come to the U.S.," he wrote to her. "I would go back if possible."

ABROAD IN THE CITY

Innocent of technology, armed with an archaic British vocabulary, they had been seen off from Africa to become a new, educated Dinka elite.

"We hope they will get all the chances of life," said Joseph Kuir Maker last fall, as one of many flights left Africa from a tiny Kenyan airstrip. Maker, a former official in southern Sudan, had helped watch over the group for a decade. "They will get education in all things. They will be the people to build up this nation and they will be the people to be defending the nation and they will be the ones doing every job."

And some seem headed that way. In Massachusetts, six months into the celebrated resettlement, 18-year-old John Alith was studying hard at Oxford High School. He had decided not to try out for football, concluding that "if you have a small muscle like this one the possibility of getting an accident is there." And his interest in Edgar Allen Poe had grown: "It demonstrate the macabre. It demonstrate the darknesses, the badnesses."

But he didn't see his future in literature. "My blood," he said, "is telling me to be a doctor."

Bol Thiik, 18, had become a strong runner on Winchester High School's track team, and was headed to a summer job at a camp on a lake in New Hampshire. He had begun to notice social differences on trips in and out of Winchester.

"Here in America, the poor person is the fat guy, and the rich person is the thin one, and I don't know why!"

Six months after his arrival, he still saw America as a "second heaven."

Their older compatriots came in with the same otherworldly naiveté. Never having used an alarm clock, one household of Sudanese refugees in Chelsea had developed their own system for waking up: Every night, one of them was designated to stay up all night, waking up his housemates when the sun rose.

And 21-year-old David Diing found his whole understanding of human skin color thrown into disorder by posters for the Blue Man Group. (Although, he added, gravely, "I have not seen them physically to confirm that.")

Without the protection of host families, though, the older Sudanese also have had to face serious, adult situations. On a June night in Chelsea, one of the refugees received a deep gash in his arm during an altercation with a neighbor. The neighbor said she slapped him after he swatted at her 10-year-old daughter, who had been teasing him on the porch of their house, but denies that anyone in her family cut his arm. (Police suspended their investigation because the victim was unable to identify his assailant, said Sergeant Thomas Dunn.)

Since then relations in the apartment building have improved, and have even become friendly, thanks to the intervention of a Spanish-speaking volunteer. But the incident sent waves of anxiety through the apartments of resettled Sudanese throughout the area.

"I flew 36 hours above the sky to come here from Africa," said the young man, who now has a wound snaking up his forearm. "I was innocent. I did not know where I am going. I was not expecting to come get such a thing here."

THE QUIET ZONE

They had been informed that the transition might be rocky. Before leaving Africa they received a packet of information that contained, alongside instructions not to engage in female circumcision or polygamy, a graph of their projected happiness over time. The graph starts high, with arrival in the United States, then spikes during the "honeymoon" stage, in the month after arrival. The line plummets during "Stage 2: shock/depression." A few months later, the happiness graph rallies and lifts toward "Stage 4: balance."

The promise of reaching Stage 4 was not much consolation to the 11 young men in Lynn, who spent much of their first weeks in the United States holed up in a small apartment playing cards and chatting in Dinka, recreating the life they had left in the camp. For three days after they arrived, in an apartment so cold they had "smoke" coming out of their mouths, they didn't step outside, Garang said.

Outside was great confusion. They wondered what kind of death waited on those streets labeled "DEAD END." The words "QUIET ZONE" posted on a tree outside their apartment made them wonder what would happen if they made noise. Warned in Africa about the aggression of American drunks, they crossed the street warily every time they went near a bar.

They were crestfallen every night when their neighbors, returning home from work, passed them by wordlessly instead of stopping to chat. And as the young men walked the streets, too tall and too dark to blend in, comments rang out from the sidewalk. Garang began to believe the advice of an elder who had warned him,

"even if you're in America, you're still in the bush."
They came home, the unfamiliar epithets ringing in
their ears, and tried to figure out what they meant.

"We know that in Africa a gang is a group of thieves,
and we wonder why people call us gangs," Garang said.
"We realize here in America, 'gang' is not depending on
a group of rebels alone. Whenever you walk in a group
you will be called a gang."

All those complaints paled, though, beside the growing fear that they were not going to receive a proper
education. That was the promise that drew them out of
the cattle-herding villages in the first place. Imagining
work in the United States, they had a vague picture of
themselves in an office, or wild hopes of finding employment at a Sudanese-style cattle camp. Now, having
come as far as America, without marketable skills, they
were interviewing for jobs washing dishes and loading
laundry.

No one was more depressed than Garang. He had left
Africa six months short of graduating from secondary
school, hoping to return to his country as a doctor or a
teacher or a priest. Now he found himself applying for a
sanitation job at Logan Airport.

"You talk of a graph having honeymoon, depression,
and balance, but for me it start by depression, and I
don't see the possibility of the other two come in,"
Garang wrote to the woman who had taught cultural orientation at Kakuma. "The only thing which can solve
my problems is education and not money."

'I AM READY TO WORK'

The official answer to their troubles, however, is
money—and finding a way to earn it.

Upon arrival, resettled refugees are entitled to $428 a
month in federal cash assistance, in addition to transportation money for up to eight months. But resettlement
agencies encourage them to get into the work force—and
end federal payments—as soon as possible. Agencies
help arrange for adult education or night school classes
once the refugees are settled in their jobs.

So for refugees intent on enrolling in school, the first
few months "becomes a little bit about the dream de-
ferred," said Robert Meek, director of resettlement at

the International Institute of Boston, which arranged the Lynn group's resettlement.

Because of the employment push, the average refugee resettled by the International Institute is off assistance in 4.5 months, said Westy Egmont, the agency's executive director.

"That's a remarkable testimony to the economy and immigrant culture," he said. "Countries like the Netherlands…provide social welfare [for a longer period], but people end up dependent on the state."

For the Dinka, who would be the first in their ancestral line to do anything but subsistence farming or cattle herding, the quest for a job has meant learning everything at once.

Alison Lutz, an employment coordinator for another resettlement agency, Catholic Charities International, recalls driving a young Sudanese man to a job interview, getting out of her car, and watching him clamber after her out the driver's-side door, not knowing how to open his own. On an employment application, another listed his emergency contact number as 911.

To the Dinka, who consider self-promotion deeply shameful, the job interview itself was a challenging concept. Twenty-five-year-old Joseph Garang (no relation to John), while waiting for an interview for a janitorial job at an Old Navy store, expressed some doubts about the training he had received at the resettlement agency.

"How am I to say I am a hard worker, and I will come to work on time? What if I am not?" he asked. The boss "will disqualify me, saying I am not a truth person."

Across town, in Chelsea, John Garang explained that he had grinned through interviews at the Omni Parker House and Walmart. He shook hands firmly, and he made eye contact, but he couldn't help laughing afterward. If he ever behaved that way in Africa, his reputation would never recover.

"People see you, they will laugh so much you will start hiding from them," he said, shaking his head incredulously. Asking for work in Africa, "you just say, 'I am ready to work.' Not, 'These are the adjectives to describe myself.' What Americans like is to keep smiling. It really is quite funny," he added, "to smile when you

do not like it. I don't know if they realize is not gen-
uine."

Still, when he went to interview for a job working the
night shift at a coffee shop, he said what he was supposed to say.

"The man ask me what time are you available,"
Garang said. "I said I am available when you need me.
He said how much money do you require. I said any
amount that you decide. He ask me also which shift do
you want. I say any that you choose. He say when do
you want to start. I said I will start when you like."

But the man didn't call.

'ANOTHER PLACE'

One by one, the young Dinka men in Lynn began
leaving the quiet of the apartment for jobs. The first to
leave was Alier Agok, who took his place at $11.53 an
hour beside one Haitian, one Liberian, one Vietnamese,
two Chinese, two Puerto Ricans, one Dominican, and
one Salvadoran in the laundry room of the Omni Parker
House.

The laundry room was all compressed steam and
pounding extractors, which caused a painful throbbing
in the place where, two years ago, an arrow had lodged
above Agok's left ear. After he returned from his first
day, he said he understood why "all the men in America
they have a hump like a cow."

Agok's thoughts, as he shook out pillowcases on the
evening shift, were about the future, about saving
$5,000 for the cows he needs to trade for a Dinka bride.
He felt sure he would not be in the laundry room for
very long, and had heard of a less taxing job that quickly
became his ambition: security guard. But at this point,
he cannot see ever saving enough money to buy a car or
own a home or pursue an education.

Sometimes, in the laundry room, he thinks about
what it would be like to go back to Sudan and fight in
the rebel army.

"Sometimes I feel this is not America," he said. "All
the people are not speaking English, and I hear that this
is where the English came from. America must be another place. We are just on the way to America."

For his part, John Garang watched his roommates

leave for work but made no gesture to join them. By the beginning of his third month here, he had given up in disgust on the job interviews. His vision of the future now centered dreamily on Salem State College.

Garang spent hours sprawled inside the apartment, poring over test preparation books. He left on a recent Thursday for what seemed to him like his last shot at charting his own course: the Test of English as a Foreign Language, which foreign students must take to attend most four-year colleges in this country.

Garang had been gently warned by his pastor at St. Stephen's Episcopal Church that he couldn't expect to pass the test, whose grammar and reading comprehension sections regularly stump recent arrivals in this country.

But he set off that morning, anyway, full of hope. It had become clear what he had to do.

The following Sunday he went to St. Stephen's, a parish that has swelled with Africans from former British colonies. Garang asked to make an announcement, and climbed up to the pulpit.

"I am here to thank you for what you have done," Garang told the congregation. "When I first come here, I was thinking that Americans don't concern of other people. I was thinking if there is any possibility, I will go back to Africa. But when you show concern it bring a change in my life.

"One of the very great changes is that three days ago, I took the TOEFL exam. I passed the exam, and it is because of you people."

Someone started clapping. The clapping spread, and someone pumped her fist in the crowd, and a full house of worshipers hooted and cheered. John Garang stood there, smiling.

African and American

DECEMBER 30, 2001

MARENG, Sudan—Two months ago, a man walked 15 miles through the bush to tell Nyanwel Joh that her son Deng was alive and attending high school in America.

He also told her: America is another country. It is not located in Africa. If you walked, he said, it would take three months to get there.

America was the fourth place Nyanwel had ever heard of outside the stretch of plain where she lives, after Ethiopia, Kenya, and Khartoum. But looking at photographs of Deng hunched like a gangsta rapper on Huntington Avenue, or with arms slung around his classmates at Arlington High School, she allowed her mind to slip its old boundaries.

"When I look up, I see blue unending space. At night, I see the stars and moon. Horizontally I see the end of the earth, the end of the sky, and beyond that I cannot imagine," she said, and fell silent.

A few moments later, she ventured, "I wonder if you live the same as we do there."

There was much in his life that Deng could not have explained to the woman who, 14 years ago, sent him away from the village to become a different kind of person.

He could not explain Avogadro's number, or the wind chill factor, or financial aid, or why, after all he had been through on the way to America, he had nearly wept to see a man beaten in the film *Uncle Tom's Cabin*. A year after he arrived in Massachusetts, Nyanwel's son—now a tall 18-year-old known as John—was eligible to receive a green card, which gives him permanent residency in the United States.

Like the other Massachusetts high schoolers who left the same Sudanese village that same day, he was looking out at the dark street from lighted windows this Christmas. And although his future in America was far from assured, he also knew for a certainty that he didn't belong in Mareng anymore.

When news of Deng's whereabouts arrived in his mother's village, a 2,000-year-old way of life stopped and rearranged itself.

Head men carrying umbrella spokes and hammered metal crosses walked out of the bush and converged on the homestead Deng had left. His elderly aunts got into the sorghum wine and trilled girlish songs about bulls, finally collapsing into a deep sleep on a corner of a tarpaulin. His brothers called a truce in their hut-burning feud over the family's 10 remaining cows.

And his mother, Nyanwel, who has shrunk with age and hunger to the lightness of a wren, slaughtered a goat and boiled it in pond water.

"I just heard the name of America,"she said. "I don't know whether you go there by car or by foot. I don't know where it is located. I don't know whether America owns cows. According to the stories I have heard, it contains white people.

"Since he left, I am failing to imagine how he lives," she said. "I only pray to God to bring him back to me."

The choice to send Deng away was partly hers. In 1987, with southern Sudan racked by its fourth year of civil war, word came from the Sudanese People's Liberation Army that several hundred children from Mareng were to be taken from their homes. They would be led in the direction of Ethiopia, where, parents were informed, they would be taught to read.

It was the month of Mareng's chief joy, the cattle camp, where every year villagers forget the hunger of August and guzzle cow's milk to see how fat they can get. Young boys covered themselves with ashes. Pale smoke rose around white song-oxen.

Nyanwel's older sons, 19-year-old Panchol and 14-year-old Koryam, had no desire to leave. But her strong-willed 5-year-old saw the other children preparing to go, and he grew eager. Nyanwel—who had borne 10 children in a mud-walled hut and lost six in infancy—agreed at last. Deng went.

She expected to see him again at school holidays.

Fourteen years later, when his message reached her, he had passed from the hands of the southern Sudanese rebel movement to the Ethiopian government, to the Kenyan government, to the United Nations, and finally to the United States, where he was already in his second year at Arlington High School.

Some of the children who had left Mareng with him had drowned in the terrible crossing of the Gilo River, and others, too tired to continue, curled up beside the road to die. Those who survived were stranded in a Kenyan refugee camp until their story inspired the U.S. State Department to arrange the largest resettlement of children since the Vietnam War.

Last winter, Deng and more than 3,100 other young men were flown to the United States and delivered to subdivisions and apartment buildings, where a small army of volunteers has worked to ensure that the cattle-herders' sons successfully make the transition to Western life.

The view in Sudanese villages like Mareng, where many of the boys' families still live in the pre-modern state they left, is quite different. When the process is complete, the parents ask, will they still be our children?

Under a tamarind tree, in the glow of the news about Deng, one man questioned whether the children would want to return to the village, where progressive-minded local officials still promote the wearing of clothes as "an indication that you are somebody, that you are not an animal."

Until 1993, he said, villagers here still worshipped a piece of zinc named Lorpyo.

People are happy here, he said, but only until they leave.

"He will not fit with the condition of this place. Here life is very simple. You have five or six cows and you run after them," said Garang Kuei Mel, 48, a longtime official in the humanitarian wing of the rebel movement.

"Most of these people are illiterate. You will not waste your time reading books about Shakespeare.

"These are stories," he added, with some contempt. "You do not tell stories to people who do not read or write. They will not make use of you."

Nyanwel Joh — who has never been told what year it is, or how old she is, or that the Earth revolves — was not thinking about his return. Instead, she appealed to Deng to save the family from a gathering catastrophe.

The message she sent him from Africa was this: Your brothers have become enemies. Nuer raiders left us with only 10 cows, and the younger, Koryam, used them to marry. Furious at the usurpation of his birthright, the elder burned our hut down.

Without cow's milk, Deng's mother reported, I am starving.

She also added, sweetly, almost as an afterthought, that she was considering joining him in America.

"If there is a vacancy," she said.

ARRIVAL IN THE U.S., AND THOUGHTS OF HOME

John Deng, suburban 10th-grader, had shaken off the sadness that gripped him on the day of his arrival.

He flew in on Dec. 20, 2000. Moving airport sidewalks had come at him first, and they were followed rapidly by hothouse vegetables, climate control, and the complex night machinery of New York City. He watched with fascination a beer can talking on television. He complained with hurt dignity about the teenagers in Roxbury, whose pants revealed their buttocks.

But the worst injury seemed to be to his self-esteem. His eyes still red from jet lag, Deng shook his head at the realization that his people had somehow been left out of 2,000 years of human progress.

"In part of education we are so backwards and in everything we are backwards," he said. "We are very backward in English speaking. Maybe our country is so backward."

For months after they landed, many of the boys were still dreaming about hump-backed cattle. They drew them on notebook paper and gave them to their teachers for Valentine's Day.

They thought about home. During the long years at the refugee camp, Deng's cousin Peter Thon had ached to return to Mareng; it took all his friends' efforts to convince him that village life is useless. Now, on the other side of the world, Thon shuttled from one high school class to another with only the foggiest understanding of the information he was being given.

This spring, as a math teacher scribbled long columns of numbers on the blackboard, he turned to a near-stranger beside him and asked, "Can you find my father?"

Some of that longing faded this year, replaced by more local aspirations. In the spangled interior of the Burlington Mall, 14-year-old Philip Mou darted like a homing pigeon into Abercrombie and Fitch, where he spent most of his savings on a shirt that read, "Got a Sister?" William Wol, his tribal markings now set off by gold spectacles, had focused his affection on Arlington High School's track team.

When he saw photographs of African cattle, Wol still broke out in a luminous smile and thrust his arms into the air in imitation of their long horns, as 20 generations of his ancestors would have.

"I still love them," he said of the cows. "But I do not think I will be with them."

Their embrace of their new home did not mean they were succeeding as they had expected. Many of the boys under 18, who had been desperate to go to school, found themselves struggling. Those over 18, fed directly into the work force, worried that the education they had been promised would never come at all.

It was an outcome that had troubled Francis Mading Deng, a top U.N. official who is himself the son of Dinka cattle-herders, from the moment he heard about the resettlement.

"At best, maybe a few will distinguish themselves. But a lot of them are going to just disappear into situations where they make ends meet in a basic way," he said, from a book-lined office in Manhattan. "Then the country loses them, their own people lose them, they themselves fundamentally lose that clear sense of identity and purpose."

If there was a living exception, it was John Deng, who matriculated at Arlington High School and tore off like a racehorse through the new curriculum. He turned his attention to the Holocaust, to the volume of spherical objects, to the awful triangle of the Atlantic slave trade. In the group home where he lived, he regularly clashed with his house parents over disciplinary matters—but he was a conspicuous top student. A year after he arrived, his report card listed an A in English, an A minus in chemistry, and an A plus in Algebra 2.

"He had an outwardly rebellious body language,"

said Walter Mau, an engineer who began tutoring Deng over the summer. "But he showed me his math, and I was astounded."

Franco Majok, a case worker for Lutheran Social Services, said many of the minors were frustrated at their performance in school. Deng was different.

"Deng can make it," he said.

AFTER SUCCESSES, A SETBACK

On the anniversary of their arrival, the boys' house in Arlington was crowded with tutors and volunteers and neighbors' children. Albino Mayar had learned to sing the "Dreidel Song" and Philip Jok had acquired a fuzzy elf hat; in the corner of their room stood a small artificial tree. They unwound tangles of ribbon and ripped paper off a slim box that contained the board game Monopoly. Their dreadful first week in this country—when they huddled around heaters and thought their skin was shrinking on their bodies—seemed faint and almost forgotten amid the lights and music of Christmas.

The one face missing was John Deng's.

Deng was arrested the Sunday after Thanksgiving after a fistfight with one of his roommates. When the police arrived, a resettlement worker was already on the scene, and pleaded with them not to arrest him.

"She states that residents of Sudan have a difficult time managing conflict in the United States and learning the customs and laws, but are trying the best they can," reads the police report in the case.

Despite her plea, that morning found Deng posing in profile for a mug shot. Two weeks later, a house parent called the police again to report that Deng had shouted an obscenity and thrown a shoe.

Only gradually, after Deng had been placed in a temporary foster home, did his roommates realize that the incidents could, at the very least, jeopardize his immigration status.

At worst, if he was convicted and immigration authorities stepped in, they could result in deportation.

It was a predicament that troubled his old friend Philip Jok, who had accompanied Deng for years.

"Fighting is something printed in the blood of Sudanese generations," Jok said. "We cannot say we are not going to."

John Deng waited in a foster home this Christmas, puzzling over the lawyer who had not yet asked him whether he was guilty. In school he was laboring through *Go Ask Alice*, the 1971 antidrug parable that purports to be the diary of a good girl turned junkie-stripper. He had been assigned an essay about racist hate mail. He was working on finding the mass of an atom of aluminum.

He thought about his bird-boned mother at the moments when he thought she might be cooking dinner.

He thought about his brothers' archaic rage.

"If I go there, I may say that is really kind of primitive. They are really just quarreling like that is the end of the world," said Deng, in English that has loosened to near-fluency over the last year. "I will tell them, the world is wide."

This is how he celebrated the day of his arrival: Half married to the Western world, half living in a place he can barely see through memory.

But as proud adults remarked on the enormous changes he has seen in the past year—the year he first encountered the light switch and the microchip—Deng did not give America any credit for transforming him.

If he changed at all, he said, it happened long before he had even heard of America.

The great change came in one day, when he held hands with the other children and left Mareng.

"I am not like my people anymore, and I am not like the rest of the other worlds," he said.

"I am just between," he said. "I am just Deng."

Writers' Workshop

1) Reporters often write more than one story about an event or an issue. Whether it's a sewer bond issue, a court case, or the saga of "The Lost Boys of Sudan," the challenge is the same: provide the reader with enough information without bogging the story down. Ellen Barry describes her approach as "telegraphing the background in a few sentences." Compare how she varied the summary of the Sudanese exiles' tale in Parts Two through Four. What strategies does she employ? How does she handle attribution? What surprises you about the way she writes these sections?

2) In Part Three of her series, "Illusions Fade in Reality of City Life," Barry describes examples of racial animosity that the young Sudanese men encountered in their new home. In her interview she makes an argument for including more examples of the racial epithets hurled at the "lost boys"; her editors decided otherwise. Whose side would you take? To prepare for the discussion, read these two articles on Poynter's website: "An Essay on a Wickedly Powerful Word" and "Nigger: A Case Study in Using a Racial Epithet."

3) "Good ethical decision-making often means choosing alternatives that allow you to minimize harm and maximize truthtelling," says Bob Steele, Poynter's ethics group leader. In her interview, Barry describes a rape charge filed against one of the Sudanese immigrants she profiled in "The Lost Boys" and discusses the newsroom debate about whether to include that information in the series. How was the issue resolved? Do you agree with the decision? How would you have handled the situation if you were Barry or her editor?

4) Newspapers are often accused of "dumbing down," that is, writing for the lowest common denominator. On page 240 Barry describes one of the "lost boys" as "mordant." Do you think the average reader would know what that word means? Take a random survey and see how commonly understood the term is. Use your findings to discuss how news organizations should write to their audiences.

Assignment Desk

1) Barry gravitates toward stories about frontiers. Study her definition of the term on page 256. Using her yardstick, try to identify frontiers that exist in your community and write a story about one of them.

2) Builders would never lay a foundation without a blueprint in hand. Yet planning news stories—organizing information into coherent, appropriate structures—is an overlooked activity for all too many journalists. Barry uses a simple but effective ordering device: organizing her best quotes to create a story skeleton. See if you can X-ray her stories to find the skeleton of quotes. Try her approach on your next story.

3) Using the background sections in Parts Two through Four of this series as a model, report, write, and revise a background section about a running story in your community.

4) Barry is able to describe her vision for her award-winning series and the way her dream affected her reporting and writing decisions. What's your vision for the story you're working on right now? Write it down. Consider how that vision will affect the choices you make as you develop the story and have to make decisions on such things as whom you interview, how you organize your story, the details and relevant action you include, what you leave in and take out. Ask your editor to consider the same issues and discuss where you agree and disagree.

5) "The Lost Boys of Sudan" series demonstrates the value of teamwork and collaboration as a way to improve your own work. Browse the gallery of photos by photographer Bill Greene on the companion CD-ROM and read Barry's description on page 265 of the lessons she learned about reporting from her photojournalist colleague. Invite yourself as an observer on an assignment with a photographer. Answer these questions: What surprised you? What did you learn? How can you apply what you observed to your own reporting?

A conversation with
Ellen Barry

CHRISTOPHER SCANLAN: What was your job at the time you got this assignment?

ELLEN BARRY: Wandering around New England doing stories from small towns. I couldn't have conceived of a better job for me. I did a lot of weird stuff that dovetailed amazingly with what the paper was looking for. I was constantly shocked by that. I never thought of myself as a daily reporter. I mean, I'm interested in some pretty weird things, like a paralyzed girl in Worcester, who was considered a sort of Catholic miracle worker; UFO sightings in the very northern part of New England; the politics of rural New England; the sociology of small towns and how life in rural areas is different from cities. Cultural boundaries were always something that I wanted to write about.

Could you put a name to your territory, your central interests or concerns as a reporter?

I really like writing about frontiers, the different psychological conditions in sparsely populated territory, the different values of life, the different ways people look at the government. I like writing about people who leave one kind of life and come to another.

What is a frontier in your mind?

Fewer services, a weaker center, probably more natural adversity. But I also write about people on night shifts and what I consider to be a frontier, people who force themselves into uncomfortable spaces.

Did you ever study journalism formally?

I took one class with a great professor, Fred Strebeigh, who taught narrative journalism. He was a magazine writer and he did a great job of showing us methods and techniques and the way people structure stories, and we would dissect them. He taught us about rhythm in sentences and short sentences and long sentences. In that class, I started reading people who are still some of my favorite writers.

Who are those writers?

Joan Didion, Mark Singer, Tracey Kidder. I didn't adore all of those people, but I really learned. I read Anne Fadiman's *The Spirit Catches You and You Fall Down* shortly before I started this series, and I was blown away. I thought it was one of the best nonfiction pieces of journalism I had ever read.

What did you learn?

I realized that you could use a very strong personal voice in newspapers. I had grown up reading the Style section of *The Washington Post,* and I realized that you don't have to play by the rules. The best people have always been storytellers with strong voices. But it certainly gave me a lot of confidence to try it in the work force. In one of my very first assignments, I had a long excerpt of a verbatim discussion between a mail-order bride and a raunchy New Jersey broker.

Where was that first assignment?

I got a nonexistent internship at a recently defunct weekly called the *Moscow Guardian* in Russia. I arrived there to discover that all of the people who had hired me had recently decamped, stealing a car by way of back pay. I had studied Russian and I wanted to work overseas. I didn't really want to work for a local daily where I'd have to do three stories a day. I had worked for a local weekly briefly in college, and I can remember being so frustrated with the way things were supposed to be written that I would write two versions—one for myself the way I thought it should be written and the other version for the paper.

How do you read?

You learn to read stories and ask how this reporter found out this fact, what led her or him to ask this question. That's something I automatically do now: work backward and figure out the reporting process, because you don't just magically have a full notebook. People have certain things or certain types of people they gravitate to—the town clerk, the person in the back of the room. I used to read the Style section in sort of a predatory way. There were certain reporters whom I would read enough to know how they got their ideas or what kind of people they're most likely to talk to.

What was the genesis of "The Lost Boys of Sudan" series?

It was a one-day story. I went to the airport to meet a group of the young men and had some of the most interesting conversations I had ever had reporting. I was meeting Sudanese teenagers who had been here for one day, and they were both full of impressions and lacking the words to explain them. I had a conversation with a young man. I asked him what he had eaten, and he said, "They have fed us some things here in America, but I don't know what they are." I asked, "Is it a vegetable? Is it a meat?" And he said, "It's a bread, but it's very small and it's also very big." I went down every kind of bread I could think of: "Was it a croissant? Was it a muffin?" And he said, "It's very tiny and it's also very large and square." It turned out that he was referring to cereal. I think I had sparks coming off me when I left that night.

Did you file that night?

It ended up being a Sunday story, but they didn't put it on the front, and I was hopping mad because I knew I hadn't done the job that I had wanted to do. I thought this was the strangest and most magical assignment I'd ever had. You could physically see that they were seeing the industrialized world for the first time and you could be with them. They spoke this beautiful, broken, poetic English—and it was just this moment that wouldn't be duplicated. Four days later I was working on a different story, and this photographer, Bill Greene, called me up.

His editor, Catie Aldrich, was taken with the story. At that point they were thinking it would be an occasional photo project over a year showing acculturation. So this is a photo project. I just wrote the captions. Seriously.

What was your vision for the series? How did that affect your choices and decisions on such things as subjects, structure, imagery, voice?

I really wanted to sustain the magical feeling of the first story. I didn't want to write about injustice, or the travails of immigrant life, or the political overlays our readers might put onto it. What was induplicable, though, was the wonder, the way things looked from their naive point of view—to get that across without making fun of them (by the end, I called it "Refugees Say the Darnedest Things"). I couldn't try to be funny at their expense. The voice was dreamy, sometimes, too; again, I was trying to capture their experience.

You have that wonderful line about the boy "whose name refers to the gray-brown color of a favorite cow." This didn't strike me as the kind of information that's offered without prompting. How did you get that?

You would know within a few hours of meeting any of this group of guys that they have about a half-dozen names, and one of them is a cattle name that describes a valuable cow. I probably asked everyone, "What does your name mean?" I started to find out that their names meant things like "poverty"; there were a number of boys named "cold"; most of them were named after ordeals. There was a name that meant "the child before me died." I found that very moving because I think they come from a group of people who marked time by hardship, especially now.

In Part One, you write, "An older boy asserted that North Dakota is colder than Nairobi, but this was impossible to confirm. Another was enraptured with the idea of Albany, and dreamily repeated the phrase 'Albany, New York. Albany, New York,' a spot whose

distance he estimated at a million, or possibly 2 million, kilometers." And in Part Two, "He had not been informed of Communism's rise, or its fall, until that morning."

I hear something in that voice that I like very much, and I can't put a name to it.

That is sort of deadpan.

Why deadpan?

Because in a way it speaks for itself. It was terribly funny and terribly pitiful. Your sympathy just goes out to them because they're naive. Maybe a lot of people don't like immigrants, but we love naive people. I knew that there was a danger, especially as I kept writing about them, that it would seem like I was making fun of that, and the truth is that all of that naiveté is gone. These kids I quote as asking why the elevator doesn't fall underneath them—they don't say those things anymore and they never will, and it takes so precious little time to stop being amazed by the world around you. But that was just the greatest thing, to be there when they were going through that.

So you were concerned about whether you were condescending or making fun? How did you wrestle with that?

The occasional narrative series form is really a hazardous one because so much changes after each story. You're sort of coping with the Heisenberg effect every time you publish.

What's the Heisenberg effect?

You change the reality by observing it. You write a front-page story about an obscure person and their life changes, and so what you're writing about changes. And if you're doing a massive front-page series about a resettlement project, every time you write a story you're going to change the reality.

But, fortunately, we had this great experience on the first story. Not only were the young men I wrote about not at all upset by the story, the social service people and resettlement workers were really happy with the story; and there was an enormous outpouring of sympathy and aid and donations for the boys. And this not only made them trust us much more, but it also made me much less afraid, because I had fear and trembling. I knew that I liked the first story I wrote, but I had fear and trembling that this would be mortifying to vulnerable 17-year-old immigrants. But not only was that not the case, it was completely the opposite. I think that they enjoyed it, at least the first one.

You said you reconstructed some scenes, such as the ending of Part Three in the church. How do you decide if and when to reconstruct a scene that you haven't witnessed? What's your standard for using quotes and other details in a reconstruction?

That was not a very organized process. If you're following one family or one person and you miss a crucial moment, you are obliged to reconstruct it. In this case, my reporting was very scattered, and often (as with the "gate started crying" comment at the end of the first story) I got an account from one of the young men and just thought it was too good to lose. So in those situations, I interviewed as many people who had been present as possible. If I suspected that someone wasn't being honest in his account, I wouldn't use it. But a lot of times, it was more interesting to hear their version than to be there—like when they came home from the job interview and said, "Why should I tell them I will be on time every day, when I do not know whether I will be on time every day?"

Reporters covering a continuing story often have to recap background. You had to do it three times. How do you sum up a complicated story without making it read like boilerplate?

By the end, I was really telegraphing the background in a few sentences. It felt sort of moronic but I knew there were new readers. I was leaving out the suffering, the starvation, the politics of the war, the politics of the

State Department. I just tried to keep it out of the foreground.

What were the kinds of ethical dilemmas the series posed for you?

There was a rape charge that came up during the year. Do I make that part of the series? I wrote that as a metro story. Now that was a very difficult decision. I actually felt that I shouldn't because, while it could in some ways teach people something about the culture gap and what that meant, given that I'm trying to represent a large population, to make a very big emphasis on this one man seemed to me to be misleading. One of my editors really wanted that story, and I wasn't sure how I could do it fairly, given that it hadn't gotten to trial and, at this point, it was only an allegation. Bringing publicity to it was going to very clearly make the situation much worse.

In this building, we really talked it back and forth. I actually did a week of research into the legal definition of rape, into cultural argument in the courtroom. I think we made the right decision in not overplaying it. But I'm sure there are people, even among my editors, who disagree.

To whom does the reporter owe allegiance in a situation like this—the subject, a private person who would not normally be written about, or the readers?

The question is, is it fair when you're writing about obscure people who would not be in the paper, to blow something up to the proportions that we have when it's not representative of a mass experience? I thought, in the case of the rape, that it absolutely had to be reported because it's a public safety issue and because, if I spent a year writing about a resettlement and failed to mention this very serious criminal charge, it would be irresponsible of me. I just thought that I had no choice at all.

Writing about the charges against John Deng, that was much more equivocal in the sense that, first of all, it's not a very serious crime; second of all, the consequences could be dire; and third of all, publicity could absolutely alter the consequences, considering that it's a situation in which deportation is a legitimate fear, even if it's an outside fear. And so that was my worst dark night, trying to figure out how to write that story in a way that didn't blow up whatever happened inside that house.

Were there ramifications as a result?

We still don't know. I think it would be a travesty if he was deported as a result of a fistfight with his room-mate, which was one punch. But I also think that type of thing happens. I was asked to go to his hearing and speak in his defense, but my editors said, "No, you can't do that." In some ways the article speaks in his defense.

Were there racial issues that you confronted?

They took out a lot of epithets that were too nasty to put in the paper. I had a long list, a long list of horrible words—really bad stuff and they [the editors] decided not to put that in the paper, which I thought was a shame because the thing that was so piercing about that conversation is that they had no idea—the things they were saying to me, they didn't even know you aren't supposed to say them. And someone had been calling them these names and they had no idea what that indicated. You know what I mean? And for a well-meaning liberal, it's just tragic to hear that, in their first week in the United States, they would have people calling them monkeys or saying they're apes from the jungle.

Why did you put them in and why would you have preferred that they stayed in?

Because you just have this enormous pity at the idea that they will have to learn that there is racism. They have to learn that they're slotting into American society in a spot that they were not warned about, that they did not know existed. They were elite where they came from, but they're underclass here, and probably it's going to be a very, very uphill climb for them not to be underclass. And that's what I was thinking about in that whole piece, that without a superhuman focus, it would be very easy for them never to hoist themselves out of that track.

Do you think your readers would have benefited from reading that?

From reading those words? Yeah, in the sense that when I had that conversation it just broke my heart, because we're going to have to teach them about race in America. I think most Africans actually had a lot of warning about that, but these guys just had no information.

I really wanted to do that story because I thought that all those issues came up all over the country in the sense that these boys could be settled in a predominantly African-American neighborhood or could be settled in a white suburb. You know, is it more important for them to identify with African Americans or with white Americans? They had a lot of preconceptions about African Americans, and they weren't all positive. They associated America with white missionaries and with English people. They just thought people here were all going to be white. Most of their real troubles seemed to be cultural.

Are there things you've learned about that challenge that help you do the work and be sensitive?

I've learned from people I work with—like Mitch Zuckoff and other people at *The Boston Globe* whom I really admire—that it's always best to be up front. You know, don't surprise your source too much, and don't be afraid of telling them what you're really doing. In the case of John Deng, that was the most agonizing process because he was so vulnerable and I was writing about his arrest. I read it to him and that made all the difference, I think, in terms of trust between us, in terms of our continuing relationship. He didn't ask me to change anything. When I got out of college I would never have thought you'd ever read [your story to the subject]. Everyone's always going to be so upset that you shouldn't do it. But Mitch had done that with his series, and I talked to him about it. I do believe in it, especially if it's a private citizen.

Why?

I'm not certain that I would have read it to the resettlement workers, who certainly have an idea of what they want to appear, what they think is most important. John Deng is a private citizen. I'm writing about his life. He would never be on the front page if it weren't for me and, in this case, it seemed to me to be fair. There are plenty of stories I would not do that with, but I just went over to his house and I said if there's something that's not true, please stop me.

Did you read it to him aloud?

I didn't show him the text. I read it to him, and he didn't have anything that he wanted me to correct.

What did you learn from collaborating with photographer Bill Greene?

He taught me to just sit in the back of the room, to go there every day, to not be shy, to be there so much that you're not there. I was still self-conscious about asking people for liberties, and he's not at all. As a reporter, you become far too self-conscious about imposing yourself on situations or of staying too long or coming too early or coming too often. But Bill definitely taught me that it is easiest if you come consistently enough and without being embarrassed and without being self-conscious. It means every time you enter a situation, it's better. He knows if you miss a moment, you can't reconstruct it and that is the main thing I learned from working with him. Also, he had such a great, easy relationship with sources. I was the one who was always agonizing over whether we were going to lose access, or whether what I wrote was going to offend someone, or whether I was going to compromise any of my sources. Every time we printed, I thought it could get cancelled, that we could get shut out. Which was true; we could have. There were times when he was shooting and I was working on other stories, and he would call me and say what he'd seen. He absolutely contributed to my reporting, probably more than I contributed to his shooting.

Did you work with a particular editor on the series?

I filed to Steven Heuser, an editor from the *Boston*

Phoenix who is now at the *Globe*. John Yemma, the projects editor, stewarded the whole thing.

What was the role of the editor in this?

Steven just tried to sedate me the entire year. He said if there was a prize for worrying about a story, I would get it. I trusted his judgment about line editing and a lot of the planning was very solitary, and I would yap at him for hours and hours, and he would sit there nodding like an oracle.

What was his greatest contribution in your mind?

Working on something by yourself for a year, in which you're sacrificing a lot of things for it, turns out to be very hard. I guess it would be like writing a book, which I hope some day I'll do. You're not on the starting rotation anymore, and I sometimes felt like the people who sat next to me must have thought I didn't have a job, and I was off the front page. I was trying to do a Sunday story every week and I just disappeared in some ways. So it was incredibly important to have a few people in the newsroom who were with me, and he was always on my side.

I want to talk about your writing process. How do you get story ideas?

It sort of depends on the job, but a lot of times in my old job (at the *Boston Phoenix*) I used to get them from the Yellow Pages. I used to have to do these profiles with alarming frequency—a 700- to 800-word feature every other week. I must have been stuck on the B's because I did baby models and bronze baby shoe salesmen and baby modeling agencies.

How do you fatten your notebook?

I am trying to teach myself to describe how someone looked, actually writing down descriptive text. Some people have just such an incredible talent for that, and I don't really, but I am working on it. My attention tends to be caught by phrases or the way people talk. This whole series is completely fueled by the way of talking of people who have a somewhat archaic, somewhat biblical vocabulary.

What's your process after you've come back with a fat notebook?

Mitch Zuckoff had done the "Choosing Naia" series two years before (*Best Newspaper Writing 2000*) and he really helped me with the process. The most important thing, I think, was his advice to empty my notebook after every single day of reporting, then compile a big binder of notes for use when I was ready to write. That binder was my salvation; there is no way I could have retained the detail I needed without it. It also meant that my work was spread out evenly, that I was extremely familiar with my notes.

Then I look through my notebooks. I figure out the things that you come back and tell your family, the things you have repeated 10 or 12 times and seen people react to. When I sit down, the first thing I do is transcribe all the best quotes. In most of these stories, I built the whole thing around either quotes or anecdotes. I know what the top is going to be; I usually know what the bottom is going to be. I know I'm in trouble if I don't know those things before I sit down. Then I use the quotes that I think are going to be turning points or important hinges, and I build it starting from that as a skeleton.

What else do you have to know?

I have to know that I have enough. If you're sparse on reporting and you sit down to write, then you're inventing.

How do you know when you have enough?

You don't. You definitely know when you're scraping by.

When you have so much material, what governs the decisions on what stays, what goes?

You don't want to overdo. I could have put in twice as many little moments such as Bol Thiik saying, "The gate started crying." But you devalue them if you load too many of them. You want to use a few things that people will really remember. So you end up tossing a lot of babies off the sled.

Was it very painful to leave things out?

No. I'd love to spend five years on it and, yeah, I have a drawer full of stuff, tapes that I never transcribed, notebooks I haven't read through since I wrote them. I have a huge amount of stuff that I didn't use.

How do you overcome that hurdle?

I just think you learn timing and you learn how to set things effectively, strategically. You just don't want to overload the best moments. If you have a line like that beautiful note that's at the end of Part Two, "Do not worry about me a lot, but I will always be the first one to worry about you," you want that to be suspended at the end of the story so people will never forget it, that they'll be as affected as I was when I first heard it. There are probably beautiful things from that same conversation I could have used, but you just want to show off that one line to its best advantage.

When you visit journalism classes, what do you tell them about quotes?

I feel so strongly that, in general, the best line should not be yours. I'm not sure that most newspaper writers pay enough attention to that. The idea that the moral to the story should not be in your mouth, it should be in someone else's. That's when I feel most satisfied. If you talk to people long enough, they'll say something that's much better than you could have come up with, because it was about their experience and because they had the ability to express it and because they spoke very well.

What was the low point of the series, and how did you get past it?

The worst part was actually around Sept. 11, when I was

waiting for approval for Part Four. Working on something like this for a year means you take yourself out of
rotation and delay gratification, something I had done
joyfully and gratefully. But Sept. 11 just made me want
to be back in the lineup. My friends were all rushing off
to New York. At that point our editors were not as invested in "The Lost Boys," for reasons I could understand,
but I had such a fire in the belly about the project—I believed in it so much—and I felt like it might have been
the wrong year to sequester myself.

I got past it by throwing up my hands and taking other assignments. Actually I went to Afghanistan, on the
condition that I had a month upon my return to finish the
story. In the end, I was very lucky that the editors here
took a leap of faith and sent me and Bill to Sudan.

**What was the most important lesson you learned
from reporting and writing "The Lost Boys of Sudan"?**

Your most important tool is your own enthusiasm and
the trust of your editors. Institutional support, great
planning, the advice of editors, etc., are all vital, but
there are times when you're going to be on your own.
It's your risk. It's your responsibility.

David Finkel

Finalist, Non-Deadline Writing

David Finkel has been a staff writer at *The Washington Post* since 1990, working on the national, magazine, and foreign staffs.

A native of Reading, Pa., Finkel joined the *Post* after spending nine years at the *St. Petersburg Times*, where he was a general assignment reporter. A 1977 graduate of the University of Florida, he began his newspaper career in 1978 at the *Tallahassee Democrat* where he covered, among other things, the Ted Bundy serial murder case.

At the *Post*, his assignments have taken him to Afghanistan, Pakistan, sub-Saharan Africa, Kosovo, and across the United States. He makes his fourth appearance in *Best Newspaper Writing*, having shared the prize for distinguished writing in 1986 and appeared as a finalist in 1988 and 2000. Finkel is married, has two daughters, and lives in Silver Spring, Md.

In "The Road of Last Resort," Finkel launches a multipart narrative that surges, stops, shivers, and chokes along with the refugees ever moving toward a place that is surely better than where they are. He journeys with refugees through Afghanistan to a Pakistan border gate where, amid caked dirt and hungry children, frustration meets desperation, with only more of the same waiting on the other side of the fence.

The road of last resort

MARCH 18, 2001

TORKHAM, Afghanistan—He is standing unsteadily on the eastern edge of Afghanistan, a hollowed man with an unbuttoned coat, a torn wool cap and dust-coated eyebrows. Dead fields. Dead crops. Dead animals. A dead village. That's where he has come from. He ran out of money. Then he ran out of food. That's why he is here. He left nine days before. He spent the first day walking, and the next eight squeezed into vans that took him past more dead fields, more dying animals, more dying villages. And now it is down to this for 30-year-old Abdul Qahar: a final journey of 200 yards.

"Pakistan," he is saying of what's ahead.

There will be work. Or at least food. Or at least water. There will be help.

All he has to do is cross the border.

Just moments out of the van, he begins walking, still too far away to see what awaits him. He can't see the solid metal gate blocking most of the roadway. He can't see the hundreds of people like him—without proper documents, without money for bribes, without any possessions other than their filthy clothes—who are surging toward the small opening, trying to press their way across. He can't see the Pakistani border guards who are waiting with wooden sticks and instructions to let no more undocumented refugees through. He can't hear the sounds of people being hit, hard, and he can't see the flinches and retreats.

What he can see: He is almost, almost there.

"I'm desperate. I can't think. I don't know where I'm going," he says and steps forward into the crowd.

* * *

Each day, step by invisible step, the population of the world is shifting.

Just as one man, on one day, is trying to find his way out of Afghanistan, so are a vast number of other people on similar journeys, all over the world, in swelling numbers, motivated by fear of war, hunger's ache, the need for a little money, the desire for a lot.

How many people are on the move at a particular moment no one can precisely say, but over a year's time the number is in the tens of millions. There are, at the moment, an estimated 12 million refugees around the world, and another 25 million people who are displaced within their own countries by conflict, and tens of millions who leave one life behind for a new one, crossing borders however they can. They are being smuggled out of China, or being trafficked out of Africa, or crossing the Rio Grande, or floating amid cattle herds across the Zambezi River to shield themselves from gunfire, or traversing the Strait of Gibraltar in rubber rafts even though an estimated 3,500 people have died doing that in the past decade.

The journeys take days, weeks or longer. Success means arriving unnoticed. Failure comes in the form of visibility, such as when 910 dazed Iraqi Kurds end up on the French Riviera after the decrepit freighter smuggling them in is run aground. Or when 58 Chinese are found in England, suffocated in the back of a truck that was supposed to be carrying tomatoes. Or when 150 people, most of them children and women, freeze to death after having arrived in an Afghan refugee camp.

Those journeys, the visible ones, which is to say the failed ones, are what make headlines, reminding the world that such journeys are taking place. But the invisible ones, which is to say the successful ones, or the ones whose outcomes are not yet certain, are also transforming.

What can a journey mean? What is it to be such a person?

For the most desperate, the ones who aren't heading toward something good as much as away from something unbearable, the journey, in its origins and execution, can be a matter of life and death. And no place was more extravagant in its desperation in the early months of the year than this one: Afghanistan.

It is a broken place from border to border, where the worst drought in memory has left 22 million people increasingly desperate, and two decades of war have left the country in ruins, and the extremist policies of its Taliban rulers—no music, no TV, no cleanshaven men, no

schooling for women, no cliff-size statues of Buddha—
have left it ever more isolated from the rest of the world.

So bad has the situation become that in the past year
700,000 Afghans have abandoned their homes and begun journeys like Abdul Qahar's, a number so large that
at times the country has seemed stitched with lines of
fleeing people, a place entirely on the move.

BUILDUP TO A CRISIS

A Taliban checkpoint: men in black turbans and black
eyeliner and shouldered rifles, a dead sticker bush fes-
tooned with fluttering ribbons of confiscated cassette
tapes, a chain across the road slowly lowered.

Then nothing.

A dead-looking village.

Then nothing.

A broken bridge and a detour across a dry riverbed.

Then nothing.

A few sheep. A few camels. A few nomads.

Then nothing. Nothing. Nothing. Nothing.

This is the landscape of southern Afghanistan, the
part of the country to first feel the drought. It is where
the mountains that define so much of Afghanistan flat-
ten into plains, and the plains turn into desert, and the
desert gives way to shriveled grazing land, and dying
orchards, and vanished rivers, and wells that no longer
reach water.

"Critical. Worse and going to worst, by the day," is
how Fayyaz Shah, who runs the World Food Program's
office in the southern provincial capital of Kandahar,
describes the situation. "I mean the people are going
backward and backward. In some villages, you come
across children—I'm sorry to use this word, they're acting like animals. They want food. That's it. That's all
their life is. The search for food."

It has been building to this point for three years. The
first signs of impending crisis began showing up here in
the form of endlessly clear skies and lowering water
tables. Month by month things only grew worse. In 1999,
a prediction that 60 percent of the harvest would be lost
turned out to be optimistic. By spring of 2000, people had
begun to leave. By summer came the eerie sight of a long-
lost Soviet helicopter, the crew's skeletons still inside,

exposed when, after a decade, the 130-foot-deep lake it had crashed into went completely dry. By last fall, truck convoys were dispatched deep into the Rigestan Desert in search of 25,000 nomadic families living in small riverbank encampments, whose water sources were gone, whose animals were dying, who were stranded and in grave danger of dying as well.

One by one, out came the families, in the backs of trucks, or hanging onto the sides, or seated on top, or, in a few urgent cases, brought out by helicopter. The drought was now firmly in place throughout Afghanistan and journeys toward every border were under way. The numbers kept increasing and soon grew to include the rescued of southern Afghanistan, who came to Kandahar, regained their strength and pushed south toward Pakistan.

Months later, perhaps half are gone. Maybe they're in Pakistan, Shah says, or maybe they found a way to cross into Iran, or maybe they're encamped somewhere in the southern dunes. His concern of the moment is no longer them as much as the other half, the 14,000 families still in the vicinity of Kandahar, who are living in conditions that are growing more desperate by the day.

In a place called Talacon, for instance, which is 20 miles outside of Kandahar, 1,600 families are stuck on a remote patch of land that doesn't even qualify as a formal encampment. It's just a place with groupings of tents here and there, not even tents, really, but dead willow branches supporting pieces of torn cloth, appearing from a distance like wind-blown litter ensnared in the brush.

There is no drinkable water here other than what puddles up out of a small spring. There is no medical help. There is no food other than the wheat sacks that the World Food Program brings once a month. There are no latrines. There is no heat on sub-freezing winter nights except from whatever brush can be built into fire. There are only people, filthy and needy, who have nowhere else to be.

"I used to beg," says a woman who lives in one of the tents, a widow with eight children, describing what life was like before this place, starting to cry simply because someone is taking a moment to listen to her. "Now I can't even beg."

"I feel cold, all the time," says the woman in the next tent, whose name is Gul Maida, who came here four months ago, and gave birth to twins in the tent three months ago, and is feeding them spoonfuls of dirty water because she is too weak to produce milk. One is wrapped in a green cloth, the other in brown. "I haven't named them yet," she says.

"'If you're desperate, there's a place for you,'" is what the man in the next tent, Mohammed Essa, says he was told, explaining how he ended up here. He had just arrived in Kandahar with his wife and two sons after begging their way onto trucks for nearly a week, and was standing lost in a market, wondering what to do next. So he came here, and 25 days later, he says he thinks he is going to die.

"Can't you see?" he says, showing how thin he is. "Isn't the cold killing me? Isn't the hunger killing me?"

He holds out his hands. They are encased in thick dirt. He points to his wife, who is both deaf and mute and looks back at him with a frightened expression. He shows what he owns in the world, some blankets and a pot. He points to his sons, one 8, the other 6.

"I want to leave this place," he says.

"Pakistan," he says of where he wants to be.

"Tell me," he says. "How do I go?"

'UNBELIEVABLE MISERY'

It is a question being asked not only in Talacon, but in western Afghanistan as well, by people whose journeys have brought them as far as a flat, treeless, useless, windswept patch of dried-up dirt. This is the place where 150 people, mostly children and women, froze to death in the course of a few nights in late January, and where a few weeks after that a convoy of cars approaches and rolls to a stop.

Years ago, this was the site of an animal slaughterhouse. Now it holds tens of thousands of miserable people who had hoped to make their way into Iran but are stuck instead inside of Afghanistan in a camp near the city of Herat, watching a man named Kenzo Oshima step out of one of the cars.

Oshima is the U.N. undersecretary for humanitarian

affairs and emergency relief, who has been dispatched to officially look around. There is a kind of script to these visits, and Oshima follows it for the next hour.

Here are the children lined up for their daily bowl of high-protein porridge. Here are men carrying 110-pound sacks of wheat on their backs to their tents. Here, at this tent, is a man in torn slippers talking about the slow death of his animals. Here, at the next tent, comes the sound of a child's wet cough. Here, at the next, is a woman hunched over trying to build a fire from a few bits of brush, whose child was one of the 150 who froze, who is the only one not to turn away when a gust blows dirt into hair, into mouths, into eyes.

"I saw a sea of people living in unbelievable misery," Oshima will say after his visit.

He will say this in the course of issuing an urgent appeal for help so that money can be shaken loose from governments that have "donor fatigue," which is a polite way of describing how weary the world has become of Afghanistan's never-ending struggles: the ascent of the Islamic fundamentalist Taliban, which now controls 90 percent of Afghanistan and is fighting for the remainder; before that the daily atrocities of a civil war; before that the 10-year Soviet occupation. "We believe at least 1 million people are at risk of famine," Oshima will go on, trying to shift attention away from the Taliban and back to those suffering, saying they will need at least $250 million to survive. Meanwhile, people across Afghanistan are begging for whatever they can get.

Once begging was rare in Afghanistan; now it is commonplace. South out of Herat the road is lined with children who spend their days throwing handfuls of dirt into potholes whenever a car approaches, hoping that whoever drives by will toss them some money. North, on the road to Turkmenistan, it is even more bleak: brown land, no other color at all, and no people either except for the occasional person who can be seen hacking runty bushes out of the ground, which he will then drag to the side of the road, hoping someone in need of kindling will give him some money.

Not that there's no chance at all. Not that no one has money. Northeast of Herat, toward Uzbekistan, in the town of Karukh, inside a dingy hotel, a truck driver named Ghulam Sarwar is taking a break and eating lunch as he nears the end of a three-day trip. Normally his load would be wheat. But of course there is no wheat, so his load this day is 35 men who had walked from their village to a truck stop, where they flagged him down and said they were willing to hand over the money they'd gotten from selling what remained of their livestock in exchange for transport to Herat.

"They don't even have money to eat," Sarwar says, shrugging, "so I'm eating, and they're outside." And there they are, in the back of his truck, packed so tightly that no one is moving except for a man who reaches into his pocket and takes out the one possession he has brought with him.

It is a handkerchief. But what it really is is a love letter because that's what love letters are in a place where girls are prohibited from going to school and the female illiteracy rate is estimated at above 85 percent. Maybe a woman can't write what she feels, but she can embroider, and that's what this man has brought, his love letter, white as bridal linen and embroidered with red flowers, which he uses to wipe his eyes while he waits for the truck driver to finish lunch, so he can be taken to Herat, where he hopes to find work, where there is no work to be found, where everyone eventually ends up at the slaughterhouse.

Maslakh. That's the word in Afghanistan for slaughterhouse, and that's the name of the camp, and that's where, two days after Oshima's visit, there is another death.

"A child," says Noor Ali, one of the Taliban who oversees Maslakh, just a few hours after the child was buried. "He got trampled, under the crowd." And before he can finish explaining how such a thing happened, it becomes apparent when another car comes into the camp.

In the car are three men who have come to distribute a few piles of clothing. They are men with charitable intentions, in other words, but as soon as they stop, the car is surrounded by dozens of people, and then very quickly hundreds, who press in, looking, now touching, now trying to get the doors open. Now the driver is panicking. Now he's trying to back up. Now he's inching forward. Now he's picking up speed. Now he's trying to shake off the pursuing crowd by veering off the road, but still they follow, and now he is speeding through a field that has been turned into a bathroom for tens of thousands of people and is covered in feces, and still they follow, and now he is racing past the graves. And now, without stopping, without slowing, he is throwing the clothing out of the car.

The crowd descends. Noor Ali watches. So does Hans-Christian Poulson, who oversees the U.N. humanitarian operation in Herat. "Just for a few rags, a boy is dead?" Poulson says quietly to Ali. They keep watching. A fight breaks out. There's nothing much they can do. Here comes another car.

"It's undignified to make the crowd run around like beggars," Poulson says.

This time it's a fistful of money, tossed into the air.

"They are not beggars," he says.

Here comes the crowd.

GETTING TO THE GATE

If he'd wanted to, Abdul Qahar could have journeyed to Maslakh. His home is in north-central Afghanistan, up in the deep snows where there is intense fighting between the Taliban and several opposing factions, and where it's just as difficult to go in one direction as another.

His decision, though, was to go east, to a crossing into Pakistan called the Torkham gate, which is the spot where more people have crossed out of Afghanistan than anywhere else: millions fleeing the Soviet occupation, tens of thousands since last fall, and now one more, who has no idea of what's just ahead.

"I'm happy," Qahar is saying, now perhaps 100 yards from the gate.

What he doesn't know, not yet, is that last November Pakistan began severely limiting the hours the gate would be open and restricting the influx of refugees to only those with valid documents, saying it couldn't cope with the numbers of destitute people coming across.

"I'll find something to eat," Qahar says.

More than a million Afghan refugees remain in Pakistan from the last big exodus, during the Soviet era.

They have taken jobs, says Abdul Hafeez, a Pakistani official in charge of refugees. They don't pay taxes. They wreck the roads. They cut down the trees. They use up the water. "No," Hafeez says, "we don't want any more."

"I'll find work," says Qahar, who comes from a place where there is no TV or newspaper and where radio signals are no match for the mountains, who simply followed word of mouth from the mountains down to Kabul, and then east on the decaying road to Jalalabad, and then all the way east to the Torkham gate. "Anywhere I can find work I'm willing to go," he continues.

And moments later he comes to a stop.

As would anyone seeing this place close-up for the first time.

There is the gate, just up ahead, but it is open only a sliver, which has things in turmoil: a long line of trucks with blaring bird-whistle horns, men in turbans and ripped shoes, women covered in head-to-toe *burqas*, children everywhere, minibuses disgorging more people, now a wailing ambulance at the back of the line — all trying to get through the sliver. This is what Qahar finds himself in the midst of. It is dust and truck exhaust and shouting and the drumroll of footsteps under everything else, and the closer Qahar gets, working his way toward the front of the pressing crowd, the more the chaos increases.

Because most people, he is beginning to understand, aren't getting across. They try, and then they try again, and then they become the men standing slightly to either side of the gate, up against barbed wire, six inches from Pakistan, which might as well be back in the mountains.

"Four days," says one man, of how long he has been here.

"Nine days," says another.

Trying. Failing. Trying. Failing. This is what they are doing, the men say, because what else is there? They say they stay near the gate until it closes, and then they find somewhere to sleep, and then they start another day. There are scores of such men. All seemingly the same. But in fact some of the faces change from day to day because people tend to retreat after a while and find other ways across.

One route: north of Torkham, and over the unguarded wilderness that defines so much of the 1,400-mile-long border between Afghanistan and Pakistan. The problem with that, though, is the Pakistan side is controlled by tribal factions and there is a history of robbery, of assaults, of murders, of viciousness.

Another route: farther north, through the mountains. But that is a journey of weeks, on foot, through deep snow, over dangerous passes, also leading to tribal lands.

Another: a road between Jalalabad and the border, less a road, actually, than tire tracks leading up the barren hills. It is a smuggling route for trucks carrying loads bound from Iran through Afghanistan to Pakistan. TVs. Tires. Air conditioners. Refrigerators. They are taken as far as the trucks can go, where they are then offloaded into a village of warehouses, where they are strapped onto donkeys and camels. A camel can hold six tires, say the men who run the warehouses, a donkey four; the rest of the trip is a seven-hour walk; the traffic is steady; refugees aren't welcome.

The option of choice, then: Torkham—at least until people find out what Abdul Qahar is finding out now.

"They won't let me go," he says.

It has taken him nine days to get here. He has eaten only bread. He is hungry. He is thirsty. He is exhausted. He has no idea what to do next. It's 3:25 in the afternoon.

The gate closes at 5.

"What can I do?" he says.

Four o'clock.

Back on the Pakistani side. A border guard is hitting a man so hard to drive him back into Afghanistan that dust from his clothing flies into the air. Now a guard is driving another man back by slapping him in the head. Now another guard is swinging a stick at a man who is charging through carrying a crying little girl. Now another guard is grabbing a teenage boy by the ear and twisting it so hard the boy sinks to his knees.

Back on the Afghanistan side. Qahar has retreated.

4:57: The gate starts to close. People rush. Sticks swing. People fall, get up, rush, are hit, fall again.

4:59: Closed. Chained. Locked.

Five o'clock: Qahar has not made it through. Neither have the ones who are looking over the top of the gate to the other side. They see a wide-open road leading to food, to water, to money, to work, to whatever. To everything.

They see a sign. "Welcome to Pakistan," it says.

AND THEN PAKISTAN

Pakistan: where there are roads and telephones and TVs and computers and Coca-Cola and Sony and Mc-Donald's and a man named Amiruddin Deen, who is the newest arrival in this place of abundance.

Drought, he says, telling the familiar story. Money gone, food gone, fighting, snow, three days on a bus, a detour in Jalalabad when he heard about the Torkham gate, a walk through the hills, and, at long last, finally, here.

He looks around.

"I've never seen such a place," he says.

Its name is Jalozai. It is just south of the city of Peshawar. It is 80,000 people, all from Afghanistan, ones who made it across.

"Tie it tighter," one of them says now to Deen.

They are tying pieces of wood together, three pieces in all, two that have been stuck in the ground and one as a crossbar.

Now they are draping a piece of pink plastic over the wood.

Now they are spreading the plastic out into a triangle and weighing the edges down with rocks.

And now Deen is crawling into his new home.

It isn't even a tent, like in Maslakh.

It isn't even a piece of cloth, like in Talacon.

It's just a plastic covering over a patch of useless dirt, which is in a useless field, which over the past few months has been turned into a home for people with nowhere else to go. It's not even an official refugee camp because the Pakistani government, worried that 80,000 will be just the beginning, will allow nothing that would suggest acceptance. It will not allow humanitarian organizations to bring tents. It will allow only water that's trucked in. It will allow only skeletal medical help. It will allow the U.N. refugee agency only occasional access. It won't allow the World Food Program in at all, meaning there is no dependable source of food.

"Everything," says a neighbor of Deen's, when asked what he needs.

"Everything," says another.

"Everything," says another.

"A hellhole," is how Yusuf Hassan, a spokesman for the U.N. refugee agency, describes Jalozai. "Jalozai," he goes on, "is turning into a death camp"—and indeed there have been deaths: In January dozens died from exposure; in February, from various illnesses; in March, on the day Deen arrived, they were burying a child who'd been bitten by a snake.

This, then, is where Deen has come to.

And where Abdul Qahar, who knows no better, is hoping to get to.

And where 80,000 journeys have led.

How do such journeys begin?

"You have patience until the day comes when you know you can't survive," says Ghulam Mohammad, who has been in Jalozai for 45 days. "You close your eyes and say, 'Let's get out of here.' That's what you decide."

How do such journeys end?

That's what Deen is wondering as he looks around in bewilderment. Red-eyed and weary and with no idea of how he will survive, and how his wife will survive, and how his three children will survive, he is already thinking about his next journey, to the place he wishes to be most of all.

"My home," he says.

Back, somehow, to Afghanistan.

Lessons Learned

BY DAVID FINKEL

This isn't the easiest story from which to suggest lessons because the reporting of it was such a singular experience. The idea for the story was simple enough: write about the enormous topic of global migration by finding people making migrations, going along with them, and chronicling the narratives of their journeys. Next, to taper an idea that could be done on six continents in hundreds of ways into manageable form, we decided to do a series of stories that would evolve as a chain—wherever one ended, the next would begin; in effect creating a journey of journeys. We also decided that for this to work, the series should build forward from a starting point of the worst place in the world, and that's why this story took me to Afghanistan.

So much for simple. So much for manageable.

My plan was to follow a single family as it crossed from eastern Afghanistan into western Pakistan. Because of difficulties obtaining a visa, I ended up on a plane that took me to western Afghanistan, a turn of events that caused me to adjust my reporting from a piece featuring a single family to one involving many people in many places. I think this broader view ultimately helped the piece, but at the time, realizing I had lost my organizing frame, I remember feeling a building sense of failure, that I had traveled a long way to do a story I was now not going to be able to do. Two gloomy days later, I began to see the possibilities in the new approach.

I needed to know whether the man I highlight in the lead of the piece made it from Afghanistan into Pakistan, but the Taliban didn't want me hanging around the Afghanistan side of the border crossing, and the Pakistanis weren't too keen on my hanging around their side, either. Finally, the Pakistanis agreed to let me remain until the gate closed for the day. But then came total weirdness: Insistently hospitable, the Pakistani soldiers brought me a chair to sit on and tea to sip, and there I sat and sipped under their watchful eyes while, a few feet away, surging refugees were being slapped, clubbed, and beaten back into Afghanistan.

The fixer/interpreter I hired to navigate me safely through Afghanistan ditched me at the last second because CNN was willing to pay him much more than I could. He gave me as a replacement his brother—who, in spite of assurances otherwise, had never been a fixer or an interpreter and didn't have much interest in being one. I remember the drive to Talacon: The whole way there, I did role-playing with him, trying to teach an increasingly resentful man the basics for interpreting what he was about to encounter.

And then…he saw it. And in his reaction to these invisible people—"I didn't know this existed," is how he put it later, after he had managed to stop crying—is the lesson to be gotten from this piece. It's not a lesson about the mechanics of what we do—every story requires adjustment, just as every story has its weirdnesses and version of bad translators. Neither is it about technique—anyone who reads and studies narrative journalism knows the importance of observation, scene, and authenticating details. All are present in this piece, but so are what I will always think of as flawed sentences, imperfect transitions, and organizing decisions to be eternally second-guessed. So why dwell on those?

But I also see when I re-read the piece a hard-fought attempt at the mission we all share, which has to do with being a witness to present-tense life, and that's where the lesson resides. One rainy day in the worst place in the world, I got to meet a man whose only possession to ground him on a wretched journey between here and there was a love letter in the form of a perfectly white handkerchief. I feel honored to have seen him. I take some pride in asking about the handkerchief's meaning rather than assuming it wasn't a question worth asking, and, to repeat a word, I feel honored to have written about him and given him some visibility. Maybe he matters, maybe he doesn't. I think he does, and that's the lesson I'm comfortable drawing from this piece, and I'm certain can be drawn from every other piece in this book as well. It matters, what we do. To go, to see, to witness, to feel, and to pass it on, that's a decent thing. And if there's no lesson in that, at the least, there is a reminder.

Dexter Filkins

Finalist, Non-Deadline Writing

Dexter Filkins crossed the Tajik border into Afghanistan in early October and has stayed throughout the war, reporting for *The New York Times* on the human drama unfolding amid air raids and ground assaults.

He was a finalist for a 2002 Pulitzer Prize for his international reporting. Before covering the war, Filkins was the New Delhi bureau chief for the *Los Angeles Times*, covering the subcontinent for three years. He was a reporter for *The Miami Herald* from 1987 to 1995 and started in the *Herald*'s West Palm Beach bureau. He has a master's degree in international relations from Oxford University and a bachelor's degree in political science from the University of Florida. He grew up in Cape Canaveral, Fla.

His writing in Afghanistan delves deeply into the rugged, barren world of war and the people pulled inexorably into its destructive vortex. It shines a lyrical, personalizing light on the faces of men and boys fighting against and for the Taliban, helping readers see the sometimes-invisible difference between those deeply committed to a cause and those hard-pressed to explain how they came to be in such a desperate place.

That is the story in "After Defeat, Journey to Uncertain Fate," a raw, discomfiting snapshot of the moments between surrender in a brutal war and the ominous future awaiting a truckload of prisoners.

After defeat, journey to uncertain fate

NOVEMBER 28, 2001

KHULM, Afghanistan, Nov. 27—Like some lost caravan, the trucks rumbled across the steppe bearing their wretched cargo, 800 Taliban prisoners bound for an uncertain fate.

The prisoners, crawling and writhing on one another like turtles in a pet shop, were the sorry byproduct of the Northern Alliance's most recent victory. Until Monday, the Taliban soldiers had been hunkered down in the northern city of Kunduz, and when the Northern Alliance laid siege to the place for the last two weeks, the Taliban troops faced the choice of surrendering or fighting to the death. First they retreated, then they gave up.

It was a defeated army this, all rags and filth and lowered heads. Flies swarmed around men with matted hair, and fights broke out in the tangle of bodies for the tiny corners of space. The air around the trucks reeked so powerfully that the guards wrapped their faces with their scarves before they approached.

Some of the prisoners, the still unbroken ones, were bound, and some were bound to each other, lest they jump from the trucks. The rest were suspended in their misery by the threat of Kalashnikovs.

"Terrorists and invaders, come to ruin our country," huffed Agha Muhammad, the chief alliance guard, walking down the line of trucks with a walkie-talkie and a long stick. "I wonder what they are thinking now."

The prisoners had come to this spot, a way station in the parched vastness of northern Afghanistan, to wait for some word on their final destination.

They had run out of Kunduz toward the west as the Northern Alliance rolled in from the east, and it was their misfortune that another anti-Taliban warlord, Abdul Rashid Dostum, was waiting for them as they came out.

Because these Taliban were foreigners, mostly illiterate young men from Pakistan, they were not being allowed to return to their homes—unlike the Taliban from Afghanistan. The future of the foreign prisoners is murky, with

Northern Alliance commanders bickering over whether they should be tried and executed or turned over to the United Nations.

General Dostum captured and disarmed this group on Monday, and sent them toward his base at Mazar-i-Sharif. But as he did so, another group of Taliban prisoners was mounting a violent uprising in the fort, at Qala Jangi, where he had intended to send them. Suddenly, Qala Jangi was out of the question, and so the 14 truckfuls of prisoners had come here to wait.

Recent Afghan history is not encouraging when it comes to the fate of such large numbers of prisoners. For example, the northern city of Mazar-i-Sharif has been the scene of two massacres over the last five years as it has changed hands between the Taliban and their rivals.

In the weeks leading up to the Taliban's collapse, Northern Alliance troops often spoke of the hordes of foreign soldiers who they maintained were arrayed against them. The phrase "Arabs, Chechens and Pakistanis" was uttered so often that it seemed to have been drilled into the mind of every alliance soldier. Yet few independent observers had ever seen many foreign soldiers outside of Northern Alliance jails.

Here, in the desert, was a large group of foreign fighters the likes of which the Northern Alliance had talked about for so long. The guards described the prisoners as "Arab, Chechen and Pakistani" but in fact the group appeared to be almost entirely from Pakistan.

With Kunduz now under its control, the Northern Alliance appeared to be giving these prisoners all the consideration it might afford a pile of spent bullets. The trucks sat motionless in a row next to the road, with the prisoners remaining inside them. The guards, bored by the inactivity, threw large stones at any prisoner who allowed an arm or foot to drape over the side.

Some of the feet were bare.

"Water!" cried the men, who talked in Urdu, Punjabi and Pashto, the languages of Pakistan. They gestured to the guards, their hands motioning up and down toward their mouths, as if dipping into a well.

"Water!"

The guards lazily tossed up a few jugs where hundreds were needed, those that went up setting off more squabbles and lurches of the human scrum. When the guards walked away, the men in the trucks quietly sent word that they had not eaten or drunk since they had surrendered.

They had not been allowed to leave the truck to relieve themselves since they left Chardara, the village outside of Kunduz where they had surrendered several hours before.

After some haggling, the guards agreed to allow one prisoner to speak. His name was Muhammad Tadamia, age 30, and he stood before a Western reporter a filthy and confused man. The ride from Kunduz had caked his hair and skin in dust. He had lost a shoe somewhere inside the truck, and he cracked his knuckles over and over as he spoke.

Mr. Tadamia said he was living in Karachi, the Pakistani port city about 800 miles away, when he was inspired by a call from an Islamic leader, a man he recalled as "Mullah Brother," to go north to fight in the jihad against nonbelievers. So Mr. Tadamia, who said he could not read or write, went north to Kunduz, marching out of his home country three months ago with several hundred of his Pakistani brethren.

Describing this, Mr. Tadamaia marched in place in front of the trucks, and dozens of his comrades laughed and guffawed.

"I am just a Talib," Mr. Tadamia said, marching in place. "I am just a Talib."

Mr. Tadamia said he was not sure why his army had surrendered, only that he had been ordered to do so by the senior Taliban leaders in Kunduz, Mullah Fazel and Mullah Dadullah. The American bombing had been terrifying, he said, and he figured that that had something to do with it.

Mr. Tadamia said the Northern Alliance troops had treated him well so far, but as he spoke his eyes wandered to Mr. Muhammad, the guard standing within earshot.

When the interview was finished and the guards prepared to lead Mr. Tadamia back into the truck, he was asked if he intended to fight again. Mr. Tadamia shook his head and did not wait to answer.

"I will never fight in the name of jihad again," he said.

As he walked back to the giant truck that held his comrades, Mr. Muhammad, the guard, picked up a large stone and hurled it into Mr. Tadamia's back.

Lessons Learned

BY DEXTER FILKINS

For much of the time that I covered the war in Afghanistan, I felt like an undersized quarterback running for my life, hounded by 300-pound linemen with bad intentions. I was always out of time, always exhausted, never comprehending. Yet what a thrill it was. There is a line from *Moby-Dick* that goes, "The great flood-gates of the wonder-world swung open." So it was in Afghanistan, a land of camels, boulders as big as skyscrapers, soldiers with eyeliner. I'll never forget those crazy days. Here, at risk of reducing the anarchy to a flash card, are a few of the things I learned there.

■ **It's not about brains, it's about stamina.** Covering a war in a Third World country is an exhausting enterprise. Every road is a swamp, no one speaks English, and there are no press releases. Staying awake and alert day in, day out, was the toughest challenge I faced. Twenty-hour days were routine, for weeks on end. Advice: Train for a marathon.

■ **Think like a camera.** War is an extraordinarily visual event. Armies move; people die. If you are fortunate enough to see such things, throw out the language of throw-weights and weapons systems. Take readers to the front with you. Show them what you see. Six months later, all I remember are the images: the contrails of the B-52s, the Pakistani prisoner with one shoe, the charcoal that lined the eyes of every Taliban soldier.

■ **Don't take too many notes.** You're not at a city council meeting. War, by its nature, does not lend itself to neat, categorical descriptions; it's chaos. Better to look, feel, and smell. Sit on the hill and watch the bombers. Run your hand along the caked mud of the Taliban pickup. Pull the blanket back and look into the corpse's eyes. Then close your notebook and write. Think about what you saw. Keep the notebook closed, and write some more.

I learned this lesson writing the piece featured in this book. I had not counted on finding those prisoners in the middle of the steppe and, finding them, I was too exhausted to take more than a page of notes. But it was such an unforgettable thing to witness, these filthy men herded into trucks, and I think the dearth of facts worked in my favor. Lacking notes, I wondered: Who are these people? How did they get here? Where are they going? The images kept flooding my mind and, lacking anything else to write about, I wrote about them.

■ **War is not about tanks, or guns, or even about who wins. It's about people.** The central fact of war, or about any cataclysmic event, is that it puts ordinary human beings under pressures that are inconceivable to the rest of us. That's what is interesting about war—what it does to people's souls. I remember standing on a hill outside the besieged city of Kunduz and listening to three young Northern Alliance soldiers recite the number of family members they had lost in the country's endless war. Five, six, and four, said the boys, all with eyes as dead as a shark's.

Surely that is why we are here, to look into lifeless eyes and tell the world what we see.

John McCormick
Editorial Writing

John McCormick is deputy editorial page editor of the *Chicago Tribune*. He joined the paper as an editorial writer in 2000, after serving as *Newsweek*'s Chicago bureau chief for 13 of his 18 years with the magazine.

The Chicago area and Midwestern states are home base for McCormick, personally and in his career. He lives in the western Chicago suburb of La Grange Park with his wife, Dawn, and their two sons, Michael, 13, and Conor, 10. He was born in Dubuque and grew up in Manchester, Iowa. He went to college at Northwestern University's Medill School of Journalism, where he had majors in political science and journalism.

His entrée into journalism was as a copy clerk at the *Chicago Daily News*. His first job after graduating from college was as a reporter and columnist at the Dubuque *Telegraph Herald*. He covered local government, labor,

Chicago Tribune

and energy before becoming a roving columnist responsible for news and feature coverage in Iowa, Wisconsin, and Illinois. For 18 months, he and another reporter were dispatched to produce a 200,000-word look at the history and likely future of the Mississippi River Valley and its people.

At *Newsweek*, the Midwest was his assignment. He was responsible for generating cover stories and other projects, including looks at the decline of the nation's industrial workforce and how the development of the atomic bomb affected the physicists involved. He focused on policy questions through the lives of the people they influence: how a welfare recipient claws her way into the mainstream economy, and why juvenile court judges often return children to the parents who abused them.

When he joined the *Tribune*, his boss, Bruce Dold, was bringing new ideas to the editorial pages in terms of original reporting and late-breaking editorials. Nine months later, McCormick was named deputy editorial page editor.

McCormick's voice is fresh, forceful, and passionate, verging on anger in the kicker of a Sept. 11 editorial that warns terrorists of America's unfinished business, approaching poetry in mourning the murder of a Chicago cop. His winning pieces inform, encourage, demand, and decry, rising above the seductive trap of cynicism, reaching beyond the traditional borders of stoicism.

—Pam Johnson

From the dust
will come justice

There is an instant, before the grief sets in, when shock carries us from one moment to the next. It is our bridge, our momentary defense against the unimaginable.

This time the shock must carry us further than usual. The unfolding events of a sunny Tuesday morning will touch thousands and thousands of American families.

The grief will be as widespread as it is deep. It may be days before friends and acquaintances of the innocents realize their losses. Not since our wars—most recently Vietnam, and World Wars I and II and Korea before that—will so many be touched by the taking of lives.

The urge for a complete and instant explanation is as understandable as it is fruitless. No doubt that day will arrive, though even then it will not satisfy.

The events of Tuesday, shocking though they may be, aren't entirely a surprise. In recent years, terrorism experts have warned of this nation's vulnerability to sneak attacks, via biological weaponry, suitcase bombs or the kind of suicide attack from which modern transportation can't protect itself.

And yet we had grown complacent. Security had become routine, even a joke to many air travelers: Yes, yes, I packed my own bags.

Our carefree moments are over, buried in the gray dust that coated the dazed onlookers on streets of lower Manhattan after the first of the day's many tragedies.

From this day forward, our lives and our institutions will not be the same. This nation's sense of relative isolation from the kinds of disputes that have put the civilians of other lands squarely in harm's way—from the Middle East to the Congo to Northern Ireland to Sri Lanka to Colombia—now vanishes. If, as suspected, the assaults of Tuesday are in fact the work of murderers with international agendas, then our comparative indifference to world affairs likely will vanish with it.

Suddenly, with so many lives having tumbled like dominos, many of our most earnest concerns and obsessions—Did you see that hit on Monday Night Football? Do you think the lake will still be warm this weekend?—seem petty beyond belief. If a slowing economy already had brought pause to what, in retrospect, felt like a carefree era, this well-planned attack jars us into what passes, too sadly, for the modern world.

Often it is foolhardy to speculate on the American psyche. But we have just become a more serious people. The bombing of Pearl Harbor ended the lives of some 2,400 U.S. military personnel and 1,200 civilians. Tuesday's conflagrations claimed many more lives.

On this day, someone set out to frighten us. And succeeded. That we must admit.

Yet it would be dangerous to succumb in ways that would hearten the terrorists responsible for these acts.

That term, terrorist, comes not so much from the strength of the perpetrator, but rather from his ability to destroy the confidence of those he targets.

As Tuesday blossomed so tragically, most Americans were left to stare at screens filled with smoke, sprays of water from fire hoses—and expressions of fear for those who had suffered as well as those who would suffer next.

The fear, like the shock, is abundantly sensible. But not if we as a nation let those be our destinations. That would please those whose cowardice expresses itself in the capture of commercial airliners and the targeting of American landmarks.

For all that we as a people are feeling, this is a moment for quiet resolve. This nation has known 225 years of challenges and surmounted the lot.

It is reasonable to expect that America will change. Our losses will exceed this day's realization.

And yet the terror should not rest here. It should, and, in all likelihood, eventually will be turned back at those who today celebrate this broad river of American blood. In their twisted minds, this must be some mission of revenge.

But if our response is rooted in nothing more noble than vengeance, then that, too, cannot fully satisfy us.

The point here must be justice, the principle that inexactly has guided this country throughout its history.

That justice may not be swift. It is important, though, that it be sure.

For those who on Tuesday tore a part of America's heart, there must be one uneasy assurance: Life is long. We are not finished. And it is now they who must feel the terror.

Children, praying for peace

OCTOBER 14, 2001

This is a confusing time for children. On television, they see grainy video of cluster bombs splashing into targets in Afghanistan. They also see President Bush explain the need to drop those bombs. And yet, in houses of worship and in some schools, they are encouraged to pray for what most kids really want: peace, and the sense of calm that accompanies it.

In many Roman Catholic schools, for example, students who know their nation is boldly waging war also are repeating the prayer of St. Francis of Assisi, one of the most humble and lyrical works of Christendom: "Lord, make me an instrument of your peace. Where there is hatred, let me sow love; where there is injury, pardon; where there is doubt, faith; where there is despair, hope...." Elsewhere, many other children earnestly voice the parallel prayers of Muslim, Jewish and other faiths—or the spontaneous words that spring from their own young hearts.

Squaring the horror of war with entreaties for peace is difficult business. It's complicated further by the fact that for believers, prayer is the most personal of expressions. Suggesting that any other person should pray, let alone for what, would be fatuous and unwelcome.

But that noble principle doesn't begin to help parents who aren't sure how to help their kids understand something on which mainstream Jews, Muslims and Christians largely agree: the concept of a just war. For those who think the current military operation fits the rigorous demands of that concept, waging war while praying for peace is a profoundly acceptable paradox.

That sentence is anathema to pacifists, many of whom have lived their faith in recent weeks by urging that this nation either turn the other cheek or attempt to gain legal convictions of those who sponsor terrorism. Pacifism requires guts, especially when a rising chorus of cries for justice demand not legal action, but military.

In the face of unarguable danger, though, pacifism

can be a worthy conclusion in desperate search of a logical rationale. And when that danger is so palpable that it has already obliterated some 6,000 lives, pacifists determined to put their principle above all others can fall into a tempting trap: the accusation that those who disagree with them want only vengeance and blood.

Not necessarily. The regrettable truth is that some people need to be fought to keep them from annihilating innocents. Writing last week in *The Wall Street Journal*, National Public Radio host Scott Simon, a Quaker, noted: "About half of all draft age Quakers enlisted in World War II, believing that whatever wisdom pacifism had to give the world, it could not defeat the murderous schemes of Adolf Hitler and his cohorts."

Peace, then, isn't best defined as the short-term absence of fighting. Instead it embodies the long-term goal of safety and calm after an injustice is punished, or a threat eliminated. Some children can best comprehend this when it's likened to standing up to an injurious bully, or using medicine to stop a ravaging disease.

Even when invoked, war must be played by moral rules. Islam, Judaism and Christianity generally concur that war should be a last resort; should be fought for the right motive, such as self-defense; should inflict the least possible harm on innocent parties; and should produce benefits that outweigh its terrible costs.

Wherever possible, war also should not march alone. Diplomacy should continue. So should kindness. Bush's call for American children to come to the aid of malnourished or starving Afghan children gives parents a golden chance to teach the difference between hatred and help.

Even that mix of messages—let alone the broader suggestion that one can pray for peace while waging a just war—can confuse the youngest among us. That, of course, is why they have parents or grandparents or other grown-ups in their lives: to explain what to a child seems inexplicable. If we are willing to do the job.

The fact that so many countries have banded together in this effort makes it easier to explain. So does the significant, and unexpected, vote last week by a 56-nation group, the Organization of the Islamic Conference, to implicitly support a targeted campaign against the Taliban.

On the afternoon of Sept. 11, more than a few children came home from school frightened by the thought that a war had just begun—and that they would somehow have to fight it.

The temptation for parents was to say that's impossible. But it is more honest to explain that unless some courageous people stop global terrorists now, what those children feared could come true after years of nightmares like Sept. 11.

The renaissance
of Black Chicago

MARCH 11, 2001

Michael Chandler's black sedan glides unnoticed down the streets of North Lawndale on Chicago's West Side. It was here that Chandler, then 15, watched the sky over his parents' house turn orange as commercial strips along Pulaski Road and Madison Street erupted in flames after the killing of Rev. Martin Luther King Jr.

Chandler is now 48 and represents North Lawndale as the alderman of the 24th Ward. It's a mostly poor area still scarred by vacant lots and dilapidated buildings. But Chandler can point to some remarkable changes: the attractive shopping center anchored by a Dominick's food store and a 10-screen Cineplex Odeon theater; block upon block of newly built homes near the old Sears headquarters; the big community center and indoor pool now being built; the stylish stretch of Millard Avenue that appears to have been airlifted in from Lakeview; the new Albany on the Park Townhomes off Ogden Avenue that black families purchased for $250,000 apiece. "I'd never say we've made it until we bring everyone along," Chandler says. "But there is real progress here. I say that with confidence."

Chandler could be speaking for much of Black Chicago—both the neighborhoods and the populace. The past decade has seen substantial improvements by almost every social, educational or economic measure. Most of this growth has come, not from the good works or wishes of outsiders, but from determination within the African-American community itself. Chandler is correct: much has been done, and yet much remains to be done.

This concrete progress, as opposed to the well-meant but often empty hopes of earlier years, is happening repeatedly—but not uniformly—throughout Black Chicago. Yes, many areas remain bleak and dangerous for those who must live in them. Still, as many numbers and neighborhoods attest, the overall changes are as crucial for the long haul as they are lacking in instantaneous drama. Slowly but surely, many of the statistics and images that document the difficulties of African Americans here, and elsewhere, have begun to reverse.

This is not the portrait of Black Chicago that most of us see in TV news reports of murders and drug busts. That media fascination—the only view many whites ever get of black neighborhoods—would have us believe every block is swathed in yellow police tape.

But look closer. This week, early numbers from the 2000 U.S. Census should document not only the big growth of the Latino population here, but also the freer movement of middle-class black families throughout the metropolitan area. That easier migration reflects important facets of both race and class: Rising fortunes have given more black families the means to live in safe neighborhoods and send their kids to good schools.

The pending release of census data prompts a look at other measures of black Chicagoans over the last decade. Crime rates are down. So are teen pregnancies. In Chicago's public schools, the black dropout rate is down, the graduation rate is up and many more African-American students are taking Advanced Placement courses. The number of low-income census tracts in the Chicago area has dropped by 12 percent, with the percentage of residents who live in them (many of whom are black) declining 22 percent. Future census data will show sharp increases in employment and income. Another plus: the razing of CHA high-rises that not only dead-ended many families, but also overwhelmed and stigmatized entire black neighborhoods.

Why the progress? Conventional wisdom says black advances stem largely from a record-long U.S. economic boom that, despite its current perils, is now marking its 10th anniversary. And yet many African Americans disagree with that simplistic view, telling survey researchers that the more important reasons include the work of black churches and a culture of black self-help.

Those notions dovetail with changes in the way blacks view themselves. Three measurements:

■ Michael Dawson, chair of political science at the University of Chicago and a student of black attitudes, says his most recent polling found plenty of pessimism about race relations, but "the highest economic confidence among African Americans that I've ever seen."

■ In 2000, majorities of U.S. blacks and whites (64 and 67 percent) told researchers from the U of C's National Opinion Research Center that they are better off than their parents were. But black respondents were more likely than whites (74 to 57 percent) to say their children's lives will be better than their own. And the share of African Americans who say blacks are *at least* as hardworking, intelligent and non-violent as whites leaped 20 points in 10 years, to about 75 percent. As NORC's Tom W. Smith concludes: "There's certainly no veil of pessimism dominating the black perspective."

■ In 1999, Princeton Survey Research found majorities of black respondents saying welfare reform has meant not only more jobs for blacks (57 percent), but also more black self-reliance (63 percent). Blacks were more likely than whites to say that their incomes, job opportunities and quality of education had improved.

Drawing broad conclusions about black Chicagoans, not just in the city but in the diaspora fanning out more than ever to the suburbs, risks generalizing too much about a community with lots of subgroups and opinions. What's more, skepticism about progress abounds, among both blacks who see enduring injustices and whites who don't grasp improvements among blacks.

Some of that is understandable. This is a metro area of 8 million people, most of whom have deeply rooted opinions about race and class. It's in the interest of many—whites, mostly, but a few blacks with a stake in the status quo as well—to minimize what's begun to occur. Or who, at the least, still hold impressions of Black Chicago that haven't changed as much as the city has.

But in the aggregate, the evidence is inescapable.

Look around. Scores of new houses and rehabs dot the streets that flank Drexel Boulevard on the city's South Side—places that haven't seen new construction in a half-century or more. More houses have popped up from once-weedy lots near Lake Park Avenue. But the clash of old and new images can be jarring. A few blocks west, near Cottage Grove Avenue, a lot advertised as "Prime Bronzeville Vacant Land" sits next to a dilapidated house flanked by two junked jalopies.

But the investment is telling. New homes in chancy

neighborhoods represent not only the calculated aspirations of the families who buy them, but also the long-range faith of flinty-eyed lenders now investing money in neighborhoods that many of them long ignored.

In North Lawndale, recent buyers include people who have always lived there as well as others who, in order to be closer to their families and jobs, have returned to Chicago from Oak Park and other suburbs. In the struggle to better their neighborhoods, they win a few and lose a few. Last month, for example, Chandler got the city to trim trees and add lighting on Lawndale Avenue—and then gathered for three nights with dozens of his constituents for what he calls "positive loitering" to drive away the drug dealers. As North Lawndale improves, Chandler also is preparing black residents for the arrival, just now starting, of white families. "Remember," he drolly tells constituents, "you can't discriminate against people over the color of their skin."

The comeback of many black neighborhoods would be more convincing if more retailers would get into the act. There's an appalling lack of even middlebrow stores in many areas, a throwback to a time when businesses followed customers out of the inner city. The hope now is that census data will persuade them to return to areas where per-capita income is on the rise.

Which raises a question: Whenever the economy fades, will Black Chicago's progress fade with it?

Perhaps, especially for the so-called bottom third, the former welfare recipients now in the most marginal jobs. But many African Americans are in a stronger position than they were during the brutal double-dip recessions of 1980-82. Today's professional and skilled workers are often more entrenched and experienced, arguably less vulnerable to panicky downsizings.

The future, though, isn't entirely bright. By many measures, the improvements of the last decade leave African Americans well short of whites. Too many students aren't getting the parental care and educations they need; too many neighborhoods must some day absorb an unskilled prison population that is disproportionately black. Dawson, the U of C prof, worries that poor blacks are being pushed from a reviving inner city to the borders of Chicago and some suburbs beyond. He also warns that accumulation of family wealth—housing equity, investments, retirement accounts—is inadequate. Politically, the growth of Hispanic Chicago could mean bitter rivalries over resources and clout.

Progress, then, is no reason for Chicago to turn its back on the needs of black citizens. Too many remain a people apart, living lives that are separate and unequal.

But neither should all of us overlook the many improvements that for too long have been elusive.

Those working to rebuild communities devastated by the loss of jobs and rise of crime should be proud. They have created more than a glimmer of something this city has long needed: the renaissance of Black Chicago.

Blood money and the Bears

JULY 15, 2001

Imagine the frustration of those in City Hall and Halas Hall who have worked so hard to get a new football stadium for the Chicago Bears.

There's the mayor, Richard Daley. The team chairman, Michael McCaskey. The city planners, architects and elected officials who did just what Daley and McCaskey wanted—and who don't like hearing that they are desecrating a war memorial on Chicago's lakefront for private gain. They're all so gosh-darn weary from long years of effort. They just want it all to end.

Of course there is frustration, and then there is frustration. Imagine you're no older than one of the Bears' wealthy young draftees. But imagine that, instead of packing up your Porsche to head to football summer camp, you're lying face-down in a European farm field, coughing toxic gas out of your lungs. Imagine your heart pounds with terror. Imagine realizing that, even if the cool mud beneath your cheek doesn't feel so bad, the hot, sticky wound gouged by one of Kaiser Wilhelm's bullets is slowly bleeding the life out of you. Chances are you'd want it all to end, too.

In the years after World War I, this city vowed to honor its fallen soldiers. It also showed respect for the many who considered themselves unlucky to be alive: veterans poisoned or crippled or shell-shocked in the supposed war to end all wars. Chicago dedicated its proud new Soldier Field to war vets—and swore that it would never, ever forget the catastrophic personal price they had paid for our freedom.

But, hey, so what? Last week the Chicago Park District Board curtsied dutifully to the plan by Daley and McCaskey to put a big, repulsive bowl inside skeletal remains of Soldier Field. Without discussion or public comment, the five board members present—Mona Castillo, William Bartholomay, Margaret Burroughs, Anita Cummings and Gerald Sullivan—unanimously voted to fast-track the $582 million project.

Even brief discussion would have exposed this ram-rod civic malpractice for what it is. As a *Tribune* story put it: "In essence, a private sports team will use public money to build a public stadium to be used primarily for the benefit of the privately owned team." And yet the public gets only pretend hearings and hurried voice votes on that project's grossly unattractive design.

* * *

But the sham vote wasn't last week's greatest indig-nity. Daley and the Bears expect some big corporation to take leave of its senses and pay perhaps $250 million to puts its name on a ruined war monument for the next 30 years. Veterans groups are angry, and the lip-service inclusion of a memorial wall in the new design hasn't bought them off. In fact, veterans young and old have packed the few public sessions where the stadium plan has been considered.

So, figuring that everybody's got a price, the Bears— no doubt with City Hall's approval—now have offered the soldiers blood money, just like compensation paid to a victim's descendants: If you people stop screaming about our stadium deal, we'll cut veterans causes in for $200,000 a year. We and the park district will decide where the money goes. And we'll all pretend this bribe is a heartfelt honor to the brave war vets whose children still grieve at their graves. "This has been in the works for a long time—pretty much since the beginning," offers a Bears spokesman. Sure it has, and the rising temper of veterans had nothing to do with it.

Maybe some veterans will grovel for the money; every group this big has its little Judases. But other vet-erans, many of them fighting the last public battle of their lives, should resist. They should not sell their souls—or the legacy of veterans who are not here to fight. They, like the rest of us, should protest all the loud-er, even as Daley tries to rush the stadium deal and stifle debate.

As he showed with another bout of histrionics when asked last week about the opposition, the mayor is rat-tled. He doesn't want a stadium that people ridicule to sully his own legacy. Nor do he, McCaskey and others already stained by this fiasco want their children's chil-dren apologizing decades from now for a monstrosity they put on Chicago's supposedly protected lakefront.

* * *

But the opponents won't go away. As more Chicagoans see depictions of how out of scale this bad marriage of new and old architecture would be, Daley and McCaskey's only escape route is to project an air of inevitability. Forget it. This deal is done. You people need to shut up and move on.

Maybe Daley and McCaskey will prevail. But their refusal to open up the process for real public debate must first withstand a court challenge from Friends of the Parks, an advocacy group steelier than its prissy name suggests. The first judge on the case has shown he may not buckle as quickly as Daley's cronies at the Chicago Plan Commission, the City Council, the Illinois legislature and the governor's mansion.

Daley and the Bears must reopen the question of siting and designing this stadium.

Their plan meets their needs. But this is a public stadium on public ground, paid for with public money. Neither Daley nor the Bears can violate Chicago's lakefront, especially when neighborhoods such as Comiskey Park's would avoid the pitfalls and encourage other development on the South Side.

The Bears' crass, desperate offer of money for silence should energize opponents of this carelessly designed stadium plan. Too many scared and lonely young Americans died in European farm fields—and too many Chicagoans promised to remember their ultimate sacrifice by christening Soldier Field—to let a mayor and a private company ride roughshod over honor.

At some point, it will be the people of Chicago who grow weary of hearing Daley and the Bears say they just want this over. When what they really mean is, we just want our way.

Eric Lee, and all
that went right

AUGUST 24, 2001

So much went right Sunday night. So many of the attributes of big-city police officers that virtually all citizens
agree is the ideal.

When he started his shift, Eric Lee was just what
Chicago's drug- and gang-ridden Englewood neighborhood needs more of: a veteran officer, a former Marine
with a magna cum laude university degree, whose personnel file spoke to his nine years of good judgment on
the job. He had volunteered to be a tactical officer, an
especially dangerous line of police work. He had passed
up his once-every-month options to "bid out" of Englewood for easier duty in a less stressful district. Friends
say he liked the people of Englewood, enjoyed the uphill struggle to make their lives safer.

When Lee and two partners spotted a down-and-out
man being pummeled in an alley, they hurried to help
the victim and announced that they were the police. In
some cities, complaints about "disengagement" are on
the rise—assertions that officers too often look the other
way, don't want to take risks, avoid confrontations that
could lead to accusations of misconduct. But Lee and
his partners engaged, just as they'd been trained to do.

When the assailants fled, Lee didn't open fire. In a
rapidly unfolding situation that surely had his adrenaline pumping, he stuck well within police department
guidelines on use of deadly force and "proportional response" to the threat posed by the assailants.

When one of those assailants unexpectedly fired,
dropping Lee, his partners, too, showed restraint. They
had every reason to fear for their safety—and thus every
legal right to shoot the shooter. Even those who accuse
some cops of being trigger-happy couldn't have
squawked. Instead, Lee's partners arrested a convicted
felon, confiscated his still-loaded gun—and filed the reports that accuse him of killing their friend.

When they learned what had happened, Lee's other
friends back at the station flung black arms around

white shoulders, and vice versa. They cried colorless tears on blue shirts. They poured out sorrow in a moment that revenge or frustration or anger might have kidnapped.

So now the most vulnerable of Chicago's citizens no longer have Eric Lee, just as they no longer have Brian Strouse or James Camp or John Knight or Michael Ceriale, the four other policemen—all tactical officers—who have been shot to death since August of 1998.

Their deaths came as shocks but not, unfortunately, as surprises. Police work is risky. Lee, like the others, had chosen to make it more risky by pursuing the toughest challenges, and often the toughest criminals.

When police officers break rules or laws, and citizens die, there is a proper cry for justice. But when it's the officers who die, many of us recalibrate our reactions. We may mourn, but because we expect officers to work in harm's way on our behalf, too many of us accept the odds that some of them won't come home.

Eric Lee's wife and his 6-year-old daughter don't have that intellectual luxury. They must go Friday to his funeral.

Writers' Workshop

Talking Points

1) The distinction between editorials and news coverage has always been fuzzy for readers. How important is this issue to a newspaper and its credibility with readers? What kinds of steps could news and editorial staffs take to clarify roles for the reader?

2) John McCormick talks about how some editorials are written with specific elements of the community in mind. What might be reasons that editorials would be written to different groups of readers?

3) Discuss various leadership roles editorial pages can play in generating public discussion of community issues, beyond exercising their institutional voice.

4) If you could build your version of the ideal editorial board, what professional and personal qualities, values, and skills would you require?

5) McCormick talks about newsy editorials, original reporting, varied moods and tones, and sorting out complexities. Only in the Soldier Field editorial does the *Tribune* attempt to achieve a change in direction on a public issue. Discuss whether this veers from traditional editorial pages. How does it serve readers and the community?

Assignment Desk

1) Read editorials for several days. Pick three of differing styles. Describe the style for each and what was effective and not effective.

2) On Sept. 11, McCormick had 55 minutes to write his editorial about the terrorist attack. He talks about outlining as a critical writing step. Read "From the Dust Will Come Justice" and identify key points that might have been in his outline.

3) Write an editorial on an issue about which there has been a news story. Answer these questions: To whom are you writing? What's the editorial's purpose—to educate, to spur action, to

sort out complexities, other? What additional reporting might be needed? Draft a quick outline of which points you want to make.

4) Now take that same news story and write an editorial that has an opposing view to what you wrote. What points are on your quick outline? How difficult was it to shift perspectives?

A conversation with
John McCormick

PAM JOHNSON: What attracted you to journalism? What was it you wanted to accomplish?

JOHN McCORMICK: I'm a believer that a newspaper should be the poor man's university. I had grown up in a small place. We didn't think of it as the end of the earth; we thought it was the center of the earth. But it was a place in which people were very interested in things that happened far away—big emphasis on public education in states like Iowa and Minnesota and Wisconsin, and big emphasis on world affairs. It's a big export area. You would sit in cafés and hear people talk about grain prices in Rotterdam. So this was something of a window to the world. There were two windows. That was one and the other was sitting late at night with a radio under my pillow listening to far-off 50,000-watt clear channel stations. But I especially liked the way the newspapers brought that world to places that couldn't see it.

What led you to the editorial position at the *Tribune*?

In college I worked as a copy boy at the old *Chicago Daily News*. I was Mike Royko's night copy boy for a time. I didn't know him all that well. I don't mean to stretch this. I never researched a spelling of the word "boo" for him or anything else. That newspaper had an editorial page, but I had no idea where it came from. I then worked at the newspaper in Dubuque, the *Telegraph Herald*, for a wonderful guy named Jim Geladas, who didn't like editorials. I remember a year in which he won a national editorial writing contest and his sardonically telling a couple of us that he had won this national award for submitting five editorials. He was really glad that was the rule because we had only run five editorials in the prior year, literally five. And again, it just wasn't part of my experience.

So then I went to work at *Newsweek,* and there I saw something completely different. I worked in the bureau in Chicago for 18 years and, during that time, I was either participating in or responsible for the coverage of 10 Midwestern states. I learned an entirely new way to read a newspaper in a hurry, which was to glance at the front page, to glance at the metro front, and go straight to the editorials. It was through the editorials that I would learn whether a story was just a flash in the pan in a city that I didn't know as well as my own. I would get the context from the editorial. I'd learn why it was important. I'd call New York and say, "We ought to do something on this." It wasn't the front page that was teaching me that; it was the editorial page.

Did that create an interest in doing that yourself someday?

No. It didn't. Nor did it create a disinterest. It just wasn't on my screen. A good friend of mine, Bruce Dold, joined the editorial board of the *Tribune* around 1990, and I had known him before that time and had worked with his wife, who had free-lanced for *Newsweek*. Eventually we became neighbors and I got to know him better and he would talk about his job. It was through that that I grew interested. It seemed like a way to be able to write in a manner that cut through a lot of the conventions of news coverage, that made it simpler to say to readers, "This is what's really going on here." Bruce called me the Thursday before Labor Day in 2000 and said that he might have a job opening—he had just become the editorial page editor. Five days later, I signed on.

That's a good set-up for talking about your success with editorials in such a short period of time.

It was a very abrupt switch. I had never written an editorial or sat in on an editorial board meeting. When he hired me, Bruce said, "When I say editorial, I want you to think about what that entails and the standard image of what an editorial should be, and then I'd like you to forget all of that because I don't want to do that."

He talked about wanting to have editorials that—this is my phrase, not his—added value. There were two things he did *not* want the job to consist of: a) pieces that simply repeat the news and then plop some opinion at the bottom. He wanted fresh reporting. And, b) he wanted to break the standard motif of the event happened on Monday, it's in the paper on Tuesday, there's an editorial on Wednesday. He really wanted to get away from that. He runs an extremely newsy editorial page.

On the night that the U.S. Supreme Court essentially decided the presidential election, there were TV correspondents standing in the wind rifling through a fairly lengthy decision trying to figure out what the heck it meant. About 9:45 it became clear, and Bruce and I were on the phone. We can go without squeezing anybody's shoes in the newsroom until 9:30 for a first edition. The question was, could we go till 10:30? So he calls the desk. The desk says fine—we have a news desk that loves newsy editorials. I plop down at the computer at home. Bruce races off for a bureau to re-engineer the page. We're done about 10:15. I won't say it happens every week, but it happens every month. So that's something that we try very, very hard to do: live by the credo that there is no tomorrow.

The ASNE judges described your editorials as "strong without being preachy." Do you agree?

I go back to Royko, whom I admired not so much for his individual columns but for his ability to do four a week, decade after decade. I thought that his secret was—in the best sense of the word—"moodiness." Not only did I not know where he was going to be on many issues, I truly didn't know whether he was going to be lighthearted on Monday, blistering on Tuesday, sardonic on Wednesday, cheerful on Thursday. You just didn't know. His column had differing moods, unpredictable moods. We talk about the mix of editorials on a given day—some days you want to be light about a subject, some days you want to be serious. The test has to be: "Am I doing something that brings readers into the paper or am I driving them away?" They don't need to be here. They can live long, rich lives without reading what journalists produce.

One of the things I try to do is figure out for each editorial to whom it is written rather than what the tone will be. The tone tends to follow to whom it is written. Then I can take a guess on where their heads are going to be by tomorrow morning or Sunday morning or whenever, and go to where I think they will be.

So you don't write every day for everybody?

There are occasions when you're trying, for example, to move the voters in a Democratic primary election. You're addressing readers who have a certain amount of civic interest at a minimum. That's what I mean. I don't mean writing to movers and shakers. I mean whom are you trying to reach and, more important, are their minds reasonably well coalesced around a certain set of thoughts? If so, do you want to shepherd that along and say, "Yep, keep going"? Do you want to toss a grenade and try to restart the discussion?

There are two things, and we're going to get to one of them later, but one thing that a newsmagazine drummed into me was that you have to be mindful of what the issue is going to be next week. Where will people's heads be next week? It seems to me the perfect editorial is sitting on the newsstand when everybody shows up to cover the story.

Let's talk about the editorial you wrote the day of the terrorist attack, "From the Dust Will Come Justice." Was that in the Extra?

We had two Extras that day. The first, and that's when this was written, was an eight-page wrap, and that was your basic newspaper Extra going to newsstands. But Ann Marie Lipinski, the editor of the paper, and our publisher, Scott Smith, decided to do two. The other would be a 24-page Extra delivered to all home subscribers that afternoon. So we actually had three editions being prepared simultaneously—the first Extra, the second, and then the paper of Sept. 12. Bruce walked into my office at about 9:20 on the morning of Sept. 11 and gave me a 10:15 deadline. We did a little bit of tweaking for the second edition, but it's basically the same piece.

It was a morning of such shock and disbelief. What was going through your mind about how you would

talk to your readers? How did you go about collecting your thoughts?

You've now come to the second thing I learned in the magazine world. The people whom I really admire as newsmagazine writers spend more time outlining than writing. You can walk halls and see people sitting with four different colored pens and hurriedly doing outlines. These are people who don't need to do outlines to write well. They do outlines to write *extraordinarily* well. I'm going to come back to what you asked but it's a mechanical point, which is to divide the job into four components and to get to a point that it's automatic, with the first two being, "What do I want to say?" and "In what order?" The basic junior high outlining exercise. And then separately, okay, now it's time to write and to try to improve that as I'm going along.

The point for me when I'm in a hurry is to not have to keep all of what I want to say in random access memory —not to have all of the stuff swirling through my head. You know that terrible feeling when you're sitting, your fingers are on the keyboard, you're looking to your left at your notes, and don't know what to do next. That is not an experience I enjoy, and I try to eliminate it whenever possible, especially in a deadline situation.

So the question then is, okay, what do we want to say?

In 1970 I was at Northwestern, and this was right around Kent State. The Vietnam War division in the country was probably at its zenith. My dad wrote to me on a notepad from his little furniture store. It's about a couple of other things and then there's a paragraph that says:

"Don't become discouraged over the plight we are in at the present. We have come through revolution, wars, depression, the 'Four Horsemen,' and we will pull through this. It takes courage, optimism, hard work, a belief in a Supreme Being, and just plain guts, plus a love for one's fellow man whether he be a saint or a stinker. Keep the faith. Love, Dad."

That is a note that, in moments like that, has just stuck with me and it popped into my mind. I had no idea where people's heads would be by the time they read the editorial. So I then went to the second default: If he were alive, what would my father say to my two sons? That's what that editorial is. That's what I think my father would say to my sons, and it's the theme of that note, which is to slow down, don't get carried away, put this in perspective, and then the sentence that's in the kicker, "Life is long."

How challenging was that editorial to write?

Once I remembered the note, it wasn't that hard to do an outline. I think I was writing by about 9:40, so there was plenty of time. I find that the least effective work I do is when I don't take the time to outline it, and I was mindful of that because I didn't have any brilliant thoughts. This was going to have to be a workmanlike exercise.

One thing about outlining. People have wildly different ways and they all call it outlining. But there's one thing I notice when I read editorials I admire and when I read ones I don't. The people who it seems do some sort of outline force themselves to make their thoughts track, and I feel like I'm reading an article. Other times I feel like I'm reading a group of very well-written sentences. But it isn't an article. It doesn't have any architecture that draws the reader from beginning to end. I can tell where they stopped to go get a cup of coffee and came back and started writing about something else. There isn't a linear nature to the piece, and that's the only thing I wanted to do on Sept. 11 — to try to be linear and come down to the kicker. I didn't know when I started how to get there, and so that was my little cross that morning while other people were carrying far, far heavier ones.

I went out at one point to check something in the newsroom because there was a serious difference of fact between something I saw on the wire and something I saw on television. I remember people were doing things in a hurried but orderly, calm fashion. The place knew what to do with that story and there was a sense in my mind that, you know, John, this is game time. Whatever you've got, it's got to be today. There are not that many days in a career that hugely matter. I knew the newsroom was going to do a great job. The question was, were we?

Did you get reaction to that editorial from readers?

We did get reactions, but not so much to any one editorial.

We later met and decided that some editorials were going to be written speaking to policy—you know, it would be great if Washington would do such and such. But some—the "Children, Praying for Peace" editorial falls in this category—would try to help readers sort through the complexities and deal with whatever they were going to have to deal with over their kitchen tables or in their workplaces or schools or churches or wherever. And we did get a fair amount of reaction to that. Though I can't say to one editorial.

How did "Children, Praying for Peace" originate?

In the kicker, there's a mention of kids coming home from school and being frightened a) that there would be a war, and b) that they would have to fight it. On the 11th, my wife, Dawn, told me what occurred when our sons came home from school. One at the time was 12 and he had not yet seen the video of the planes hitting the World Trade Center. He's a take-it-in-stride kid. But I have a 10-year-old—he's the child in the kicker—who was very unnerved by this. And I did not know how to process that. My initial thought was, "We really need to assure him that that's false, that's not realistic. Older people fight wars. Ten-year-olds don't have to do it."

And over the next couple of days or weeks, it occurred to me, you know, what if he's right and I'm wrong? He just might be right if this threat goes on and on and on. So that was pretty much where the editorial came from—that and talking to other parents. And just the sense that I thought kids were getting very mixed messages. My kids go to a Roman Catholic grade school, and at the school they're praying for peace and that's fine. That's what I want them doing. But at the same time, they're coming home and they're seeing the president on the news saying we need to go to war. That conflicts with what seems to me to be children's own natural inclination to want peace. How do you juxtapose these two things in a way that makes sense for them?

Were you writing to parents?

Yes, primarily—or to people who are around kids.

Grandparents, teachers, and so forth. I remember feeling that we were all grappling with that. Pacifist voices were rising, and then bellicose voices were shouting down the pacifist voices. We were dealing with what our reaction should be and should we be all of one mind. If you remember, a forest of trees gave their lives for editorials about dissent. My concern was that I could see that my kids weren't processing it very well. As adults we know how to factor protests and dissent and majority sentiment and authoritarianism. But, as kids, they just seemed intimidated by it all.

"The Renaissance of Black Chicago" editorial is very different from what we've discussed so far. Through facts and details you built a picture different from what many Chicago residents might have thought was the circumstance today.

The attempt was to be persuasive not with words but with facts. That's fairly simple writing. There isn't any sizzle going on in that piece. Again, who's this written to and where are their heads at? It's written to a primarily white audience that probably doesn't get to all parts of town and may be dealing with notions from a long time ago. I could pluck a hundred people off Michigan Avenue and take them blindfolded to some of these neighborhoods and peel off the blindfold and they would have no idea where they were. But I knew this was going to be a little bit of a sell.

This goes back to reporting and the extent to which editorials are reported versus the extent to which they are screeds. There's a difference between telling me a story and showing me a story, and this was going to have to be a "show me a story." If people have preconceptions, I can sit here till I'm blue in the face pontificating that Black Chicago has changed, and it's useless.

If, on the other hand, we stack up a combination of facts—townhomes in what people see as a devastated area are in fact brand new and going for $250,000, and there are African-American families snapping them up as soon as they're built, or attitudinal studies that show black Americans still are very concerned about interracial situations but they've never had a more optimistic view of their future—that to me is compelling.

That editorial is a great big duffel bag into which I wanted to stuff as many convincing, compelling facts as I could and offset that with the very clear acknowledgment that this is a job that's started, not finished.

How strategic in your writing was the image in the lead of the black sedan gliding unnoticed down the streets of North Lawndale?

The scene had to start somewhere and I thought if you have black cars moving silently down streets, readers don't necessarily know if that's good news or bad news. I was riding with an alderman I knew from another story. I had found him to be, first, realistic and, second, bullish. As he took me down streets that he had taken me down three years earlier, the streets appeared to me to have been airlifted from other parts of town. This is an area I sometimes drive through on my way to work—but not the side streets. Which goes to the point for journalists: Are we people who write as though we always drive to work the same way? Or are we satisfied with the familiar? Is the reporting there or not?

Sometimes, you do all the reporting, then you set the notes aside and write the piece. But you've got the reporting to back you up. This piece did not seem to me to be something on which I could set the notes aside. I would have to mention this block and that block, mention this survey finding and that, the appearance of such-and-such street, the fact that lenders are making substantial home loans in neighborhoods where lenders haven't made loans in decades. These had to be the selling points because if I just say, gosh, you ought to drive there, things are better, you're going to shrug and say, "Right, it's just one more do-gooder who wants me to believe things that I know aren't true."

I wanted to get people past what they think they know. I care that people form their opinions based on the best facts they can get.

I wanted it to be: "You know what? In parts of town you may not have seen lately, substantially different things are happening on the streets and in people's heads. Now you go do with that what you want, but you can no longer talk about how 'they' don't take care of their neighborhood." I just want the conversation to come up to speed with what's really occurring.

"Blood Money and the Bears," about the renovation of Soldier Field, was your most stinging editorial. What made that style fit this circumstance?

We've run 14 editorials on various facets of this topic, and this is your old-fashioned crusade to stop or change a project. It was definitely an uphill fight. The style of our mayor has greatly benefited the city. He is a get-it-done kind of person and consensus largely depends on what he decides the consensus is. On one level we really like that. But it's a bull-in-a-china-shop style and sometimes we don't like it.

This struck us as a situation in which he was trying to get a stadium built, which is a good thing, but was doing it by wrecking a war memorial. In the years after World War I, even at the dedication of this particular stadium, there had been a very strong commitment not to forget what soldiers had sacrificed. We felt this was just being ramrodded and the piece speaks for itself.

This goes to the mood point we talked about earlier. Some days you want to be in this mood and some days you want to be in that mood.

I don't associate the tone with outright attacks on him. It was more the process. Does that say something about how the target is defined?

No matter how visceral the feelings may be, we talk about what the person *does* and not what the person *is*. The tone doesn't hugely differ from the tone of many of the other editorials on that particular campaign.

Gauging the right tone can be tricky business. On Sept. 11, I called a guy who was a prosecutor in the Oklahoma City bombing case to ask if he would write an op-ed for us. And, as we were on the phone, the second tower collapsed and he said, "Oh, my God, there goes my law firm." His Chicago firm was just completing or had just completed a merger with a New York firm and this was the New York office. He knew only a very few people there, and I believe most if not all were out of the building.

But a toggle switch flipped in my mind that whatever we said was going to be read against a tableau of probably hundreds, if not thousands, of people who had lost their lives. I'm extremely grateful that someone has given me a prize for these pieces, but a lot of unfortunate things had to happen to bring this about. I just hope we don't forget that. In writing some of these things it's really important to keep in mind that in writing about a stadium, I can take certain liberties. In writing about Sept. 11 or writing about police officers being killed, or anybody being killed for that matter, I've got to be careful. We are privileged to write about things without having to experience them.

Was that something you tried to keep in mind when you were writing the Eric Lee editorial?

I have a lot of friends who are cops, and for the most part these are people who try every bit as hard to do their jobs well as people I work with at the *Tribune*. They sometimes feel that we're only interested when things are going wrong. The police department has over 13,000 sworn officers and their view is that, like any community of 13,000, there are going to be some who don't deserve respect, but a lot of others who do.

This was just a striking example. One thing about writing about a police officer is that it's not that hard to find out how unblemished or blemished the individual's record is. And with that in hand, I began to learn about the guy. The news stories were helpful because it appeared that he was a wonderful guy. And it was not hugely difficult to piece together what had happened that night, some of which hadn't made it into the stories.

For example, I didn't initially know that the assailant was still armed when he was arrested. The other officers would have had every justification in shooting him—not in executing him, I don't mean that. But this was a live-fire situation, and they made it a point of capturing him rather than taking a more drastic action. I checked that six ways from sundown. He had fired at them. They're entitled to fire at him, end of story. Again, it was in the reporting that this little factlet came through.

We do not automatically write an editorial every time a Chicago police officer is slain. In fact, one was slain a few days ago and we won't be writing about it. But this was a situation in which a community that really needs officers like Eric Lee had him and was robbed of him, and that got under my skin.

In Officer Lee's editorial you again establish the importance of the reporting. Are editorials growing away from just offering opinions?

Bruce [Dold] talks a lot about what the reader is going to learn. Do the readers really learn to think about something in a new way or do they just learn the *Tribune*'s opinion? Are they coming away with information that they didn't have when they got there? Between talk radio and TV, public affairs talk shows, and *Nightline*, there is no shortage of loud voices. If what we are is another one, that does not strike me as a winning offering. What we should offer is the *knowledgeable* opinion. I don't think that forceful writing by itself is enough. People are surrounded by too many forceful words.

You once referred to the precision journalism movement of the 1970s and to teachers who opened your eyes to things that you couldn't see. How do those experiences explain you today as a journalist?

Starting with Franciscan nuns and moving up through Jesuits in high school and then also at Northwestern, I felt like I was being taught basic, effective writing, how to read or see something and figure it out and tear into it. I remember a teacher in high school who spent a lot of time teaching logic and fallacies, and to be wary of argumentative writing and speech. I remember it was very rigorous.

When it's time to write, there are things I don't have to think about. Thanks to those teachers, it's automatic. I'm convinced that high school is much more important than college because this is where you get the basics or you don't. No one in college is going to ask you to diagram a sentence.

The professor I remember most from Northwestern

was Ray Mack, whom I barely knew. I don't think I ever said a word to him in college. He taught big courses and I took every one I could. He taught unsentimental concepts about race and class and power. And that's something I really keep in mind with the editorials I report and write. Am I saying this because it's the sentimental thing to say or the journalistically orthodox thing to say? It's the realization that disadvantaged though they may be, the poor are sometimes right and sometimes wrong just like the rest of us. And trying to be rigorous, "Jesuitical" in the thinking. What do we really think is the right thing here rather than whom do we really want to support? Those can lead you to two different and sometimes clashing conclusions. Emotion is a wonderful thing, but it sometimes covers a lack of research.

So is that where precision journalism fits in?

There was a journalist named Phil Meyer who was with Knight Ridder and who in the early '70s wrote a book, *Precision Journalism*. He got some grant money to bring 25 reporters and editors from big and small newspapers around the country to Northwestern to do two things. He was trying to teach the use of computers to help journalists do their own survey research, and also to help us manipulate existing data sets to find interesting patterns.

There was very early work on trying to measure everything from why traffic accidents occurred in one city to patterns of drug flow in another. Reporters were realizing that journalism was becoming harder to do because there were more facts available, and it wasn't always just the official version. You could check the official version for yourself in a lot of different areas.

What Phil Meyer was really trying to do was to get us to think more like social scientists and less like reactive reporters. He wanted us to be able to write with authority and to know that what we had were the real facts as opposed to the facts we were being told.

It was really about getting a lot of the sentiment and the emotion parked on the side. And again, this is the classic "show me a story" versus "tell me a story." I keep going to that word "rigorous," methodically researching material. I don't do database work anymore. But it stays with you. When an interest group comes in and presents its survey or its data, this background allows us to ask much tougher, much more informed questions about how this was done and under what circumstances.

It sounds like you want to help people with the context of what's going on around them and you want that to be precise.

I think a lot of people are in journalism to change the world. Others are in journalism to set the record straight, and I think that's a high calling. There's so much information. There's so much misinformation, some of it intentional, most of it just inept. We try to bring order to the world, and I know how corny that sounds, but I believe it.

I've always thought of myself as a newspaper person. I spent 18 years at a newsmagazine, which I enjoyed very much. What I got from moving between the newspaper world and the magazine world is that I'm not quite sure what editorials are, but I do know what persuasive essays are.

If you are out to do dutiful, virtuous, and worthy work—three adjectives that in the magazine world will get your story killed the fastest—it's not going to survive the internal competition for space. You've got to be there with compelling facts. I never felt that environment was competitive in the sense of people trying to stab one another's backs. It's competitive in that, frankly, unlike a newspaper, there's a very limited amount of space. So it's the stories that are competing and the stories are going to sell themselves on the impact they have, on whether they are interesting, whether they go to things people are talking about. That forces you to be less interested in yourself, I think, and more interested in the readers. And that for me was a good experience because before I went to a magazine, I was more interested in what I wanted to write about and what I thought I had to say. Having been humbled for 18 years by how little that mattered was, for me, a good experience. On the page, these editorials don't speak for me. They speak for the *Chicago Tribune*.

StarTribune

Kate Stanley

Finalist, Editorial Writing

Kate Stanley joined the *Star Tribune* as an editorial writer in 1980 after graduating with an English literature degree from the University of Minnesota.

Her editorials address legal issues, social policy, international affairs, and medicine. Her 1997 editorial series on medical care at life's end, "Learning to Die," was recognized with several national awards, including the Society of Professional Journalists distinguished writing award and as a finalist for the ASNE award for editorial writing.

Stanley received the Walker Stone Award from the Scripps-Howard Foundation in 2002 for her editorials on topics including concealed weapons legislation, homelessness, teen pregnancy prevention, and mental health.

A New York native, she lives in Minneapolis with her husband, Richard Rose, a physician, and their daughters. In their back yard is a magnolia tree that has given life to a *Star Tribune* tradition. In the editorial "Star Flowers," an annual title Stanley writes when the tree's first spring flowers bloom, her literary roots show in an ode to a city's resilience and shivering soul.

Star flowers

MAY 5, 2001

A magnolia in Minnesota is an improbability. Spring upon spring, its flowery audacity startles the landscape. Especially in the wake of such a bleak winter, such loveliness is mystifying. How strange to live at a latitude that leaps so quickly from bitter ice to blossom! How remarkable to see a delicate southerner outlast northern tyranny. But here on the tundra, that's how it happens: Winter ends not with a whimper, but with bursts of white laughter.

Do you suppose the magnolia is a Buddhist, or simply an optimist? Impossible to tell, for trees are uninclined to speech. Either way, the magnolia seems to know something human beings strain to grasp: Hard weather happens. Cold and dark, like loss and change, know their way around the world quite well. When they show up for a visit, there's no sense in acting surprised. Better to hunker down, learn the lessons a storm can teach, and contemplate the morrow.

Somehow, this is not the human way. We interpret life's storms as betrayals of life's promise—imagining that the original deal involved a rose garden. We can't get used to Mother Nature's sense of justice—to the way weather and time crash so heedlessly through our lives. Thus no matter how much warning the forecaster grants, we're never quite ready for what's coming. We feel tricked when rough weather descends. Our dreams freeze in mid-plot, and we curse the cold for wrecking the play. We rage against common circumstance—lamenting our ordinary losses as personal affronts.

This isn't at all the magnolian approach—not that the trees are telling. Observation proves the point: As you wander about town, you'll hear no whining from the star flowers. Their philosophy calls for wordless transcendence—and for blooming where they're planted.

And they're planted in so many unlikely patches: Hidden in a Minneapolis back yard, a grand teenager of a tree has cast off frigidity in a storm of 500 blossoms.

Rising unceremoniously from a ditch, an ancient magnolian trinity spills its seasonal offerings onto a lonely road. Huddling against a St. Paul rooming house, a forlorn little shrub has mustered just two delicate flowers—each exulting in the implausible made manifest.

Ask the magnolia, or ask the men under the bridge, and they'll tell you the truth: The world dishes out enough ice, wind and cruelty to break every tender branch and every beating heart. And indeed, its perpetual onslaughts leave behind many a snapped limb and mind.

It's the same story year after year, but amazing all the same. Somehow, and more than sometimes, the world's fragile creatures manage to prevail against its harsh winds. Astonishingly often, it seems, life's cold crucible forges remarkable things. From its vessel come prisoners who free their persecutors. Sufferers who become healers. Beleaguered children who grow up wise and strong. Their presence in the world seems so very unlikely—for how can a bitterness leave room for beauty?

There are philosophers who will tell you how, but let them speak another day. In this season, we keep faith with the magnolia—which abides against odds the wintry dark, and proclaims the light with a shower of stars.

Lessons Learned

BY KATE STANLEY

Here's a secret the journalism professors don't tell you: Writing—especially editorial writing—is a spiritual endeavor.

It may seem to be about crafting clever arguments to nudge the doltish to do the right thing, and surely it is that. But if you hack away at it long enough, you come to see that it isn't just about arranging words in the proper persuasive order. It isn't just about hectoring society toward betterment. In the end—or do I mean in the beginning?—editorial writing entails paying attention to deeper human stuff. You know the stuff I mean: Death. Love. Loneliness. Cruelty. Weather. Gardening. Beauty.

It sounds sort of mushy. It isn't, not if you take the task seriously. Acquiring tactical skill is the easy part. More daunting—and more delightful—is venturing into the uncharted territory of reflection. You can't say much about how life ought to be lived—how society ought to be organized—if you haven't considered the matter. Writing thoughtfully requires looking out—and looking in. It entails cultivating consciousness, conviction, wonderment.

This is where the magnolia tree comes in—the one sitting in my back yard. In the 16 years since I planted it as an elfin shrub, it has worked its way into my mind as a sort of talisman—an emblem of all that is right, and not right, with the world. It's one of Minnesota's most delicate trees and earliest bloomers, and when I see it preparing to do its spring thing, I gear up to write my annual magnolia editorial.

I can't say why I do it, exactly, except that I must. It forces me to undertake an annual conversation with my readers. It's a chat of a special sort—about matters too elemental to address without the aid of metaphor. I've written four of these annual essays now, and I have it in mind to write one every year so long as the tree and I are on speaking terms.

The magnolia editorial has become a springtime mainstay at the *Star Tribune*: It always carries the same headline and the same first sentence—and then launches into some sort of philosophical banter about the world's odd ways. It's partly about Mother Nature, partly about her silly and brave human offspring. How it turns out depends largely on what's in my head when the blossoms burst. I will admit to occasional moments of panic as the day draws near—and was utterly terrified the one time it seemed I might be out of town on the fateful day. But it all tends to work out. The magnolia always finds its way into words.

It's a weird kind of thing to put on an editorial page, I suppose—speaking as it does so generally and whimsically about the human heart. But readers seem to like it well enough, and my editors are tolerant, and I can't really imagine not writing about the magnolia.

In truth, I think it is essential that I do. These pieces are the sort editorial pages ought to publish more often—and not because they are "light" or "offbeat" or offer a "change of pace" from the conventional editorial onslaught. (The magnolia, I can report, takes umbrage at such demeaning justifications.) They are essential because they speak fundamentally about the human quest—the yearning for beauty, for justice, for good, for transcendence.

These evanescences are tricky to write about well. It's easy to fall into a vat of rhetorical syrup somewhere in the first paragraph and then be sorry you ever started. Somehow the magnolia helps keep me out of the syrup and on the straight and narrow. Its blooming spurs me to mull the matters that preoccupy thinking people but that nevertheless seem "too big" to talk about. But they must be discussed now and then, for no matter what Madonna says, we don't live in a merely material world.

Thus the editorial voice can't just argue about the brass tacks of economics and foreign affairs and social policy. It can't just lament what is wrong and cheer what is going right in the "public sphere."

If the voice is to resonate with readers, it must also wonder and weep and sing. It must acknowledge in subtle and poetic terms what every writer, and every reader, cannot help but notice in rare moments: that the mere fact of existence is amazing, bewildering, and worth dwelling upon.

THE SUN

Stephen Henderson
Finalist, Editorial Writing

Stephen Henderson is the associate editor of *The Baltimore Sun*'s editorial page. He previously worked as an editorial writer for the *Lexington* (Ky.) *Herald-Leader* and the *Detroit Free Press*, and as a reporter for the *Free Press*, the *Chicago Tribune*, and the *Sun*. He has been in his current position since moving to Baltimore with his wife, Christine Kloostra, in July 1999.

His work, which has always sought to inspire positive change, has been honored with more than 10 national awards, including the 2001 ASNE Distinguished Writing Award for Editorial Writing.

His 3,000-word editorial "Justice Denied" (excerpted here), like much of his writing, is an opinion wrapped in a story, challenging readers to think hard about the fairness of the death penalty and the disparate values that underlie justice.

Justice denied

DECEMBER 2, 2001

Two brutal crimes.

Two disparate punishments.

In the eyes of Maryland criminal justice officials, Cheryl Ann Griffin's vicious rape and murder didn't merit the kind of vengeance sought for slain police Officer Vincent J. Adolfo.

No matter that Griffin, a single mother, was attacked while reading the Bible in her bed, strangled and struck nine times in the head with a hammer.

Baltimore City prosecutors would allow her attacker, Troy A. Emery, to plead guilty to second-degree murder. They wouldn't bother to prosecute the sexual assault at all.

Thirty years in prison was the sentence Emery drew, and 10 of those were suspended. In early 2003, thanks to good-time credits, Emery is scheduled to walk free after serving fewer than 15 years.

Adolfo's killer, by contrast, would face the ultimate punishment for his crime. Baltimore prosecutors made clear from the beginning they would seek the death penalty for Flint Gregory Hunt, a heroin addict who shot Adolfo to death after the young officer tried to arrest Hunt for stealing a car.

Most cop killers in Maryland never face the prospect of execution. And to date, no others have lost their lives for murdering a police officer. But Baltimore prosecutors brought the full force of the law down on Hunt anyway.

A jury complied with the state's attorney's wishes, and Hunt became the only Maryland prisoner executed for killing an officer.

Two brutal crimes.

Two disparate punishments.

For years, death penalty proponents have maintained that differences such as those found between the Adolfo and Griffin cases are insignificant. There are good explanations, they say, behind prosecutorial decisions to seek death on behalf of some victims but not others.

Proponents scoff at calls for a halt to executions

while a serious inquiry into Maryland's death penalty takes place. They have been unwavering in their assertions that fairness—not randomness or discrimination—is the driving force behind capital punishment in this state.

Their beliefs rule the day in Annapolis. Polls say their thinking is in line with that of a majority of Maryland residents.

But that position could never make sense to Gregory Gerard Hunt Jr., whose interest in the Adolfo and Griffin murders is quintessentially personal.

Flint Gregory Hunt was his father.

His mother was Cheryl Ann Griffin.

In America, we teach children to respect the judicial system because it's fair. We say it doesn't matter whether you're black or white, rich or poor, male or female. The law exists to move beyond those distinctions in pursuit of a more noble ideal: justice for all.

But that's not the message the state of Maryland sent to Gregory Gerard Hunt Jr. It taught him that the idea of justice in state-sanctioned killings is a con—a false notion that masks a system whose standards for taking life are duplicitous and arbitrary.

When he was just an adolescent—12 when his mother was killed, 18 when his father was executed—the law schooled him in an unfairness that would faze most adult minds.

Death penalty opponents, defense attorneys and even some judges have long complained that the nature and circumstances of the crime—which is how the law itself defines who's eligible for death—have little to do with who ends up on death row in Maryland.

The standards aren't clear, so it winds up being about race. Or geography. Or, perhaps even more frightening to contemplate, it's just about chance.

Part of the problem is that there are 24 state's attorneys in Maryland—each with his or her own take on how to interpret the state's death penalty statute. Some seek execution for all death-eligible murders; others don't do it at all.

What's absent is a statewide guidepost, a judicial guardrail to protect against imbalances or abuses.

Mr. Hunt's life represents an uncanny but telling

convergence of all that shadowy unfairness. He sits at the nexus of everything that's wrong with the death penalty in Maryland.

Not surprisingly, he doesn't want to talk about what happened to his parents. Mr. Hunt, now an adult living in the Baltimore area, did not respond to efforts by *The Sun* to contact him for this editorial. So, we cannot know how he managed to cope with such tragedy, or how he moved beyond it.

But his parents' stories are worth exploring—particularly in advance of the 2002 legislative session, which will undoubtedly include debate about the future of the death penalty in Maryland.

Flint Gregory Hunt and Cheryl Ann Griffin provide enough reasons for us all to reconsider whether Maryland should ever again take life in the name of justice.

[The full text of this story can be read on the CD-ROM included with this edition of Best Newspaper Writing.]

Lessons Learned

BY STEPHEN HENDERSON

Flint Gregory Hunt was his father.

His mother was Cheryl Ann Griffin.

So ended the first section of one of the most difficult editorials I've ever written. And so marked the critical turning point in a piece that I believe both defines and stretches the traditional parameters of argumentative writing.

Without question, "Justice Denied" is an editorial: It expresses a strong point of view, presented logically and with supporting facts. But it is also much more: a tale of unfairness, replete with narrative passages and colorful language; a story of sorts with a clear beginning, middle, and end; and in some ways a personal journey through Maryland's complex and bizarre death penalty legislation and the mess that it has produced.

Only the first two sections of the piece are reprinted here. The others went on to recount (in great detail) both murders discussed in the opening passage and to explore the reasons why the legal system handled them so differently. In the end, the piece returns to Gregory Gerard Hunt Jr. and a letter he wrote to Maryland's governor, begging for his father's life to be spared.

I needed all the typical skills I employ each day in my job to write this editorial: strong reporting skills and an eye for the importance of logic and argument building.

But because this piece required a marriage of traditional editorial writing with other literary and even feature-like elements, there were also some not-so-typical lessons derived from its writing.

One is the importance of a central theme—in this case two sentences—around which the entire piece revolves:

"Flint Gregory Hunt was his father.

"His mother was Cheryl Ann Griffin."

Those were the first words I wrote in this editorial, and once I had them down, the rest of the piece was about how to work up to that point, and what came after. Of course, those two sentences weren't obvious from the beginning. It wasn't until I was deep into the reporting and had talked the piece through with several other people that they came to me.

But without them, I'm not sure the piece would have worked.

Another lesson has less to do with writing than with smart risk-taking and good thinking, I suppose.

When I came across the story that was the impetus for this editorial, it would have been very easy to shuffle it off to the news department for a big Page One blowout or a features centerpiece. Traditional editorial thinking might have prevented me from seeing the possibilities for our department.

But I was sure we could make this an editorial—a powerful, well-crafted argument that was strengthened by strong storytelling. And I had an editor who was open to the idea, too, a fact that can never be underestimated.

In the end, the risk paid off. We had been writing about the death penalty for nearly two years when this piece was published. And to date, no other editorial (including one that helped win an inmate's commutation) generated the kind of response this piece did. More people wrote letters. More people called. More people stopped me at parties or on the street to tell me how much they either liked or disliked the piece. Even many death penalty proponents admitted that the editorial forced them to reconsider how fair capital punishment is in Maryland.

To me, that's the goal of any editorial. And I'd never hesitate again to break out of the traditional editorial form to achieve that goal.

Steve Lopez
Commentary

Steve Lopez's first lessons in holding scoundrels accountable came at the dinner table when he was a boy. There he heard his mother's dry quips and his father's contributions about powerful people who mistreated the working class. That indignation and sarcasm, as well as compassion and powerful storytelling, mark his columns today.

Lopez was born in California and grew up near San Francisco. He earned a journalism degree at San Jose State University and began reporting as a sportswriter. He's worked at seven newspapers including *The Oakland Tribune*, which he joined in 1977. He went to the *San Jose Mercury News* in 1983, and *The Philadelphia Inquirer* in 1985. In 1997 he became columnist and editor-at-large for *Time* magazine. In 2001 he returned to local column writing by joining the *Los Angeles Times*.

His column is published three days a week.

Along the way he has published four books: *Land of Giants* is a collection of columns; *Third and Indiana* tells about young life on the streets of Philadelphia; *The Sunday Macaroni Club* looks at abuse of power during a campaign; and *In the Clear* is the story of a small town trying to save its soul in the midst of a murder investigation.

He also has received the H.L. Mencken and National Headliner awards for column writing, the Sigma Delta Chi and National Headliner awards for magazine writing, and the 2002 Sigma Delta Chi award for column writing.

His wife, Alison Shore, is a writer and editor. Of his two sons, Jeffrey, 24, and Andrew, 22, he says, "I'm proud to say they are young revolutionary anarchists who protest mainstream media as public enemy number one."

—Karen Brown Dunlap

When love stands bravely against unbearable grief

OCTOBER 24, 2001

The visits began two days after her husband was killed aboard American Flight 11 when it crashed into the World Trade Center.

Prasanna Kalahasthi, a 25-year-old dental school student at USC, would stop by the campus office of Nadadur S. Kumar, a stranger who would become a friend. She would sit in the same chair every time, the one by the big picture window, and speak dreamily of a love that had come to her like a sweet surprise.

Kumar, like Prasanna, was from southern India. He, like Prasanna, had an arranged marriage.

"She was deeply in love," says Kumar, associate director of the Office of International Services. In the weeks that followed her referral to his office, Kumar would come to admire this beautiful, wounded young woman. She was small in stature but filled with strength, and with a grace known only in love and in grief.

Such plans they had had, Prasanna and her husband, Pendyala Vamsikrishna, a 30-year-old technician for a Silicon Valley company.

They wanted to get Prasanna through the demanding two-year graduate program she had begun only a few months earlier, and establish her career somewhere in the United States. He would go with her wherever that might be. Then they were going to start a family.

Vamsikrishna traveled frequently in his job—far too much for his liking. They had missed each other so much, Prasanna had gone to visit him in Boston a week before he was killed.

"I should be spending more time with you," he told her as he had many times, according to Kumar.

Kumar says Vamsikrishna was to leave Boston on Sept. 10, but hadn't finished his job, and rescheduled for the following day on American Airlines Flight 11.

"He boarded the plane and left her a message," says Kumar. He told her he would be home by lunch, and would surprise her with a meal he was going to prepare.

Prasanna would wake to his message, and to the televised image of Flight 11 crashing into the tower.

That can't be him, she thought. It looks like a small plane, not a jet.

That can't be him. They had such plans.

"Her father flew to Los Angeles and said, 'I'm going to take you home,'" says Kumar.

But Prasanna told him L.A. was her home now. A brother was moving into the apartment she and her husband had shared near the USC campus, and she also had a new, extended family that included Kumar and her classmates.

"She said the best way for her to remember her husband was to stay in the program and complete it," says Kumar, who remembers her saying these words:

"His memory is only going to strengthen my resolve."

In their regular chats, Kumar reminded Prasanna that therapists were available to help her. But he knew she wouldn't go for it.

"In India, from a cultural point of view, going for that kind of counseling is treated like a stigma, like admitting that something is wrong," says Kumar, 48.

The customary way to deal with such a tragedy is to lean on family, and particularly elders. So Kumar took Prasanna home with him the very first day they met and introduced her to his wife and mother-in-law.

In dozens of almost-daily telephone calls and visits, Prasanna seemed to be progressing, says Kumar. As a Hindu, she believed in an afterlife, and she believed she would be reunited with her husband one day.

Just once did she mention the terrorists who had killed her husband and more than 5,000 others on Sept. 11. "She said whatever differences people have, this is no way to resolve them," says Kumar.

Only in retrospect was her call of last Thursday somewhat unusual. She called Kumar about 3:30 p.m. to chat about nothing in particular, which was something of a departure. She called friends and relatives that day, too.

But no one had any idea what was to come.

Her brother, the one who had moved in with her, was out of town. A receipt suggests Prasanna had gone to the

Home Depot in Tustin a few days earlier and bought some nylon rope.

On Friday afternoon, Kumar got an urgent call from USC colleagues. Los Angeles police were at Prasanna's apartment and he was asked to go there immediately.

At the door, an officer asked him if he thought he could handle the task of identifying the body of the young woman inside.

"Yes, of course," he said, holding onto a slim hope.

She had said more than once that her husband would have wanted her to finish school. This couldn't be Prasanna, the woman whose strength had been an inspiration.

What he saw in the apartment, he instantly knew, would be with him always.

Prasanna had strung the rope over the Nautilus equipment her husband worked out on. Without warning or explanation, she had taken her life, too much grief to carry through a world gone cold.

As Kumar left the apartment, he was asked by police to sign a form, but he couldn't.

"My hands were trembling."

He did not sleep that night, haunted by the image. Asked if he's OK now, he says: "I don't know."

It's as if the Prasanna he knew was the ghost of a woman who died on Sept. 11, crushed by grief.

Kumar's wife tells him he is absent even when he's in the room. He finds mesmerizing beauty in the subtlest gesture of his 7-year-old daughter. He marvels at the complexities of the mind and the mysteries of the heart.

"I keep wondering if I missed something," says Kumar, his face full of shadows. "Maybe I should have dropped everything when she called on Thursday."

He missed nothing. Prasanna revealed only what she chose to, then followed after her husband, taking a love without limit to a world without end.

Amid the ruins,
a separate peace

SEPTEMBER 15, 2001

NEW YORK—Midnight came and went, and Manhattan couldn't sleep.

"Look at this. Just look at this," Vincent Bury said as he aimed his yellow cab toward the smoke. "That used to be a beautiful view of the towers, but I'm going to tell you something. You see all these people out here? Everybody helping out in whatever way they can? They tried to break us up, but this city's never been more unified."

Vincent Bury drove slower than any cabby has ever driven in New York, loving his wounded city. The heavens thundered with an advancing storm, and flashes of lightning illuminated American flags that hung from fire escapes.

A few poor souls wandered the streets like ghosts, photos of missing loved ones taped to shirts or strung around their necks. They were consoled by people they did not know and would never see again.

"Look at this," Vincent Bury said again, his heart full.

He turned a corner at 15th Street and 11th Avenue to find a group of teenagers cheering. "Thank you Thank you Thank you," said the signs they held. They were spending the night at the intersection to greet rescue workers who came up for air after digging with their hands for hours. Digging for miracles. Ambulances lined the streets, waiting for a call.

On a normal night, Vincent Bury would have been driven off the road by angry motorists leaning on horns. But they passed politely, letting him mourn in his own time. He calls himself the last white native New York cabby, and he is different in another way too. Instead of ramming fenders and bumpers, like you're supposed to do to let off steam, he meditates.

"The inner self never dies," he said, and he was sure something good was going to come of this tragedy.

"Where to now?" he asked.

"A Hundredth and Riverside. The fireman's memorial."

Bury parked on Riverside and got out of the car with a camera. He said that in his 49 years, he had never seen the fireman's memorial and its twin statues of Courage and Duty. He wanted to take the memory home to Brooklyn with him.

A little earlier in the evening, an advertising man named John Avery had left his Upper West Side apartment to walk his poodle Gracie. Avery had been in a state of shock over the attack on New York, but the shock was becoming sadness and anger. A co-worker lost her husband in one of the towers, and it was hitting Avery in a way it hadn't until then.

He was thinking, too, about the estimated 300 firefighters believed to have died under the rubble of what used to be an American symbol.

Three hundred.

Avery walked two blocks to the memorial that has stood since 1913. Firefighters never hesitate, he was thinking as Gracie tugged on the leash. They take chances with their own lives to save others, and there is a striking gallantry about them. The bravery, the bond, the cut of the uniform.

On this night, candles had been left at the memorial, and they flickered in the breeze of the coming storm. Bouquets were laid about, and some well-wishers had written anonymous notes of thanks and sympathy.

"The whole world is a very narrow bridge," said one. "Words can not express our sorrow," said another.

Avery's eyes filled, and anger floated just beneath the sadness. President Bush and the rest of America have to have the guts to root out terrorists wherever they are, he said, his voice deepening.

"We must go after the terrorists and anyone who harbors or finances them. It's not about revenge; it's about protection. If we don't do it, this can happen again. But if it's about revenge, we've sunk to the morality of the terrorists."

The storm had moved across the Hudson, bringing with it a drenching rain that sent John Avery and Gracie the poodle home.

Vincent Bury took a picture of the memorial, which has the following inscription:

"To the men of the fire department of the city of New York, who died at the call of duty. Soldiers in a war that never ends."

Vincent Bury drove away at funeral speed, in touch with both the living and the dead. It rained like everyone was crying all at once, and it seemed to me that New York had never been more beautiful.

Love and prejudice at work and home in city of immigrants

NOVEMBER 12, 2001

Mohammed Meah fell in love with a girl in Bangladesh, but couldn't have her as his wife. Her family, which had money, wouldn't allow it because Meah's family was poor.

Meah, who was raised Muslim, took his broken heart and traveled as far away as he could. He joined the foreign ministry and was assigned to a post in Seoul, where one day the phone rang in his apartment.

It was a South Korean woman named Young Moon. She had dialed the wrong number. Meah, who had learned some Korean by then, tried it out on her. When they couldn't understand each other, they tried English.

A few months later, she called back and they talked some more, and several months later they decided to meet. They liked each other instantly and became good friends, and over the course of a few years, the friendship became a romance.

"I don't know how or why she fell in love with me, or why I fell in love with her," says Mohammed.

But fall in love they did, and once again, Mohammed's heart would be broken. Moon's parents were deceased, so she went to her brothers for their approval, and they forbade her to marry Mohammed.

As a modest, uneducated man from one of the world's poorest nations, and a mere messenger at the Bangladeshi ministry in Seoul, Mohammed was not good enough for her.

"They told her that if she married me, they would never speak to her again," says Mohammed, whose eyes glisten when he tells the story.

Marriage to a South Korean was also prohibited by the Bangladeshi ministry, so Mohammed quit his job and moved to Los Angeles in 1990 to look for work. The plan was to get settled, then send for Young, who would defy her brothers and come marry Mohammed in America.

The job he found was at a 7-Eleven on 6th Street, where he worked 10 to 15 hours a day, seven days a week, for four years. That's how long it took before he had saved enough money to send for his future wife and start a home with her.

Finally, in 1994, Young Moon came to Los Angeles and married Mohammed. A year later, they had a son they named Steven, who would be raised to know Islam as a religion of peace.

The apartment was too small for comfort, and so was Mohammed's paycheck. But they scrimped and saved, and he quit 7-Eleven and bought a little grocery store for $14,000 in 1997. Ben's Market is on 6th Street, just west of MacArthur Park.

"You see this?" Mohammed asks, pointing out the paneling, the lighting, the clean white walls. "I remodeled it myself, little by little. I have very many bills," he says, reaching under the counter for a 4-inch stack of them. "But it's OK now, thank God. We are doing very well."

A good many people might not think of this Westlake neighborhood as paradise. But given his journey, it's close enough by Mohammed's measure.

He's with the woman he loves. He takes his handsome son to an Islamic school in the morning on his way to work. He bought "the ugliest house" on a nearby block, nurtured it with sweat and hard-earned money, and now, he says, "it is the top one on the street." He was even sending a few dollars to his mother in Bangladesh.

But in the aftermath of Sept. 11, Mohammed's heart was broken a third time.

It was easy enough to write off the first customer who mocked his name and cursed him. But it happened again, and again, and again.

Go back home, he was told. Go back to the Middle East. Go back to Afghanistan with Osama bin Laden and the other terrorists.

They were mostly Latinos, he says. Immigrants themselves in an international city built and rebuilt by simple desire, a city re-imagined a million times over. If America could be theirs, how could it not be his?

Mohammed informed some of them that Bangladesh and Afghanistan are nowhere near each other, but he wasn't confrontational. That was partly because he's a man of peace, and partly out of fear.

Arab Americans and Sikhs were being attacked in

America—killed, even—by ignorant thugs retaliating for Sept. 11. If someone harmed Mohammed, who would take care of his wife and son?

"I can say only that they did not have good qualifications," Mohammed says in his gracious way, though he is hurt that some of his tormentors were regular customers. "They were not having very good education. Some just see my skin color, or they know my name is Mohammed, and that's why they do this."

Then, when he hoped it had ended, in walked a man with a knife. He stood at the door, flashing steel and calling Mohammed a terrorist.

"Come on over here," he said. "Come on over here, so I can slit your throat."

Mohammed, terrified, didn't move an inch. If the man came closer, the security camera would pick him up, giving the police something to go on.

Maybe Mohammed's would-be assailant was aware of that. For whatever reason, the knife-wielding man left as suddenly as he had appeared, never to be seen again.

Mohammed closed his shop and went home in tears, and his eyes fill again as he tells the story. "I was never afraid in my life until this," he says.

He closes earlier in the evening now, because his wife trembles until he gets home safely. At home, he tells his son, Steven, that theirs is an Islam of peace, and that with a life of hard work, honesty and good will, Steven will make his parents proud.

Truth be told, Mohammed says, the news hasn't been all bad since Sept. 11. For every insult he received, he also got a promise from a loyal customer vowing to watch out for him. He's still wary in the store, given these uncertain times, but the support of his customers has been a source of pride.

As if to offer further proof of his standing as a productive citizen, Mohammed insists on closing the shop for a while to show a visitor the fixer-upper he bought a year and a half ago.

The woman who waited four years to be with him waits now on the porch of their two-story clapboard house. It's a lovely house, and she is lovely, too.

"It was in very bad shape," Mohammed says of their home. "Little by little, we are fixing it."

Playing footsie with a dragon's basic instinct

JUNE 13, 2001

All I have to say is this:

If my wife were to tell me that as a special Father's Day gift, she was going to put me into a cage with a 7-foot lizard, I would start sleeping with one eye open.

I might check in with the life insurance agent, too, and see if there were any recent changes in the policy.

You know the story.

San Francisco newspaper editor Phil Bronstein came to Los Angeles with his wife, actress Sharon Stone, and special arrangements were made for him to have some private time with the Komodo dragon at the L.A. Zoo.

Bronstein, as I understand it, was instructed by the zookeeper to remove his white sneakers before entering the dragon's domain, so the beast would not mistake his feet for rats.

Now look. I have worked for seven newspapers and a lot of editors, and none of them came within eight yards of normal.

But if you had scraped them off a barroom floor at 2 a.m. and asked if they'd enter a cage with an animal that might mistake their feet for rats, they would have had the sense to stand clear. They don't even like contact with readers, let alone exotic animals.

Have you seen pictures of this Komodo dragon, by the way? Its head looks like a boulder with eyeballs. The dinosaurs in *Jurassic Park* looked friendlier, and they were eating SUVs.

Bronstein apparently likes these things, though. Or at least Stone managed to convince him that he would.

"No, really honey. Just scratch him behind the ears and he'll roll over on his back."

So he goes in with the lizard while Stone watches from outside the cage. The same Sharon Stone who got rich and famous playing a woman suspected of whacking her lovers with an ice pick.

Not to read into this. But Stone and Bronstein hadn't been married 10 minutes when, out of the blue, he develops a heart problem. And then, with a rebuilt ticker and no note from his cardiologist, she sends him into the cage with a dragon.

Basic Instinct II: Return of the Dragon Lady.

"Of course I loved my husband, detective. Why do you ask?"

And what does this dragon do upon realizing that a member of the media has dropped by unannounced?

It goes for the newspaper editor like a shark after chum. It chomps down on his big toe with the jaws of life and won't let go.

Maybe the dragon has read the *Chronicle*.

Maybe it knew that Bronstein and Stone hadn't paid admission to the zoo or made a donation, either, as others in the privileged and pampered set have done before getting the royal treatment.

Bronstein, having married into show business, makes like Crocodile Dundee. He manages to free himself from the Komodo dragon and escape through a trap-door, and they run him to the hospital for foot surgery.

Happy Father's Day.

All things considered, it could have been worse than a big toe. Joe Brown, a *Chronicle* spokesman, said Bronstein was in stable condition and was doing some work Tuesday from his hospital bed.

My guess is that across the country, newsroom reporters are taking up collections to send their own editors to the L.A. Zoo.

It's a shame that when he visited L.A. to tell us we could take our energy problem and drop dead, no one arranged for President Bush to get a special tour.

The dragon, by the way, is doing fine, not that anyone asked. Lora LaMarca, zoo spokeswoman, described a dragon that seemed to be quite pleased with itself.

Maybe this is a north-south thing with the lizard. LaMarca confirmed the dragon never bit anyone from L.A. Next time the San Francisco Giants come down to play the Dodgers, someone ought to arrange for Barry Bonds to stop by the zoo.

LaMarca says the dragon that ate Phil Bronstein is now unavailable for private viewings, but that's a big mistake, if you ask me. This thing is world famous now, and it could be worth a fortune.

I'd bet the mortgage that people would pay for a chance to tempt fate. If you have faith and your heart is pure, He'll protect you in that cage, won't He?

Bronstein must not be a believer. Or maybe there's a cosmic force for universal justice, and it says that if you're going to win Sharon Stone as your wife, at some point you're going to be attacked by a 7-foot reptile.

From one hack to another, Phil, if she starts hinting at something special for Christmas, run for the hills.

A few Coors Lights might blur the truth

JUNE 29, 2001

It was about 8:45 Thursday morning when I walked into the Hermosa Beach Police Department with two dozen Krispy Kreme doughnuts and a 12-pack of Coors Light.

In college, that was a typical breakfast. But in this case, I was conducting a scientific experiment to determine how many beers a man has to drink before he's legally hammered.

Roger Clinton, the ex-president's half brother, went on *Larry King Live* last week to talk about his legal problems, which include but are not limited to a DUI arrest in Hermosa.

Clinton, who lives in Torrance and plays in a band, denied selling presidential pardons to friends. He also denied he was driving under the influence in Hermosa on Feb. 21 even though he flunked three blood-alcohol tests after being stopped for driving erratically.

"I had had about two beers," he told Larry King. "Two Coors Lights."

My first thought when anybody in trouble appears on *Larry King* is that they are guilty as sin, because no matter what you've been accused of, you know Larry will keep it cordial.

Had Mussolini been a guest, King would have asked a question or two about the fascista thing, Mussolini's attorney would have cut him off, and after a commercial break and a call from Idaho, King would have asked Mussolini if the balsamic craze was just a fad.

Sgt. Paul Wolcott greeted me at the station house in Hermosa. At precisely 9 a.m., as Wolcott and Sgt. Tom Thompson looked on, I cracked open my first beer and bit into a glazed doughnut.

It felt kind of like a hillbilly picnic, but that was apropos. The Clinton clan did not grow up in Paris.

By a lucky coincidence, Roger Clinton and I each go about 205 pounds, so our alcohol tolerance might well be about the same. Our taste in refreshment is not, however. I'd have had him locked up for his choice of beer alone.

Around 9:45, I'd slugged back my second can, and it was time for my test.

At exactly 10 a.m., I blew into the same device Roger Clinton had used. You're under the influence if you blow a 0.08 percent, Wolcott says, and Clinton ran up a 0.10 on his first try.

Mine came up 0.01.

Geez, this Roger Clinton is no Billy Carter. Two wimpy Coors Lights and he's in the tank, with 10 times the damage those same 24 ounces did to me. Unless, of course, he didn't tell Larry King the truth.

"Keep drinking," Sgt. Thompson said.

I had my third beer by 10:15, my fourth by 10:30. And a couple more doughnuts, too. They gave me my own desk to drink at, and Wolcott did some paperwork in the corner under a movie poster of John Wayne in *The Sands of Iwo Jima*.

At one point, they took me outside for the field sobriety test that Roger Clinton flunked, calling it a "Jane Fonda" workout on *Larry King*. Touch your nose, walk a line. That kind of thing.

I passed like a champ.

"How do you feel?" Wolcott asked.

"Great," I said. "I just can't believe I'm getting paid to do this."

While sipping my beer, I perused the *Times* and noticed that Roger Clinton was on Page 1 again. Reporter Richard Serrano's story said congressional investigators have evidence suggesting Clinton might have pocketed $50,000 for trying to arrange clemency for a convicted heroin dealer from New Jersey.

The dealer is related to the Gambino crime family, so let me state publicly that nothing personal is meant by this little beer-and-doughnut social.

Investigators also claim to have found "a couple hundred grand" in travelers checks cashed by Clinton, which can only mean that his band is doing really, really well.

Mark Geragos, Clinton's attorney, assured me there was no truth to any of the pardon-peddling allegations. As for the DUI, he claims without explanation that the blood-alcohol tests were inaccurate, and that Hermosa police had no probable cause to arrest Clinton. They did so, he says, as a matter of "political profiling."

You might say it was a strain of political profiling that led to pardons for 47 people, including Roger Clinton, as one of President Clinton's last acts in office. Roger had a 1985 conviction for cocaine distribution wiped from his slate.

While I chugged beer, Wolcott reviewed the police report, and it seems that although Roger told a national television audience he'd had only two beers, he told Hermosa cops he'd had four or five.

"Go ahead and have five and we'll test you again," Wolcott told me.

The fifth went down like water. I took a deep breath and blew a 0.04.

Five Coors Lights and I'm only halfway to jail.

When they brought Clinton into the station, they gave him two more tests on a more reliable machine.

He blew a 0.08 the first time, a 0.09 the second.

Kind of ironic that in 1998, President Clinton campaigned for lowering the legal limit to 0.08 in all 50 states, saying: .

"To people who disregard the lethal threat they pose…lowering the legal limit will send a strong message that our nation will not tolerate irresponsible acts that endanger our children and our nation."

I can't remember the last time I drank before lunch, but in Hermosa, I dusted a six-pack by 11:15 and they hooked me up to the same machine where Clinton blew his 0.08 and 0.09.

My first shot was 0.05, the second was 0.06.

Reality TV is all the rage, and I think we've got a concept here.

Roger and me, a keg and a Breathalyzer.

Have your people talk to mine, Larry.

Writers' Workshop

Talking Points

1) Steve Lopez's columns are peopled with interesting characters. Some have major roles; others are mentioned in passing. Notice the number of people mentioned in a column. What purposes do they serve? How do writers include many people without causing clutter?

2) The columns mock an editor, an actress, and a president's brother. Who are others skewered in the columns? What are the fair targets for a columnist's ridicule?

3) Writers are taught to "Get the name of the dog," as a reminder to get the details in a story. In "Amid the Ruins, a Separate Peace," the dog, Gracie, appears. What purpose does Gracie serve? What difference does it make to use the name?

4) In "When Love Stands Bravely Against Unbearable Grief," Lopez takes on the difficult task of building a column around a person he had never met. Additionally, information on Prasanna Kalahasthi was limited. What do we know about her? How did Lopez know each fact? What else would you like to know about her? Is that missing information crucial to the column?

Assignment Desk

1) Most of the columns are written in chronological form. Consider other forms of storytelling. Now try writing one column in another form.

2) Lopez challenges Roger Clinton's claim on drinking by creating a demonstration. It draws out the facts and makes Clinton's claim appear ludicrous. Consider a recent claim in the news and devise a demonstration that supports or undermines the claim.

3) Lopez said his former editor, Bob Maynard, encouraged him to write, not a humor column, but a humorous column. Write a humorous column. What's the difference in writing humor and writing humorously? Why is humorous writing difficult?

4) Some readers said the column "When Love Stands Brave-ly Against Unbearable Grief" appears to support suicide. What part of the column might lead to that conclusion? Rewrite that part. How does your change affect the column?

5) Write five column ideas that capture the essence, issues, diversity, humor, and human stories of your area.

A conversation with
Steve Lopez

KAREN DUNLAP: Why did you become a columnist?

STEVE LOPEZ: I was a sportswriter for two years, then a news reporter for five years at *The Oakland Tribune*. Bob Maynard took over the paper and asked me to start a column. I did it there for about a year and have done mostly column writing since then, but not exclusively. I've been a columnist off and on for over 20 years.

What effect do you want to achieve with the column?

It's different every day, and I think that's the only thing that's kept me at it. Sometimes the purpose is just to highlight or illuminate a story that's in the news. Sometimes it's just to do my own reporting and dig up a story. Sometimes the attempt is a little bit of humor. Sometimes the purpose is to smack someone. All these different things keep me going. I don't think I would have survived more than a couple of years if the column was the same subject matter or the same treatment and tone. One thing I try to achieve is to keep readers guessing a little bit, keep them wondering, "What's he going to do next?"

Do you feel that you have to report a column?

I think the biggest mistake columnists make is to think that they have something important to say, and they forget the thing that sustains most columns, which is reporting. That's a bit of a generalization because there are all different kinds of columns. For some columns, the purpose is not to report, it's to pontificate. But even then, the thing that keeps a column fresh is to go out on the street, to knock on some doors, to do your homework, to make the phone calls, and to do your own original reporting.

Does your reporting ever come into conflict with the news reporters?

For me, an important part of writing a column is to be in the newsroom, to be in the thick of it so I can see and hear what's going on. I can also develop relationships with the reporters. I'm at my seventh newspaper, so I keep going into cities where I know nothing and the people who know the most about each of these cities have ended up sitting around me in the newsroom. Their eyes and ears are a tremendous resource for me. It's obvious that it's in self-interest and maybe it's even selfish, but I think reporters like working with columnists. And I'm not bashful at all about dropping reporters' names in the column when I mention their stories. You've made them a part of this process, and I think they appreciate that.

Having worked as a reporter myself, I know that there are often things you know about a story that just don't make it into print. And oddly enough, those things are often the essential truth about the story. You're required to do a little bit of a "he-said-she-said." Your duty is objectivity and fairness and covering all sides in this, and you end up not being able to get to the heart of what this is about. You can kick that over to the columnist, who has some sense of the background of the story. A column ought to be about getting to the heart of it.

Are you often the subject of your own column?

No, but I am sometimes. I'd been writing quite a few columns about the scandal in the Catholic Church, and had not really done one on who I am and where I come from. There had been all of this criticism from people saying I was a Catholic-basher and a fallen Catholic and an ex-Catholic who had an ax to grind. I wrote about my experience in the Catholic Church and about how, in the brief time I was in the church, I was taught to ask questions. It brought a different element to my coverage of the issue. I gave up a little bit of me, and I guess that's part of what I'm talking about when I say you've got to give up just a little bit of yourself for a column to stand out as something different in the paper.

What are your guidelines for telling about yourself?

You have to leave a little bit of mystery about yourself, because when people have you completely figured out, the game is over. It's like performance. Jim Naughton [former executive editor of *The Philadelphia Inquirer* and now president of Poynter] used to call writing a column a "high-wire act." I like to think the reader sees something on stage and wonders a little bit more about what's going on behind the curtain.

What are your cues that a column is not working?

I just feel that my heart's not in it. I ask, "Would I read this thing? Is the idea big enough? Am I advancing a story that people already know about? Am I giving them something new and different to think about? Am I going to entertain them? Am I going to inform them?" And, you know, by 2 or 3 o'clock you should have answers on most of those things. Every few weeks I'll find out at 3 o'clock—you know, the deadline is 5—but I'll just think at 3 o'clock, it's time to cut my losses, just dump it, move on to something else. And, of course, if you move on, you've got to pick one that you know you can write and report quickly.

Who do you bounce your column ideas off of?

My editor, 90 percent of the time, is Sam Enriguez. Sam is an assigning editor, and one of the things that works for me is that Sam is a Los Angeles native. I had specifically requested, when I came here, that I be assigned to an editor who knew L.A. I was probably going to need to be saved from making a fool of myself because of my ignorance about L.A. So they gave me to Sam.

In general, how have editors helped you?

Sam is great at seeing the essence of each column. After a long day, he'll look beat. He'll read my column, and I wonder if the column is putting him to sleep. Then he'll bolt up, point to a paragraph, and say: "That's it. That's the essence of the whole thing." I'll think I need to move the paragraph up, but he'll tell me, "No, just tease it up. Create a better set-up by an early mention of what is to come." I often write on deadline. I turn columns in and wonder: "Did I pull this off?" Then there's Sam telling me that I did.

David Tucker was my editor in Philadelphia [now in Newark]. He understood that I wanted columns kicked back to me. He was willing to comply. The best thing I got from him was being challenged.

My wife, Alison Shore, has been a great editor. She's a medical writer and editor, and she has a great eye. When you're a columnist, you need someone with that sharp eye to help you.

What's the writing process like for you?

Well, the column is due at 5. My plan is to start writing by 2. Beginning to write the column is at least 75 percent of the writing time. When I start writing the column, I'm usually not done with the reporting. I'm waiting on a half dozen calls. Maybe I'll even start writing the column knowing that I have to go out on another interview or just go out on the street and check something. So the writing of the column is not always *just* the writing of the column. It's still putting the whole thing together.

I might write the first sentence 10 different times. Take a look at it, and it's not quite right. It's the right thought, but it's not the right wording. Or it's the right wording, but it's not the right thought. Finally, I get it in shape and write the second sentence and rewrite it several times until I finally get it right, and then realize that it doesn't go with the first sentence. So it's just this constant inching forward and refining one sentence after another to try to create this sense that the reader is being pulled through this thing somewhat seamlessly.

Some would say it helps to go on and force yourself to finish, then go back and edit. Have you tried that?

I think I do that. I'll go through and just write it, but it's never just a straight write-through. It's the same process of writing and then discarding and writing again and working your way through. Sometimes I look at my computer screen and all I've done is cross out the first paragraph about 20 times. What I have to do is stop thinking and just write this thing and get it in shape to turn in, and then maybe I'll have some time to refine it.

Part of that is training that was drilled into my head at the *San Jose Mercury News*. They hired a writing coach for the summer. This guy would pull me into a little glassed-in office and sit at a desk about 3 feet away and hold my columns in his hands and proceed to read the columns aloud to me in this little tiny room. I don't mean to dismiss the kind of torture that goes on in parts of the world when people in lockup are tortured one way or another, but this was torture. To have a guy in this little chamber read to you your own work from columns that were published and went out to hundreds of thousands of people, and you begin to hear, you begin to squirm, and you'd rather that they were using thumb screws. This guy was reading my work and I would think, "That's not quite what I meant to say" or "That is what I meant to say, but that's not how I meant to say it." And just constantly embarrass myself with how sloppy and incomplete my work was.

What was his purpose?

His purpose was, as he used to put it, to get me to write with my ears, to listen to the words, to consider cadence, rhythm. To remember that there were a million reasons a reader did not have to read your story. They've got a million other things to do in a day, and if you give them any reason to walk away, they're going to take it. Especially with a column he said, "You've got to write with more authority and with voice. You've got to draw them into this, and you've got to keep them there; if you lose the cadence, if your train of thought is hard to follow, if your language is flat, sloppy, they're walking away, and you've failed in your mission."

And so every time he came to something that didn't quite work, he would stop and we'd figure out what it was that went wrong and rewrite it. We'd start up again and go back through and hope that we made it safely through that pass, and we'd make it through but then go off a cliff somewhere else in the story.

In your winning collection of five columns, three are

very serious, and two are humorous. Humorous writing can be more challenging than other forms. How did you begin writing humor?

I think I always wrote a little bit of humor, and I think it's one reason Bob Maynard called me into his office and said, "I want you to write a column." A lot of newspapers have a problem with humor. They're not quite sure how to get much of it in, and there are a lot of people who write humor who are not funny. I think anybody who shows any kind of a knack or an instinct for it will get a chance. And so I guess Bob Maynard saw something in my sensibilities, my story selection, and my treatment of some stories that led him to think that I could occasionally write, not a humor column, but a humorous column. I tried it and some of them worked, but I also wrote some just horrible columns at *The Oakland Tribune*. Just hideous.

I think that if I were to go into psychotherapy, it would come out that my writing goes back to my mother and my upbringing. My mother's a very darkly humorous person who always had a quip. Her parents are from Sicily and Naples. She could just size something up. We grew up with these dinner-table quips and summations of people and events and things. Another part of the humor is that this was a working-class environment, blue collar all the way. My father's family were immigrants from Spain, and here we were in this little industrial armpit of the Bay area—Dad driving a truck and just sure as all-get-out that somebody was trying to screw people, people with power or those damn Republicans. Somebody was out to get us, and what are we going to do about it and let's find a way to get at them.

The column, for me is about holding people to a higher accountability, sort of getting even, and holding up hypocrites to public ridicule.

Is that the background for this passage? "All I have to say is this:

"If my wife were to tell me that as a special Father's Day gift, she was going to put me into a cage with a 7-foot lizard, I would start sleeping with one eye open.

"I might check in with the life insurance agent, too,

and see if there were any recent changes in the policy."

Is there any money associated with this award?

Yes, there is.

I should send it to my mother. I mean, this sounds just like her. And my father'd be there adding something to it.

So I see this thing in the news and here are these celebrities who have this privilege that we don't have, doing something stupid. Thank God for newspaper columns. Here's your chance to come in and balance things out a little bit.

When do you draw the line between the things your mother could have said at the table and the things you can write about in the column?

I don't think that I have drawn any lines. There are times when I've gone overboard. There are times when you've got to hammer somebody. But in a case like this, a guy goes into a cage, you don't want to hammer, you want to poke fun.

In the story on Roger Clinton, you use a device of drinking and trying to match his breath analyzer test. You have a way of visually presenting how ridiculous some things are. Do you have a name for that?

Yes. Desperation.

Do you remember what motivated you to take on the big task of drinking Coors Light?

First of all, I saw Roger Clinton on *Larry King,* and that set off a big flashing light. Here's Roger Clinton saying, "I really only had two Coors Lights." So I'm thinking, what a joke. Here're these Clintons. My God, they're just shameless. Walking away from the White House with everything that wasn't bolted down, arranging all these last-minute pardons for campaign contributors, just the most shameless stuff you could imagine. And here's Roger. Billy Carter might have been somebody for him to aspire to. Now he's on *Larry King*.

So I think, "How do we get him?" Sure, the police have been known to plant evidence and make things up, but this guy looks like he has a six-pack for breakfast. So I called the police and said, "Did you see Roger Clinton on *Larry King*? Would you mind if I come in to the police station with some beer and if we do an experiment and see how many beers I have to drink before I get up to his level?" They thought about it. Long pause. I don't think they get a lot of requests like this. And the guy says, "Well, come on in." I said I would have to come early in the morning because I think I wrote the column the day that I drank the beer.

So I stopped at Krispy Kreme. I bought two big boxes of doughnuts and I had a 12-pack of Coors Light and I show up at the police station, still thinking that they're going to throw me out. But they saw the doughnuts and said, "Come on in." So here I am. They give me my own desk and I'm sitting there drinking beer thinking, "I can't believe I'm getting paid to do this." I'm even expensing the doughnuts and the beer and they're watching me and giving me this breath analyzer test, and it's all very goofy and juvenile, but there's a point to be made. I drank a six-pack before lunch and did not get anywhere near the legal limit. It was a way of just debunking Roger Clinton's whole goofball claim.

"Amid the Ruins, a Separate Peace," was published on Saturday, Sept. 15, four days after the World Trade Center attacks. It was written while everyone was watching the news and reading special editions of newspapers. One of the big questions for columnists is how to find something fresh, particularly in an event that everybody's covering.

Well, we got to New York in the evening and pulled into a hotel that was maybe 40 blocks from the scene. I was on West Coast time and kind of wound up and wanted to go out on the street. I had just moved to L.A. from New York so I knew New York City, and one idea I had was to go to the fireman's memorial, which is way uptown. I was thinking I didn't want to write little feature stories because the paper's going to have plenty of features and hard news. I've got to try to capture the emotion and the craziness of this whole thing.

So I hailed a cab to take me down to Ground Zero, and the cabby just starts talking like a poet. He was sad and he was awestruck by how people were coming together to get through this thing. There's this running commentary as we're going through New York. And you know the cheapest trick in the book is to interview the cabby, and as he was talking, I was thinking to myself, "Dammit, I wish I'd met him on the street. I just can't bring myself to write a column about a cabby because everybody, every journalist, will say, 'Oh, yeah, nice work. Hail a cab and write a column. That's really difficult.'" But the guy just had so much to say, and I thought the hell with it. Readers are going to read it, not journalists, and that's who I'm writing for. The guy's got something interesting to say and the tone of it is right and so I just went with it. I pulled my notebook out and started quoting this guy. When we got to the memorial, I took over and he was kind of a secondary figure in the thing. When we got to the fireman's memorial and the storm was coming in, it was just this dramatic moment that captured the craziness and the darkness of the whole thing.

Consider this sentence. "Vincent Bury drove slower than any cabby has ever driven in New York." Obviously hyperbole. Obviously unsubstantiated. When can a columnist get away with that?

It's not meant to be taken factually. What do you think of when you think of cabbies in New York? You think they're all driving too fast and recklessly. So in a dark, serious, somber column, here's another tone. Here's a lighter touch, a conscious effort to keep from just totally depressing the reader.

We don't know much about the men in your column, Vincent Bury and John Avery. We don't have their addresses or descriptions of them. We don't have things that verify they exist. We don't have much except the writer's word. In a world in which columnists have been shown to have made up characters, how do you indicate to readers that yours are real?

I think there's enough in there. I think that John Avery is described as a marketing guy, so if somebody wants to find out whether I made this guy up, they'll find out that he works on Madison Avenue. And with Vincent Bury, the fact that you're talking about a guy who calls himself the last white native cabby in New York, it's not going to be too hard to find out whether such a person exists.

So it's the detail that you provide about them that authenticates them.

Yeah. But you know what? There's a certain level of trust that has to be accepted between reader and writer, and I feel like I can't be held responsible for other columnists' sins. I'm there talking to these people so the reader can believe it or disbelieve it. I will often add a note about somebody, just on the chance that somebody is thinking this person is completely made up.

Would you find questions from your editors offensive?

I don't think editors have to ask. I think that if you're doing your job, if you're working, if you're reporting, if you're out on the street, if you're engaged in the column rather than going through the motions, I think the editors know that. I think my editors know that I'm working. And as you look back on those scandals, there was a lot of evidence that those columnists were no longer working. They were running on fumes. And so I think it becomes fairly obvious to editors.

The kicker says, "It rained like everyone was crying all at once, and it seemed to me that New York had never been more beautiful." How did you decide on that as the ending?

When I was done working the story on the street, it started pouring, and I went back to the hotel and thought, "How fitting." So I knew I had my ending. I knew I had the beginning once I talked myself into writing a column that involved the cabby. The column begins with me getting into the cab and it ends with the sky just wailing.

And you know it ended up being relatively easy to write.

The sound of the rain was haunting to me. So was another sound. We stayed at a hotel where families of victims were staying. They had come to New York looking for any sign of loved ones. I wrote about being in my hotel room and being awakened at night by the sound of the person next door crying. All you have to do is describe being awakened by the sobs of someone next door, and it tells a big part of the New York story. It's not something that you're likely to see in other stories because you can't personalize it quite like that. But for me to say that in my hotel room I hear somebody crying next door brings readers from L.A. into the hotel, into New York, into the middle of this unbelievable tragedy.

How do you keep that heightened sense of what's going on around you?

I think a lot of people in New York were just numb. I know I was numb because on about the fourth day I was talking to my wife, and she said, "There's something wrong. You just don't sound right." She said she was watching at home and was just destroyed by this thing. But I sounded like, "I'm working on another column, I'm out here in Union Square," and she was right. But then it hit me. I met a family that I wrote about twice and a complete stranger, a dad, threw his arms around me after telling me about his daughter. He laid down a picture of his daughter, lit a candle over it, and I asked him to tell me about her. He said she had just moved to New York, she worked in the World Trade Center tower that was first hit and it hit at about the floor she worked on. She was a wonderful girl and so he steps forward and hugs me and in tears tells me to say good things, and turned and walked away, stopped once more and said, "Say good things." So when that happened and when I saw somebody looking so all-American, it made it real for me for the first time.

The tragedy of New York came to Los Angeles in your column, "When Love Stands Bravely Against Unbearable Grief." Did this column follow a news story on the death?

No. It was not in the news section. I learned about it from a *Los Angeles Times* reporter whose wife works at the University of Southern California.

You never met the central figure in the column and few family members seemed available. How did you report the column?

I went to USC and had a meeting with three people who knew Prasanna. I realized one guy knew her much better than the others, so I arranged to spend more time with him. The family was unavailable. I remember checking out a few things to make sure what he told me was correct.

What was the reaction to the piece?

Some readers felt I had endorsed suicide because of the ending. Their point was that the woman needed help. Maybe she did the right thing. Who are we to know? She chose not to go on, and I reported her decision. Some readers thought I romanticized her decision. I was taken aback. When I reconsidered, I had no regrets.

Love emerged in a different way in the column, "Love and Prejudice at Work and Home in City of Immigrants." How did you find Mohammed Meah?

A reader sent me an e-mail and said, "There's this guy who has taken a really dumpy store and, with all of this immigrant pluck, has transformed it and it has become an important part of our little community. I walked into the store one day and he didn't seem right. I asked what was wrong, and he started crying as he told me about people coming and threatening him, telling him to go back to his own country because he was Muslim."

So why did you go?

Well, it was still post-9/11, and I had written columns from New York and Washington and different places halfway across the country. When I got back to L.A., I thought I'd see how feelings were playing out here.

When I went to the store, the guy just wanted to show me what he'd done to the store and was so proud and talked about the house. I asked, "When did you move here?" and he just sounded so proud and so heartbroken that I said I wanted to hear the whole thing.

You wrote the column like a series of almost separate stories. It starts with a one-paragraph story of love found, love lost, in Bangladesh. It goes on to the strange story of somebody calling him and they end up talking, and there again is a longer story of love found. The third story is love lost again. Then there's another story of them coming here, building a home and a store. Then there are two stories of threats, one the general one, then a man specifically coming in with a knife. It ends with a story of support and achievement.

I thought that I would tell the story chronologically, beginning with how he lost the girl he loved, found another one, moved to America, really struggled, finally bought a house, transformed this store, is raising a son, and here's 9/11 and, all of a sudden, it's all about to unravel.

Tell me the best story that you came across while doing this that you did not include in the column.

As I wandered around the neighborhood asking neighbors about this guy, I could see this was a once-grand neighborhood that had fallen into complete disrepair. It's next to a notoriously dangerous park, and as I wandered around, I saw all of these signs of rebuilding, including the refurbishing of a forgotten building that is becoming a luxury hotel.

There was a story about the community. There was a column about the L.A. story, of waves of immigrants coming here and bringing something to the community, but I decided to focus on Mohammed's story.

What's your favorite type of column?

I don't think I have one. It's always fun to poke at a newspaper editor, so the one on Sharon Stone's husband was fun to do, but the one about the woman who committed suicide just takes you into a different world, and the tone is entirely different. What's wonderful about my job is that at the start of each week, I rarely know what I'm going to be writing about or where I will be going. I think what I like best is not any one particular type of column, but just the idea of the endless variety.

Leonard Pitts Jr.

Finalist, Commentary

Leonard Pitts Jr. joined *The Miami Herald* in 1991 as its pop music critic. Since 1994, he has written a syndicated column of commentary on pop culture, social issues, and family life. His most recent book, *Becoming Dad: Black Men and the Journey to Fatherhood*, was released in May 1999.

Born and raised in Southern California, Pitts has lived in Bowie, Md., a suburb of Washington, D.C., with his wife and five children since 1995.

He has been writing professionally since 1976 when, as an 18-year-old college student, he began doing freelance reviews and profiles for *SOUL*, a national black entertainment tabloid.

Pitts was a finalist for the Pulitzer Prize in 1992. In 1997, he was awarded the first-place prize for commentary by the American Association of Sunday and Feature Editors. He has been honored by the Society of Professional Journalists, the National Association of Black Journalists, and the Simon Wiesenthal Center, among others. He is a three-time recipient of the National Headliner Award. In 2001, he won the ASNE Distinguished Writing Award for Commentary/Column Writing.

His initial column on the Sept. 11 attacks, "We'll Go Forward From This Moment," is an angry and defiant open letter to the terrorists. It circulated the globe via Internet, generated upward of 30,000 e-mails, and was later set to music, reprinted in poster form, read on television by Regis Philbin, and quoted by Rep. Richard Gephardt as part of the Democratic Party's weekly radio address.

We'll go forward from this moment

SEPTEMBER 12, 2001

It's my job to have something to say.

They pay me to provide words that help make sense of that which troubles the American soul. But in this moment of airless shock when hot tears sting disbelieving eyes, the only thing I can find to say, the only words that seem to fit, must be addressed to the unknown author of this suffering.

You monster. You beast. You unspeakable bastard.

What lesson did you hope to teach us by your coward's attack on our World Trade Center, our Pentagon, us? What was it you hoped we would learn? Whatever it was, please know that you failed.

Did you want us to respect your cause? You just damned your cause.

Did you want to make us fear? You just steeled our resolve.

Did you want to tear us apart? You just brought us together.

Let me tell you about my people. We are a vast and quarrelsome family, a family rent by racial, social, political and class division, but a family nonetheless. We're frivolous, yes, capable of expending tremendous emotional energy on pop cultural minutiae—a singer's revealing dress, a ball team's misfortune, a cartoon mouse. We're wealthy, too, spoiled by the ready availability of trinkets and material goods, and maybe because of that, we walk through life with a certain sense of blithe entitlement. We are fundamentally decent, though—peace-loving and compassionate. We struggle to know the right thing and to do it. And we are, the overwhelming majority of us, people of faith, believers in a just and loving God.

Some people—you, perhaps—think that any or all of this makes us weak. You're mistaken. We are not weak. Indeed, we are strong in ways that cannot be measured by arsenals.

IN PAIN

Yes, we're in pain now. We are in mourning and we are in shock. We're still grappling with the unreality of the awful thing you did, still working to make ourselves understand that this isn't a special effect from some Hollywood blockbuster, isn't the plot development from a Tom Clancy novel. Both in terms of the awful scope of their ambition and the probable final death toll, your attacks are likely to go down as the worst acts of terrorism in the history of the United States and, probably, the history of the world. You've bloodied us as we have never been bloodied before.

But there's a gulf of difference between making us bloody and making us fall. This is the lesson Japan was taught to its bitter sorrow the last time anyone hit us this hard, the last time anyone brought us such abrupt and monumental pain. When roused, we are righteous in our outrage, terrible in our force. When provoked by this level of barbarism, we will bear any suffering, pay any cost, go to any length, in the pursuit of justice.

I tell you this without fear of contradiction. I know my people, as you, I think, do not. What I know reassures me. It also causes me to tremble with dread of the future.

In the days to come, there will be recrimination and accusation, fingers pointing to determine whose failure allowed this to happen and what can be done to prevent it from happening again. There will be heightened security, misguided talk of revoking basic freedoms. We'll go forward from this moment sobered, chastened, sad. But determined, too. Unimaginably determined.

THE STEEL IN US

You see, the steel in us is not always readily apparent. That aspect of our character is seldom understood by people who don't know us well. On this day, the family's bickering is put on hold.

As Americans we will weep, as Americans we will mourn, and as Americans, we will rise in defense of all that we cherish.

So I ask again: What was it you hoped to teach us? It occurs to me that maybe you just wanted us to know the depths of your hatred. If that's the case, consider the message received. And take this message in exchange: You don't know my people. You don't know what we're capable of. You don't know what you just started.

But you're about to learn.

Lessons Learned

BY LEONARD PITTS JR.

Andrea Yates and the death penalty.

This is what I was chewing over in my head as I drove my daughter to school: the question of whether it was morally defensible or served any practical purpose to send this emotionally disturbed killer to her death. By the time I dropped my daughter off and turned for home, I had my arguments lined up, my lead pretty well decided, and I was ready to write.

It was a little before 9 in the morning, and it was deadline day. The 11th of September.

By the time I got home, of course, the world had changed. My world. Your world. *The* world.

For a long time, I sat there numb and dumb watching television, watching Katie and Matt and Tom and Peter and Dan try to make sense of the incomprehensible. At some point, I realized two things:

1) It was still deadline day.

2) Nobody cared about Andrea Yates.

I was obligated to say something about this, couldn't not write about it. The problem was, I had no idea what to say. How in the hell could you know what to think, find words to encompass this obscenity—while it was still under way, no less?

As sometimes (rarely) happens, I started to write without really having much idea where I was going. High in the piece—it eventually became the lead—I said, "It's my job to have something to say." Which sort of encapsulates the internal monologue I was having in that moment: me reminding myself that I get paid to provide opinions and that, at any moment, the phone was going to ring and there'd be an editor on the other end demanding one.

But I didn't know. There was so much I—*we*—just didn't know.

So I said the only things I *did* know: that the events of this day had left a bottomless anger and that out of this violation of our country, there would certainly come resolve. Those sentiments seemed small against the immensity of the moment. Less an insightful analysis than just the raising and shaking of a bloodied fist.

The writing was fast. My Sept. 12 column was one of those in which the words just come and editorial changes in the original draft are small and few. Strong emotions, anger in particular, have a way of clarifying thought, making writing flow. This is something I've always known, but writing that column reinforced it for me in a powerful way.

Sometimes, this clarifying carries the danger of making a piece strident and simplistic. Other times, it makes it simple, direct. I hope and believe this was one of those other times. There are, I guess, moments for the shaking of fists. Indeed, moments when that is the only response decent people have left.

I filed the column without thinking much about what I had written. Didn't spend much time second-guessing the opinions I had offered. That's rare for me; I am an inveterate tinkerer. But truthfully, I didn't care. There were, to put it mildly, bigger things.

I met my deadline. I went back to watching television.

THE PLAIN DEALER

Connie Schultz

Finalist, Commentary

Connie Schultz is a columnist and feature writer for *The Plain Dealer* in
Cleveland. After working for 15 years as
a free-lance writer, she joined *The Plain Dealer* as a beat
reporter in 1993 and switched to writing general assignment features in 1995. She began the Sunday magazine
column "Life Happens" in 1998. A native of Ashtabula,
Ohio, Schultz is a 1979 graduate of Kent State University.
She is the mother of two children, Caitlin and Andy.

Her columns and essays earned her three writing
prizes in 2001: a National Headliner Award, an American
Association of Sunday and Feature Editors Award, and a
Cleveland Press Club Award.

In the column "Inside Out," Schultz tells readers about
an adolescent girl struggling with the fallout when word
gets out that she might be a lesbian. Schultz effectively
intermingles her own story about a friend who is a lesbian
with that of the teen's, providing the story with provocative, unexpected turns.

Inside out: The price we pay to be different

DECEMBER 30, 2001

The first thing Annie wants you to know about her is she's unhappy her real name is not being used.

She has been through a lot in the last two years and, at 14, ardently feels she is strong and wise enough now to be immune to others' judgments. Annie also believes in the sincerity of those classmates who say they are sorry for what they did and trusts that even those who never apologized no longer want to hurt her.

Annie's mother is far less confident in the good intentions of her daughter's classmates and understandably so. She is a devoted parent, a mother lion who stood steadfastly by Annie as she plummeted from her lofty seventh-grade perch of popularity into an abyss of loneliness and isolation. The parents of the kids who targeted Annie either didn't know about their vicious campaign or, worse, knew and didn't care. Small wonder her mother is cautious.

Here is Annie's crime: At the beginning of seventh grade, she confided to her closest friend at a slumber party that she thought she could be attracted to girls.

She didn't name any particular girl. She didn't even say the word lesbian. Like most middle-schoolers, she was in the foothills of her sexuality, tentative about the climb and honest enough to admit she wasn't dead-sure which way she was going.

"I had a boyfriend at the time," Annie told me. "But things were starting to change with me. I was more open with myself and I thought, 'I don't have to choose my sexuality now.' I was straight until proven otherwise, but I was more open about it."

Annie chose the wrong person to trust.

"My friend flipped out." She told everyone.

The campaign against Annie was swift and savage. Overnight, virtually everyone abandoned her. They warned other girls that Annie might "have the hots" for them. Their boyfriends, led by one of the most popular boys in the school, shouted "dyke" and "lesbo" when they passed Annie in the hall. Rumors of her lesbian relationships, all false, propagated like dandelions on a vacant lot. In the locker room, Annie was so afraid girls would think she was looking at them that she stared at her locker as she changed into her gym clothes, which she wore under her school clothes so no one would see her undressed.

Annie, already in treatment for depression, started to crumble. "I couldn't believe I lost my best friend over this. She had told me her deepest secrets, but I never, ever thought to betray her. She ruined my life. I felt really alone."

One day in computer class, she signed on to discover someone had changed her screen saver. Annie thought she had to follow the teacher's rule never to interrupt the computer's start-up, and so she sat still and helpless as the class erupted into gasps and giggles over the bright red letters scrolling across a black background:

You are a fag…You are a fag…You are a fag.

After that, Annie started missing school. Lots of it. Her depression dramatically worsened and she began seeing a therapist twice a week. She was on three medications for depression. Her physical health deteriorated, too. An honors student in seventh grade, she missed so much school that only a medical dispensation allowed her to pass eighth grade and enter high school.

In a desperate attempt to stem the harassment, Annie's mom reached out to the most vicious boy's mother, whom she had known for years. The woman's response was chilling: "My son," she announced, "says it's true, that your daughter *is* a lesbian."

It was a sobering moment for Annie's mother to realize just how wide and deep ignorance can run. It also was an empowering one. She went to the school and calmly informed the administrators that she would sue them if they did not rein in their students.

Her threat worked. The kids were yanked in with their parents and within days the harassment stopped. Several of the kids eventually apologized to Annie. The ringleader was not one of them.

"A lot of people grew up," says Annie. "They were afraid of what they don't understand and sometimes what they don't understand is themselves. Now a lot of people come to me with their problems. I think they figure, 'Now you can tell Annie anything because she's been there, only 10 times worse.'"

Annie says she holds no grudges, but she would like to ask a few questions of the kids who taunted her.

"I'd really like to ask them, 'Was it really worth it? Did it make you feel better about yourselves? How do you feel about it now when you see that I've made it through it all?'"

In the last couple of years, Annie has grown from a shy sprite into an elegant young woman. She smiles a lot as she talks, but she also seems vulnerable. Her confidence is hard-earned, but it is fragile. It is not easy to be authentically ourselves at any age. Annie, though, seems ahead of most of us.

"I've realized you don't ever have to be sure of who you are, and I mean that in all kinds of ways," she says now. "I used to be so fake, worrying all the time what others think. The good thing is the outer me and the inner me are the same person now. I could spontaneously combust at any moment and be happy with who I've become."

My friend Jackie tears up hearing about Annie. "There's such a poignancy to her," she said. "If she *is* gay, there will be the possibility of rejection with every new person she meets."

Jackie is one of my closest friends. She is a mother, an actress, a high-level manager, a surrogate aunt to my daughter and a touchstone for me. We are shamefully competitive when tackling Martha Stewart projects, believe hundreds of problems are easily solved by a quote from *Auntie Mame* and regularly shop for groceries together, giggling down the aisles in tandem as we talk each other into things we really don't need. Her partner, Kate, describes our chatter as twin talk, that language understood only by kids who spent their first months of life in the same womb.

Jackie also is gay. She was the mother of a toddler when she fell in love with a woman. She was in her early 30s, married to a kind and decent man who never suspected what Jackie had been afraid to admit even to herself most of her life. Now she jokes that she should have known something was up when her first adolescent crush was on Liesl, the oldest Von Trapp girl in *The Sound of Music*.

I met Jackie several years after her divorce but long before she was openly gay. She still laughs over how she blurted out that she was a lesbian at our first lunch. I can't share in the laugh because her motive behind that moment of honesty still rattles me. At that time, Jackie was a self-described stealth lesbian. When she met me, though, she was so sure she had found a good friend that she didn't want to risk rejection later if I had a problem with her being gay.

So she told me. And that was that.

By the mid-1990s, Jackie was becoming exhausted from living a half-life. She was still afraid of rejection, but was more afraid that she was losing herself. Then Robbie Kirkland, a gay teenager in Cleveland, killed himself.

"Robbie was 15," Jackie said last week, her voice catching in the way it so often does when she mentions his name. "He was my son's age. His family had been so clear with him that they loved him no matter what. And it wasn't enough."

That's when Jackie decided to find her own courage. "I realized I need to be brave not only when I'm safe, but when I'm not so safe," she said. She's now open at work, at church and in her various volunteer jobs, including the local theater community. She and Kate held their commitment ceremony in October 1996. Their new house is under construction, and they are downright giddy over the recent birth of Kate's first grandchild.

They are a family. They are part of our family, too, and there are moments when I find myself fiercely protective of them. Last summer, for example, Jackie was stunned into silence when a fellow cast member in a musical production loudly opined in the dressing room that homosexuality was just plain wrong. Jackie didn't say a word.

I was angrier than Jackie. "Why didn't you say anything?" I asked her, ready for battle.

"It was a temporary relationship," she said, her face tired. "And, besides, one of the straight women let her have it." She gave me one of her wise, motherly looks. "I keep telling you, we need you straights on the front lines."

Meanwhile, Annie is back in the trenches. For the first time in two years, she is no longer afraid to go to school. "I have more courage now. I raise my hand and volunteer in class to put myself in the spotlight. It's my way of saying, 'I'm back and I'm not going to be the girl missing school anymore because of what others think of me.'"

Maybe Annie is gay. Maybe not. Either way, she is changed by the judgment of others. In her own, soft way she is a warrior, and that makes Jackie hopeful.

"I hope that my generation will have done its job to make the world a more hospitable place for gay kids," she told me on our way to the grocery last weekend. "I don't want them to have to choose between going underground or committing suicide."

Lessons Learned

BY CONNIE SCHULTZ

Sometimes you have to wait it out.

For more than a year I had wanted to write a column about the eighth-grade girl who was suffering almost unbearable cruelties at the hands of her classmates after confiding to a friend that she might be attracted to girls. Every time I tried to write, though, my fear of making it worse for her won over my reporter's urge to pounce.

When I first heard about "Annie," she was already on three medications for depression and could drag herself to school only half the time. Classmates were calling her "dyke" and "lesbo" in the hallways. Her closest friends shunned her, warning other girls that she might have "the hots" for them. One day in computer class, her screen saver was changed to read, *"You are a fag…You are a fag…You are a fag."*

I knew if I hung in there, kept in touch with the family, eventually the moment would come when I could tell Annie's story. I checked in with them periodically to see how she was doing, stockpiling notes.

I waited. And waited.

Then one day I ran into the mother, who told me Annie had turned a corner. She was now in high school, her grades had improved, and she was actually getting involved in extracurricular activities. A few days later, the parents agreed that I could take their daughter to dinner.

Finally, I had my column.

My editor, Ellen Stein Burbach, had listened to me talk—and rant—for months on end about the vicious campaign against Annie. When the time came to write, she agreed that I should include the voice of my close friend, Jackie, who also is gay, which gave the column heft and a larger context. She also urged me to write longer and keep myself out of it as much as possible. Sometimes simply telling another's story is opinion enough.

Reader response to the column continued for weeks. Despite changing her name and not mentioning the school, Annie's classmates quickly figured out that she was the girl in the column. That turned out to be a good thing. The ringleader, who had never apologized, called Annie sobbing and asked if she could ever forgive her.

"Sure," Annie said. And then they talked about clothes.

Promoting better journalism through community focus

The move to honor photojournalists in the annual American Society of Newspaper Editors competition was several years in the making and had many champions. Led by *Austin American-Statesman* editor Rich Oppel, ASNE's president in 2000-2001, the Community Service Photojournalism Award became a reality last year.

Poynter's Kenny Irby, one of the early advocates for recognizing the storytellers who carry cameras, joined an advisory group of seven high-powered photojournalism leaders in early 2000. That group included Sonya Doctorian, then with the *St. Petersburg Times*, Steve Rice of the Minneapolis *Star Tribune*, Marcia Prouse of *The Register* (Orange County, Calif.), Mike Smith of *The New York Times*, and Patty Reksten of *The Oregonian* (Portland, Ore.). Oppel appointed Zach Ryall, the *American-Statesman*'s director of photography, and AME Sharon Roberts to lead the way in defining the new award category.

Newspapers of the 21st century face many challenges as journalists strive to produce content that is relevant to readers' lives. The Community Service Photojournalism Award, fully presented on the CD-ROM included with this edition of *Best Newspaper Writing*, honors photographic reporting that offers compelling visual content and has had such an impact on the community that changes came about as a result.

ASNE has chosen to make the advancement of community service photography one of its primary goals, acknowledging the fact that words and pictures go hand in hand as newspapers work to inform, educate, and strengthen their communities.

J. Albert Diaz
Community Photojournalism

J. Albert Diaz has been a staff photographer for *The Miami Herald* for eight years. He was born in Matanzas, Cuba, and came to the United States by boat in 1965. After graduation from high school in Miami, he joined the U.S. Navy and became a photographer's mate. He was accepted into the Military Photojournalism Program at Syracuse University and later was stationed in San Diego, where he worked as a photojournalist and writer for Navy publications.

In 1985, Diaz left the Navy and returned to Miami to work for *The Miami News* as a photographer. When that newspaper closed in 1988, he joined the staff of the *Los Angeles Times*. In 1994, he returned to Miami as a photographer for the *Herald*.

Diaz lives in Broward County with his wife, Nury, and their children: Grace, 19, Emily, 13, and Jason, 11.

Lure of the Burbs

From the land rush of the Old West to modern-day suburbia, Americans have searched for paradise. In south Florida, that paradise has been found in the former swamplands of Broward County. Now the rapid growth has subsided as the county nears being built out. The boom has hit a wall: the ever-fragile line between encroaching development and the federally protected Everglades National Park. The challenge is to keep paradise found from becoming paradise lost.

Broward is a place where communities are born and lifestyles flourish, a true glimpse of American life and the product of a nation built by different cultures working to a harmonious coexistence. And if it looks cookie-cutter on the outside, it is anything but that inside.

The photographs by J. Albert Diaz, accompanied by a story written by William Yardley, eloquently address the issues and raise many questions about the future of Broward County, and the whole country, as urban sprawl becomes a major challenge to our way of life.

The reader response was enormous and the paper provided a venue for community discussion on how to curb growth and handle the pressures. The photos hit a nerve in the best sense of community service.

—Adapted from The Miami Herald ASNE contest entry

A conversation with
J. Albert Diaz

KENNY IRBY: What drew you into this project and how did it get started?

J. ALBERT DIAZ: I work in the Broward bureau of *The Miami Herald,* and this project started in early 2000. My inspiration was personal: It is a project of my own life experience. Five years ago I moved to Silver Lakes and it's the area I cover. It was also professional: It is the community itself and the people searching for a piece of paradise that inspired me to pursue this project.

What would you say was the central objective of the project?

My main goal was to offer our readers pictures that captured a little part of what life is like in a suburban community. They have a real interest because they [the residents] have concerns about the consequences of over-development and buildout. I wanted to show people both inside and outside the community what the impact looked like. They were already living it.

How did you approach such a massive project?

I had worked on some other picture stories that were somewhat related. I made suggestions to my editor, Alan Freund, and our director of phototography, Maggie Stebber. Maggie urged me to write up a proposal, and everybody thought it was a great idea. I worked on this project almost all of the time—on my own time, in my down time, in between assignments. I just kept working on it. As a staff we had endured Elián, the election recounts, and Sept. 11. What really kept me going was that I knew it was an important story and a combination of our collective enthusiasm.

Over the course of the coverage, how did your reporting relationships play out?

The reporters were very involved and knew the official people to contact. Everybody knew what to do and we trusted one another. The entire paper got behind my vision. I worked most closely with the lifestyle reporter, Bill Yardley. He helped me focus. There were some times when I got discouraged, but Maggie, Bill, and Alan were always there. My family was great, too.

What surprised you about this project?

I think that it is interesting and gratifying that most people are much the same. It was very interesting to realize that we all want a place to call home and to be safe and the freedom to live our lives our own way. I tried to show that there is a diverse group of people living in harmony.

Of all the segments of the project, what was most difficult?

Without a doubt, it was the closing picture. Alan and I talked about how to show the encroachment on nature. We wanted the perspective from the Everglades. I went out there a dozen times. Alan kept telling me that it was there and that I could do it. Then, finally, the gator showed up and I was there.

Say a word about feedback and reaction to your

work by the community?

It is gratifying to hear that the judges saw my vision. I wanted to inform and create emotion. I wanted a historical document of this experience in my community.

We have gotten a ton of e-mail and people have been talking about the project everywhere. My personal favorite so far was an e-mail that simply read, "I grew up in South Florida. You captured the essence of living here." The paper has been viewed in a favorable light as a result of the coverage.

You obviously spent a great deal of time on this story. How do you feel about the end result?

What is most gratifying for me, because I am a true believer in community journalism, is that I contributed to a historic project that allows a group of people to see themselves. This project confirms that you do not have to go halfway around the world to report meaningful stories. No disrespect to those who travel a lot. This is a different kind of challenge: to unearth the images right in your back yard. I am so interested in telling the story of people living their daily lives.

In the spirit of sharing, what was the single greatest lesson that you learned during this project?

It is really important to document, not just do illustrative photojournalism. I hope that people will do more documenting and actually spend time with people and not rush the moments. It takes a lot of work to document. In my view, an illustration is someone's concept or idea of what a situation is. These are sometimes graphically appealing, but with a message that often is not honest. Documentary photojournalism is informational — it goes beyond the quick-hit shot or setting up a picture. And that is the beauty of documentary photojournalism: It is real life.

Let's talk about some technical issues. What type of cameras did you use?

I am not big on the digital camera as a daily tool, especially not for working on big projects like this. Film still has a lot more latitude when you are doing long-term documentary work because still film holds better quality. I used two Canon film camera bodies, the A2 and EOS-1 with two zoom lens, the 70-200 mm and 24-70 mm zoom.

What was your film preference?

Fuji 800 is the film I love. There were many situations in which it worked like a charm. I must have exposed a combination of 200 rolls of Fuji 200, 400, and 800.

The vast majority of your work is taken in available lighting situations. Is that intentional?

Indeed it is. I think flash photography takes away from the spontaneity and detracts from the moment. I really wish that I were invisible when I am working. I am more interested in capturing moments. I'd rather have a great moment in bad lighting than great lighting and a mediocre moment.

How important is the photographer-to-subject relationship for you and how do you build good rapport and relationships?

A lot of people accept me because I am not pushy. I try to show real interest in their lives and that I really care and respect their privacy. I give it as much time as it takes.

Every situation is different, and most times you are trying to get into peoples' homes to see their real lives. Sometimes I don't even take pictures in the beginning. I just talk. This story had a large number of hit-or-miss situations; relationships were not the real challenge.

Then what *was* the greatest challenge for you?

My greatest challenge was that this story had a lot of different events and twists. There was an uncertainty about finding images that showed the emotion I knew was out there: angry homeowners and frustrated parents. The town hall meeting images showed the effects and frustration of urban sprawl. To find those situations meant that I had to enterprise and be there.

What were your research tools and how did you find the right situations?

Believe you me, I read our paper. The hometown *Herald* was a great resource, as were the community newspapers. They had all kinds of information that gave me picture possibilities. I really had this story mapped out in my head. It was almost edited in my head because I lived it (this lifestyle). It was not a typical or traditional project. This project was very personal for me.

What was your editing and support structure?

I did all of my own processing, pre-editing, and film cataloging. I made some black-and-white proofs as a record, and every so often I would meet with my editors for input and discussion about my direction. I kept most of this story in my head.

Can you offer a look into the overall editing process?

I did most of the editing as I went along. We did the final edit as a team. I had about 50 pictures that I really felt told the main story. I was trying to create a little journey for the reader/viewer. David Walters was the picture editor and page designer. The final layout was being done in Miami and I made several trips there. I was very pleased with the final result.

How do you respond to the notion of finding a story that only you can tell?

It is indeed a story that I can relate to. I moved to this community, and everyone was drawn to this area. I feel I can relate to every picture in the story on an emotional level. You cannot be distant.

There has been lots of industry discussion about the difference between feature hunting and enterprise photography. Which model does your project fit into?

This was enterprise photography. That is when the best work is produced. It is something that photographers feel a commitment toward and they go out prepared with a purpose in mind. And this is history. In 30 years, I hope people will look back and see that I made a statement about how people were living here at the turn of the century. I wanted people to see the diversity within this community. We [journalists] have a very important job of informing and sharing. Yes, I had to go out and find the situations, but I did not find them by wandering around. I lived this life and I was reporting what I knew to be happening.

Los Angeles Times

Gail Fisher

Finalist, Photojournalism

Gail Fisher is photo editor/special projects for the *Los Angeles Times*. A native of Akron, Ohio, Fisher joined the *Times* in 1983 after working at the *San Bernardino County Sun* in California for three years. Fisher has received the Robert F. Kennedy Journalism Award for outstanding coverage of the problems of the disadvantaged, and also has won the Community Awareness Award twice from the Pictures of the Year competition. Her photographs and her multimedia and editing skills have been recognized on a national level from the National Press Photographers Association and Society of News Design to the American Society of Newspaper Editors.

Fisher earned her bachelor of arts degree from Miami University in Oxford, Ohio, and her master of fine arts degree from Ohio University. She has two children, Whitney, 16, and Zachary, 12.

Crashing Hard Into Adulthood

Janea, Monique, and Jesse are foster care leftovers—too old or too troubled to be adopted and too vulnerable to be returned to their unfit families. Passed from relatives to foster families to institutionalized group homes, they have ridden the system to the very end. Now at 18, the state launches them out of foster care into the streets, flop houses, and jails.

Los Angeles Times photographer Gail Fisher conceived the idea of following these youngsters in their first year on their own. What Fisher seeks always are those compelling, decisive moments when her subjects are revealed for who they are. Her aim is to lose herself and hide her camera, leaving readers with a deeply affecting sense of lives observed without artifice. The "art of becoming invisible," she calls it.

The results are extraordinarily unvarnished portraits that probe and illuminate. Fisher's photos don't judge or distort. Instead they lead us to understand. Her heartbreaking work for "Crashing Hard Into Adulthood" pulls back the curtain on a world that must be seen.

—Adapted from the Los Angeles Times ASNE contest entry

Lessons Learned

BY GAIL FISHER

As a senior photo editor at the *Los Angeles Times*, on occasion I have the opportunity to initiate and photograph in-depth stories. A few years ago the *Times* published a series on the kids in the foster care system, focusing on the cruelties most had endured. It left me questioning what happened to such kids when they reached 18 and aged out of the system.

After weeks of research and navigating miles of red tape with foster care authorities, I was granted access to interview foster kids who would be aging out but were still in the system. Ultimately, I believe we were granted access, first, because of our persistence and, second, because of the long-term commitment we were making. Fortunately, we were appealing to a presiding judge who trusted us.

Writer Phil Willon was assigned to the project. Together we interviewed and identified our subjects. The next year of our lives would revolve around the roller-coaster experiences of Janea, Monique, and Jesse, documenting moments that would shed some light on how they coped as young adults, on their own, out of the system—without the support of family. During their first year of freedom, they faced homelessness, violence, drugs, poverty, pregnancy, and incarceration.

By spending several days a week with the kids, we earned their trust and gained entrée into their lives. My goal as a photojournalist is to become "invisible," recording real-life moments—the mundane as well as the dramatic. I have empathy for the people I am honored to photograph and have concern for their lives and emotions. But, also, as a journalist, I am obligated not to interfere with the course of events as they unfold in front of my lens, unless people are seriously endangered.

We were there for unplanned moments of spousal abuse—when the newlyweds hit, kicked, punched, and chased each other, and then were reunited with hugs outside the Los Angeles County men's jail. We were there when Janea became homeless—sleeping in a park. And we were there when Monique was kicked out of a halfway house for single moms.

Sometimes the best stories are the hardest to get access to. With this story, it was a constant challenge. We had to obtain entry into jails, courts, homeless shelters, probation meetings, and social worker sessions. It required patience, persistence, and diplomacy when a door was shut and then finding another way in.

Looking back, I can say that "Crashing Hard Into Adulthood" was one of the most intense time periods of my career, considering the importance of the subject material, the long hours, and all the challenges presented. And it was also one of the most rewarding professionally. I feel privileged that Janea, Jesse, and Monique let us into their lives to tell their stories and illuminate problems that kids face after emancipating from the foster care system.

THE SPOKESMAN-REVIEW

Brian Plonka

Finalist, Photojournalism

Brian Plonka, a photographer for *The Spokesman-Review* in Spokane, Wash., was named this year's Newspaper Photographer of the Year in the annual Pictures of the Year competition. He started his career at age 15 at the *New Castle News* in Pennsylvania and has worked for 10 different news organizations in his 20-year career in photojournalism.

Plonka is a 10-time Photographer of the Year in various local, state, and regional contests. He has been a faculty member of NPPA's Flying Short Course and a contest judge and speaker throughout the country on numerous occasions. His wife, Kathy, is also a staff photographer at *The Spokesman-Review*. They have a 3-year-old son, Jordan, and live along the shore of Hauser Lake in northern Idaho.

The Ten Commandments

The Ten Commandments are as old as Moses. There is really nothing new about them. But photojournalist Brian Plonka was curious about how they hold up in the new millennium.

The Spokesman-Review invited Jesuits, rabbis, and other well-known theologians to have discussions with its staff. From those conversations, and his own research, Plonka determined certain representations of current thought on the Ten Commandments. He photographed them with the highest standard of skill. Consider his creative and thoughtful selection of subjects for this photo essay. Notice the range he displays as he moves seamlessly between straightforward, traditional documentary photojournalism and artistic interpretation.

Reader response was overwhelmingly positive. Letters to the editor and e-mails poured in. The newspaper gained praise for tackling such an emotionally charged subject with sensitivity and grace. It is one of those rare cases in which a sensitive subject is explained in a provocative, yet even-handed, manner, and everyone wins.

—Adapted from The Spokesman-Review ASNE contest entry

Lessons Learned

BY BRIAN PLONKA

It was about 8 p.m. one night in 1997 when the red neon glow of the Marriott sign filtered through the curtains in my room. Bad news: The cable was out and it was too late for room service. Scrambling to find a pack of matches in the room for one last smoke of the day, I found the Holy Bible staring me in the face.

I was fascinated during my younger years in Sunday school with the book of Revelation—all the 666 stuff and the world coming to an end. While thumbing through the Bible, I stumbled onto the Ten Commandments.

I had started to experiment with the picture essay and I thought the Ten Commandments would make a good subject. But the editors at Copley Newspapers didn't, so the idea sat in limbo until the coming of the new millennium and a new job at *The Spokesman-Review.*

Even though the concept was well-received by photo editor John Sale, the project was something of a problem for our editors in general. The main problem was how to put words with this story. Our features editor, photo editor, three reporters, and I came together to solve this problem. After several brainstorming sessions, we had a plan: The story would be the introduction to the history of the Ten Commandments.

We didn't want the writing that would accompany the photographs to be too long. The pictures are pretty personal, so the writers decided to do short essays with a personal perspective. This allowed the total piece to be more intimate. Two reporters wrote about three commandments and one reporter handled four.

Most reporters and photographers do very little in the way of religious reporting. Were we on the right track? About a month or so into the piece, I had already shot seven photos. At that point we brought in six theologians, ministers, and religious leaders to see what their views were on the Ten Commandments in modern society. I held my breath as they described one by one what their take was. I knew then that we had something pretty cool. Their input was incredible because of their diverse religious backgrounds.

I'm not one for much research during photo projects. I just like to go and see what happens. It was hard for me to explain what pictures would represent any particular commandment, but I had a few ideas.

Some of the choices were obvious, like adultery. In Spokane this seemed a little tough, but a flight to Reno, where prostitution is legal, is only $120 with a hotel room. After living in the West for the past few years, my way of looking at things, such as stealing, has changed. Many animals are killed just for the trophy, so after a call to the Idaho Department of Fish and Game, I found myself in a cooler filled with evidence of poaching. That commandment, along with several others, was photographed within a short distance from home. I guess I live close to a lot of sinners. But I realized after working on this for a few weeks that the Ten Commandments have taken on a different face over the past 3,000 years.

Some editors thought some of my choices were too critical. I photographed Santa Claus at the local mall for "Do not bear false witness," which I interpret as lying. However, lying is in the fabric of today's society and is accepted by millions. So when does a fun day at the mall become a little too weird? For me it was hearing parents tell their children, "If you don't sit still for Santa and stop crying, you won't get any presents."

I am not one who goes to church or practices any form of organized religion, but I do believe if you lead a good life in your heart, you will be rewarded. I also came to realize in shooting this project that the Ten Commandments are a good barometer for society.

As a rule I feel it is a photojournalist's responsibility to take readers on a trip into a world they might never know. I feel even stronger about avoiding clichés and the formulaic, predictable selection of stories covered and the way a photographer handles the vision. I'm learning that our readers are a lot more intelligent and yearn for depth in their newspapers. I feel once photojournalists reach a level of comfort in the way we see, it's time to reach for the next level. I really feel if I ever stop the learning curve or the desire to try different stories, my days as a photojournalist will be in jeopardy.

Annual Bibliography

BY DAVID B. SHEDDEN

WRITING AND REPORTING BOOKS 2001

Adams, Sally. *Interviewing for Journalists*. New York: Routledge, 2001.

Atwan, Robert, and Kathleen Norris, eds. *The Best American Essays 2001*. Boston: Houghton Mifflin, 2001.

Baskette, Floyd K., Jack Z. Sissors, and Brian S. Brooks. *The Art of Editing*. 7th ed. Boston: Allyn and Bacon, 2001.

Brooks, Brian S., George Kennedy, Daryl R. Moen, and Don Ranly. *Telling the Story: Writing for Print, Broadcast and Online Media*. New York: Bedford/St. Martins, 2001.

Clark, Roy Peter, and Christopher Scanlan, eds. *America's Best Newspaper Writing: A Collection of ASNE Prizewinners*. Boston: Bedford/St. Martin's, 2001.

Ellis, Barbara G. *The Copy Editing and Headline Handbook*. New York: Perseus Books Group, 2001.

Fedler, Fred. *Reporting for the Print Media*. 7th ed. Fort Worth: Harcourt College Publishers, 2001.

Fink, Conrad C. *Sportswriting: The Lively Game*. Ames, Iowa: Iowa State University Press, 2001.

Fox, Walter. *Writing the News: A Guide for Print Journalists*. 3rd ed. Ames, Iowa: Iowa State University Press, 2001.

Goldstein, Norm, ed. *The Associated Press Guide to Internet Research and Reporting*. New York: Perseus Books Group, 2001.

Keeble, Richard. *The Newspapers Handbook*. New York: Routledge, 2001.

Kingsolver, Barbara, and Katrina Kenison, eds. *The Best American Short Stories 2001*. Boston: Houghton Mifflin, 2001.

Leckey, Andrew, and Marshall Loeb. *The Best Business Stories of the Year, 2001*. New York: Pantheon Books, 2001.

Remnick, David, ed. *Life Stories: Profiles from the New Yorker*. New York: Random House, 2001.

Remnick, David, and Henry Finder, eds. *Fierce Pajamas: An Anthology of Humor Writing from the New Yorker*. New York: Random House, 2001.

Ryan, Buck, Michael O'Connell, and Leland B. Ryan. *The Editor's Toolbox: A Reference Guide for Beginners and Professionals*. Ames, Iowa: Iowa State University Press, 2001.

Stout, Glenn, and Bud Collins, eds. *The Best American Sports Writing 2001*. Boston: Houghton Mifflin, 2001.

Wilson, Edward O., ed. *The Best American Science and Nature Writing 2001*. Boston: Houghton Mifflin, 2001.

Zinsser, William K. *On Writing Well. 25th Anniversary Edition*. New York: Harper Resource, 2001.

CLASSICS

Atchity, Kenneth. *A Writer's Time: A Guide to the Creative Process, From Vision Through Revision*. New York: W.W. Norton & Co., 1996.

Bell, Madison Smartt. *Narrative Design: A Writer's Guide to Structure*. New York: W.W. Norton & Co., 1997.

Berg, A. Scott. *Max Perkins: Editor of Genius*. New York: Berkley Publishing Group, 1997.

Bernstein, Theodore M. *The Careful Writer: A Modern Guide to English Usage*. New York: Atheneum Books for Young Readers, 1977.

Blundell, William E. *The Art and Craft of Feature Writing: The Wall Street Journal Guide*. New York: Dutton/Plume, 1988.

Brady, John. *The Craft of Interviewing*. New York: Knopf, 1977.

Brande, Dorothea. *Becoming a Writer*. Los Angeles: J.P. Tarcher; Boston: distributed by Putnam Publishing, reprint of 1934 edition, 1981.

Cappon, Rene J. *The Associated Press Guide to News Writing*. Paramus, N.J.: Prentice Hall, 1991.

Clark, Roy Peter. *Free to Write: A Journalist Teaches Young Writers*. Westport, Conn.: Heinemann, 1995.

Clark, Roy Peter, and Don Fry. *Coaching Writers: The Essential Guide for Editors and Reporters*. New York: St. Martin's Press, 1992.

Dillard, Annie. *The Writing Life*. New York: Harper Collins, 1999.

Elbow, Peter. *Writing With Power: Techniques for Mastering the Writing Process*. 2nd ed. New York: Oxford University Press, 1998.

Follett, Wilson. *Modern American Usage: A Guide*. Revised by Erik Wensberg. New York: Hill & Wang, 1998.

Franklin, Jon. *Writing for Story: Craft Secrets of Dramatic Nonfiction by a Two-Time Pulitzer Prize Winner*. New York: Dutton/Plume, 1994.

Garlock, David. *Pulitzer Prize Feature Stories*. Ames, Iowa: Iowa State University Press, 1998.

Goldstein, Norm, ed. *AP Stylebook*. Cambridge, Mass.: Perseus Publishing, 2000.

Gross, Gerald, ed. *Editors on Editing: What Writers Should Know About What Editors Do*. New York: Grove/Atlantic, 1993.

Harrington, Walt. *Intimate Journalism: The Art and Craft of Reporting Everyday Life*. Thousand Oaks, Calif.: Sage, 1997.

Hugo, Richard. *The Triggering Town: Lectures & Essays on Poetry & Writing*. New York: Norton, 1992.

Kerrane, Kevin, and Ben Yagoda. *The Art of Fact*. New York: Scribner, 1997.

Klement, Alice, and Carolyn Matalene, eds. *Telling Stories, Taking Risks. Journalism Writing at the Century's Edge*. Belmont, Calif.: Wadsworth Publishing, 1998.

McPhee, John. *The John McPhee Reader*. William L. Howard, ed. New York: Farrar, Straus & Giroux, 1990.

Mencher, Melvin. *News Reporting and Writing*. 8th ed. New York: McGraw-Hill, 1999.

Metzler, Ken. *Creative Interviewing: The Writer's Guide to Gathering Information by Asking Questions*. 3rd ed. Needham Heights, Mass.: Allyn & Bacon, 1996.

Mitford, Jessica. *Poison Penmanship: The Gentle Art of Muckraking*. New York: Farrar, Straus & Giroux, 1988.

Murray, Donald. *Shoptalk: Learning to Write With Writers*. Portsmouth, N.H.: Boynton/Cook, 1990.

Perry, Susan K. *Writing in Flow: Keys to Enhanced Creativity*. Cincinnati: Writer's Digest Books, 1999.

Plimpton, George, ed. *Writers at Work: The Paris Review Interviews*. Series. New York: Viking, 1992.

Ross, Lillian. *Reporting*. New York: Simon & Schuster Trade, 1984.

Scanlan, Christopher, ed. *How I Wrote the Story*. Providence Journal Company, 1986.

Sims, Norman, ed. *Literary Journalism in the Twentieth Century*. New York: Oxford University Press, 1990.

Stafford, William, and Donald Hall, eds. *Writing the Australian Crawl: View on the Writer's Vocation*. Ann Arbor, Mich.: University of Michigan Press, 1978.

Stewart, James B. *Follow the Story: How to Write Successful Nonfiction*. New York: Simon and Schuster, 1998.

Strunk, William, Jr., and E.B. White. *The Elements of Style*. 4th ed. Needham Heights, Mass.: Allyn & Bacon, 1999.

Talese, Gay. *Fame & Obscurity*. New York: Ivy Books, 1971.

Wardlow, Elwood M., ed. *Effective Writing and Editing: A Guidebook for Newspapers*. Reston, Va.: American Press Institute, 1985.

White, E.B. *Essays of E.B. White*. New York: Harper Collins, 1999.

Woods, Keith, Karen Brown, Roy Peter Clark, Don Fry, and Christopher Scanlan, eds. *Best Newspaper Writing*. St. Petersburg, Fla.: The Poynter Institute. Published annually since 1979.

Zinsser, William. *On Writing Well: An Informal Guide to Writing Nonfiction*. 6th ed. New York: Harper Collins, 1998.

— *Writing to Learn*. Reading, Mass.: Addison-Wesley Educational Publishers, 1997.

— *Speaking of Journalism: 12 Writers and Editors Talk About Their Work*. New York: Harper Collins, 1994.

ARTICLES 2001

Astor, Dave. "Writers Wrestle with Width Woes." *Editor & Publisher* (May 14, 2001): 48.

Bissell, Kimberly, and Steve J. Collins. "Early Predictors of Ability in a News Writing Course." *J&MC Educator* (Summer 2001): 69-80.

Burrough, Larry. "The Long and Short of It." *The American Editor* (August 2001): 4-6, 8.

Clark, Roy Peter. "What's So Wrong with Writing Long?" *The American Editor* (May-June 2001): 22-23.

Daniel, Kelly. "An Hour with a Writing Coach Makes Her Focus on the Beginning of the End." *The American Editor* (April 2001): 19, 21.

Franklin, Jon. "Why Has Journalism Abandoned Its Observer's Role?" *Nieman Reports* (Summer 2001): 26.

Freedman, Wayne. "When to Leave Out the Details." *Communicator* (October 2001): 36-39.

Fry, Don. "Starting Writers Right—On the Copy Desk." *The American Editor* (April 2001): 23.

Gibson, Rhonda, Joe Bob Hester, and Shannon Stewart. "Pull Quotes Shape Reader Perceptions of News Stories." *Newspaper Research Journal* (Spring 2001): 66-78.

Goudreau, Rosemary. "Write Long, Just Start with a Good Idea." *The American Editor* (August 2001): 10.

Hoyt, Clark. "Emulate the Better Gettysburg Address." *The American Editor* (April 2001): 22, 30.

Krieger, Elliot. "Writing Competes with 'Survivor' as Water-Cooler Fodder, Thanks to Local Award." *The American Editor* (April 2001): 20.

Larocque, Paula. "Keep it Easy and Simple." *Quill* (March 2001): 40.

Miller, John X. "Looking for Stories in All the Third Places." *Nieman Reports* (Spring 2001): 44-45.

Overholser, Geneva. "When the Public Speaks, Do Journalists Listen?" *Nieman Reports* (Summer 2001): 23.

Rich, Carole. "Writing for the Web: Different, But How?" *The American Editor* (August 2001): 14-17.

Robins, Wayne. "Sharpening Their Lance." *Editor & Publisher* (December 3, 2001): 16-18.

Watson, Warren. "The Write Stuff." *Presstime* (April 2001): 61.

The Journalist's Toolbox

Here is a selective index that loosely follows the writing process developed by longtime columnist and author Don Murray. It references places in the book where journalists shine a light on the tools and techniques that helped make their work stand out.

Front row left to right: Pam Johnson, leadership faculty; Kenny Irby, visual journalism group leader; and Keith Woods, *Best Newspaper Writing* editor and reporting, writing, and editing group leader.
Back row left to right: Christopher Scanlan, senior writing faculty; Roy Peter Clark, senior scholar; Aly Colón, diversity program director and *Poynter Report* editor; and Karen Dunlap, dean of the faculty.

The Poynter Experience

The Poynter Institute, which opened in 1975 as the Modern Media Institute, is a school dedicated to improving the quality of journalism in the United States and wherever the press is free. Each year, the Institute hosts more than 50 professional development seminars, two programs for college students, seminars for college professors, a year-round journalism program for Tampa Bay high school students, and summer writing camps for the area's elementary and middle-school children and their teachers.

The Institute coordinates and supports the National Writers Workshops each spring, joining thousands of writers in a celebration of the craft. Poynter also has established connections around the globe with training institutes and the journalists they serve.

Poynter.

Through its publications and website, Poynter Online, the Institute connects journalists with their peers and promotes the notion that ethics is synonymous with excellence in all areas of the craft. Poynter faculty speak at journalism conventions, advise working journalists, consult in news organizations, and provide commentary on the everyday issues arising in the industry. Seven members of the faculty played a part in producing this book.

About the CD-ROM

Included with this volume is a CD-ROM containing all the images in the winners' and finalists' entry packages for the Community Service Photojournalism category. Each package is presented with the photo captions and stories that accompanied the images. We have included full-screen images that are printable at low resolution for classroom projects and an interactive cropping tool that allows for re-editing of selected photos. In addition, the CD includes photos by *Boston Globe* photographer Bill Greene that accompanied Ellen Barry's "The Lost Boys of Sudan" series and the full text versions of three finalists' stories that were excerpted in the book for space considerations.

The CD project was created by Poynter's multimedia editor Larry Larsen using Macromedia Flash. Design editor Anne Conneen of Poynter's publications department assisted with some images for the project. Kenny Irby of the Poynter faculty worked closely with editor Keith Woods and publications director Billie M. Keirstead on the presentation of the Community Service Photojournalism category.

The CD will run on both Windows and Macintosh platforms. It is designed to open at full-screen size. The Flash Player and Adobe Acrobat Reader applications are included on the CD.

We hope you find this CD useful and enjoyable.